Presidential Profiles Washington to Trump

Enneagram and Myers-Briggs Perspectives

Jane,
I hope this gives you interesting information about the Presidents.

by Herb Pearce

Best to you in everything you do! Herb

Acknowledgements:

I would like to acknowledge my chief editor Jan Larivee for an amazing job. Many other people helped edit chapters in the initial stage: Connie Farley, Sherry Greene, Felice Katz of Graphics to Go, Steven Orzack, Sue Johnson, Helene Martel, William Buonopane, Ariane Cherbuliez, Stephen Wingate, Cathy Reuben, David Anick, Linda Glazer, Emily Page, Rick Charnes, Reed Synder, John O'Leary and Cliff Putney. Many others helped in encouragement, title suggestions and emotional support. Thank you so much for your contributions.

Photo on front cover, author: Cuvafitness
/commons.wikimedia.org/wiki/File:Mount_Rushmore_"The_Presidents".
jpg, Mount Rushmore, South Dakota

INTRODUCTION

This book explores the personalities of all United States Presidents, with the addition of understanding their Enneagram and Myers-Briggs personality types. It's a challenge to discover the real personality of each president due to the abundance of myth and image-making that surrounds the office in general. This includes exaggerated anecdotes and stories, debunking from opposed political parties, inaccurate or contradictory information, patriotic rewriting of history and skewed perspectives. I've read many articles and books, quotes from people who knew them, diary entries, historical analyses and watched documentaries about the presidents. I have gathered and studied in depth a great deal of presidential information. All this research has been combined with my own experience with the Enneagram and Myers-Briggs. In this work I have attempted to reflect the basic personality structure of each president with strengths and weaknesses, complexities and contradictions.

Many presidents came from moneyed or prestigious backgrounds, though some were middle class and some were from poor backgrounds. Eleven of the presidents were generals, though most were politicians by trade. Many were lawyers though some were merchants, educators or businessmen. I have concentrated on providing descriptions, incidents, stories, and quotes from the presidents themselves or political commentators that reflect a relatively consistent personality makeup of each president during his lifetime. The focus is on the entire life of each president before, during and after his presidency.

Pressure to be ambitious, family background and marital partner, historical trends of the time, and regions of the country also reflect upon the Type that I have chosen and will comment on.

There are 44 Presidents including Donald Trump, as Grover Cleveland, president number 22 and 24, had two non-consecutive terms; that is, he won, then lost, then won again. It's traditionally been labeled as 45 presidents (Cleveland counted twice) and in the book, I do that, president number 1, president 2, president 3, etc. through 45.

My type conclusions come from a number of sources – books and articles, The History Channel Presidential TV documentaries, National Geographic and other TV network specials or miniseries that I read articles about for historical accuracy, hundreds of articles and book reviews online, history lectures and author book reviews downloaded to YouTube, talking to historians, studying many paintings and photographs, attending lectures about presidents at the Massachusetts Historical Society in Boston, visiting presidential sites such as the Adams Estate and an eight-day visit to presidential mansions in Virginia, and thousands of hours of reading related to American history, my minor in history in college and my 28-year-plus experience teaching the Enneagram and Myers-Briggs. My four years in the US Navy contributed to my understanding of how military history fits into the presidency. I was a sailor on the USS Intrepid aircraft carrier which is now a museum in New York City. I was among the first race relations teachers in the Navy.

I typed every president independently, based on my research and years of typing people, before I looked at how others have typed the presidents. I've been an avid student of American history since elementary school.

I think our presidents reflect American culture and people's process of growth, as well as the many factions in American society at any point in its history. The struggles between those factions represent the struggles between rich and poor, big business and small enterprise, independence and interdependence, trust and fear, regional, cultural and racial divides and degrees of maturity and immaturity. History swings back and forth from the tried and true to experimentation, between what has worked in the past with what modern life and change bring to bear.

A focus of the book will be on Enneagram type dynamics, as well as the Myers-Briggs type, which I decided to add after I had typed each president in the Enneagram. The research into the Myers-Briggs types helped me change some of the Enneagram types of the president. I consider myself more a specialist on the Enneagram, though I have taught the Myers-Briggs for over 20 years.

This is also a basic history, though not a comprehensive one of the presidents and certainly not a major history book of historical documentation. Each president's presentation is a summary of some political facts and biography, and just as important, personality. I try to give stories and evidence that reflect the types. Each chapter is unique, with no regular structure presented for each president.

There is often debate and disagreement by the experts on the details and interpretations about each president's motivations and behavior. I try to pick out relevant features that many historians will agree on, and find a balance between the personality strengths and limitations of each president.

Presidents are ranked very differently by historians based on what criteria they consider important. Washington, Lincoln and Franklin Roosevelt, for instance, are usually ranked highly, though some historians or ranking systems rate those presidents at the bottom of the list. Presidents in office during times of war are often ranked higher than peacetime presidents. Presidents can be rated on the economy or prosperity, foreign relations, relationship to Congress, record of promoting peace, conservatism, conservation of land, promotion of business and corporations, minority rights, equal rights record for more modern presidents, public opinion, legislative record, honesty, toughness, power, relationship to the military or other categories.

I make comments on subtypes at times, type aspects other than the dominant type such as secondary type (type used secondarily and often mistaken as the core type), wings and also maturity levels. Articles at the end of the book explain types, subtypes and wings more thoroughly. I make personal comments at times on the presidents, their wives and their influence, their legacies and the historical policies of the United States government.

By all means, feel free to disagree with my analyses. Each typing is based on many hours of research and thought. There were occasional shocks to my system of what I had previously thought or had been taught about some of the presidents. I do believe if I missed the core type of a president, my type analysis is likely the secondary type or certainly an important type feature of that president. Several of the presidents I've been in debate about regarding type for years, and I make comments on that and the process I went through in typing. Feel free to communicate with me regarding type and your opinions.

The purpose of the book is to give a human understanding of how each president saw the world in general and also how he responded to it from the perspective of his Enneagram and Myers-Briggs makeup. This process was also a way for me, and hopefully you, to understand the Presidents and American history a little more in depth. I make more comments from the Enneagram perspective than the Myers-Briggs, though the two systems often are intimately related.

I love the typing process, as it helps to understand the complexities of a human being and how each person tends to uniquely think and act. A deeper purpose of the book is to understand and value differences and to have better communication with different personalities. The Presidents model for us great strengths, and also limitations, that we can learn from through reflection.

At the end of the book, especially for those not familiar with the Enneagram or Myers-Briggs, I've included a description of the Enneagram types from my first book, *Enneagram Basics* and from my second book, *Enneagram Beyond the Basics*, I've included information about the Myers-Briggs and the correlation between the Myers-Briggs and the Enneagram types, as well as touching on instinctual subtypes, wings and stress and secure types. I've also included a summary of the Enneagram and Myers-Briggs types of the Presidents. Read more from my *Enneagram Basics* and *Enneagram Beyond the Basics*, as well as my book, *The Caregiver's Enneagram,* to understand the Enneagram more in depth. There are also thousands of Enneagram sites on line.

Each presidential chapter has a more detailed description of that President's Myers-Briggs type with references within that chapter. I encourage more research and debate about the US Presidents and type perspective. Toward the end of the book, for the more modern presidents, I've included parts of some articles written by others regarding the personalities of each president.

In the heading of each presidential chapter, I included an epithet label for each president, my determination of his Enneagram and Myers-Briggs core type and the inclusive dates of the presidency. I start out each chapter with the birth and death years of each president.

I intend to give lectures and presentations to groups and organizations on the topic of US Presidents, Personality and Type and welcome invitations to do so.

Herb Pearce, January 6, 2018

Table of Contents

George Washington, Founder and Model, Type 3, ISTJ, 1789-1797

(1732-1799) Myths, especially about our first president George Washington, are rampant, making it especially difficult to get to the truth about him. Most early biographers and historians were invested in seeing our Founding Father as perfect and godlike. The intention of the myth was to promote a glorified image of George Washington as the Father of our country, an honest statesman and a man who sacrificed everything for his country. The real truth is somewhat different. It takes courage to see our first president as a real person with flaws and strengths.

Washington sounds like a Type 1 Perfectionist in most school history books but the actual George was far from honest and very far from perfect. As a matter of fact, he lied outrageously much of the time, particularly in his younger years. He could be quite deceitful and became enraged if anyone spoke negatively about him. The image he wanted to portray was one of being modest, moral, and a paragon of integrity.

In reality as a Type 3, he expected special treatment, had to be top dog at any cost and tried very hard to hide his weaknesses. The culture of leadership in his time idealized a person of high morals and integrity and he attempted to reflect those values to his constituents. To his dying day, he altered reality to fit how he wanted others to see him. His legacy in the country and the perception of his role in its founding, was ever present in his mind.

As a 3, George and his compatriots led an active public relations campaign to hide his flaws and to promote the myth of his idealized character. The new Americans needed someone to worship who could clarify the confusion, the violence and the chaotic circumstances that brought the United States into creation. Congress looked for a leader who could create stability and lessen the fears of people who invested in the Revolution and the founding of our country.

In the Image Triad of the Enneagram, Washington was a Type 3 with 2 and 4 wings, with a leaning toward 4. He deeply protected his image by withholding information that would reflect badly on him even if others suffered. He exaggerated details to make himself look good and sacrificed those who competed with him. He was jealous of anyone getting more attention, blamed people if they made him look bad, took credit for others' success and seldom took responsibility for his mistakes or flaws. Most of these negative attributes were more apparent in his youth and the years during the Revolution. In his late 40s, 50s and 60s he matured, though he continued to overreact to anyone who would, in his opinion, make him look bad.

On the plus side, he lived up to the model of an action hero, which is a code name for type 3. He was tall (over 6'2"), handsome in a rugged outdoorsy way, active, dynamic and athletic. He was an accomplished horseback rider, a surveyor, designed military uniforms as well as interior home decorations, was an accomplished dancer (ladies were always waiting in line to dance with him), and he was adept at gambling.

George was a leader in politics and the military, and could be innovative. He had the biggest whiskey distillery in America. He entertained and surrounded himself with many important people even though by nature he was more of an introvert than an extrovert. As a type 3 his image and accomplishments were central to who he was and saw himself to be.

He was an innovator, trying out new farming techniques, using current technology and was very productive as a plantation owner. He could be reliable if you were on his side and he paid his debts. Washington turned down payment for being Commander of the Revolution and President of the United States, although that was probably more to create a positive image than to save money for the country. He was one of the richest men in America, if not the richest, and enjoyed playing the part of what was perceived to be the most successful and famous person in colonial and early federal America. He loved money and property - his portrait on the dollar bill is appropriate. I'm surprised it's not a higher denomination though his portrait is more circulated as a $1!

He had a knack of picking the right people to work for him; who could make good decisions and make him look good. He could praise others, but only if they supported him and allowed him to take most of the credit. He attracted attention from others due to his wealth, background, energy, appearance and desire to lead. This suited him as a 3 since 3s love getting attention from people whose admiration they seek. To a 3 being envied is desired.

George was raised as gentry. He was not born in the top tier of Virginia aristocratic society but quickly rose to that level. His ancestors in England and America were important people; landowners, politicians and community leaders. Most of his ancestors held positions of public service throughout their lives and he followed that tradition.

Not much is known of his early childhood. Washington was self-educated and possibly home schooled. He read books on his own and copied important documents to memorize practical information. George was insecure about his education, having missed college. John Adams, his vice president, said of Washington that he is "too illiterate, unlearned, and unread for his state and reputation."

Washington studied stoicism and the Greek philosopher Seneca, who focused on controlling one's emotions. He was moderately successful in masking his emotions, particularly in public but not in private. Washington's temper remained a defining feature throughout his life. According to his secretary Tobias Lear, "Few sounds on earth could compare with that of George Washington swearing a blue streak." "He is subject to attacks of anger on provocation, sometimes without just cause," said Lord Fairfax, father of George Fairfax, who was a close friend and supporter of Washington.

George admired his older half-brother Lawrence, from his mother's previous marriage. Lawrence was like a father to him. George's own father died when George was 11. This eliminated the advantage of an English education like that afforded to Lawrence. George's father was a tobacco farmer who owned many acres and slaves, and after his father's death, George inherited 280 acres and 10 slaves. He bought eight additional slaves in young adulthood.

Washington basically despised and avoided his mother throughout her life. Had his mother remarried, George would have been able to go to college, a factor that likely added to his resentment toward her. She kept him from obtaining an education, as she had been deprived herself. There was always a cool, quiet antagonism between Washington and his mother. She was hypercritical - exactly what 3s don't like.

As the eldest son, she turned to George as a surrogate husband; wanting him to manage her property and care for her. She faulted him for having his own life and he avoided her, though he did provide her with some financial support. His mother became increasingly embittered in her old age, not even attending George's wedding to Martha Custis, and he didn't attend his mother's funeral when she died at age 83!

George never bonded with his father who was frequently away on business trips. He likely had a sense of love deprivation not being close to either parent. Being oversensitive to criticism he suffered from a lifelong need for approval. He tried to have extreme self-control and silence, and manly stolidity was his guide, thus appearing as a type 1, likely his secondary type. ISTJs in the Myers-Briggs, as Washington was, often are 1s.

The military was the major path for advancement during his time in history. George's half-brother, Lawrence, was a captain in the British army. Lawrence married Anne Fairfax, daughter of Sir William Fairfax, a British colonel who had served as an English Customs agent in Barbados, as well as a justice and Governor of the Bahamas. Having a wealthy and renowned brother raised George's status. 3s love to know the right people to advance in society.

Lawrence and Lord Fairfax, devised a plan to have George join the British Royal Navy, which his mother nixed, thus angering George. Instead, Washington began his career in surveying and land speculation, which was a good move, spurring him on his way to become one of wealthiest men of his age. In the United States and in much of the rest of the world, accumulating wealth was the major focus of a successful man's working life. To be seen as successful and admired is a common ambition; even today, the drive to accumulate wealth has continued.

Wanting to emulate people in high society, Washington strove to learn the manners of rich landowners and to meet the right people. His half-brother was instrumental in this process and taught George how to fit into the best society. George's close friend's wife Sally Fairfax taught him manners, dancing, dress and high society codes. Sally's husband and Washington's close friend was George William Fairfax, son of Sir William Fairfax, the largest landowner in Virginia.

George had a crush on Sally throughout his entire life, accompanied by mutual flirting and love letters, even during his engagement to Martha! So much for George's allegiance to his friend and Martha! Apparently, it wasn't acted on except in longing, likely due to the restraints of his friend's wife and possibly his own, as scandal would have been terrible for Washington's reputation. George at that time was beneath the aristocratic station of Sally and the Fairfax's. Washington's ISTJ Myers-Briggs type likely helped in his restraint regarding Sally.

Lord Fairfax, the father of his close friend, owned more land than anyone in Virginia and took George under his wing when Lawrence married into the Fairfax family. George and Lord Fairfax, the most influential man in Virginia when George was a teenager, shared a fascination with war, exchanging books on Caesar and Alexander the Great. Through this connection with Fairfax, George secured a position as a surveyor when he was 15, which gave him opportunity to check out prime land for himself while he hobnobbed with the richest landowners.

Regarding status in society, surveying was considered a profession equal to that of being a doctor or lawyer and by age 17 George had his own surveying business. Throughout George's life he increased his land ownership, which was the easiest way to gain power and prestige. At age 20, he owned 2500 acres of land. He was a total go-getter, one of the names for a Type 3.

As mentioned, being a military leader was a primary path to success and the French and Indian War gave George the opportunity to capitalize on his position. With the help of his half-brother and Lord Fairfax, who knew the Virginia governor, George volunteered at a young age to take a missive to the French commander in the Ohio Valley, stating that England was laying claim to the land that France was occupying.

Coming back from delivering the letter, George was almost killed by an Indian scout who shot at him but misfired. After that near-death experience, Washington nearly drowned in a freezing river. He wrote about his exploits and published a journal to highlight his heroism and courage. George continued to write heroic journals throughout the French and Indian war, being a master at public relations. He wrote to his half-brother, "I heard bullets whistle past me and believe me there was something charming in the sound." It's not just the action, but also in this case the publicizing of one's heroism, that provides satisfaction for a 3.

After delivering the missive, George was then given a small military command of 60 men to negotiate with the French regarding the Ohio Valley. Instead George ordered gunfire upon 33 French regulars eating breakfast. Most were killed instantly, including the commander, as they had no time to get to their weapons. It was a massacre. George had strict orders not to fire unless fired upon and he ultimately disobeyed his orders. He then left the enemy soldiers bodies unburied, which was against the military code of ethics. Today it would be considered a war crime – the massacre, disobeying his orders and then leaving the bodies unburied. His type 3 desire to win, act quickly and gain fame, dominated his 1 side.

After the "battle," George then discovered the peace mission orders on the French commander's body. George's impulsivity and preemptive strike destroyed any trust that could have been built up between the British (George was British before the American

Revolution) and the French. This major mistake got him into severe trouble but he did his best to cover up the truth and grossly lied about the circumstances.

This massacre basically started the French and Indian War! He continued to make major military mistakes in the war due to his inexperience and audacity. He built a fort in an unprotected area whose location caused severe causalities for the colonials and British. In continued guerilla warfare against the French and Indians, he suffered heavy losses to friendly fire (due to heavy gunpowder smoke which made it difficult to distinguish the enemy from his own men). He confiscated supplies from locals along the war-path, which created much mistrust for the cause. Never admitting any errors, he blamed battle losses on "insufficient supplies and a callow soldiery." He often exaggerated enemy losses, as many as 10 times the actual amount. It's not unusual for a Type 3 looking for glory to exaggerate the truth to look good.

Washington campaigned to have a battle road go through his property, which he guessed would add land value. In the eyes of the public he was considered a war hero mostly due to his journals and friends who promoted him, despite the fact that many highly criticized him. His influence over time surpassed that of his half-brother, Lawrence. Good public relations and bragging seemed to work to his advantage.

Throughout his life, luck, volunteering to command others, and alliances with the people in power pulled him out of the mud. After the French and Indian War, he confiscated the best lands for himself, as a gift for serving the British, even though the British had promised those lands to the soldiers and not the officers like himself. His close officers got some land but not prime land like that he gave himself. He always justified his self-serving directives. In his youth, he was the quintessence of being an undeveloped 3 – action oriented, bragging and lying!

Despite his faults, Washington was our first Western "hero" – in the Ohio River Valley – an extension of Virginia. He continued to write, publish, and distribute journals of his exploits in the French and Indian War. As already stated, his stories were highly embellished to promote his courage and heroism. In the French and Indian War, he lost nearly every battle he led or participated in and never admitted the massacre of the French peace team. Instead he blamed them! He did anything to look good, even at the expense of others' suffering to hide his blunders.

To his credit, Washington was a brave and courageous soldier. In a famous battle in the French and Indian War, in which George's commander was killed and in which he then took command, he had two horses shot from under him as well as four bullet holes through his jacket. He wasn't wounded! Most of those around him were killed.

He was never wounded in battle, which is miraculous. Washington gained another command when a British officer fell off his horse and died. He felt that destiny would keep him alive and I guess he was right! Legend has it that he was protected by the Great Spirit.

Many of the successful battles, especially in the Revolutionary War, were planned and won by his fellow officers, even though George took most of the credit. His officers, on many occasions, prevented him from carrying out ill-conceived plans. He was good at picking the right men to work under him and override him when necessary.

The new Americans won the Revolutionary War due to Washington's excellent officers, his ability to wage surprise attacks and his tenacity to stay the course, despite the fact that Congress was constantly debating whether to replace him. Congress needed to create a hero and Washington fit the bill just enough to fulfill their need.

Thank God, the French stepped in to help the colonials. The last major battle that decided the Revolution, was won by the French Navy commander who countered Washington's orders without even informing him! A German commander helped lead colonial troops and Holland contributed a major loan to the colonials. Europe's support against England was a major reason the Revolutionary War turned in America's favor.

George was always a politician. Serving as a member of the House of Burgesses for 15 years beginning when he was 20, he was active in the Virginia militia and was appointed a member of Continental Congress in 1774 and 1775 until his appointment as the Commander in Chief of the Army in 1776. He won elections in the House of Burgesses by buying copious amounts of alcohol to ply his supporters to vote for him; that practice was common to win votes. He was an active Mason at age 20 and became Grand Master a year later. He was a natural born leader, active in the Virginia militia and was always on the forefront of power.

Williamsburg, Virginia played a major role in George Washington's career. Washington's half-brother, father, grandfather and great grandfather all served in the Virginia legislature. The close relationship between the Fairfax and Washington families was a catalyst for an advantage in life. George was tall, athletic and handsome in a rugged way, kind of like the John Wayne of his day. He was noticeable upon entering a room and seemed in-charge, competent and credible. He was ambitious and knew how to spin opportunities in his direction. Even though George was introverted by nature, he could be extroverted when needed to promote himself.

Washington came to the Continental Congress dressed in a military uniform each day (the only one who wore a uniform) to encourage, with as much humility as he could muster, to be chosen Army Commander. He was dignified and was aware of himself as a symbol. He always dressed well, as 3s tend to do. Appearance was especially important.

Washington appeared to reluctantly accept leadership (a bit of the Type 4 wing dramatic flair) after he was nominated by John Adams to head the Revolutionary Army. Washington actually had doubts himself about whether he could successfully command the troops, but was seduced by leadership and praise. Actually, no one else wanted the job!

George was reluctant at first to rebel against the British until taxation started affecting his own finances. He wanted to be on the right side of history and was loyal to Britain until taxation was imposed without American consent. The War was actually less about money, as the tax amount was small, than the principle of not being included in the decision-making process regarding taxes.

Washington was not outspoken like Sam Adams and Patrick Henry and other rabble-rousers. George was a person of forethought though he could be moved by passion. He had his own issues with being outspoken, but for the most part, he tried to contain himself, as he wanted to be well regarded. George felt right was on his side and he strove to be a considered a great person and model for others.

The courtship of Martha Custis when Washington was 27 lasted less than one day before he proposed! His engagement lasted much longer because he needed to wait until the French and Indian War was over. Passions were bound by ambition. He married the richest widow in Virginia. She had a great deal of land, many slaves and provided opportunity for advancement. He certainly was opportunistic – a trait of 3s. Advance, advance, advance!

Marriage of the wealthy was often a business arrangement. Even in his pursuit of Martha, George was still infatuated with his best friend's wife, Sally Fairfax. Feelings for Martha did deepen and it turned into genuine love and affection, even though it was more of a friendship than a passion according to many historians. Due to the marriage to Martha, he gained control over 17,000 new acres of land and hundreds of slaves.

George's favorite time during his life was the interim between the French and Indian War and the Revolutionary War when he could be a plantation farmer. While he was reserved in public, he could relax at Mount Vernon. He enjoyed domestic projects, family activities, entertaining guests and good conversation. He planted and harvested crops, made architectural improvements and invested in public improvements including canals, navigation of rivers and developing the nearby town of Alexandria. He did care about the public good, though he was always aware of increasing the size and value of his lands and holdings. As a 3 Achiever, he was constantly motivated to better his last win.

Washington worked to improve and expand the mansion and the surrounding plantation. He switched from tobacco to wheat as his main cash crop and he experimented with new crops, fertilizer, tools, crop rotation and livestock breeding, expanding operations to include flour milling and commercial fishing. Acreage was constantly expanded. George was a man of modern technology as is often true of 3s. He designed a 16-sided barn to thresh wheat in a more efficient and sanitary way.

It's hard to say whether George's desire to command and secure the presidency was more related to duty or fame, probably both. Historians debate, but more likely the edge was toward fame, acknowledgment and hope for glory. The importance of duty was, however, real to him and was a very valued social norm for the aristocracy. Others pressured him to lead, and George didn't resist. He wanted to be seen as bowing to pressure with a desire to serve without personal reward, which was very much the aristocratic custom of the time that continued well into the 19th century.

George's tendency to be deceptive was an asset in the Revolutionary War. He was a master at using invisible ink, and with the creation of new chemicals to read invisible -ink, he knew all kinds of ciphers and codes to hide messages. Washington had extensive spy rings of commoners who informed him of British whereabouts. He was great at leaking false messages to the enemy, exaggerating the numbers of his ranks and supplies, so he wouldn't be attacked. He was a master of disinformation. His type 3 quality of deceptiveness greatly served to his advantage!

Being a farmer, he was also adept at reading weather and could predict overnight freezes to lead his army out of harm's way on frozen rivers. He crossed the Delaware in freezing weather to surprise the enemy in a predawn attack after the German mercenaries had a drunken party on Christmas Eve. He would set numerous campfires to trick the enemy into thinking he had more troops than he actually had, after the bulk of the army had already left.

In the Revolutionary War, George was not considered a great military strategist. His best successes were surprise attacks when the enemy was unprepared. His generals, especially if given power to act unilaterally, won many of the battles they led, though as mentioned, Washington took credit. He seldom took responsibility for his losses or bad decisions. There was much grumbling among his officers and some lost commands if they opposed Washington on any level.

Congress debated whether to have another general take command and lead midstream in the war but they decided that changing the commander would be bad for the troops' as well as the public's morale and for public relations with France and Holland, whose alliance they needed. Famous Benedict Arnold likely turned to the British side due to his resentment at Washington for not promoting him. A large financial donor to the Revolutionary side disliked Arnold and encouraged anti-Arnold sentiment. Arnold's wife was British and probably encouraged him to go to the British and make some instant cash!

George constantly disobeyed Congress's orders, and politicians were very critical of Washington's military failures. George tended to blame Congress and his own subordinates. He often despaired and harbored feelings of betrayal by everyone around him, fueling rage and despair.

In a letter to his cousin, Washington wrote: "if I were to wish the bitterest curse to an enemy of this side of the grave, I should put him in my stead with my feelings: and yet I do not know what plan of conduct to pursue. I see the impossibility of serving with reputation, or doing any essential service to the cause by continuing in command, and yet I am told that if I quit the command inevitable ruin will follow from the distraction that will ensue. In confidence, I tell you that I never was in such an unhappy, divided state since I was born. If I fall, it may not be amiss that these circumstances be known, and declaration made in credit to the justice of my character. And if the men will stand by me (which by the by I despair of), I am resolved not to be forced from this ground while I have life." Certainly, as a Type 3, George had a 4 wing with a bit of dramatic flair and was always concerned about his reputation.

Quotes from biographers include: "George was alternately fawning and assertive, appealingly modest and discreetly pushy. While he knew the social forms, he could never quite restrain, much less conceal, the unstoppable force of his ambition." Historian John Ferling says, "Washington was mad for glory. He was eager to prove his courage both to his officers and to powerful figures in Virginia. And zealous for the combat that would bring the renown for which he hungered."

Washington tried to hide what he saw as his shortcomings; lack of education, wild ambition, and volatile anger, and tried to appear industrious, fair and lacking in ambition. He didn't want to appear to solicit the command but rather wanted to appear to concede to the "voice of the country."

The new country needed a figurehead – one that would promote loyalty and patriotism and provide a father image. Washington sustained enough morale during the long, difficult war to keep his image going. He suffered privations with his troops though certainly had many more luxuries as the head of the command, as he deserved. He sacrificed much throughout his lifetime to lead our new country to the best of his ability. Congress withheld information from the public about many of Washington's blunders. Keeping the image unstained was of utmost importance in managing civilian morale. The budding nation needed success and results.

Throughout his life, Washington's livelihood depended on slavery and at Mt. Vernon, he owned over 300 slaves. They worked six days a week from sunrise to sundown and the slave cabins were below par according to the journal of a well-known visitor. From different reports, his punishment of slaves was harsher than average. Whipping slaves was not an uncommon punishment and he would sell slaves, and would split up families, though he tried not to when possible. There were anti-slavery societies even in Washington's time that he did not support, even though in later years, he had mixed feelings about slavery.

Seventeen of his slaves escaped and there was a famous case of two of his favorite house slaves, one a cook and the other, Martha Washington's personal attendant, escaping from Philadelphia, the American capital and Washington's home, during his presidency. He tried until his death to recapture the slave, Ona Judge, who was Martha Washington's personal slave attendant. She escaped to New Hampshire to live out the rest of her life and was never able to see her children again. She offered to remain a slave if her children could be freed at a certain age and Washington refused to negotiate with her as a slave.

Washington did free most of his slaves upon his death, though Martha couldn't free her slaves as they were previously willed to her grandchildren. As president, he had passed a slave law in 1793 to prevent slaves from escaping and it highlighted the importance of recapturing slaves. There were heavy penalties for anyone who assisted slaves in escaping.

What about George Washington's teeth? The myth of wooden teeth is inaccurate. Several sets of dentures did have ivory, cow and even human teeth, some of which were likely his slaves' teeth, though that is speculation. Who knows how the teeth were obtained?

Whatever honesty George had, was tempered by propriety, privacy and calculation of a good outcome. His actions had to be justified by right intention. Washington was instrumental in possibly preventing an armed rebellion against Congress at the end of the Revolution. Some of his officers were plotting to rebel, as many had not been paid for their services. In an attempt to prevent the rebellion, Washington gave an inspiring speech to encourage their loyalty. He certainly modeled restraint by giving up his command of the Army when the Revolution ended. He also wanted to go back to his plantation, as farm life was a real love for him and a means to be productive.

Washington was better as a President and as a plantation owner and farmer than a military commander according to some historians, though his tenacity made him a good commander to balance some of his blunders. He showed his leadership in being the

President of the Constitutional Convention. As President of the United States for two terms, he organized and gave power to the executive branch of government and was considered a good administrator. He accepted the power of Congress. He chose men of talent to lead the cabinet and he accepted advice from those capable men. Washington helped resolve the war debt, made some Indian peace treaties despite Indian wars in the Northwest, and designated the building of Washington, D.C. He surveyed and helped in the laying out the streets of the city on paper.

Against Washington's will, Jefferson and Madison created the Democratic-Republican Party which was based on more liberal ideas and political debate, creating a schism in the government with Washington's Federalist Party. Washington was opposed to political parties, was authoritarian by nature and was cautious of too much freedom for politicians or the populace.

Washington believed in neutrality between England and France who were constantly at war with each other, with each country wanting our allegiance. He is credited with restraining himself from siding with either country and possibly from being drawn into another war with England or France, as many in the new American nation wanted.

Washington did three good will tours of the nation in 1789, 1790 and 1791 (the first two in New England and the last in the South) and was greeted with great respect. He rode to towns in a yellow coach with six white horses. Sometimes he would have the coach parked outside a city and ride in on his beloved white horse Nelson wearing his brilliant blue uniform with blazing golden epaulets. To avoid being seen as pandering to politicians and the wealthy, he stayed at public inns instead of wealthy homes. He wanted to persuade the people of the importance of a strong federal government. He certainly was the king of public relations.

As already stated, Washington was a Type 3 with a 4 wing who had a strong work ethic. He was likely a social subtype though all three subtypes of 3 are prominent in his makeup. 3s with 4 wings sometimes have issues of self-worth, are private and have darker feelings underneath. His focus was on success, constant work, accumulating wealth, promoting a positive image of importance and power and being among the elite of society. He was reserved and appeared dignified. When he was president he didn't shake hands with people, thinking that was beneath the dignity of the office.

His privacy and obfuscation of self-centered motives was paramount. Martha burned all his letters at his death, limiting our more intimate knowledge about him and their relationship. He was talented in many areas and wanted others to model themselves after him. Who knows what inner conflicts might have brewed inside him, even though his successes would have assuaged him. Despite his flaws, he was a great man and much of America is modeled after his Type 3 and 1 qualities. As previously mentioned, being a model of virtue was the image that was encouraged by many in leadership. Many men have tried to cover up their ego drive with an attempt to be seen as morally superior for their best attributes or the causes in which they believed.

In the Myers-Briggs Profile Washington would be an ISTJ, called the Duty Fulfiller, Logistician, the Trustee, and the Inspector. They are very detail oriented, pragmatic, dependable, oriented toward completion, very organized, focused on rules, rituals, regulation and authority. They have a keen sense of right and wrong and are noted for a sense of duty and responsibility. They are not known for emotional warmth and can seem aloof. They serve established institutions – home, government, schools, the military or churches. They are the bastions of society. ISTJ is a natural fit for a 3 or a 1, in this case a Type 3 who has strong 1ish tendencies and beliefs.

"The ISTJ personality type is thought to be the most abundant, making up around 13% of the population. Their defining characteristics of integrity, practical logic and tireless dedication to duty make ISTJs a vital core to many families, as well as organizations that uphold traditions, rules and standards, such as law offices, regulatory bodies and military. People with the ISTJ personality type enjoy taking responsibility for their actions, and take pride in the work they do – when working towards a goal, ISTJs hold back none of their time and energy completing each relevant task with accuracy and patience." *www.16personalities.com/istj-personality*

Washington was a natural leader who sacrificed much to model the right values and aid the new United States. He could manage the long haul, was dignified and contributed greatly to the image and reality of freedom, independence and unity, while still maintaining the higher values of the mother country of England. He wanted revolution only in a balanced state without destroying what was good. As he aged and matured, his growing restraint was a benefit to the new country.

John Adams, Political Theorist, Type 1, INTJ, 1797-1801

(1735-1826) Few questioned Adams' sense of honesty and integrity. His nickname was "Honest John." If anything, he was a bit too honest. He was serious, righteous, irascible, argumentative, relentless and thorough in everything he did. Others' agreement was not necessary, as he stood by his principles, beliefs and what he thought was right. He was a man of complexity; he was possibly manic depressive, feeling confident sometimes and at other times depressed, suspicious, doubting and insecure. His wife bolstered his spirits. Buoyed up by his strong ethical drive, Adams had a firm sense of his own mission and purpose.

As a Type 1 Perfectionist and Reformer, his sequence of strengths or tri-type is likely in the Enneagram 1-3-5 range. 1s strive hard for what is right, sacrificing for righteous principles and beliefs. There's a tendency in 1s toward rigidity, criticism and anger at the imperfection of life and how it fails to match their best ideals.

His Myers-Briggs type is likely INTJ. He was an introvert, a deep thinker and orderly and decisive in his process and conduct. As an idealist and a logical, independent thinker, he said, "I would preserve my independence even at the expense of my ambition." INTJs are analytical problem solvers and look at ways to improve systems.

The following description of INTJ is taken from: www.16personalities.com/intj-personality

"With a natural thirst for knowledge that shows itself early in life, INTJs are often given the title of "bookworm" as children. While this may be intended as an insult by their peers, they more than likely identify with it and are even proud of it, greatly enjoying their broad and deep body of knowledge. INTJs enjoy sharing what they know as well, confident in their mastery of their chosen subjects, but owing to their Intuitive (N) and Judging (J) traits, they prefer to design and execute a brilliant plan within their field rather than share opinions on "uninteresting" distractions like gossip."

"INTJs are able to live by glaring contradictions that nonetheless make perfect sense – at least from a purely rational perspective. For example, INTJs are simultaneously the most starry-eyed idealists and the bitterest of cynics, a seemingly impossible conflict. But this is because INTJ types tend to believe that with effort, intelligence and consideration, nothing is impossible, while at the same time they believe that people are too lazy, short-sighted or self-serving to actually achieve those fantastic results. Yet that cynical view of reality is unlikely to stop an interested INTJ from achieving a result they believe to be relevant."

Adams stood between 5'6" to 5'7" and was a bit rotund. Bright, learned and well read, he held a bachelor's and a master's degree from Harvard. Being a hard worker, as most 1s are, he was ambitious and fully committed to whatever he did. John was an excellent writer, speaker and promulgator of whatever he believed in, and he was articulate, convincing and passionate.

He was fair, or certainly had a strong desire for fairness. He risked his reputation to defend the seven British soldiers who were being tried for the Boston Massacre. Five of those soldiers were acquitted because Adams proved the mob instigated the shootings, and two were convicted of manslaughter. Wanting Britain to see that the colonials weren't just rabble rousers, he could be honest and fair, two major guidelines for a Type 1.

Adams was the only one of the Founding Father Presidents who didn't own slaves and Adams was clear about his opposition to slavery. Of course, he didn't come from a wealthy background or from the South where slavery was more common. Despite his opposition to slavery, in 1777 he was against abolishing it in Massachusetts, fearing opposition from the Southern states whose support he wanted in the Revolution. Massachusetts finally abolished slavery in 1783, based on a judicial decision that was related to "equal rights" in the Massachusetts Constitution written by Adams in 1780. Adams married Abigail who was even more adamant and outspoken than he against slavery. She promoted women's rights and he backed her as much as was politically feasible.

John Adams was a direct descendant of the Puritans who came to New England in the 1630s, his father was a farmer, shoemaker and deacon of the local church. Many of his New England ancestors were farmers, beer and ale brewers or ministers, the ministry being the profession that John's father wished for his son. However, John carved his own path by apprenticing to a lawyer, passing the bar, working as a lawyer and eventually entering politics.

As a child, John hunted and fished and sometimes skipped school due to his interest in outdoor activities. His father taught him a lesson by working him hard on the farm, since John said he wanted to be a farmer instead of attending school. That cured the young Adams of the farming bug and he didn't miss school from then on! From an early age, Adams loved to read. He would go into his room and read books when his parents fought. He also loved logic and deep thinking. Both parents were strong-minded and John inherited the trait.

After college, John had a stint for several years as a schoolteacher in Worcester. After becoming a lawyer, he traveled to distant villages, including ones in Maine, on the court circuit, which kept him away from Abigail and his family. He often defended Boston merchants in court, which eventually led him to become the most well-known lawyer in Boston. He had always wanted to become "a great man and have honor, reputation and make more difference than his fellows." Many 1s want to make a difference, to change the world in the right direction.

Adams developed a habit of writing in his diary, describing events and impressions of important people in history. Sometimes his annotations in the margins of the numerous books he read were as long as the original writings! Many of these annotated books still survive, residing at the Massachusetts Historical Society in Boston.

In 1763 Adams published seven essays in Boston newspapers – treatises on political theory. He wrote essays in the *Boston Gazette* in 1765 to oppose the Stamp Act and wrote in-depth analyses of historical figures and the principles of Republicanism. Adams provided one of the most extensive and learned arguments made by the colonists against British imperial policy. *Novanglus* was a systematic attempt by Adams to describe the origins, nature and jurisdiction of British concepts of constitutionality. He used his wide knowledge of English and colonial legal history to argue that the provincial legislatures were fully sovereign over their own internal affairs and his writings provided reasons for the colonials to be independent from Britain. INTJs are often great theoreticians and many INTJs are 1s.

A number of patriots sought Adams' advice about forming a new government and found his views so convincing that they urged him to commit them to paper. He did so in separate letters to colleagues, each one a bit longer and more thoughtful than the last. *Thoughts of Government* is a compilation of these letters. Many historians agree that these letters helped to spark the Revolution.

Adams was on the drafting committee to write the Declaration of Independence. Even though Jefferson wrote the main draft of the Declaration, it was highly edited by Adams. Adams was asked to write it, even by Jefferson, but he refused because he thought Jefferson would do a better job. Adams later regretted his decision, as Jefferson got all the credit and praise for this writing!

During the Revolutionary War, Adams served as the head of the Board of War and Ordnance, sitting on ninety committees and chairing twenty-five, certainly more than anyone else. As Benjamin Rush reported, he was "the first man in the House." He was a "one-man war department," working eighteen-hour days and mastering details of raising, equipping and fielding an army under civilian control. 1s are often great at detail and almost always give their best efforts. He also laid out Congress's requirements for a crucial treaty with France.

On the subject of what the president of a new country should be like, Adams suggested having a president for life or even having a monarch, though he compromised and accepted the idea of a strong president. He favored voting only by men of property, as was the custom of the time, and favored senators who were wealthy and well known. Giving people too much power worried Adams and he thought the masses were not educated or ethical enough to choose wisely. He was a Federalist in politics, believing in a strong central government run by elder statesmen, and he felt that popular votes should not determine the presidency.

With regards to religion, Adams believed that regular church service was beneficial to man's moral sense. Adams strove for religion based on common sense and reason, and he maintained that religion must change and evolve toward perfection. Hard work, self-improvement and sacrifice, all respected New England values, especially for type 1s, were his standard. He wasn't a relaxed, laid back sort of guy! He was a workaholic who tended to be uncompromising, and he made independent decisions, though he would consult others on occasion.

Adams had a vision for the future of America. In a letter to Abigail he wrote, "The science of government it is my duty to study, more than all other sciences; the arts of legislation and administration and negotiation ought to take the place of, indeed exclude, in a manner, all other arts. I must study politics and war, that our sons may have liberty to study mathematics and philosophy. Our sons ought to study mathematics and philosophy, geography, natural history and naval architecture, navigation, commerce and agriculture in order to give their children a right to study painting, poetry, music, architecture, statuary, tapestry and porcelain." Sacrificing for the future was part of his plan.

Much is known about John Adams because of all of his published writings, and the over 1,100 letters he wrote to his wife. His friend George Washington wrote letters to his wife Martha, but she burned all but three of them. John was more able than Washington to reveal his weaknesses and he hid less behind a public image. Still, he was sensitive to criticism like George Washington.

Adams won the presidency over Thomas Jefferson by a narrow margin. In those days, the runner up became vice president! The Capitol at that time was in Philadelphia as it had been for almost 10 years. The Capitol even shifted to Trenton, New Jersey for a while! No matter where the Capitol was officially, he spent much of his time running the presidency from his estate in Quincy, Massachusetts, especially in the summer when there was contagious disease in Philadelphia. Adams set the precedent for an orderly transfer of power from Washington to himself, from one president to another, which became a model for democratic process. Order is the name of the game for the perfectionist.

Adams served in the actual newly finished White House, called the President's House, in Washington D.C. but only for the last several months of his presidency. His policies resembled those of his predecessor. His cabinet, passed down from George Washington, was often at odds with him. Keeping the United States out of war with France, which had been pirating American ships, was a major focus for Adams. There actually was a quasi-unofficial war between France and America from 1798 to 1800 and it was settled by a treaty in 1800, probably the best legacy of his presidency.

Adams' successful efforts as peace minister overseas before his presidency served him well. He was constantly trying to make peace with both France and England during his presidential tenure. Both countries wanted to have America's alliance and trading rights. In addition to Anglo-French rivalry, there were serious factions in Adams own Federalist Party, as well as severe conflict with the new Democratic-Republican Party headed by Jefferson, who was Adam's vice president! Adams was a genius which was demonstrated by his ability to keep the presidency intact. The nation could have fallen apart with someone less adept.

Unfortunately, Adams signed a bill called the Alien and Sedition Act in 1798. This act basically nullified the First Amendment regarding free speech. Adams debated for a long time whether to sign it but Abigail encouraged him, thinking it would protect her husband. The bill stated that anyone could be arrested who spoke against the government and the government could deport anyone who might be a French spy. In reality, few people were arrested or deported but the bill blemished the record of Adams, one of the Founding Fathers who had written so much about freedom.

It was a challenge to find the right balance between law and freedom, in a country that was somewhat at war with itself about how to relate to foreign powers, states' rights, federal taxes, and building an army and navy. There was much disagreement. Even though Adams was strong on central government, he encouraged the development of state governments.

Many consider Adams the Father of the Navy as he had war ships built in case of a war with France. He chose policy over party, doing his best to follow what he thought would benefit the nation in the long run. He never envisioned that a political party, which Jefferson was actively engaged in creating, would occur, and he felt that divisiveness and politicking would ensue if parties were created. Adams and Jefferson were becoming at odds with each other.

Adams' faithfulness, courage, and strength in the forming of the new country had much to do with Abigail, who was also a Type 1 as well as his most trusted confidante and advisor. She kept up with current events, politics and war. The road along their farm was a byway that many colonial soldiers walked on their way to fight battles and their land was a practice marching area. A listening ear and cheery appearance were Abigail's offerings to soldiers and she even made bullets for the Revolution. Abigail and her children watched the Revolution's Battle of Bunker Hill, only two miles away, from a hill on their estate.

John had a close partnership with his wife even though he didn't spend as much time with his family as he wanted. Nearly 10 years was spent as a diplomat during and after the Revolution, serving in England, France and Holland. Several times he traveled with his sons, John Quincy Adams Jr. and Charles, to Europe. His wife, Abigail, also travelled with him and his daughter, Nabby, where they lived with John in Paris and then London. Travel aboard ship took months of preparation, bringing your own food, linens, and servants and managing seasickness and primitive conditions. French books were brought along to practice learning the language.

Abigail was quite human. In one of her letters she complained about their three-year engagement before they got married. She wanted to be more amorous physically and John scolded her playfully to be patient. They had a child exactly nine months after their wedding!

Abigail raised their children and kept the farm going during and after the War. She supported John in his commitment to the country but complained about his being away too long. She believed strongly in the Revolution and the direction of the new country and felt that her role was to encourage her husband. When Abigail died just after their 54th wedding anniversary, John said he wished he had died with her. It was one of the strongest political and romantic bonds in presidential history; John wouldn't have been the man he was without her.

John and Abigail had six children but only four survived. One was a stillbirth and another died at 15 months of age; a devastating loss for them. John loved his children but was often harsh. His son John Quincy managed to meet his father's high expectations but the other sons didn't. One son became an alcoholic and died at age 30. The other son died at 60. He too had problems with alcohol and difficulty obtaining the political success that was his father's ambition for him. Both of those sons lost considerable sums of money in bad investments. The Adams' devoted daughter, Nabby, was a constant companion of her mother and unfortunately died of breast cancer at age 48.

After serving his country for over 35 years, John retired to Peacefield, the family farm in Quincy, MA, with Abigail, where he lived another 25 years. They both enjoyed reading, talking to each other and gardening, with a particular focus on planting and tending to trees and shrubs. Many of the plants and trees at the John Adams estate in Quincy today are from his cuttings and plantings when he retired! You can visit Peacefield today and it's well worth the visit.

After the Adams' son, Charles, died of alcoholism, his widow Sally and her five young daughters moved into Peacefield, creating more life and laughter at the farm. The Adams' grandson, John Quincy's son, also lived at Peacefield when his parents were abroad. John Quincy often came and went, staying for weeks on end. The Adams' other son Thomas lived nearby.

Finally, Abigail and John had time for themselves and their children and grandchildren. Their son John Quincy became the 6th president of the United States one year before John's death. It was the first father-son presidential combo, and it was not repeated again until the Bush Presidencies. John Adams had one of the longest retirements of any president until modern history.

Adams continued to write correspondence, make political commentary, and work on his autobiography. He enjoyed learning, even becoming somewhat of an expert on compost, manure and soil development. Adams and Thomas Jefferson, had been bitter enemies, with Adams not even attending the inauguration of Jefferson. They became friends in 1812 and wrote many letters back and forth until their deaths only hours apart on the 50th anniversary of the Declaration of Independence on July 4, 1826! As he was dying, John could hear the July 4th festivities from outside his window. Abigail had died earlier when she was 73. John lived until age 91, one of the oldest presidents until modern history.

John Adams was a man of integrity and hard work, sacrificing much to maintain the United States. He was a researcher and advocate of taking the British system of law to the next step in the United States. He had a viable marriage and was able to listen to his wife's feedback to try to change some of his difficult traits to be more compromising, flexible and inclusive. His commitment and sacrifice to his country is unchallenged.

Thomas Jefferson – Renaissance Man, Type 5, INTP, 1801-09

(1743-1826) Thomas Jefferson, president number three, created a second Revolution in the United States. Whereas Washington and Adams believed in a strong central government, Jefferson believed more in states' rights, equality for all white men, and non-interference from the government. Jefferson created a new party called the Democratic - Republican Party. Thus began the two-party system, which rejected anything that resembled monarchy or limited the freedom of citizens. Jefferson viewed Washington and Adams, his predecessors, as perpetuating the monarchical tradition.

Jefferson believed in the French Revolution and the overthrow of autocratic governments, even though as president, he strengthened the power of the Executive Branch. He believed in what Alexander Hamilton said, "When a government betrays the people by amassing too much power and becoming tyrannical, the people have no choice but to exercise the original rights of self-defense – to fight the government." Jefferson fought for "the sacred fire of freedom." As a Type 5, he believed in individuality, personal freedom, the use of reason and leaving people to pursue the dictates of their own conscience.

Jefferson was a man of contrast. Whereas he was a strong believer in freedom for the common man and espoused equality, he held over 600 slaves. The slaves were almost all bequeathed to him through inheritance, but there were only a handful that he freed. He pushed the Native American tribes west without regard for *their* homeland and freedom. Jefferson, who was friendly but aloof like most 5s, had many ideas about individuality and non-interference, though those ideas mostly referred to white males.

He was an aristocrat who was in debt most of the time from overspending for fine wines, rich foods and beautiful house furnishings. He designed, built and rebuilt Monticello over many decades, loved the latest gadgets and had expansive gardens. Visitors were subject to the din produced by saws, planes and the pounding of nails in the expansion and rebuilding of Monticello. He was an experimenter, gardener extraordinaire, inventor, astronomer and an architect. He was a violinist, sang Scottish tunes, played chess, was a horseman and loved the woods. He dabbled in archaeology and paleontology. He rated his core interests in this order – scientist first, farmer second and statesman third.

As a Type 5 in the Enneagram, Jefferson was quiet, enigmatic, private and eccentric and was much more a writer than a speaker. He was awkward physically. As President, he sent the State of the Union Address to Congress to be read by someone else, and that precedent was continued until 1913. John Adams said of Jefferson that in the first Continental Congress he never uttered three complete sentences in a row but that he was prompt, frank and decisive in committees. He served on 34 committees and was a master at drafting legislation. As a member of the House of Delegates in Virginia, he drafted 128 bills that related to public education, separation of church and state, religious freedom of choice and eliminated the autocratic assigning of all property to the eldest son.

Jefferson was an inventor who loved to try new things. He invented an instrument that would duplicate any letter he wrote, a five-sided book stand to read five open books at a time, and a clock that would point to the day of the week utilizing a series of moving cannonballs that hung from the clock. Other creations include a swivel chair, a wheel cipher to decode secret messages, a machine that made fiber from hemp, a pedometer, a lazy Susan, a spherical sundial, a pasta machine and his own unique version of mac and cheese!

He grew over 250 varieties of vegetables, grafted new trees in his 1200 fruit tree orchard, had numerous flower beds, and also experimented with new varieties of non-fruit trees. His house was decorated with treasures from the Lewis and Clark Expedition of 1803 – buffalo hides, elk horns, pipes, drums, and Indian relics and these are still on display today in his main entrance room.

He drafted legislation to end or curtail slavery but never freed his own slaves. Jefferson was kinder than some slave owners, but some of his slaves were whipped by his overseer and others were sold, resulting in the breakup of families. Thousands of others in Virginia did free their slaves so Jefferson did have that option. He said he couldn't afford to free his slaves, as he was always in debt. He fathered as many as five children with one of his slaves, Sarah "Sally" Hemings. She was the half-sister of his wife Martha and his relationship with Sally spanned 38-years. This was, of course, kept very private. Sally, was the daughter of Jefferson's father-in-law's slave mistress. Many owners routinely had ongoing intimate relationships with their slaves and family relationships became entangled. The resulting progeny, being half siblings to their owners' white children, nonetheless remain enslaved.

Jefferson was intellectually optimistic but had a life filled with grief. His best friend died young, as did his wife Martha, and five of his six children died before reaching adulthood. Each loss was extremely painful, but he found ways to cope and continued to have faith in the future.

He loved ideas but had a hard time completing all the things that captured his interest. As mentioned, Monticello was in a constant state of change and repair throughout his entire life. Experimentation seemed more important than stability. 5s have a lot in common with 7s who love to learn and experiment also.

He backed the French Revolution for its ideology, rather than the reality that it turned out to be cruel and murderous leading eventually to the rise of the dictator, Napoleon. He criticized the French aristocracy but relished living in the luxury of the wealthy. He spoke highly of the common man but always lived above his own means and enjoyed luxurious living.

Many people type Jefferson as a type 7, which is probably his secondary type. In reality, he was a Type 5, the Thinker/Observer/Knowledge Seeker. Being a 5, Jefferson was measured in his speech, was very private and didn't have the animation and fast speech associated with 7s. But he had a strong connection to Type 7 as well as 1. At his core, though, he had the Type 5 characteristics of constant learning, containment, observation, privacy, and conciseness; he was quite happy to be alone to learn, study and invent. He did have plenty of visitors, due to his fame and their shared desire to have rich, intellectual conversations.

I believe Jefferson had a strong 4 wing, which provided him with an accessibility to deep experiences and feelings such as grief, a passion for art and amazing creativity. He loved the beauty of nice clothing, music, and the aesthetic surroundings of his home and gardens. In the Myers-Briggs he is likely an INTP which is a strong correlation with Type 5 - very intellectual, theoretical and brilliant thinkers who are often challenged by practicality. INTPs can easily be inventors. Shy in many ways, he loved small groups much more than large crowds. Even though he was well versed in theory, he could translate ideas into practical use. I consider him a Perceiver in the Myers-Briggs, even though he could also be decisive. He had wide ranging interests and didn't like to be overly bound by structure. He loved having free time to explore whatever arena of knowledge he wanted to develop.

INTP PERSONALITY ("THE LOGICIAN") WWW.16PERSONALITIES.COM/INTP-PERSONALITY

Learn from yesterday, live for today, hope for tomorrow. The important thing is not to stop questioning.

Albert Einstein, Type 5

"The INTP personality type is fairly rare, making up only three percent of the population, which is definitely a good thing for them, as there's nothing they'd be more unhappy about than being "common". INTPs pride themselves on their inventiveness and creativity, their unique perspective and vigorous intellect. Usually known as the philosopher, the architect, or the dreamy professor, INTPs have been responsible for many scientific discoveries throughout history."

The Unexamined Life Is Not Worth Living

"INTPs are known for their brilliant theories and unrelenting logic – in fact, they are considered the most logically precise of all the personality types. They love patterns, and spotting discrepancies between statements made in conversation or in written documents could almost be described as a hobby, making it a bad idea to lie to an INTP. This makes it ironic that the word of an INTP should always be taken with a grain of salt; not that they are dishonest, but people with the INTP personality type tend to share under-developed thoughts, using others as a sounding board for ideas and theories in a debate against themselves rather than being actual partners in conversation.

This may make them appear unreliable, but in reality, no one is more enthusiastic and capable of spotting a problem, drilling through the endless factors and details that encompass the issue and developing a unique and viable solution than INTPs – just don't expect punctual progress reports. People who share the INTP personality type aren't interested in practical, day-to-day activities and maintenance, but when they find an environment where their creative genius and potential can be expressed, there is no limit to the time and energy INTPs will expend in developing an insightful and unbiased solution."

Born on April 13, 1743 in Virginia, his mother was from the aristocracy and his father was a self-made man who was independent and industrious. He introduced Thomas to American Indians and took him exploring deep into the woods. By age six he taught himself to read Latin and Greek and he started playing the violin. Private tutors guided his education. He always had personal libraries and read extensively. He had a relative life of freedom, exploring nature, reading, learning and developing himself. At age 16, attended by his personal slave Jupiter, he was a student at William and Mary College in Williamsburg, the state capitol and the richest city in America.

In the first year of college, he frequented horse races, balls and other dances, fox hunts and card games, but eventually settled down and studied 15 hours a day. He attended special dinners each week at the governor's palace in Williamsburg where there were great conversations about the Enlightenment, fueled by the ideas of Locke, Bacon and Newton and the latest happenings in Europe; all accompanied by excellent food and wine. Intellectual enrichment was highly encouraged and added to Jefferson's native brilliance.

Jefferson became a lawyer after studying and reading law for two years and attending court sessions with the well-known lawyer George Wythe. He was admitted to the Virginia bar in 1765, his law practice dealing mostly with land cases. In the next nine years, he handled over 900 cases dealing with both common farmers and the powerful planter class.

Jefferson became an expert in estate law, drawing wills and offering counsel to other attorneys in matters related to wills and trusts. He figured out ways to avoid representing clients before a judge when at all possible. As a type 5, he preferred doing research and presenting his cases on paper. He paid meticulous attention to detail and possessed a deep understanding of English law. Politics and being a public servant was the natural evolution for a lawyer and a man of his standing and inheritance.

Jefferson, as is common for a 5, was a writer. Unlike Adams who was both a writer and a public speaker, Jefferson disliked public speaking. He was very involved in the American political cause and wrote a treatise, *Summary View of the Rights of Americans,* which served as a backdrop to ideas that were later incorporated into the Declaration of Independence. Chosen to write the Declaration of Independence, Jefferson wrote a paragraph attacking slavery that was mostly eliminated from the document. In it he basically blamed King George for transporting slaves to America and initiating the slave trade but didn't quite get around to altogether condemning slavery. Maybe his colonial guilt, and the awareness of his own hypocrisy in owning slaves, needed to be projected onto King George!

Merchants, landowners and politicians directly benefitting from the transatlantic slave trade, voted down the inclusion of a paragraph about slavery. It was hotly debated in Congress whether to include the anti-slavery passage or not. It seemed that all the Founding Fathers wanted to be seen as anti-slavery even though their very fortunes were based upon it.

Jefferson was very much in love with his wife, Martha, who often was sick or depressed, mostly it seemed from witnessing her children dying. When she died from birth complications 10 years after their marriage, Jefferson was grief stricken and stayed in one room for three weeks and spent another three weeks riding on his horse in the woods. He promised her on her deathbed that he wouldn't remarry, as Martha didn't think that their children would adjust to a stepmother. He equally grieved for each of his children when they died, but his political pursuits, Monticello and his hobbies and interests kept him going. He commented that human relationships were much more painful than the pursuit of ideas and interests and he ruminated about the nature of grief. 5s who often are INTPs, struggle with feelings and try to make sense of things with their intellect.

Even though he supported states' rights, Jefferson greatly expanded the power of the Presidency by purchasing Louisiana from France, which doubled the size of the United States, without congressional approval. Many considered the purchase unconstitutional. He also authorized the Lewis and Clarke expedition without congressional approval. He didn't like to publicize to Congress or the populace what he was doing. He was somewhat a loner who was not looking for approval, very typical of a 5. When his relationship with his slave, Sally Hemings, was exposed in the press, he never addressed it. Over time the criticism went away. He modeled an aristocratic attitude of not having to explain yourself. His privacy was of upmost importance to him.

As president, he was an eccentric and didn't follow the norm. He did away with the title, His Excellency the President, and simply wanted to be called the President. He walked to his inauguration rather than being driven by carriage. Walking in public during the inauguration parade didn't happen again until Jimmy Carter became president. He would answer his own door at the White House, greet people in his slippers and housecoat, shake hands instead of being bowed to, and invited the public for sit-down dinners instead of putting on formal dinners with people in power! He was highly criticized for not taking the arm of a diplomat's wife, preferring informality to formality.

Jefferson redesigned and added many new features to the White House. As his first act as president, Jefferson pardoned anyone jailed by Adam's Alien and Sedition Act. His daughter, Patty, served as First Lady and also gave him 11 grandchildren whom he loved.

He retired after being president for two terms and never came back to Washington in his remaining 17 years. He didn't put being president as one of his three accomplishments on his tombstone! Rather he listed: Thomas Jefferson, Author of the Declaration of Independence, Author of the Statute of Virginia for Religious Freedom and Father of the University of Virginia. He spent the last five years of his life, designing, building and hiring professors for the University of Virginia, which was a public school unaffiliated with any religion. He was the architect for all the buildings on campus! Jefferson enjoyed his retirement.

Jefferson was an apostle of change who remained optimistic about the future. He was often more theoretical than realistic though he loved to invent practical devices. He believed in freedom over restraint and didn't feel obliged to observe any tradition, as is the case for both Type 5 and INTP. He died just hours apart on the same day as John Adams, July 4, 1826, the 50th Anniversary of the Declaration of Independence. Both Jefferson and Adams had been instrumental in the founding of the country, Adams being more down to earth and Jefferson more idealistic, though both were intellects.

Jefferson supported the ideas of freedom, invention, exploration and individuality and was an experimenter and legislator who appreciated the finer things in life. He studied everything from plants to animals, ideas about government to fine art and music. He believed in freedom of religion, freedom of education and the move away from the monarchical traditions of Europe.

James Madison – Father of the Constitution, Type 5, INTP, 1809-1817

(1751-1836) "Knowledge will forever govern ignorance, and a people who mean to be their own governors must avail themselves with the power which knowledge gives." This is a classic Type 5 comment made by Madison.

Only 5 feet 4 inches and 120 pounds in weight, he had a large influence on the founding of the United States, and was the architect of many principles and guidelines for the new democratic government. Madison is considered the Father of the US Constitution; he was the author of the Bill of Rights, served as Secretary of the United States twice under Thomas Jefferson, served two terms as President of the United States, served as a Representative in the U. S. Congress four times, served in the Virginia Assembly and was President of the University of Virginia for 10 years.

Somewhat shy and reserved as is common with 5s, he wasn't prone to displays of anger like Washington and Adams. He appeared calm, yet engaged. A brilliant thinker and writer as is often true of 5s, he did his homework and was always prepared. Madison knew what he was talking about. Even though he wasn't considered a great public speaker, he could debate with the best of them, including Thomas Paine and Patrick Henry, because his knowledge was so vast. His voice was often so soft that people taking notes would leave out sentences, not being able to hear him.

He was highly influential in sponsoring and writing legislation that related to religious freedom, separation of the church and state, a system of checks and balances, the structure of the House and Senate, and a system of judicial review that became the foundation of our modern judicial review system. Madison is also considered The Father of Politics, as he knew that one had to have popular approval of the ideas that the executive branch and legislature enacted. He co-founded with Jefferson the Democratic-Republican Party, which became the modern Democratic Party. Along with Jefferson, he started the National Review newspaper to forward his ideas to the populace and counter the forces of the Federalist Party, which had a more aristocratic bent. The National Review newspaper is considered the forerunner of many modern political newspapers today.

Madison was sickly much of his life and as a child was delicate and fragile. At times he had seizures, but modern history classifies them as possibly psychosomatic in nature and not caused by epilepsy. He had malaria at various times in his life, as well as influenza, dysentery and rheumatism. He was however intellectually gifted. By the age of 11, he had read all 100 books in his father's library, very unusual for the average person, but less so for type 5s who are usually avid readers. Young Madison grew up in the wealthy home of his father's tobacco and grain plantation in Virginia, which was worked by 100 slaves.

The eldest of 12 children, he was tutored at home until he reached the age of 11. From then until he was 16 he attended a boarding school to study the classics of Latin and Greek. Madison attended The College of New Jersey, known today as Princeton University, where he was a founding member of its debating society. He studied Hebrew, history, political theory, philosophy and ethics, as well as Latin and Greek. Madison was possibly the first graduate student in America, as he continued to study with the president of the college after his graduation. He was a brilliant student and finished in two years instead of the normal three years at that time.

Madison was ill following his graduation, so he returned home and began to serve in local politics. This was the beginning of his political career. Unlike Jefferson who had many other passions, Madison devoted his life exclusively to thinking, writing, legislation and politics. Jefferson and Madison met while serving in local Virginian political offices and became best friends for life. Their closeness was reflected in Jefferson dedicating a bedroom at Monticello just for Madison who was a frequent guest.

In 1776 Madison was elected to the Virginia convention, which decided to free America from Great Britain as well as create a new state constitution. Like Jefferson, Madison's contribution emphasized the importance of creating religious freedom while harboring no prejudice or predilection toward any individual religion. He became actively involved in the pursuit of freedom for the Baptist church, which had been outlawed in Virginia.

He was elected to other governing bodies in Virginia as well as the Continental Congress of 1780 and spent years promoting Jefferson's Virginia bill for religious freedom and other reforms. Madison believed initially in a strong central government, but as time went on, he became aware of and concerned about the possible ramifications of too much power being concentrated in the federal government.

Madison's greatest contribution was his devotion to the Constitutional Convention held in Philadelphia in the summer of 1787. He showed up 11 days early to prepare for it. He previously organized and assembled a convention in Annapolis the year before to plan the Constitutional Convention. Showing up before anyone else every day of the four-month long sweltering hot gathering of the Constitutional Convention, he greeted every one of the 55 delegates from a desk in front of the hall.

He took short hand notes of the proceedings from 10am to 3pm each day and translated the notes in long hand at night. Politicking for the ideas of the Constitution, he wrote most of it himself, and kept a calm demeanor while trying to maintain harmony between the various factions at the Convention. His unemotional affect kept the reactive types in balance. He was the most emotionally mature and non-reactive of all the founding fathers.

James Madison and Alexander Hamilton wrote a series of essays called *The Federalist Papers* to promote the passage of the Constitution, which was to be voted on by each state. Madison also wrote Washington's first inaugural speech, being one of Washington's closest advisors. Later they would part ways; Madison always spoke well of Washington, even though the reverse wasn't true. In time and with Jefferson's influence, Madison came to believe in a more democratic form of government, creating a growing rift with Hamilton and Washington.

Madison was an excellent writer and all of his letters, notes, articles and legislation are contained in the seven-series set, entitled The Madison Papers. He held the position of secretary at the many conventions he attended. Madison made his thoughts very visible and could defend all of his ideas. He was well researched, well prepared and was not a person of dramatic gestures, but was rather a master of thoroughness and practicality; a visionary who thought realistically. Always five steps ahead of the next person, he considered the consequences of every decision he made. He was a master of preparation, persuasion, agenda setting, and parliamentary maneuvering. Madison showed the most mature traits of the type 5 Thinker and INTP in his patience, planning and comprehensive thinking.

Even though Madison was a centralist in the beginning, he was concerned about Alexander Hamilton, Secretary of Finance under Washington, whose focus was on supporting the privilege of the wealthy. Madison wanted to include everyone in his vision of government and the freedoms offered by the U.S. Constitution. Madison was simultaneously concerned about creating a strong trade alliance with Britain, and was worried about how that might undermine the new freedom of the United States.

One of Madison's best decisions occurred in 1794 when he met and set his sights on marrying Dolley Payne. Unlike Madison who was serious and reserved, Dolley was gracious, vivacious and attractive She was 17 years his junior and was an excellent hostess who enjoyed politics and meeting people. Everyone was drawn to her as much as Madison was himself. Serving at times as a substitute First Lady for the White House during social engagements for President Jefferson, she was an excellent First Lady in Madison's two terms. Warm and smiling, she was a beautiful woman with social graces, and had a knack for politicking without putting people off. She was loved by all, admired and respected by both rich and poor. She was the first strong political wife. Even today, many people consider her the best First Lady in American history.

Dolley was instrumental in the decoration and development of the White House. She was also famous for serving ice cream (her favorite being oyster ice cream) and decorating the White House with red velvet curtains, gilt-edged chairs, and a piano, often accompanied by of talking of a real-life macaw! During the War of 1812, in 1814, she saved national treasures, including George Washington's portrait, just hours before the British troops arrived and set fire to the White House.

Born a Quaker, Dolley gave up her religion when she married Madison. She was previously married to a lawyer in 1790. He unfortunately died, along with one of their two children, their in-laws and thousands of others in the famous yellow fever epidemic of 1793 in Philadelphia. There were many deadly epidemics throughout the colonial period of the new republic.

Dolley set the standard for the future of all First Ladies. She was so well known and well regarded that at her death in 1849, both houses of Congress adjourned, and along with the Supreme Court and President Zachary Taylor, the members all escorted her coffin to the largest funeral Washington D.C. had ever seen.

Madison was somewhat of a nerd if one were to judge by today's standards, but he was highly respected. He had the most disciplined mind of anyone in American history. No one could win an argument in the face of his brilliance. He wasn't drawn to small talk or petty arguments. Devoting his life to hard work, he dedicated the mission of the new country to educating the populace, eliminating religious prejudice and creating more opportunity for all people. Considered fair-minded and honest, he was well valued by his peers.

Madison was a Type 5 and likely an INTP (introverted, big picture thinker) in the Myers-Briggs, just like his best friend, Thomas Jefferson. He was a brilliant thinker who liked to talk about new ideas and concepts. There's a chance he could be an INTJ, but he didn't seem to have the critical edge of a Judge who sees things in a more exacting way. He seemed to have an aura of spaciousness and the more allowing attitude of a Perceiver.

He tended to accept people as they were, without needing to impose the "shoulds" of a Judge.

Despite the fact that he had never fired a gun or hunted, he briefly led a contingent of American troops in Washington D.C., during the War of 1812, to protect the city. Then Secretary of State, James Monroe, was sent to negotiate the Treaty of Ghent with Great Britain and Ireland in 1814, even though the war went on until early 1815, when Andrew Jackson won the Battle of New Orleans. News of the war's end didn't travel fast enough to stop the New Orleans battle. After the War of 1812 the country entered a lasting period of peace and respect from other nations. There was a surge of nationalism and Madison was fairly popular when he left the White House in 1817. Jefferson called Madison "The greatest man in the world."

It is interesting to note, that several rare tornadoes (described by some as a hurricane, but, in any case, a massive storm) saved the city of Washington D.C. the day after the British soldiers torched the White House. The accompanying rain put out the fire at the White House, and the British troops who weren't killed by the storm, left the city post haste. Otherwise the British might have burned down the entire city! As it was, many government buildings were burned and destroyed. Despite that, grace seemed to be protecting the new nation.

Madison was essential to the founding of the country. He was the most balanced of the Founding Fathers; different from some of the more hot-headed Founders, particularly Washington and Adams, and even Monroe. He had the brilliance of Jefferson, the commitment of Adams and the humility to step back and decline the limelight.

James Monroe – Era of Good Feelings, Type 3, ISTJ, 1817-25

(1758-1831) James Monroe, our fifth president, is the last of the Founding Fathers and the last of the Virginia Dynasty: all of the first five presidents, except John Adams, were from Virginia. All five of our first five presidents were introverts. Monroe was the last U.S. President to wear a powdered wig tied in a queue, a cocked hat and knee breeches, in the style of the late 18th century. His nickname was the Last Cocked Hat and his presidency marked the end of the Revolutionary era. A politician first and foremost, he had few hobbies other than horseback riding and hunting.

James Monroe is likely a type 3, though he had many type 9 traits: affable, inclusive, warm, low key, reserved, unpretentious, likeable, and popular. He was also bold and fearless with a type 3's bent for action and drive for success. He wasn't an intellectual like Jefferson and Madison but was an action-oriented man like Washington. Monroe was considered an aggressive expansionist, adding new territories to the United States. Although he was an introvert, he showed more warmth and friendliness than Washington. Like Washington, he was an ISTJ.

"When ISTJs say they are going to get something done, they do it, meeting their obligations no matter the personal cost, and they are baffled by people who don't hold their own word in the same respect. Combining laziness and dishonesty is the quickest way to get on ISTJs' bad side. Consequently, people with the ISTJ personality type often prefer to work alone, or at least have their authority clearly established by hierarchy, where they can set and achieve their goals without debate or worry over others' reliability." www.16personalities.com/istj-personality

As a Type 3, one of his quotes was, "A little flattery will support a man through great fatigue." 3s love to be praised by others. There is less written about Monroe than most other presidents, particularly regarding his inner personality; a possible sign of a Type 3 hiding his emotions. As mentioned above, he is likely an ISTJ, who often are Type 1s. In this case he is more likely a Type 3 in the Enneagram with Type 1 as his secondary type.

Few of his letters still exist. As a matter of fact, he burned all his papers before his death. He seems to have had an undisturbed personality, was happily married, loved his children and loved to work and serve. He championed the Bill of Rights, fought the rule of secret sessions in the Senate whereby the deliberations were concealed from the public, and as Governor of Virginia, he established publicly supported schools.

Monroe was admired by both politicians and the populace. Jefferson remarked "Monroe was a man whose soul might be turned wronged outwards without discovering a blemish to the world." He was hardworking, brought projects to successful completion and was good-natured.

Monroe was not particularly interested in legal theory or practice when he studied law under Thomas Jefferson, but according to Jefferson, Monroe chose to take it up because he thought law offered "the most immediate rewards and could ease his path to wealth, social standing, and political influence." These aspirations are consistent with Type 3 priorities. Monroe had a lavish lifestyle and liked being popular. In portraits made of him he displayed much of the reserved dignity that many of his time valued highly in positions of leadership.

Monroe was very decisive when given command, as 3s can be, and was very loyal to his superiors and his country. He had the ability to see all sides of an issue and to respect differences. He had the best traits of Type 3: action-oriented but not overly self-serving, with a quiet, warm, friendly, dignified and mature persona. His presidency from 1817-25 was called the Era of Good Feelings because it was a period of relative ease and peace.

Not everything was peaches and cream though. His Secretary of the Treasury once tried to beat him with a cane, while Monroe grabbed a pair of fire tongs and chased him out of the Executive Mansion! In another unsettling incident, the British and French Ministers drew swords against each other and Monroe drew his own to break up the fight. It wasn't unusual at that time for government officials to wear their ceremonial rapiers at the dinner table.

Monroe served as George Washington's Minister to France. After a few years had passed, he was brought home by Washington, following a dispute between them. Washington wanted Monroe to be a neutral force as opposed to being the Francophile he was. Monroe called Washington "insane and incompetent in foreign affairs" and wrote a 407-page defense of his actions in France. They did not remain friendly and, in fact, hated each other.

There is some speculation that Washington's death at age 67, in December 1799, was contributed to by his reaction of upset and anger when he found out that Monroe had just won the Governorship of Virginia. Washington had been attending to his plantation on horseback and after a long, cold and snowy ride, returned home, ranting with visitors for a long time about Monroe's election. Instead of changing into dry clothes which he normally would have done, he kept on his wet clothing which led to a cold, pneumonia and his death a short time later.

Throughout his 50-year political career, Monroe was a lawyer, serving in the Virginia Assembly, the Continental Congress and the US Senate. He served the US in many ways; Governor of Virginia four times, Ambassador to France and England during Jefferson's administration, Secretary of State and Secretary of War during both administrations of James Madison, and twice as President of the US. Monroe was also a Revolutionary War hero. He was severely wounded in battle and recovered. He was the most well-known diplomat of his time. He knew how to make friends and was strongly allied with both Jefferson and Madison. He certainly was well qualified to be President.

Despite the rigors of his political career, he was a family man being very devoted to his wife and two daughters. His beautiful, petite wife married him when she was only 17 and he was 27. His wife and daughters travelled with him during the seven years in France when he was ambassador. He grieved deeply when his son died before the age of two. His wife, Elizabeth, was an excellent hostess but was often ill and James did his best to take care of her without complaint. His daughter often served as hostess when the First Lady was unwell.

Elizabeth wasn't up to the rigors of making house calls and the constant visiting that had been the style set by the first ladies who preceded her. She was formal in a European style rather than being more casual in the American style, which caused complaint from the Washington elite. One daughter lived in the White House with her husband, and the first wedding ever held at the White House was that of the other daughter. It was small private affair.

Like Jefferson, Monroe was often in debt. Presidents weren't paid well, expense accounts were minimal, and most early presidents ended up owing money rather than making it! Monroe's lavish lifestyle added to his money woes. Many of the White House furnishings were pieces of furniture he owned himself. It took years to refurnish the White House after it was burned by the British in 1814 during the Madison Presidency. Monroe's later years were spent trying to pay back his debts. Congress repaid some of what he felt was owed him for expenses he paid during his presidency. As with most of the founding fathers, his real money was made from his plantation and the labor of his slaves.

Monroe was a man of connection and cooperation. He did three extensive tours of the United States to all regions of the country, promoting unity, modern means of transportation and trade. No president since Washington had done a presidential tour. Travel allowed Monroe to reach out to Americans and show off his relaxed and affable personality.

He was praised and applauded everywhere. I'm sure that satisfied his need for approval; 3s like receiving praise. The phrase "era of good feelings" was coined by the newspapers during his first 15-week tour of the nation in the North in 1817. He did two other tours; in 1818 to the Chesapeake and in 1819 to the South and West. The tours tied the country together and he developed many friends. In his second election, he ran unopposed except for one electoral vote and was the only president, other than Washington, to run unopposed! The single vote cast against him allowed Washington to have the honor of a perfect record having no votes cast against him.

Monroe encouraged steamship travel (he was the first president to ride on a steamboat), the building of canals and improved roads and bridges. He focused mostly on domestic affairs and supporting trade among the regions. Enterprise and manufacturing increased. During his presidency, five states were added, he was involved in Spain ceding Florida to the US and he clarified Canada's borders with the English. Under Jefferson's tenure as president, long before he himself became president, he was the diplomat who negotiated the Louisiana Purchase.

Monroe supported the Missouri Compromise in 1820, confining slavery to a northern border limit, accepting Missouri as a slave state, yet appeasing the North by adding Maine and a part of Massachusetts, as a free state. He is best known for the Monroe Doctrine, which stated that Europe was no longer to interfere with the affairs of the Western hemisphere and that the United States would not be involved in the political affairs of Europe. The Monroe Doctrine was not officially named that until 30 years after its adoption. He supported South American countries, including Mexico and Argentina, to become free of Spain and to create alliances with the United States.

Like the other Virginia Presidents, Madison had a plantation that grew tobacco and wheat. He owned slaves, about 30 or 40, whereas Jefferson owned more than ten times that amount. The plantation and the selling of crops were his primary source of income. Monroe treated his slaves humanely for his time and believed in the ideas of repatriation of slaves back to Africa, which Jefferson and many others also supported. Monrovia, Liberia, in Africa, was a city founded on those principles and is the only capital city outside the United States named for a U.S. President. During a slave uprising that was thwarted when he was Governor of Virginia, he appealed for mercy for some of the slaves who led the rebellion, though most were hanged anyway.

Less is known about Monroe than some of the other presidents who wrote diaries and letters. As already stated, Monroe was more of a man of action and compromise than a writer or scholar. The son of a prosperous farmer, he had all the advantages of early education and a good life, attending an academy as a youth and enrolling in the College of William and Mary for a year and a half before joining the Revolutionary ranks as a soldier.

After his political career, like Jefferson and Madison, he was involved with the University of Virginia. He attempted to write books about his life and presidency but never completed them. His wife died a year before him. While living with his daughter, he died at the age of 73, his death probably caused by a heart attack and tuberculosis, on July 4th, 1831 - the third of the first five presidents to die on July 4!

Some other interesting facts about Monroe: Jefferson, Madison and Monroe were friends and had farmlands that bordered each other. As an envoy to Spain, Monroe travelled by mule from Paris to Madrid to negotiate with Spain about ceding Florida to the United States. The negotiation was unsuccessful but set the stage for eventual success. By the end of his second term as president, he had served his country for over 50 years in public office, more than any other president. Samuel Morse the inventor of Morse Code, was also an accomplished artist and painted a portrait of Monroe, which hangs today in the White House.

During Monroe's presidency, he was focused on Westward expansion. Land could be bought and sold cheaply by land speculators with government support, taking over Indian lands, motivating many farmers and adventurers to move West. Goods were being transported by canal and steam ships, and better roads and bridges were built. Factories and textile looms were humming in New England and farm girls were moving to the cities to work in the factories. Cloth and consumer goods such as silverware, ready-made clothes, dishes, sugar, salt, coffee and flour were being sold in stores.

Plantations and slavery were at their peak in the South and for the most part, the economy was booming except for a short setback in 1819. Iron stoves for baking were being made and sold, and the trend was leaning toward homes being decorated with more furnishings and pictures, including portraits of the home owners rendered by itinerant painters. Spitting tobacco on the floor, a common practice at the time, became less acceptable. There was a nationalist sentiment spreading to form a unique culture independent from Europe.

It was announced in April of 2016 that the house originally thought to be Monroe's home was actually a guesthouse built to accommodate borders and generate extra money during his time as president. His actual home was within yards of the guesthouse, and the foundation of that house was discovered only recently in the spring of 2015. It is currently in the process of being unearthed; the house burned down in the 1830s. A recently discovered newspaper article, dated 1837, described the incident. I visited his guesthouse, as well as all the presidential mansions in Virginia, during the summer of 2016. It was quite an exciting trip considering the new information about Monroe's mansion and it helped foster a deeper awareness of how the founding fathers lived.

Monroe had class, prestige and a wealth of experience, which he used to propel the American nation forward. He was a man of action and commitment who tied the United States together through three Presidential tours promoting trade, optimism, expansion, transportation, growth and prosperity.

John Quincy Adams – Type 1, Diplomat, Foreign Language Expert and Highest IQ, INTJ, 1821-1825

(1767-1848) Following in his father's footsteps, John Quincy Adams was a Type 1 Perfectionist and Reformer: principled, uncompromising, honest, persistent, irascible, haughty, serious, icy, stiff and thin-lipped. He was confrontational, quick to anger, unable to make small compromises and was scornful of self-indulgence. His main luxury, though it was for health and could hardly be considered self-indulgent, was to go skinny-dipping in the Potomac River each morning when he was President. He continued his morning swim even up until his death in the US House of Representatives, 20 years after his presidency ended! He often swam for an hour and a half in warmer weather.

People would often try to steal his clothes and a few got away with it. He finally started swimming with his clothes on, as it offered more resistance to the water and therefore more exercise. He took daily ice-cold baths, scrubbed himself with a horsehair mitten, and took long walks each day (up to 6 miles). He certainly believed in exercise! John Quincy was in good health and is considered by many to be the smartest of all the Presidents with the highest IQ. He played billiards, gardened, rowed his boat, rode horseback and read the Bible every day in many different languages. 1s believe in the motto of staying busy and being productive. Never an idle minute or the devil could take over!

Like his father, he was INTJ in the Myers-Briggs. www.16personalities.com/intj-personality

"INTJs are brilliant and confident in bodies of knowledge they have taken the time to understand, but unfortunately the social contract is unlikely to be one of those subjects. White lies and small talk are hard enough as it is for a type that craves truth and depth, but INTJs may go so far as to see many social conventions as downright stupid. Ironically, it is often best for them to remain where they are comfortable – out of the spotlight – where the natural confidence prevalent in INTJs as they work with the familiar can serve as its own beacon, attracting people, romantically or otherwise, of similar temperament and interests.

INTJs are defined by their tendency to move through life as though it were a giant chess board, pieces constantly shifting with consideration and intelligence, always assessing new tactics, strategies and contingency plans, constantly outmaneuvering their peers in order to maintain control of a situation while maximizing their freedom to move about. This isn't meant to suggest that INTJs act without conscience, but to many Feeling (F) types, INTJs' distaste for acting on emotion can make it seem that way, and it explains why many fictional villains (and misunderstood heroes) are modeled on this personality type."

Adams admitted he did not possess great interpersonal skills, as he could be dogmatic and overbearing and could easily forget the courtesies of society. He had a tendency toward depression and his diary, which he kept throughout his life, was often filled with doom and gloom; I read some of his actual diary entries. A typical entry exhibited at the Massachusetts Historical Society includes, "I have an uncontrollable dejection of spirits, a sluggish carelessness of life, and an imaginary wish that it were terminated." Despite his successes, he faced many obstacles and remained depressed most of his life. As a Type 1 Perfectionist/Reformer, the self-imposed pressure to be more perfect didn't help, with a continual focus on his flaws rather than his attributes.

John Quincy Adams at age forty-five confided in his diary that he had "done nothing to distinguish himself by usefulness to my country or to mankind." In fact, he had demonstrated high character and great achievement already, with much more to come. His self-criticism made him an unhappy man. His harshness spread out to his children. The harsh Puritan background of New England haunted him, and was augmented by the legacy of his father's harshness.

He had three sons, one was alcoholic and another apparently committed suicide by jumping off a ship just prior to meeting with his father! It's unlikely that he accidentally fell overboard. The third son became a diplomat and U.S. Congressman and that helped his father's spirits. He pushed his children to work hard and be successful just as his father had done to him, but it produced negative results for two of his sons. His own father, John Adams, along with his mother Abigail, had pushed him and the strategy worked in terms of achievement, though not perfectly, considering his ongoing depression.

John Quincy Adams at the age of 10 accompanied his father on a diplomatic mission to France where he attended private schools in Paris, Leiden, and Amsterdam. He read voraciously. He translated French in the Russian Court at age 14 and eventually spoke seven languages as an adult. Being an ambassador to Russia, Prussia, England, France and the Netherlands, he spent nearly twenty years of his life overseas.

Considered one of the best diplomats in American history, John Quincy had an intellectual capacity greater than any other president in US history. Having a Master's Degree from Harvard, he also studied at several universities overseas, including the University of Leiden. For a time, he was a professor of Rhetoric and Oratory at Harvard. In addition to his learning, intelligence and independence of mind, Adams had a great capacity for hard work. His description of a day's work, written a month after he became President, tells something of his approach to the job:

Since my removal to the Presidential mansion, I rise about five and sometimes even before four; read two chapters of Scott's Bible and Commentary, and the corresponding Commentary of Hewlett; then the morning newspapers, and public papers from the several departments; write seldom and not enough; breakfast an hour, from nine to ten; then have a succession of visitors, upon business, in search of place, solicitors for donations, or from mere curiosity, from eleven till between four and five o'clock. The heads of department of course occupy much of this time. Between four and six I take a walk of three or four miles. Dine from about half past five to seven, and from dark till about eleven I generally pass the evening in my chamber, signing land grants or blank patents, in the interval of which, for the last ten days I have brought up three months of arrears in my diary index. About eleven I retire to bed. My evenings are not so free from interruption as I hoped and expected they would be.

In his biography of John Quincy Adams, Samuel Flagg Bemis argues that Adams was able to "gather together, formulate and practice the fundamentals of American foreign policy: self-determination, independence, non-colonization, non-intervention, non-entanglement in European politics, freedom of the seas and freedom of commerce. He set the stage for American foreign policy for much of the 19th century. He was the chief American peace commissioner in the negotiations at Ghent that ended the War of 1812, aided by his effectiveness as minister to Britain during the last two years of the Madison administration."

As President, he sought to modernize the American economy and promote education. He paid off much of the national debt, and built canals and improved roads when he could. He created and carried through more commercial agreements with other countries than any of the former presidents. Unfortunately, Congress and Andrew Jackson thwarted almost every project he attempted. In addition, he was maligned in the press. This was instigated by Martin van Buren and Andrew Jackson who lost the election of 1824 to Adams due to a "corrupt bargain." Henry Clay, an enemy of Jackson and ally of John Quincy Adams, cast the single tie breaking electoral vote. Jackson had won more of the popular and electoral votes than the other three candidates for the presidency in a four-way contest in which no one had won the majority of electoral votes.

Adams wanted the national government to facilitate "communications and intercourse between distant regions and multitudes of men" in America by building and improving roads and canals. The president's enemies had a field day ridiculing his advocacy of scientific investigation and of "public institutions and seminaries of learning" as the essential instruments for achieving the "moral, political, and intellectual improvement" of the American people.

He was singled out for special scorn due to his call for the "erection of an astronomical observatory for the observation upon the phenomena of the heavens". Jackson's men lampooned the suggestion that the United States build its first observatory, although no one deigned to challenge the president's report that Europe had more than 130 of these "light-houses of the skies." Andrew Jackson's men, who constantly foiled Adams' efforts in Congress, were in many ways anti-intellectual.

Adams was well known for his political life before his Presidency, having been in the Massachusetts legislature and US Senate, a diplomat for nearly 20 years and Secretary of State under Monroe for 8 years. He wrote much the Monroe Doctrine which was the cornerstone of American foreign policy. After his Presidency, he served in the House of Representatives for 18 years, the only president to do so, and he literally died at the Capitol Building at the age of 80, his wish granted of wanting to die in his beloved place of work! His life as a Type 1 Reformer was one of moral principles and actions.

Adams hated the deception and compromise required of a political campaign. It was certainly the avoidance of smooth talk and compromise that resulted in his one-term presidency. He had the same political strengths and limitations as his father and consequently suffered the same fate, losing his second bid for the presidency. John Quincy lacked the common touch, having neither the zest for nor the skill at political maneuvering required of a successful chief executive. 3s and 8s usually enjoy the sport of politics more than 1s.

One of Adams' chief blunders, though in spite of demonstrating a strong character, was his fair and high-minded treatment of his political enemies. He never fired anyone unless they were doing a poor job, even if they were undermining him. His wing is likely 9. The Jacksonians and their Whig successors judged political appointees not so much by the quality of their public performance as by their loyalty to the man or the party in power.

Adams had the notion that appointments should go not to the politically friendly but to the worthy. His moral principles, though admirable, got in the way of doing what was politically expedient.

In the 18 years following his presidency Adams served in the House of Representatives. He worked tirelessly to end slavery and spent years protesting the gag rule, which forbade Congress to even discuss the issue of slavery. He finally succeeded in ending the gag rule, thus allowing the conversation about slavery to begin. In 1839 he won a landmark case in defense of the Africans who led a rebellion on the Amistad ship; they were freed and those who wanted to go back to Africa were allowed to return. He was a champion of civil rights and he also supported women's rights, though he couldn't pass legislation to forward rights for women. He devoted his life to doing what he thought was right. Like his father, he was a Type 1 Perfectionist Reformer and an INTJ in the Myers-Briggs.

Adams was an extremely seasoned diplomat, a brilliant man of political heritage and courage deeply committed to the United States. It's unfortunate that his programs were obstructed as President. He served his country well and sacrificed almost everything to that end. Principles were above politics. Much of his best work was done in the House of Representatives where he was able to continue his unwavering dedication to just causes.

Andrew Jackson – My Way, Type 8, ESTP, 1829-37

(1767-1845) Andrew Jackson, our 7th president, was the opposite of John Quincy Adams. John Quincy had the brains and Jackson had the brawn. Jackson was known for duels and fights, acquiring power through military action, arguments and relocating or killing the Indians. He was rough and tumble, gambled, drank, swore and loved to create mischief. He threatened people, made either good friends or bitter enemies, and did what he wanted. Jackson was described as cantankerous, iron-willed and intimidating. He was the equivalent of today's Donald Trump, but rougher!

Jackson was the first of many Type 8 presidents. He did as he pleased and wasn't concerned with how others perceived his behavior. He was an ESTP in the Myers Briggs.

"ESTPs are the likeliest personality type to make a lifestyle of risky behavior. They live in the moment and dive into the action – they are the eye of the storm. People with the ESTP personality type enjoy drama, passion, and pleasure, not for emotional thrills, but because it's so stimulating to their logical minds. They are forced to make critical decisions based on factual, immediate reality in a process of rapid-fire rational stimulus response." www.16personalities.com/estp-personality

Jackson believed in the right of states to self-govern, but would threaten to use the military if a state disobeyed a federal law or order he made; he threatened to do just that when South Carolina disobeyed a federal tariff law. He distrusted wealthy people, intellectuals, federal banks and image-makers. He wanted control and would befriend and be loyal to you if you agreed with him. Loyalty was paramount to him. You wouldn't want to mess with him for fear of revenge. He was the hero of the common man, even though he ended up wealthy, with a plantation run by over 100 slaves. He felt beholden to the public; not to Congress or the courts and not even the Supreme Court.

Jackson didn't have much of an education and was a poor speller. He would threaten anyone to a duel who besmirched his character or that of anyone close to him. And as it ended up there were a lot of men he challenged. It was rumored he was in anywhere from 5 to 100 duels. At least one of them was settled when both combatants shot up in the air. He carried a bullet for the rest of his life near his heart, which he received during a duel in which he was able to take his time, aim well and kill his offender all while holding his chest to stop the bleeding. That wound plagued him throughout the rest of his life. Jackson had two more bullets lodged in his limbs from gunfights that were finally removed after twenty years. Fighting and killing were second nature to him.

He volunteered in the American Revolution as a courier at age 13 along with his brother, and they both became prisoners of war. As the story goes Andrew was slashed in the hand by a British officer when he refused to blacken the gentleman's boots. This engendered in the young boy a hatred for the British. The British invaded the Carolinas where he lived in 1780 and 1781. Those trials, and growing up in the western regions of South Carolina and Tennessee, forged a tenacious personality in him, using force to get his way and never backing down. 8s often have a rough upbringing, seeking revenge for their past and refusing to allow themselves ever to be in a weak position again.

Jackson became a lawyer in North Carolina, with a curriculum of reading, clerking, fighting, drinking and vandalism. He scandalized one town when he escorted two prostitutes to the annual Christmas Ball and he and his friends once demolished a tavern and then set the building ablaze. He loved practical jokes like moving outhouses to different locations during the night. Gambling on horse races, cockfighting and betting on any sporting event was fun and exciting to him. 8s with 7 wings like Jackson often love adventure, sport and high-energy activities.

After serving in the Tennessee House and Senate as well as being a judge, he became a commander in the Tennessee militia, fighting Indians and leading battles in the War of 1812 as a major general. In 1815 he commanded troops in the Battle of New Orleans, which occurred after the War of 1812 had officially ended. Communication was slow between Europe and America, so he didn't know the war was over! It was basically a slaughter of the British troops, with few American casualties.

Jackson fought in many Indian Wars, particularly in Florida, hung two British citizens without a trial, and is known to hang any of his troops who disobeyed orders, mutinied or deserted. He was reputed to be ruthless and razed entire Indian villages. He wasn't alone, though, in his ruthlessness; as even George Washington, before being president, ordered the slaughter of an entire Indian village of men, women and children. His fighting in Florida against the Spanish and Indians led the US eventually to annex Florida from the Spanish. Politicians liked the results of his campaigns, but there was ongoing debate as to whether Jackson should have been censured or fired because he did what he wanted, ignoring orders. Violence in his time was even more commonplace than today.

It was Jackson's audacious behavior as a battlefield commander that brought him to the White House. Losing the presidency in 1824 due to an unfair election, Jackson actually won both the popular and electoral vote in a four-way race. Henry Clay, Jackson's enemy, cast a tie-breaking vote in Congress between the top two candidates in favor of John Quincy Adams.

Jackson subsequently challenged Adams during his term as president and succeeded in obstructing the passage of any effective legislation. You didn't want to be on Andrew Jackson's bad side! He won the election in 1828 when he ran against John Quincy Adams. This was sweet revenge; he was the first Irish American president as well as the first Western Frontier President. He was decidedly a departure from the formerly elected Virginia presidents and the Adams presidents from Massachusetts. Jackson made enough money to buy a plantation in Tennessee, The Hermitage, and was a slaveholder who punished any slave who tried to run away.

His wife, Rachel, was shy and didn't like the limelight. He fell in love with her while she was still unhappily married; she was the love of his life. She was accused of adultery, due to a question about the legality of her divorce, and Jackson had to marry her twice to fully legitimize it. Political rivals used that against Jackson, and his beloved wife was shunned, causing bad publicity and avoidance from others. She preferred to stay at home at The Hermitage. Rachel died just weeks before he moved into the White House, many believing she preferred death to being ostracized as the First Lady.

The Jacksons adopted an Indian child whose mother was found dead on the battlefield, and they raised two of Rachel's nephews. Jackson was also guardian to a number of other children. It's not unusual for a Type 8 to parent and protect children. Even though 8s tend to be invulnerable themselves they often act as protectors to the truly vulnerable, especially children.

Jackson was the son of an immigrant Irish pioneer and had a very harsh early life. His father died before he was born and, along with his two brothers, was raised by his mother who earned a living tending the eight children of nearby relatives. Although he had no formal education, he learned to read early. One of his brothers died of smallpox shortly after they both were held as prisoners of war in the Revolutionary War; his mother died of cholera and his other brother was killed in that war.

Jackson was the first president to be challenged with an assassination attempt. He was leaving the Capitol building when a man aimed and fired at him with two guns that both misfired. He was quickly subdued. Davy Crockett was among those who brought down the assailant, but not before Jackson caned the man. The alleged assassin ended up in a mental institution for the rest of his life, the court declaring him insane, even though there was speculation of a plot.

John Quincy Adams said of Jackson, "He's a barbarian who could not write a sentence of grammar and who could barely write his name." Henry Clay thought Jackson was "ignorant, passionate, hypocritical, corrupt, and easily swayed by the corrupt men who surrounded him." Jefferson thought Jackson was "a dangerous man."

Jackson filled his cabinet with political cronies, whether they were competent or not. Loyalty was the most important requirement for political appointment; this is very common for Type 8s. Andrew Jackson started the new Democratic Party (which had been the Democratic-Republican Party), sometimes called the pro-Jackson party. His opponents called him a jackass, a name he rather enjoyed, and it became the symbol of the Democratic Party! As already stated, he created the spoils system—to the victor go the spoils-- many others did the same thing although not to the same degree as Jackson: giving strong supporters political jobs during his presidency. Loyalty was more important than merit.

Jackson created and supported the Indian Removal Act of 1831, which implemented a policy forcing Indians who lived east of the Mississippi to move west onto reservations, even those loyal to the American government. Five major tribes were "asked" to leave at gunpoint. Jackson was responsible for the Trail of Tears of the Cherokee Indians, in which thousands died on their march to Oklahoma. The forced march actually occurred during the subsequent presidency of Martin van Buren, even though Jackson decided to evacuate the Cherokees during his administration.

All the presidents supported the displacement of Indians and found convenient ways to break all the treaties. Some Indians attacked white settlers, but who can blame them when their land, homes, resources and lives were taken away by pressured or illegal negotiations and forced marches.

Firing and hiring new cabinet members was not unusual for Jackson. He preferred using trusted friends' advice rather than that of cabinet members. As many as five sets of cabinets were jostled around or fired during Jackson's eight years in office! Jackson managed by strong will and punishment, not caring what people thought of him. Supreme Court Justice John Marshall ruled in favor of the Cherokee Indians' plea to remain in Georgia, but Jackson displaced thousands of them anyway.

Jackson made rules, but didn't follow those made by others, typical of ruffian type 8s. The Cherokees had been model citizens in Georgia. They built houses, roads, schools and churches, raised crops, and owned businesses and banks. They modeled their lives to fit in with white values, including owning slaves, but it didn't matter. Jackson was a black and white thinker and made no exceptions to what he wanted. He was spiritually immature but was extremely powerful. Might makes right was clearly his motto.

When Congress passed a bill to continue the national bank, Jackson vetoed it. He ordered that all Federal money be sent to state banks during the time when Congress recessed, even after two of his Secretaries of the Treasury refused to obey his orders. Of course, he fired both Secretaries and hired a third who finally did obey his orders. He was censured by Congress because of that power play, but it was expunged from the record by the next Democratic Congress, in the subsequent election.

Power was the name of the game for Jackson and he would attempt to annihilate anyone who disagreed with him. Clay, Biddle and John Quincy Adams were his bitter enemies. His term and several subsequent administrations were called the Age of Jackson (1828-1850) because they were so heavily influenced by his policies and expansionist ideas. His new banking system seems to have caused the Panic of 1837 and 1839, the consequences of which were inherited by the next president, Martin Van Buren. The economic woes that ensued lasted for seven years.

After his presidency ended, Jackson retired to The Hermitage, his Tennessee plantation, but he continued to be involved in trying to steer other presidents toward policies he favored. He had many public tributes, and many admirers travelled to his home at The Hermitage.

Jackson's legacy is the formation of the Democratic Party. It motivated the creation of the opposing Whig Party, and the entire election process was strengthened by being either for or against Jackson. Jackson vetoed most bills that Congress created, more than all the other presidents before him combined. He did what he wanted and enlisted public support, not seeming to care at all about creating an alliance with Congress.

He allied himself with the people, more than the elite. At his inauguration party, he opened the White House to the public whereupon they trashed the place and took advantage of the twenty tobacco spittoons he displayed in the main room of the presidential mansion. Historians still debate about the value of Jackson's contributions, which is reflected in the discussion around whether to remove his image from the twenty-dollar bill.

Jackson could be sophisticated, warm and friendly if you agreed with him, and he was protective of any supporters who were weak or disadvantaged. He was smart and used his raw animal nature to further his cause. In promoting his belief that executive power was more important than the power of Congress or the Judiciary, he set an example for other presidents to follow. Unfortunately though, he failed to set an example of balancing the power of all three branches of the government, a reflection of his own inability to include others in his process of decision-making or receiving feedback.

Jackson was a man of action and strength, not one to compromise. He fostered ongoing prejudice and abuse of African slaves and American Indians as well as other minorities. He also paved the way for more executive power and action.

Martin Van Buren, Party Organizer, Type 2, ESFP, 1837-41

(1782-1862) Our eighth president, Dutch-born Martin Van Buren was the first President who spoke English as a second language and who was not born as a British subject. The original Dutch spelling of his name was Maarten van Buren. His last name, Buren, was the name of a town in the Netherlands from whence his early ancestors came to America in 1631. He grew up in Kinderhook, New York, populated mostly by residents of Dutch descent and he was a member of the Dutch Reformed Church. The term "OK" originated with Van Buren's birthplace of Old Kinderhook. The Democratic Party had a campaign slogan of "Vote for OK" instead of Vote for Van Buren, bypassing the possible prejudice against his Dutch roots.

Martin had a modest upbringing, although his family did own six slaves. He was immersed in politics, as his father held positions locally and also fought as a Captain in the

Revolutionary War. His father ran a tavern and inn frequented by the likes of Aaron Burr and Alexander Hamilton; political talk was always in the air.

Martin's mother was previously married and had been widowed, so he had four siblings and three half-siblings. Attending a one-room schoolhouse until the age of 14, Martin's education was bolstered when his father managed to have him apprenticed in a law office where he worked as a clerk for seven years.

At age 21 he moved to New York City and passed the bar. Alongside his half-brother, Van Buren built a successful law practice defending renters and tenants against unscrupulous landlords who unlawfully increased rents or evicted them arbitrarily. This practice gave Martin a solid reputation for helping the common folk. He also received coaching from friends as well as people of higher birth to learn how to further himself with the social aristocracy of his day.

In 1807 he married his childhood sweetheart who was his first cousin. The couple had six children, five sons and a daughter, only four of whom survived to adulthood. All of the remaining Van Buren children rose to positions of success in their chosen fields of law, politics and the military.

In addition to being a lawyer, Van Buren decided to engage in New York politics and joined the Democratic-Republicans of the Thomas Jefferson/James Madison camp, which had been the political choice of his father and his family's friends. The Jeffersonians espoused limiting the power of the federal government, the defense of individual rights and protection of local and state power. Van Buren tried to unify the Democratic-Republican Party which was bedeviled with rivalry and infighting. His predilection for keeping his political alliances and loyalties quiet, earned him the reputation of being devious and unprincipled. The truth was that he was trying to build alliances with disparate groups without losing support from any of them. Someone stated that he "rode to his object with muffled oars." Silence was used to his advantage.

His reputation of having many courtroom successes enabled him to win a seat in the state Senate, where he became head of the Bucktail contingency of the Party (they actually wore tails of a deer on their hats). As a senator, he promoted the Bucktails, which emphasized party loyalty, "machine politics," patronage posts and the spoils system.

By nature, Van Buren was a quiet man who worked well behind the scenes. He never revealed anything controversial, so no one ever really knew his actual point of view. "He made carefully calculated inquiry: asking for information, seeking others' opinions, considering, shrewdly reconsidering, checking for problems, traps, pitfalls. He absorbed information and sought commitment, giving in return as little as he could." He was so adroit that one of his adversaries commented that, "Van Buren glides along as smoothly as oil and as silently as a cat." His enemy had the right lubricant in mind but the wrong animal; Van Buren was no cat, "but a most stealthy fox," quoted from the book *Presidential Temperament*.

Van Buren was the architect of the first nationwide political party, the Jacksonian Democrats, or Democratic Party, which evolved out of the Democratic-Republican Party. According to Van Buren, "Without strong national political organizations, there would be nothing to moderate the prejudices between free and slaveholding states." He was seeking a means of preventing a concentration of power in the Federal government and was attempting to focus power in a party that would mediate between regional differences. He is considered the father of the political machine known as the Democratic Party.

Van Buren was most likely a Type 2, with a strong Type 3 wing; he was probably a Social Subtype, focused on public image, giving of himself, personal connection and creating alliances. He was happy to control things from behind the scenes, and preferred to wield his influence quietly while enjoying a great amount of power. With image, success and winning, being his Type 3 wing components, there were also elements of cautious Type 6 and peacemaking Type 9 included in the snapshot. He was positive while hiding anything negative. he was a master of impression management.

In Van Buren's autobiography, he left out anything too personal that might be considered unpleasant, including details of his marriage, although he loved his wife. He showed only the cards he felt the world should see. Type 2s can appear to be like Type 6s, because of their ability to look beneath the surface, while not revealing what they see. As a smooth Type 2, he withheld his own opinions, while encouraging others to vocalize theirs. He was quite social and engaging, with a seductive capacity of getting others to reveal their positions without bringing attention to his own. He was a genius at pulling differing factions together.

Once he whispered a request into a woman's ear at a political gathering, for her to promise not to divulge to Andrew Jackson how much he admired him. So, of course, the comment made its way back to Jackson, resulting in Jackson's constant trust in and promotions for Van Buren. Van Buren certainly possessed a seductive edge, and was a master of political maneuver. "Ease and grace of movement, meticulous dress and grooming, the glow of health and good cheer – all suggested the drawing room or a caucus more than the battlefield," quoted from the book, *The Presidency of Martin Van Buren*.

Friends as well as enemies respected his cleverness. While his allies admired him as an able politician, his enemies (including the outspoken Davy Crockett) portrayed him as nothing more than a small-minded, unprincipled opportunist. He was interested only in personal power and prestige, they declared, and they awarded him a number of nicknames, including "the Little Magician," "Weasel," and "The Wizard," paraphrased from *Presidential Temperament.*

In 1817, his wife died of tuberculosis. Despite his grief and having to raise four sons on his own, he remained in the Senate and went on later to become the state's attorney general. He continued to unite the Democratic Republicans in New York. Politically powerful, he was elected to the US Senate in 1821, and although he maintained his primary residence in Washington, D.C., he retained control in New York, unifying the party and creating a nationally growing political organization. Van Buren never remarried.

His skill at uniting the party played a large role in getting Andrew Jackson elected president in 1828. Jackson was a two-term president, the last two-term president until Abraham Lincoln was elected 25 years later. The six presidents following Jackson, including Van Buren, had only one-term presidencies.

Van Buren interacted well with different ethnic, income and social groups, which was an enormous help in becoming a great political organizer. He mingled with upper class society, as well as enjoying camaraderie in barrooms, like the tavern in which his father owned when he was a child. Van Buren was a key advisor to the President during Jackson's eight-year term. In Jackson's first term, he rewarded Van Buren's support by appointing him Secretary of State. He then went on to become the Vice President during Jackson's second term as President. That appointment as Secretary of State and Vice President was Van Buren's gateway to becoming the next president.

Van Buren was the first and only vice president elected president until George H. W. Bush in 1988. Other vice presidents rose to the presidency only via the sitting president's death or assassination. Jackson said of Van Buren, "he was a true man of no guile." Van Buren in truth was wily and Jackson was likely deceived by Van Buren's adept political maneuvering.

Van Buren was noted for treating his opponents well and creating minimal enemies, typical of Type 2s. Type 2s can also be quite controlling, knowing exactly what they are doing as they move toward their intended outcomes. Van Buren used carefully crafted words to protect himself and could easily give the impression he was promising something that he, in fact, was not. He managed the daunting task of holding the party together while trying to unite Northern and Southern factions.

Van Buren would hold a post for a short time and was quickly appointed to a higher post. For instance, he ran and won the governorship of New York to bolster Andrew Jackson's chances of winning the presidency. Gaining New York support was the tipping point to a Jackson victory. He resigned as Governor as soon as he was appointed Secretary of State.

As Secretary of State, Van Buren was very effective negotiating boundaries between Maine and New Brunswick, Canada, making reparations and settlements with France over property that had been seized during the Napoleonic Wars, creating a treaty with the Ottoman Empire to gain access to the Black Sea, and negotiating trade agreements. He sided with Jackson on domestic as well as international politics. Van Buren seemed to have had a both a pleasing and peacemaking side that allowed him to create alliances and take the time necessary to make well-considered decisions.

He knew how to win favor from, and ally with Andrew Jackson during Jackson's presidency. His boss was his ticket to his success. As Secretary of State and Jackson's right-hand man, he allied himself with Jackson's unpopular opinions. The Secretary of War to Jackson began "dating" a married woman by the name of Sue Eaton, while her husband was still alive. Soon after Sue's husband died the couple married and the prominent political wives of Washington, DC. Immediately ostracized her. Jackson demanded that his cabinet members' wives include Sue socially, but the situation reached an explosive point when most of the cabinet members refused to encourage their wives to engage with her. Van Buren offered to give up his cabinet post as a result of this conflict, which set the stage for Jackson firing all his cabinet members, except Van Buren, who remained a staunch ally. John Calhoun, Jackson's first term Vice President, was relieved of his command, and his wife, the force behind the ostracism of Sue Eaton, was in turn ostracized by Jackson.

Up until that time, vice presidents could oppose their own presidents. Van Buren was blatantly mocked, "When Jackson dances, Van Buren plays the fiddle." Van Buren certainly represented the power behind the throne, as is often true for Type 2s. Van Buren remained in Jackson's cabinet, while the other insubordinate members were quickly banished.

Van Buren's presidency was mired in an economic depression brought on both by the bank policies of Jackson, and by England withdrawing money from the United States. Van Buren's opposition to the annexation of Texas was unpopular, and many were critical of the Indian removal policies that were created by Jackson but implemented by Van Buren. Thousands of Indians died during the "Trail of Tears" march, which took place during the Van Buren presidency.

Border disputes with Canada and Britain led Van Buren to strengthen his diplomatic skills to avoid war with Britain. His presidency took place during a time period of increased tension: slave and free state balance was perilous, controversy around abolition, temperance, women's rights, racial tensions between free blacks and poor whites in the north, along with the Irish conflict with the Scottish and English, among others. American history has always been fraught with conflict, and Van Buren's skills were stretched to the limit.

Van Buren continued to have a close connection to his four sons. Two became his private secretaries, while his other two were politically active in Albany, New York, keeping their father informed of the political climate there. Van Buren ran for the next presidential nomination, was defeated, then ran for president on a third-party ticket for the Free-Soil Party in the next election, and lost again. After those losses, he spent more time with his children and grandchildren, dying at the age of 79 in 1862, during the Civil War era. His legacy was less about his actual presidency and more about his creation of the Democratic Party and the uniting of the factions within it.

Van Buren was described as optimistic, cheerful, and prone to laughing and smiling, all strong traits of Type 2s. He was an engaging conversationalist, loved dinner parties, and had impeccable manners. He happily granted others the lead in conversation. He was our first professional politician, and as mentioned, was nicknamed the "red fox" and "little magician." He was often commented about or made fun of as "little" because he was only 5'6" tall.

Van Buren was a definite challenge to type in the Myers-Briggs. I believe he is an ES<u>F</u>P, adaptive to the specifics of the moment, while being as strategic as an ES<u>T</u>P. He was always planning how to keep his party together, hobnobbed with everyone to win favor, while keeping his views to himself, unlike an ESTP who vies to be the center of attention and is always outspoken. He had strong feelings and an intensely personal component, so it's likely he was an ESFP, which is more resonant with a Type 2. His T and F seem close. He was strategic, adept at maneuvering things in the moment and adaptive to the best political win. He was not an idealistic man; he was practical, down to earth and always focused on uniting his political group.

"ESFPs are born entertainers. They love the spotlight, and all the world is a stage for them. Many famous people with the ESFP personality type are indeed actors, but this type loves putting on a show for their friends, social chatting with a unique and earthy wit, soaking up attention and making every outing feel like a party. Utterly social, ESFP's enjoy the simplest things, and there's no greater joy for them than just having fun with a good group of friends.

It's not just talk either – ESFP's have the strongest aesthetic sense of any personality type. From grooming and outfits to a well-appointed home, ESFP personalities have an eye for fashion. Knowing what's attractive the moment they see it, ESFP's are not afraid to change their surroundings to reflect their personal style. ESFP's are naturally curious, exploring new designs and styles with ease." www.16personalities.com/esfp-personality

William Henry Harrison, Indian Fighter, Frontier Governor, Type 3, ESTJ, 1841

(1773-1841) Born into Virginia aristocracy to a father who was a gentleman plantation farmer, William Henry Harrison had the privilege of growing up in an elite and wealthy family. His father was governor of Virginia, a signer of the Declaration of Independence and a passionate patriot. His mother traveled in the upper echelons of society, and enjoyed the friendship of both George Washington and Benjamin Franklin. An ambitious boy, he was the youngest of seven children. He had a solid education having the advantage of being tutored at home while young. He attended three years at Hampden-Sydney College in Hanover County, Virginia where he studied Shakespeare, military history and classical literature. His father decided William was to become a doctor, and sent him to Philadelphia to study with the renowned physician Benjamin Rush, but Harrison chose a career in the military, which very much disappointed his father.

William learned about the military from his father, who was a captain in the Revolutionary War. The family's home and possessions were destroyed in the war by the famous traitor Benedict Arnold. At age nine, young William watched his father march off to war to fight in the Battle of Yorktown. Like many boys, he admired the profession of soldiering, and fostered particular dreams of becoming an officer.

Granted a military commission from George Washington, much of Harrison's life was focused on fighting Indians in the Northwest Territories, which included the area currently known as the states of Indiana, Ohio, and Michigan. He fought bravely, was decisive, aggressive and a respected leader. Harrison was an aide-de-camp to generals, and was involved in building, fortifying and defending army forts. He created treaties with Indians that he did not honor, killing as many Indians as possible and simultaneously destroying their villages.

A contemporary of the famous expedition leaders, Lewis and Clark, he served with both men in the army and in government. He was considered equally as instrumental in adding vast amounts of western land to the United States. When he could not destroy or relocate Indians he would attempt negotiating with chieftains, and became well known for his trickery and deceit. He acquired at least 50 million acres for the government while spending as little money as he possibly could spare. He was intent on fostering Indian dependence on the government, and on forcing them further west, sanctioned by presidential policies. Money, bribes, liquor, trumped-up charges to engender fear of the government, and killing and lying were his standard tools. Some 3s aim to win at any cost.

During the time that Harrison was posted at Fort Washington, twenty-year-old Anna Symmes moved to a nearby town with her father, the newly appointed judge for the region. Anna was soon smitten with the handsome young Harrison. Her father disapproved, believing his daughter was worthy of a better and wealthier match. The young couple waited until Judge Symmes travelled to another part of the territory and promptly eloped. When he returned and learned of their marriage he asked of Harrison, "How, sir, do you intend to support my daughter?" William replied, "Sir, my sword is my means of support."

For Harrison, the marriage was politically advantageous. The Symmes family had inside connections with local land speculators, something the new son-in-law quickly exploited. By 1798, Captain Harrison saw the army as a dead-end career and resigned his commission. His father-in-law remained unimpressed with Harrison, writing a friend, "He can neither bleed, plead, nor preach, and if he could plow, I should be satisfied." Finally, the judge used his contacts in Washington to further his son-in-law's ambitions.

The new President, John Adams, named Harrison Secretary of the Northwest Territory. In 1799, the territory was allowed to send a delegate to Congress for the first time, and Harrison was elected. He played expertly to the voters by reforming land-buying policies, allowing them to buy large purchases, while siphoning off some of the money for his own pocket. He was a mover and a shaker, and as a typical Type 3, he excelled when it came to action, money and fame.

Being a Type 3 Achiever, William was confident, charming and was a master of witty one-liners. He could regale his listeners with dramatic stories and, as a friend recalled, "he was more entertaining than the most stirring romance." Harrison was well connected and intelligent; he was also hard working and practical, while being a fun companion.

By 1800, the Harrisons had three of what would eventually be ten children, although only four would survive to see their father in the White House. That year the Northwest Territory split into the Ohio and Indiana Territories. President Adams named Harrison Governor of the Indiana Territory where he served in that capacity for the next 12 years. The Indiana Territory was comprised of what is currently all, or sections of, Indiana, Illinois, Michigan, Minnesota, and Wisconsin. Harrison built a palatial home, a veritable mansion in the wilderness he called "Grouseland," located near his headquarters in Vincennes, Indiana. It became a political as well as a social epicenter for the territory; hosting officials, friends, and meetings with Native Americans.

Harrison enjoyed as much luxury as he could, consuming gourmet food and owning fine possessions. Relishing both power and fame, he aimed toward being president at some point in his future. Although it seems apparent that at this time he hoped to become president some historians disagree. However, serving in the military has historically been a path to becoming president; eleven presidents rose to that office following their tenure as military leaders. Most were 1s, 3s or 8s, called the aggressive types.

Initially, I questioned whether Harrison was a Type 3 or a Type 8, as both types have an affinity for power. Type 8's are more down-to-earth, they're straight-talkers, and have more focus on power, than image. Harrison shows more signs of the positive image oriented Type 3; he was not considered a straight talker, by any means.

Typical of Type 3's, Harrison was acutely aware of his social position and was quite pretentious. Though generally respectable, he was a professional office-seeker, with a tendency to follow the directions of others in power. His career ambitions took priority over a moral higher purpose. Harrison is likely an ESTJ, a socially oriented, natural leader.

According to the website truity.com, "ESTJ's are conventional, factual, and grounded in reality. For the ESTJ, the proof is in the past: what has worked and what has been done before. They value evidence over conjecture, and trust the results of their personal experience. ESTJ's look for rules to follow and standards to meet, and often take a leadership role in helping other people meet expectations as well. They concern themselves with maintaining the social order and keeping others in line.

ESTJ's often take on a project manager role at home, as well as at work, and excel at setting goals, making decisions, and organizing resources to accomplish a task. The ESTJ wants to achieve efficient productivity and typically believes this is best accomplished when people, structures, and systems are well organized." (www.truity.com/personality-type/ESTJ

Harrison speculated in land, invested in mill enterprises, and was reputed to be an honest administrator with some. To his credit, he was instrumental in improving the roads and other infrastructures in the region. He fought in a number of battles against the Indians, who were often in alliance with the British. Harrison was also instrumental in the success of The War of 1812 and was considered to have been a good general, but his focus was as much on building fame as in fighting to win. For the last 20 years of his life, he held positions in the U.S. House of Representatives, the Ohio State Senate and the U.S. Senate, as well as serving a short stint as ambassador to Columbia. He lost more elections than he won however.

In addition to his military successes, he was most recognized when, after losing a presidential bid in 1836, he ran again and went on to victory in 1840. The presiding President, Martin van Buren, was unable to relieve the country of an ongoing economic depression. Van Buren was considered vain and uppity in spite of being very inclusive of common folk. William Henry Harrison, a born southerner and war hero, seemed to be a perfect antidote to the staid Van Buren and offered the country a welcomed change.

The Whig Party that Harrison represented flooded the electorate with posters and badges extolling the virtues of their colorful, down-home "log-cabin-and-hard-cider" candidate. He was the hero of Tippecanoe, an Indian battle over 25 years before the election, in which Harrison's forces won solely because they vastly outnumbered the Indian Confederation. Harrison's forces actually experienced more casualties than did the Indians.

It is said that before he died, Tecumseh, the chief of the Indian Confederation, placed a curse on Harrison proclaiming that he would die in office and that an American president would then die in office every 20 years hence. That is exactly what happened; every 20 years since then the sitting president has died while in office. Those unfortunates including Harrison are Lincoln, Garfield, McKinley, Harding, Franklin Roosevelt, and John Kennedy. This "curse" was only broken when Ronald Reagan survived his assassination attempt!

Harrison was born in a mansion to an aristocratic family, so the "log cabin and hard cider" candidacy was a pure concoction. His election team offered "Old Tip" to the electorate, transforming a genteel blue blood into "One of Us." It became one of the most successful public images constructed in an American presidential race. While his opponent Van Buren tried to run an intelligent, issues-driven campaign (not the best of strategies when one's country is mired in financial depression), Harrison's campaign went straight for emotional appeal, creating a false image for the candidate by deceiving the electorate.

Since Jackson's presidential campaign of 1832, politics had become a form of entertainment for the masses. Campaign rallies, meetings, whiskey, bonfires and barbecues were now firmly entrenched in the American way of life on the campaign trail. The Whigs adopted these tactics from Jackson (whose campaign was managed by Van Buren) and added balloon rides, coonskin caps and music, to turn the tables on the Democrats.

One group of Whig Party members pushed a ten-foot, paper-and-tin ball emblazoned with pro-Harrison and anti-Van Buren slogans for hundreds of miles. Others handed out whiskey in log cabin shaped bottles supplied by the E.C. Booz distillery. Thus, arrived two popular additions to the American vocabulary: "keep the ball rolling" and "booze." The Whigs mass-marketed their candidate, flooding America with cups, plates, flags, and sewing boxes with Old Tip pictured on them. Countless popular songs left little doubt about who was supported by the Whigs.

Harrison won by a landslide, but his presidency lasted only 32 days. He was the oldest president of that time at age 68, and that record stood until Reagan became president at age 69, and Trump became president at age 70. By the time he made it to his inauguration, Harrison was completely worn out. He spoke for two hours (the longest inauguration speech in US history) bareheaded during a snowstorm, and without a coat. His feet were soaking wet and he caught a cold that transitioned to pneumonia. He was probably trying to prove his strength and dispel the concern that he was too old to be president, but his efforts backfired.

His doctors swung into action, bleeding and blistering him, feeding him calomel and laudanum, ipecac, castor oil, even "seneca" (pure Pennsylvania petroleum). They rubbed him with mercury and even used a remedy involving live snakes. It was rumored that he was poisoned, but after exhuming his body in recent history, there is no evidence to that effect. It is little wonder that after a month of such treatment, the man who was considered quite old at that time in history, expired on April 4, 1841. Although some suggested that he died from dysentery, as a result of the White House being near both a swamp and a cesspool, it is quite likely the remedies killed him!

Harrison was considered a cultivated man. He was known for helping to expand the country via negotiations with the Native Americans and either their relocation or elimination. He was well liked, and was considerably instrumental in the governance of new western territories. He projected a positive image, played the political game well and built a substantial career. His wife lived another 20 years beyond Harrison's demise.

John Tyler, First Vice President to Become President Following Death of His Predecessor, Type 1, ISTJ, 1841-45

(1790-1862) John Tyler was the 10th US president. He was the first Vice President to become President following the death of his predecessor. There was no precedent yet established for a vice president to take over the office when a president died. Tyler took the reins at once demanding that his inauguration as President be held within three days. At this juncture, he returned any mail addressed to him as Vice President rather than President!

Some cabinet members wanted Tyler to retain the cabinet chosen by Harrison. Tyler stated, "I, as President, shall be responsible for my administration," and suggested that anyone who wanted to buck his authority resign. He set the precedent for succeeding vice presidents when a sitting president died. From Tyler's example emerged the idea that vice presidents should be chosen to run based on their capacity to be president. This idea was not considered in the US Constitution and it took until the 20th century to clarify it.

Tyler was born in 1790. His aristocratic family owned both land and slaves, making their money farming tobacco. He and his seven siblings were privileged in education and had easy access to power and prestige. Born in the same county in Virginia as Harrison, Tyler was the last of the US Presidents from Virginia in the 19th century. His father was a personal friend of Thomas Jefferson and a former governor of Virginia.

Tyler was educated for three years at William and Mary College, graduating at the age of 17. He apprenticed to a well-known lawyer and became a Virginia legislator when he was 21. This set the stage for the rest of his life in politics.

Some interesting facts about John Tyler include: he had the most children of any other president, 15 in total, eight children by his first wife and seven by his second! His first wife died of a stroke 18 months after he took office. She was the first of three First Ladies to die during their husband's tenure as president. Tyler then became the first president to marry while in office. Julia, his second wife, was 30 years younger than he. One of Tyler's sons was interested in pursuing Julia, but his father, being president and very gallant, had more to offer and won her hand. As the story goes, Julia's father was mortally wounded when a defective cannon, ironically called the Peacemaker, misfired. This happened on a frigate undergoing its maiden voyage on the Potomac River. During that tragic incident, the Secretaries of State and of the Navy were also killed. Julia, who was on board along with Tyler, fainted upon hearing the news. The President caught her as she swooned and carried her off the ship in his arms; they were married soon afterwards in a secret ceremony.

John Tyler's grandson, Lyon, from Tyler's second marriage is alive today in his late 80s and currently lives in John Tyler's plantation house. Both John Tyler and his son fathered children in their 70s! Over 300 feet long, the plantation house is the longest frame house in America. It includes a 68-foot-long dance floor built for Julia who loved to dance. The modern dance of the time was the Virginia Reel which required a lot of room. Tyler called the plantation Sherwood Forest because he felt like a political outlaw. I was privileged to have a private tour of the house, which is quite stunning, as well as the 25 acres of beautiful terraced gardens.

As a southern aristocrat and an avid proponent of states' rights, Tyler opposed a national bank, a formidable standing army and a strong federal government. He supported the expansion of slavery for any new state and for citizens in those states to determine their own destiny. He wanted the Southern plantation way of life to continue, being a plantation owner and slaveholder himself. He advocated for state legislatures choosing electors to vote for the president rather than having presidents elected by popular vote.

His life was one of public service. He spent time as a state legislator, a US House Representative and a Senator. He resigned when he was a US Senator to protest against pressure to vote for a measure sponsored by Andrew Jackson. He openly spoke out against Jackson on the Senate floor, and had the courage to speak his mind whenever he felt called to do so, as Type 1s tend to do.

As president, Tyler was derisively called His Accidency and His Ascendantcy by his foes because he wasn't elected. Known for vetoing Congressional bills, he was voted out of his own Whig Party because of his refusal to go along with party politics! All of his entire cabinet except for his Secretary of State resigned after the second attempt by Congress to pass a national bank act. Tyler was called "the President without a party."

Tyler was known for his stubbornness and unwillingness to compromise. A Type 1, he was called "Honest John" but he alienated more and more people, particularly politicians. He had a lot of popular support, as many people loved his honesty and states' rights focus. Even his popular support faded however, when he vetoed two particular bills. The first called for a new national bank and the other for higher tariffs. Mobs protested outside the White House yelling, throwing stones and hanging him in effigy! He armed the White House staff and calmly waited for the crowds to disperse.

As an active president, Tyler supported westward movement and expansion of the United States, allowing land to be bought cheaply by settlers. Treaties were made with Great Britain over boundary disputes with Canada, and he advocated for the annexation of Texas. He opened trade with China and protected and prevented other nations from interfering with Hawaii, which eventually led to it being one of our territories.

Tyler's greatest legacy set the precedent to the right of succession from the Vice President to President, which wasn't finalized by law until the 25th amendment in 1967! His greatest foreign policy achievement was opening diplomatic relations with China.

His photographs indicate a Type 1 – tight jaw, pursed lips and a lean, angular look. Of course, slow camera shutter speeds back then probably made everyone look serious. He stayed thin and wiry his entire life. Strong beliefs made it hard for him to compromise. Typical for 1s, his moral values and strong opinions took precedence over everything, even politics.

Tyler had a dignified charm and the grace of a southern plantation owner but he felt awkward and judgmental of people outside his class. Some considered it his vanity but biographer Robert Seager said, "What appeared to be vanity was an ingrained shyness and discomfort in the presence of people with dirty fingernails. He hadn't had any experience with these people and he was too diffident to gain any." 1s like to be clean!

Tyler was modest, reserved, and had a stoic character with a preference for working informally with others as equals. As an ISTJ in the Myers-Briggs, he was quiet, unbending, definite in his views and unconcerned with what others thought, as long as he followed his own conscience. He loved structure, detail and predictability. Tyler was a strict conservative and believed in a literal interpretation of the Constitution. He joins George Washington and James Monroe, both ISTJs, as well as the next president, James Polk. ISTJ is a common type among our presidents, with many more to follow.

After his presidency, John Tyler retired to his plantation while his family continued to grow larger. Before the Civil War, he chaired a peace conference in Washington D.C. in an attempt to prevent a civil war and keep the Union but no compromise could be reached. He then voted to secede from the union as a loyalist to his state of Virginia. He also became a Representative in the Confederate Congress but died of a stroke in 1862 before he took office. When Tyler died his demise was ignored by Abraham Lincoln, the sitting President, because Tyler was considered a traitor to the United States.

His wife, Julia, lived another 27 years after Tyler's death. In 1864 during the Civil War, she moved from Virginia to New York. In the midst of extreme controversy, she continued to advocate for the Southern cause, as she believed in slavery and the Southern plantation way of life. She eventually moved back to Richmond, Virginia where the active and beautiful "Rose of Long Island" passed away in 1889.

During the time of Tyler's presidency, Morse code was invented and the first telegraph line was completed between Washington D.C. and Baltimore, Maryland. Transportation was improved with better toll roads, canals and railroads, and Florida and Texas were added to the Union. Texas was officially added as a State late in Tyler's final year as President. This act led to the Mexican War soon thereafter. Public education for whites was increasing and religious sponsored colleges were burgeoning. The North was industrializing at a rapid pace – factories producing shoes, textiles, guns, machines, clocks and furniture were on the rise, while cotton, sugar, slaves and smaller towns were the major focus of growth in the South rather than the cities in the North. The country was heading toward a major war between North and South.

Tyler set the precedent for the Vice President to succeed the President when his predecessor died and therefore awakened the country to the importance of seriously considering the power and importance of choosing the right Vice President. Tyler was independent and strong. He supported the idea of presidents having executive power; crossing their own party if need be, and following their conscience regardless of the consequences. As a Type 1, he stood his ground on what he thought was right. He is considered to have done poorly as President by historians. However, the book entitled *Recarving Rushmore* ranks him as the number one President of all. This is because he kept peace in the country as well as in our relations worldwide while managing to simultaneously develop the American economy. The book also lauds him because he was conservative and honest.

James Polk, Type 1, ISTJ, Expansionist, 1845-49

(1795-1849) James Polk, the 11th president of the United States, is considered to have been one of the most active US presidents. Just as Jefferson nearly doubled the size of the country, Polk did the same during his administration. He was an expansionist; through war and negotiation he acquired all the territory that makes up the current Western United States. Winning the controversial Mexican-American War gave the United States California, Arizona, New Mexico, Nevada and Utah. Negotiation and threat of war with England over the Canadian boundary gave the US Oregon. He accomplished all four of the goals he set for his administration – the acquisition of the Southwest and Oregon territories, the lowering of tariffs and an independent Treasury system.

Polk was a Type 1. He was very goal oriented and success driven, similar to a type 3 but with a perfectionistic drive. He was a workaholic, a micromanager, who was grim and serious. He didn't allow drinking or dancing in the White House, though that was probably due as much to his wife's standards as his own. Gaslights were installed in the White House for the first time, which allowed him to stay up all night working when he needed to. He requested the national budgets be directed to him so he could detail them out instead of allowing the Department of the Treasury to handle them. 1s often do the best job and hesitate to delegate to someone else for fear the job won't be done right.

He was our fourth ISTJ president. Others include Washington, Monroe and Tyler. The following section from Truity.com explains: "ISTJs are responsible organizers, driven to create and enforce order within systems and institutions. They are neat and orderly, inside and out, and tend to have a procedure for everything they do. Reliable and dutiful, ISTJs want to uphold tradition and follow regulations.

ISTJs are steady, productive contributors. Although they are Introverted, ISTJs are rarely isolated; typical ISTJs know just where they belong in life, and want to understand how they can participate in established organizations and systems. They concern themselves with maintaining the social order and making sure that standards are met well and precisely."www.truity.com/personality-type/istj

As is typical of 1s, Polk wanted to be in charge of every detail of every decision. This included being in charge of war strategies with American generals in the Mexican-American War, an agenda that dominated his presidency. The Southwestern territory that included California, Nevada, Utah, the majority of New Mexico and Arizona, as well as part of Texas, was ceded to the United States by Mexico following the war. In the case of the Oregon territories, he negotiated a financial arrangement with Britain.

Growing up in North Carolina, James was the oldest son of a successful farmer and surveyor. The family moved to Tennessee when he was 10, which some people believe was a strain on his already questionable health. At 17 he had surgery to remove stones in his urinary bladder. In those days, there was no anesthetic for surgery except drinking alcohol. The successful outcome of the surgery provided an additional benefit: the ability to attend school. Ill health in his early childhood had been a barrier to formal education.

He enrolled in the University of North Carolina at 20 where he graduated at the top of his class in mathematics and the classics three years later. He then apprenticed with a law firm in Tennessee, and entered politics as a state legislator at 27. He got a late start and died young at age 53, but accomplished a lot in his life. Polk was in the Tennessee legislature and was a US Representative for seven two-year terms. Four of those years he served as Speaker of the House of Representatives. Andrew Jackson's influence propelled much of his career.

At age 29 he married Sarah Childress. She was from a prominent family, and was intelligent, very active, had social graces and loved politics. Her role as a hostess and the support of her husband was instrumental in his success. They discussed politics, he sought her advice and she monitored his health. They made connections with important politicians and she was liked by everyone. Loyal to close friends of Andrew Jackson, including future president Franklin Pierce, John C. Calhoun and his wife; Polk and Sarah made alliances that furthered his career. Andrew Jackson was a strong supporter of James Polk's career, and Polk was often referred to as "Young Hickory." When he was president, Sarah was referred to as the "Presidentress," referring to her strong influence on her husband.

Sarah's strict Presbyterian background forbade her to attend the theater, drink or dance and certainly not go to horse-races. She didn't play music at the White House on Sunday. They never had children which gave them the time necessary to be a truly political couple. Some think that his operation at age 17 prevented him from fathering children.

As a 1, Polk was not an easy man to know; his lifestyle was austere. He could be inflexible and tended to over manage. By reputation he was known as a man of duty, integrity and dignity. He maintained control at all times. During his presidency, he kept a diary in which he wrote with despair of the tedium of entertaining visitors who sought appointments to public office. Other presidents commented on how awful office seekers were for them also. He must have liked steadiness, as he had the same cabinet members throughout his tenure. He could have easily been elected twice but held to a publicly made promise that he would serve only one term. The decision to honor one's word is a common trait of Type 1 people.

Polk went on a tour of the South for three months after he was president and was warmly welcomed by throngs of people. Unfortunately, he contracted cholera, which was spreading through the South, and died a premature death at 53 at the end of his tour. His wife, Sarah, lived for 41 more years after Polk died, and wore a black dress as a symbol of her mourning the entire time! She received many visitors and was held in great esteem. Even during the Civil War, dignitaries of both sides would visit, as the Polk mansion was honored as a safe zone. James Polk was considered to be the strongest president to serve in the era between Jackson and Lincoln, as he accomplished everything he set out to accomplish.

Polk did have his detractors. Lincoln called Polk a liar and strongly criticized him for instigating an unjustified war (the Mexican-American War). He thought Polk was a dictator and wished the wrath of God on him! Congress passed the war resolution to declare war on Mexico by a narrow vote. It was controversial, similar to the Vietnam War in modern history. Ulysses S. Grant who fought in that War, later assessed it as unholy and "the most unjust war ever waged."

Polk was lacking in charisma and magnetic and was rather modest, unpretentious and matter of fact. John Quincy Adams said of Polk, "He has no wit, no literature, no point of argument, no gracefulness of delivery, no elegance of language, no philosophy, no pathos, no felicitous impromptus; nothing that constitutes an orator, but confidence, fluency and labor." Polk was aristocratic, honest, stubborn, aloof and independent.

As a classic Type 1 Perfectionist, Polk tended to be formal, stiff and humorless and was more concerned with maintaining his own dignity and the dignity of the office than he was with being admired. He was disciplined, diligent, intelligent and responsible. He tended to be quiet and did not confide in many people, trusting the dictates of his own conscience. He worked 12 hours a day on average and didn't delegate responsibilities to others, but rather did things himself. Polk was especially admired by Harry Truman who was also a 1.

Polk rarely left Washington and regarded pleasure as time wasted. He didn't believe a president should take vacations but rather should be a classic nose-to-the-grindstone, hard worker. “No President,” he observed, “who performs his duty faithfully and conscientiously can have any leisure.” He didn’t like receptions, dinner parties, concerts and other entertainments in the White House and avoided them if possible. Speaking about Congress, he said “There is more selfishness and less principle among Congress than I had any conception of before I became President of the United States.” From the country’s perspective, his greatest achievement was in the expansion of US territory. He was a man of his word.

Zachary Taylor, Rough and Ready, Type 8, ISTP, 1849-50

(1784-1850) Zachary Taylor, president number 12, a general and war hero in the Mexican-American War of 1846-48, never voted in an election, including his own, and never held a political office before being voted in as president. A career soldier, he fought in the War of 1812 and in many Indian wars, and established a series of forts on the Western frontier. He owned three plantations in Kentucky, Louisiana and Mississippi with hundreds of slaves.

Taylor was born into a well-known family of planters in Virginia. They moved westward to Kentucky and eventually owned over 10,000 acres of land and over 25 slaves. The family lived in a log cabin until they were able to build a large brick home. Taylor was descended from the Elder William Brewster, who was a leader of Plymouth Colony in Massachusetts. He was also second cousin to the fourth president, James Madison and father-in-law to Jefferson Davis, the head of the Confederacy.

Known as "Rough and Ready," he shared the hardships of camp and fort life with his troops. He appeared unkempt and disheveled, fought hand-to-hand combat, was a career soldier and eventually became a general. He commanded a number of military forts in the West and South. Even though he was an "Indian fighter," he also protected Indian interests when he could. Even as a child Taylor knew he wanted to be in the military; his family lineage included soldiers who participated in past wars. He received some education but was not a man of letters nor was he partial to deep introspection, yet he was intelligent and thoughtful. Taylor could read well but barely wrote, as he attended school sporadically and his family moved a lot.

Taylor was likely an 8 with a 9 wing, a leader who was decisive and opinionated, yet able to compromise. He was direct, frank and outspoken but also gentlemanly, courteous, congenial and friendly. He was cautious in his speech when necessary, which attests to his strong 9 wing. He was also quiet, observant, insightful and focused on efficiency and structure, yet did not over plan in his battle preparations. He completely trusted his ability to decide in the moment. Abrupt at times, he could be authoritarian. He was known for ignoring orders from above and doing what he wanted; this is not unusual for an 8. Taylor had many contrasting qualities.

He was a bit shy meeting new people but warmed up quickly. He stammered a bit and was thoughtful before speaking. Although his image was gruff, particularly his manner of dress, Taylor was, according to biographer Holman Hamilton, "a gentleman, inherently gracious, even gallant where women were concerned, and an affable and agreeable host."

Taylor was a shrewd observer of men. Grant said that he cared little for fancy uniforms and spoke little but that on paper he was very clear in his directions, intentions, and action plans. He was practical and a top-notch general. Most of his career was devoted to the military, interspersed with periods of being a plantation owner and overseeing his land as a gentleman farmer. He wasn't a died-in-the-wool slave states' rightist, like other presidents. Some Myers-Briggs practitioners have typed him as an ESFP though my evidence and intuition indicate he was an ISTP. If my assessment is accurate it would make him the only ISTP president.

www.personalitypage.com/html/ISTP.html

Portrait of an ISTP – The Mechanic

"As an ISTP, your primary mode of living is focused internally, where you deal with things rationally and logically. Your secondary mode is external, where you take things in via your five senses in a literal, concrete fashion.

ISTPs have a compelling drive to understand the way things work. They're good at logical analysis, and like to use it on practical concerns. They typically have strong powers of reasoning, although they're not interested in theories or concepts unless they can see a practical application. They like to take things apart and see the way they work.

ISTPs have an adventuresome spirit. They thrive on action, and are usually fearless. ISTPs are fiercely independent, needing to have the space to make their own decisions about their next step. They do not believe in or follow rules and regulations, as this would prohibit their ability to "do their own thing". Their sense of adventure and desire for constant action makes ISTPs prone to becoming bored rather quickly.

ISTPs like and need to spend time alone, because this is when they can sort things out in their minds most clearly. They absorb large quantities of impersonal facts from the external world, and sort through those facts, making judgments, when they are alone.

ISTPs are action-oriented people. They like to be up and about, doing things. They are not people to sit behind a desk all day and do long-range planning. Adaptable and spontaneous, they respond to what is immediately before them. They usually have strong technical skills, and can be effective technical leaders. They focus on details and practical things. They have an excellent sense of expediency and grasp of the details which enables them to make quick, effective decisions.

ISTPs are optimistic, full of good cheer, loyal to their equals, uncomplicated in their desires, generous, trusting and receptive people who want no part in confining commitments."

Taylor was able to deal with Indians as equals and contemporaries rather than enemies. He could ward off wars with diplomacy and peace, while simultaneously carrying out the presidential agenda of moving the Indians westward. His Type 8 with 9 wing made him calm in battle and deadly in his strategies and fighting. However, he could be forgiving after the battle, a quality that served him well as president. He seemed to have empathy for Indians but nonetheless killed them if they failed to comply with government wishes. He could be tough, even hanging his own soldiers if they were traitors or cowards.

He had a good family life. His wife Peggy set up house each time they moved to be near his military posts, and they lived in the best style they could, considering the circumstances. They had six children, one son and five daughters. Two daughters died in infancy; one of his surviving daughters married Jefferson Davis. Taylor objected to the marriage because he didn't want his daughter to marry an Army officer but the young woman ignored her father's wishes and married Davis anyway.

Taylor naturally wanted his daughters to marry men who were civilians, not unusual as the Army presented a rough life for soldiers and their spouses and families. Due to Taylor's objection, Davis resigned from the Army and Taylor was appreciative, although tragically his daughter died three months later. His daughter Mary acted as White House hostess because her mother Peggy was in poor health. Their son became a famous Confederate general.

Taylor didn't care if he won the presidency or not as he would have been just as happy serving on a military post and then return to his plantation. "I don't care a fig about the office of president," he said. Of all of our presidents, he was the one most unconcerned whether he won or lost the election.

He didn't learn that he had won his party's nomination as a candidate for President until weeks after it was announced. He instructed the post office to deliver only postage paid letters and one of the letters that was withheld informed him that he had won the nomination from his party! Taylor didn't even take the president's office immediately as he was stationed on a military outpost and it took a while to travel to Washington, D.C. Taylor's wife prayed every day that he wouldn't win the election as she didn't want to be a president's wife and would rather go home to their plantation.

He had been chosen as a candidate because he was a popular general and for no other reason. President Taylor himself thought he was unfit to command the country. He had been instructed during the campaign to keep his mouth shut about specifics of his policies (he didn't have many specific policies) and let the Whig leaders speak for him. They thought they could control him if he won.

Much to their horror when he was elected, Taylor had different ideas than the Whigs and spoke and acted according to what he wanted. He was a president who was able to see beyond party politics and said what he thought. He defended the South's right to continue owning slaves and the North's to attack the practice of owning of slaves. He became the last Whig to be elected president and the party was torn asunder by the fight of northern and southern Whigs over the slavery issue. Taylor was a Unionist and didn't believe in extending slavery to the West simply in order to keep the country together.

Taylor was a simple man. When he was asked whether he would run for president, he said, "such an idea never entered my head, nor is it likely to enter the head of any sane man." He shared in his troops' hardships, yet also had a luxurious wilderness house as well as his plantations to go home to when it was all over. He was ignorant of politics, though both parties courted him to run for president; it being less important who he actually was than the image the parties thought people wanted. He basically ignored his cabinet as well as the Whig press and set up and ran his own newspaper. He was absolutely independent and decisive which are traits of Type 8.

He was sensitive to slights against him. As already stated, in battle he was calm and deadly but almost always magnanimous after a battle and settled on fairly good terms with the enemy. He was known for negotiating with the Indians and settling things peacefully when possible.

He died a quick death. At a 4th of July celebration in DC, everyone was warned against drinking water and eating raw fruit, as there had been a cholera epidemic. In the heat of the day, he drank lots of water and upon returning to the White House he ate loads of cherries and iced cucumbers and drank iced milk. He had terrible diarrhea, which caused severe dehydration and vomiting. He was dead in three days! He had served 16 months in office. His last words were, "I regret nothing, but am sorry that I am about to leave my friends." There has been a fair amount of speculation that Taylor was poisoned and recently his body was exhumed in order to find out. It was then proven that he died of natural causes. Lincoln gave a speech at his funeral.

Some additional facts about Zachary Taylor:
He rode his horse side-saddle in battle. He was known to have a perfect spitting tobacco aim – never missing his sand filled box across his office.

Millard Fillmore, Compromiser, Type 9, ISFJ, 1850-1853

(1800-1874) Millard Fillmore, our 13th president, was the second of nine children and was born in a log cabin. He grew up in poverty on a farm in New York State where he attended school for only three months a year and learned to read on his own. He studied a dictionary meticulously. Apprenticed as a cloth maker at the age of 14, he was virtually a slave to his master. He borrowed enough money to pay off his abusive owner and walked back 100 miles to his parent's house. Starting regular school when he was 17, he was tutored by his teacher Abigail, who was only 19, and whom he eventually married when he was 26.

Abigail supported his desire to read and be successful. She encouraged him to read challenging books to develop his mind. Fillmore trained to be a lawyer with his father's support, and thanks to the backing of local lawyers, he became successful. He was elected to the state legislature three times where he supported legislation banning the imprisonment of debtors, then was elected to the US House of Representatives four times.

Over time he became nationally known in the Whig party and attempted to formulate compromises between the Northern and Southern factions who were divided over the slavery issue. Having risen to the position of Vice President of the United States, he succeeded Zachary Taylor, who died after serving only 16 months in office. While Fillmore was Vice President he lived alone, in a single room in the Willard Hotel in Washington, D.C. His wife had decided to go back home to Buffalo, New York when he became Vice President, but she then joined him at the White House when he became President.

Fillmore was considered attractive, well-dressed and in good health most of his life, though he gained weight as he aged. He was likeable, spoke slowly, was a pragmatist and he was able to accomplish goals through the art of compromise. Common sense was his guide and he appealed to reason more than emotion.

Millard was quiet, easy-going and had a live and let live attitude. He also had perfectionist qualities and was loyal to values, beliefs and traditions. His warm and easygoing nature attracted many friends. He was not particularly ambitious but his friends continued to encourage him to run for office. Gentle wisdom was the gift he offered but some described him as “second-hand, commonplace, mediocre, undistinguished.”

Fillmore was soft-spoken yet he was a persuasive advocate, tending to be conciliatory, sympathetic and charitable. He was likely a Type 9 with a 1 wing. Almost every adjective that describes him points out the traits of 9 – easygoing, common, warm and not overly ambitious. 9s have been promoted to the presidency because of their willingness to compromise, avoiding conflict and getting along with the majority of people they encounter.

He was a compromise vice presidential candidate being from the North, though he wanted to appease the South. He didn’t want to abolish slavery and as president, supported the Compromise of 1850. It included the Fugitive Slave Act, which allowed slave owners and their representatives to pursue escapees and return them to their owners. Fillmore's support of that measure enraged abolitionists and, nearly started the Civil War in the 1850s. His desire to compromise as a Type 9, created as much conflict as it solved.

During his presidency, Fillmore was fairly successful in foreign policy. Trade opened up with Japan, which actually commenced in Pierce's term, Hawaii was protected from European colonists, and England agreed with the United States to refrain from invading and colonizing any South American countries. Several unsuccessful attempts were made to take over Cuba (similar to a Bay of Pigs invasion) by private interests who wanted to establish a presence there with the intention of expanding the slave trade. Fillmore was cognizant of this attempt and didn't stop it. Even though the U.S. government had nothing to do with these ventures President Fillmore was blamed for them. He supported freedom from dictatorships in Eastern Europe but walked a fine diplomatic line so that we could maintain alliances with those governments.

He never gambled, drank or smoked and preferred quiet times with his family to loud parties (9s have a strong distaste for noise and chaos). He didn't hold many parties at the White House, because his wife was unwell and he would rather listen to his daughter play piano, harp or guitar while he read or worked. He often worked late into the night. Meanwhile, his family preferred to retreat to the countryside rather than stay in Washington, D.C.

He was likely an ISFJ, as were a number of other presidents. "The ISFJ personality type is quite unique, as many of their qualities defy the definition of their individual traits. Though possessing the Feeling (F) trait, ISFJs have excellent analytical abilities; though Introverted (I), they have well-developed people skills and robust social relationships; and though they are a Judging (J) type, ISFJs are often receptive to change and new ideas. ISFJs are true altruists, meeting kindness with kindness-in-excess and engaging the work and people they believe in with enthusiasm and generosity.

There's hardly a better type to make up such a large proportion of the population, nearly 13%. Combining the best of tradition and the desire to do good, ISFJs are found in lines of work with a sense of history behind them, such as medicine, academics and charitable social work." www.16personalities.com/isfj-personality.

The White House was in disrepair in the 1840s and visitors often complained of springs in the furniture popping out and stabbing them. He also installed the first running water bathtub in the White House. The first permanent library in the White House was established with the important assistance of his wife, Abigail. Abigail loved to read, tend the garden or listen to music. She had been a teacher before Fillmore was elected president and was the first First Lady to hold a job after marriage. During her time as First Lady (1850-1853), she made certain the White House had a music room and three pianos, and she made additions to the White House library. She was an intelligent, cultured, well-read woman who offered wise counsel to her husband.

Fillmore's beloved Abigail died unexpectedly of pneumonia, just a month after Fillmore left office. She caught a cold listening to Franklin Pierce's inaugural address, traditionally held outside in January. His 22 years old daughter died soon after her mother's death from cholera, a common cause of death. Both were devastating losses to him, one right after the other.

During Fillmore's time as president, industrialization was happening at a rapid pace. Clipper ships travelled around the Cape of Good Hope at the tip of South Africa, expanding trade to the East. Whaling vessels were capturing whales for sperm whale oil to boost industrial output. Immigration was increasing, women's conventions were being held, which inspired the suffragette movement and the beginnings of civil rights for women. Craftsmen were organizing unions though factory workers were not yet included in the movement at this point.

Gold was discovered in California and people began pouring into San Francisco and the West Coast. The country was becoming bi-coastal. *Uncle Tom's Cabin* was written by Harriet Beecher Stowe and the Underground Railroad was established to transport slaves to the North or Canada. The country was becoming increasingly divided over slavery. Politicians during Fillmore's term got into fistfights and cane fights. It became so contentious that Congressmen began carrying pistols into Congressional session.

Fillmore opposed the Masons, was somewhat anti-Catholic and believed in limiting immigration. Even though he was against slavery, he acquiesced to pro-slavery elements in an attempt to keep the country together. Fillmore is faulted for trying to ally with everyone, which is not unusual for a 9. When he died in 1874 he wasn't deeply mourned by the country. Fillmore is generally not thought of as having been a strong president. However, considering the unrest of the country during the time he resided as President, many think he is underrated.

"Among the chief magistrates of our country there appear more brilliant names than Fillmore's, yet none who more wisely led on the nation to progress and prosperity, making her name great and preserving peace in most perilous times, without invoking the power of the sword, or one who could more truthfully say, "*These hands are clean.*" Without being a genius like Webster or Hamilton, he was a safe and sagacious statesman. He possessed a mind so nicely adjusted and well balanced that he was fitted for the fulfillment of any duty that he was called to perform. He was always ready to give up everything but conviction when once convinced. A single public act, The Fugitive Slave Law of 1850, honestly and unflinchingly performed cost him his popularity. Posterity, looking from a distance, will perhaps be more just. All his acts, whether daily and common or deliberate and well considered, were marked with modesty, justice and sincerity."
www.milliardfillmore.org

"God knows that I detest slavery, but it is an existing evil, for which we are not responsible, and we must endure it, till we can get rid of it without destroying the last hope of free government in the world," said Fillmore.

Fillmore ran for president twice again but lost. He remarried some five years after his wife died. Active in political and civic causes when he retired to Buffalo, New York, he became the first chancellor of the University of Buffalo, the head of a number of civic committees and the founder of the Buffalo Historical Society.

Fillmore was considered the leading citizen of Buffalo, welcoming distinguished visitors such as Abraham Lincoln and presided over conventions and other gatherings. He was against the Civil War, believing Lincoln could have prevented it, a position shared by a number of historians. Many people never forgot his support of the Fugitive Slave Act and some citizens even smeared his lavish house in Buffalo with black paint when Lincoln was assassinated in 1865. He died at the age of 74 and his second wife outlived him by seven years.

Fillmore's foreign policy choices were more powerful than his domestic leadership. He was a president who added to the peace and prosperity of the United States in spite of the contention over slavery, but lacked a sense of vision. He tried too hard to please everyone. He did to best to heal the country with compromise but dissent continued its course toward division.

Franklin Pierce, Type 7, ESFP, Appeasing the South, 1853-57

(1804-1869) Franklin Pierce was the 14th President. He won the presidency on the Democratic nominating ballot as a dark horse compromise candidate. Being a northerner, he understood that his best chance of winning the presidency was to support slavery in the South. Holding to that position, he won against his opponent Winfield Scott, who had been his commander in the Mexican-American War. Pierce received a political appointment and served as a brigadier general, despite having no military experience.

Franklin's father, Benjamin, was a Revolutionary War hero and served twice as governor of New Hampshire. Benjamin was an extravert who loved his eight children and the constant activity of many business and political friends as well as that of the neighborhood kids who were always welcomed to visit his home. Their large house was not only a home but also an inn, tavern and stagecoach and mail stop. It was a family business and his wife and all the children participated in running it. The home and inn was located in Hillsborough, New Hampshire, and was situated on a road considered to be a major road or turnpike, though still being a country road. Franklin, like his father who was friendly and extraverted, grew up with a good education in local schools and private academies.

Starting college at age 15, Franklin graduated from Bowdoin College in Maine and he later married the college president's daughter Jane. The first two years at college were largely spent partying though he became a serious student in the last two years, graduating near the top of his class of 15 students. He was president of one of the two debating societies. At college he started a lifelong friendship with fellow student Nathaniel Hawthorne, who supported Pierce's political ambitions throughout his life; Hawthorne wrote political pamphlets to promote Pierce's career. Law school in Northampton, Massachusetts was Pierce's next step and he did his law apprenticeship with a former New Hampshire governor as well as a New Hampshire judge. Pierce soon started his law practice across the street from his home and tavern, which became a major political gathering place in Hillsborough.

At the age of 24 Franklin was elected State Representative of the New Hampshire State House and Speaker of the House two years later. Eventually he became a U.S. Representative and Senator. Though he didn't author legislation, he was quite well liked by his peers and was a strong supporter of Andrew Jackson. Distinguished as a trial lawyer during times when he wasn't serving in government, he had a large following among courtroom attendees who especially enjoyed his unique skill of appealing to juries' emotional sensibilities. He won most of his cases. Pierce was an ardent supporter of the Constitutional right to freedom of religion, and he successfully defended the religious community of Shakers from being driven out of New Hampshire, as well as the Catholic Church in Concord, New Hampshire where religious prejudice was in play.

Attending trials was big entertainment in those days. His wife, Jane, encouraged Franklin to continue practicing law rather than entering national politics, which she hated. Unfortunately, his dedication to a career in politics drove a wedge between them. From New Hampshire, he led Polk's successful presidential bid prior to running for his own presidency. Jefferson Davis, who later became the President of the Confederacy, was a strong political ally and Davis's wife Varina, was a close family friend.

Married to Franklin when she was 28, Jane, who came from the nearby county seat of Amherst, New Hampshire and grew up in an established family, was Franklin's opposite. Whereas Franklin was very social and knew how to hobnob, Jane was shy, religious, intellectual, and withdrawn. Franklin loved attention, liked to drink and was a southern sympathizer.

When he occasionally had too much to drink, he could be undignified and make a fool of himself. Once, while attending a play with friends, they were ejected from the theater for loud behavior and subsequently instigated a street fight. Pierce was impetuous and boisterous; loving the stimulation of political life. As a Type 7, he loved excitement, fun, entertainment and high energy. His Type 7 nature was softened by a 6 wing, which tempered the 7 qualities with a proclivity for developing loyal friendships and relationships. Despite his outgoing personality, periodic bouts of depression plagued him.

Jane was of opposite political views. She preached temperance and was a northern abolitionist. She hated politics, alcohol, Washington D.C. and the social crowd. He loved parties and politics. They were certainly a pair of opposites and it caused difficulties in their relationship. Nonetheless they loved each other, and, in spite of their differences he genuinely cared about her throughout his life and tried his best to please her.

Jane had grown up with a Congregationalist minister father with a rigid Calvinistic background, which contributed to her more serious nature. She was prone to digestive and respiratory problems. Some speculate that the tight corsets of the time contributed to her breathing problems. Being married to Franklin required quite a bit of change in residence. They lived in boarding houses in Washington, D.C. and different parts of New Hampshire and Jane often visited her sisters, mother and aunt in Massachusetts for relaxation and family connection. Preferring to live in one place, traveling was stressful for her.

Jane tried to fit into Pierce's political life, even attending Congressional meetings, attempting to keep up on the latest political news, visiting politicians' wives and attending social events but it was a challenge for her introverted nature and delicate constitution. She preferred to be a mother, visit relatives, occasionally play the piano and read. When she was feeling well, she rode horses and took walks. She missed Franklin terribly when he was away. As president, Pierce welcomed Jane's nieces and nephews to visit his wife at the White House anytime.

In 1840, Pierce denounced drinking and, in 1841, gave up his Senate seat to be with Jane and their son, and focus on his successful law practice. They purchased and moved into a new house in Concord, New Hampshire in 1842. He was out of politics for almost 10 years. The only exception to his retirement from political life at that time was a two-year period from 1846 to 1848 when he accepted an appointment as a brigadier general in the Mexican-American War. According to some, he didn't seem to be cut out to be a military leader. "I hate war in all its aspects. I deem it unworthy of the age in which I live." He was criticized for being a coward even though he fought courageously in many battles and was ordered to remove himself from a major battle due to an injury. He was unwillingly confined to his tent, sustaining a concussion after being thrown from a horse. Franklin very much wanted to emulate his father and two brothers who were all noted for their military careers and heroism. He was given a hero's welcome when he returned to New Hampshire.

Pierce's beloved wife Jane bore him three sons. All unfortunately died; one at birth, one at four years old of typhus and another, their beloved son Benny, at eleven years old in a tragic train wreck. This accident occurred, with both parents present, two months before Pierce took presidential office. Jane became very depressed, particularly with the death of her adored son Benny. She barely ever came out of her room in the White House the first year, accomplishing only some of her social duties and then was gradually able to do more. She did manage however, even in that difficult first year, to emerge for dinner each night to eat with her husband and guests. It was the custom of the time to grieve for a year and a half the loss of a child and two years for the loss of a husband. Wearing black and limiting social engagements was considered the custom. Pierce had to fulfill his political duties as president despite the fact that he deeply grieved along with his wife.

Franklin's presidency started out on a bitter note on a bitterly cold day. His 20-minute memorized speech (he was a good speaker and debater) asked for support from the American people for the grief he was still experiencing from the loss of his son. He emphasized his desire for American expansionism and for peace and prosperity in the nation.

His wife didn't attend the speech or inauguration; rather, she was writing an apologetic letter to her dead son. She wondered if he lost his life because either God was punishing them for the sin of her husband becoming president or because He wanted her husband to devote all his time to the presidency. Calvinist beliefs were linked to the idea that God had a deeper purpose for everything that happened, and a tendency toward predestination.

Pierce appointed future Confederate President Jefferson Davis as his Secretary of War, which alienated many in his party. His vice president William King died of tuberculosis after six weeks in office, and was not replaced by another vice president. Things got off to a rocky start.

The main controversy of the Pierce presidency was his support for the Kansas-Nebraska Act of 1854. Senator Stephen Douglas pressured Pierce to go along with the Act which he had written in support of the Kansas and Nebraska territories having the right to choose whether to become a slave or free state through popular vote. That was in direct violation of the Missouri Act of 1820, which limited slavery above the 36th parallel, thus preventing the proliferation of slavery in the North. Northern abolitionists were outraged.

Murderous activity erupted in Kansas with pro-slavery and anti-slavery forces fighting and killing each other in many parts of the state and Pierce was blamed for a majority of the fighting. Failure to set a limit on the spread of slavery, annihilated any consideration of nominating him for a second term. He had already supported and enforced the Fugitive Slave Act legalizing the forced return of captured slaves to their owners and punished anyone harboring or aiding slaves.

Pierce felt he had to compromise with the South to keep the nation together but he ended up alienating the populace in the North where he lived. He discounted the gravity of Northern opposition to the expansion of slavery. Type 7s avoid conflict when possible, particularly 7s with a 6 wing as Franklin probably was; they prefer harmony and creating alliances. They can live in a fantasy that things are rosier than they actually are and that positive thinking can fix things.

Pierce tended to give into pressure groups, exhibiting weak leadership, in the opinion of some historians. Border disputes with Mexico, pressure to take over Cuba to give the South easy access to slavery, attempts to annex Nicaragua for slave land, and pressure to annex lands for Stephen Douglas to build a transcontinental railroad in the Northern Territories, all led to constant, unresolvable controversies.

Some historians believe Pierce accomplished many of his goals as president. He extended the national boundaries via the Gadsden Purchase from Mexico, which later became southern New Mexico and Arizona. This completed the boundary of the present day 48 state continental United States. One of Pierce's goals was to support US expansionism. He was a strong believer in Manifest Destiny and wanted to add Alaska, Hawaii and Cuba to the US Territories. He is credited with starting discussions to purchase Alaska and sent ambassadors to negotiate with Hawaii and Cuba to add those territories.

"The policy of my administration will not be controlled by any timid forebodings of evil from expansion," Pierce said during his inauguration speech. "Indeed, it is not to be disguised that our attitude as a nation and our position on the globe render the acquisition of certain possessions not without our jurisdiction eminently important for our protection, if not in the future essential for the preservation of the rights of commerce and the peace of the world."

The successful Canadian Reciprocity Treaty was a trade agreement stating that the United States could supply Canadian Provinces north of the United States boundary. The US established trade with Japan for the first time. The national debt was reduced 60 percent from 75 million to 30 million. The tariff was strongly lowered, the Army and Navy were modernized and the authority of the Attorney General was strengthened. The Pendleton

Act established the Civil Service Department, which reduced occurrences of nepotism and politically motivated appointments.

Pierce's relationship with the Indians was better than that of some presidents. More treaties were honored, though that is challenged by the fact that Indian agents from the U.S. Government were constantly lying, bribing and forcing them to give up lands for white settlement and railroad expansion. In his second annual address, in December 1854, Pierce urged Congress to increase military force to protect settlers in Indian Territory. "The settlers on the frontier have suffered much from the incursions of predatory bands," he said. "The recurrence of such scenes can only be prevented by teaching these wild tribes the power of and their responsibility to the United States." A triumvirate of politicians, railroad companies and land spectators formed the Indian Ring, a "union of dishonor that bought off congressmen, bilked the public purse and expropriated Indian homelands," Clifford Trafzer wrote in his 2009 book "American Indians/American Presidents." "Indian agents forged blatantly corrupt deals, negotiating dozens of treaties with eastern tribes that had already been relocated to Kansas. The new treaties removed them a second time, and additional treaties forced other tribes to give up lands to make room for whites."
www.indiancountrymedianetwork.com/history/events/franklin-pierce-fierce-protector-of-white-settlers-in-indian-territory

There was no corruption in his office other than that of the US policies against the Indians and there was international peace and prosperity in the nation. He is generally ranked poorly as a President but much evidence contradicts this idea. The Kansas-Nebraska Act and his perceived later issues with alcohol marred the legacy of his otherwise successful administration.

He wanted to please everyone and his stance on the slavery issue led to trouble. It's possible that Pierce was a Type 2 (Helper), as he was loyal and generous to his friends as well as the many who sought his help, but his need for stimulation and charismatic nature, points more in the direction of 7. Many 7s are likewise very generous and giving.

Franklin was agreeable, open, compliant, congenial, likeable, charismatic, attractive, charming and a good talker. He had a magnetic personality. Type 7s love action and stimulation, they prefer to avoid having to feel any "negative" feelings. They can get depressed, though do their best to avoid it. Rather, they try to maintain excitement, activity and positivity to stay above the pain, or have addictive tendencies to enable them to forget. He came from his father's tradition of being driven to succeed and had a high tolerance for differing opinions. His wife's depression and anxiety, difficulty coping with challenges and physical sensitivity, likely increased his own anxiety. There's a strong correlation between Type 7 and ESFP, his likely MBTI type. www.truity.com/personality-type/ESFP

"ESFPs are vivacious entertainers who charm and engage those around them. They are spontaneous, energetic, and fun-loving, and take pleasure in the things around them: food, clothes, nature, animals, and especially people.

ESFPs are typically warm and talkative and have a contagious enthusiasm for life. They like to be in the middle of the action and the center of attention. They have a playful, open sense of humor, and like to draw out other people and help them have a good time."

Pierce, as mentioned, was also extremely giving and had strong elements of Type 2 The Giver. He travelled to Ohio to retrieve and take care of his two young nieces when his brother and sister-in-law died. He supported Nathaniel Hawthorne, his close friend and author by giving political jobs to him: Customs Officer in Salem, Massachusetts and US Consul in Liverpool, England. He paid for Hawthorne's two children to go to college, as well as paying for others' education and contributed resources to his extended family of siblings, nieces and nephews.

He trekked through snow or bad weather to check on the welfare of his friends in need. He gave away many of his possessions and constantly helped friends, going out of his way to promote people in their careers. Very devoted to his wife, he took care of and was attentive to her in many ways. Pierce was a generous man.

Pierce took care of Hawthorne in his dying days. Sophia Hawthorne, Nathaniel's wife, said to Pierce "I would not trust my husband in any hands now excepting just such gentle and tender hands as yours." "How singular it is that you should be the guard angelic of Mr. Hawthorne again as once before." Pierce took a trip with Hawthorne with a hope of helping him recover from his declining health. Unfortunately, Hawthorne expired on the trip. Pierce had also been particularly caring of Hawthorne's ill daughter many years before.

Pierce held to the moral position of wanting to keep the Union together and avoid war. Although he opposed slavery in principle he felt the abolitionists inflamed the situation by forcing the abolishment of slavery. As Pierce perceived it, he strongly disagreed with Lincoln's instigation of war. He felt war was to be avoided at all cost. It was upsetting to Pierce that the slavery issue went unresolved and he was unable to generate national peace and the approval he wanted. He was a strong critic of Lincoln, particularly over Lincoln's suspension of the writ of habeas corpus, which gave authorities the right to hold prisoners indefinitely without a trial during the Civil War. However, Pierce continued to support the Union as Lincoln did.

Pierce was an active man. He enjoyed taking long brisk walks each day and swimming in the ocean. He was optimistic and spontaneous but also suffered from depression sometimes. This was possibly due to his wife's depression and his closeness to her, as well as guilt about the difficulties his wife endured as a politician's wife.

A persistent cough due to chronic bronchitis stayed with Pierce his entire life. He felt he that had done a good job as president but it pained him that he wasn't offered the opportunity to run for a second term. He was offered the nomination to run again in 1860 and 1864, which he declined.

His wife Jane gradually withered from tuberculosis. A two-year trip to the West Indies after Franklin's term expired, to improve her health failed but increased their bond. He travelled extensively with her to other islands and to Europe and took care of her. It was possibly the best period of their marriage. She died in 1863 at the age of 57. Apparently, they were closer after the presidency ended and when they were travelling but he became more depressed after her death.

According to some accounts, drinking was problematic on and off for Pierce but not during his presidency. Jane placed his wine glass upside down during dinner. Pierce went through long periods being abstinent. Alcoholism was more common than today but it's debatable how serious his problem was. He was reprimanded for drinking during his military service, though that was a common problem in the military. To counteract his drinking image, he joined a temperance movement in his thirties and even got the town of Concord to outlaw drinking.

When Pierce left the White House he retired to Concord, New Hampshire before leaving for his travels with Jane. After she died he continued drinking now and then, bought a summer seaside residence in New Hampshire and spent more time alone though he did have visitors and would visit his relatives. He apparently drank more just before his death. He succumbed to cirrhosis of the liver at the age of 64. The literature varies widely on issues of his drinking, depression, and his final years.

One of his biographer's Roy Franklin Nichols said, "He lacked a sustained feeling of self-confidence and was desirous of approbation. Consequently, he endeavored to be gracious and accommodating to all those who sought favors." He didn't have the force of a Jackson or Lincoln but was more assertive than most biographers attested to. Pierce was a generous and kind man; he tried to heal the nation and to live up to what he thought best for the country. He attempted to satisfy the conflicting needs of the North and South, tried to prevent war and did much to strengthen the United States.

There are many myths about Pierce, including the idea that he didn't have an agenda as president. He actually had very clear goals: to expand US territory, to improve trade relations with foreign powers, to have an honest administration and to strictly uphold the Constitution. He upheld all of these, though he had a difficult time trying to maintain peace regarding the slavery issue. Another myth was that he was weak and easily manipulated. Pierce was both moralistic and legalistic and vetoed bills not in alignment with his beliefs. He had very high principles. He had the same loyal cabinet throughout his administration with no resignations.

New Hampshire's only US president, the house where he lived most of his first 30 years is open to the public in Hillsborough, New Hampshire. The personally guided tours are very informative and well worth the visit. It provides a comprehensive view of Franklin Pierce's life. His house in Concord New Hampshire where his family lived between 1842 and 1848 is called the Pierce Manse. There one can gain an intimate perspective on Franklin Pierce's life.

James Buchanan – Conservative, Type 6, ISFJ, 1857-1861

(1791-1868) The 15th president was James Buchanan, the only president who was never married and the last one born in the 18th century. He was one of the most politically experienced presidents: for five years he maintained his law practice while serving in the Pennsylvania House of Representatives, and then served 5 terms in the US House of Representatives and 10 years in the US Senate. He was also Minister to Russia under Andrew Jackson, Secretary of State under James Polk and Minister to Great Britain under Franklin Pierce.

Buchanan mistakenly thought the acrimony between the North and South could be handled by convincing the two factions to abide by constitutional law, especially in light of the Supreme Court's Dred Scott decision of 1857. That ruling reinforced the South's right to own slaves as property, stating they had no rights and certainly shouldn't be US citizens. He tried to solve the ever-widening divide by enforcing the law rather than demonstrating moral leadership and navigating difficult negotiations. Northerners were uninterested in enforcing constitutional rights; they felt the Dred Scott decision was morally wrong. Southerners demanded approval for what they saw as their moral right and freedom to own slaves. The North could barely tolerate allowing slavery to continue where it was already entrenched, never mind, allowing its' expansion into the new territories of the West. Most of these territories were annexed after the Mexican-American War ended in 1848 and the Northern states didn't want the new Northern territories to become slave states.

The South's economy had been based on slavery for generations and the soil was farmed first for rice, then tobacco and, eventually, for the large-scale production of cotton that "needed slaves" to do the grueling fieldwork required to produce cotton. Of course, many Northerners were complicit in the slave trade; it insured their profitability, particularly in the manufacture of cotton cloth.

Before his nomination as president Buchanan lived abroad acting as Minister to Great Britain. He wasn't engaged in the growing discord around the slavery issue in the United States and therefore hadn't spoken publicly about his views on slavery. This helped him to be chosen for nomination, as he wasn't a controversial or outspoken figure. Buchanan actually favored the South, even though he tried to be neutral. Living in boarding houses before being president, he roomed with pro-slavery Southern politicians and was possibly influenced by them.

For instance, he supported a pro-slavery constitution for Kansas, which upset many in his Democratic Party. It is claimed that he bribed Congressmen who voted for it. This is uncorroborated and seems unlikely given Buchanan's reputation was one of honesty and he was concerned about following rules. The majority of the populace in Kansas wanted a free state but Buchanan favored the pro-slavery minority.

Eventually Kansas became a free state in 1861 after the vote of a 4th state constitutional convention. For years there were 2 state capitals, one being pro-slavery and one anti-slavery. War-torn Kansas was filled with people entering the state to vote illegally; there were 55 deaths and constant bloody fighting. Many pioneers in the state simply wanted to own a farm and had no interest in the slavery issue, one way or the other, but Bleeding Kansas became the touchstone for the conflict to be worked out among white people.

The Democrats split into North and South factions during Buchanan's administration, the Whig Party faded out and the Republican Party emerged to take a strong stand against slavery and the expansion of slave territories. Eventually there was the anti-slavery Republican Party in the North that included some who were sympathetic to slavery, and the Democratic Party in the South that was mostly pro-slavery.

The country was severely divided and eventually 11 states from the South seceded from the Union. It's probable that no one could have resolved the split. The country was heading toward war and Buchanan didn't know what to do. He refused to take a strong stand either way, claiming the secession illegal, yet believing the government was powerless to prevent it. A Peace Convention was held in February of 1861, presided over by former President John Tyler in an attempt to prevent war. A series of amendments to the Constitution were proposed to create peace but those proposals died quickly in Congressional debate. Meanwhile the South gathered arms to prepare for war and the North followed. Buchanan left it to his successor, Lincoln, to decide how to deal with the impending disaster of war.

The only US president from Pennsylvania, Buchanan was the second of eleven children born to a successful merchant in the rural southern part of the state. Attending local schools, he entered Dickinson College at the age of 16, graduated with honors and then went on to study law. He was very successful as a lawyer and amassed a small fortune, being ambitious in the manner of most presidents. He tried to get himself nominated three times before his party finally nominated him as a candidate for the presidency in 1856.

After being in the Pennsylvania legislature for five years, he became engaged to Ann Coleman, the daughter of a rich iron mill owner. Her parents were opposed to the engagement. They thought Buchanan was after their money even though Buchanan was rich enough at the time that he didn't need their fortune. Rumor had it that he was seeing other women while he was betrothed to Ann. The rumors were probably untrue, but just two days after ending the engagement Ann died, likely a suicide caused by those rumors and/or family pressure not to marry him.

The family forbade him to attend her funeral, which caused great distress for Buchanan. He vowed never to marry, though, according to some biographers, he carried on flirtations throughout his life. Other writers dispute that claim. On the other hand, there is speculation that he might have been gay; he lived with Rufus King for over 10 years who later became Pierce's vice president. They appeared together often and were snidely referred to as Aunt Miss Nancy and Aunt Fancy. Buchanan is a good example of how rumors and political attacks make it hard to assess what is historically accurate.

Buchanan has been described as charming, diplomatic, genial, loyal to friends and constituents, principled, graceful, elegant, compassionate, forgiving, and courteous. Others describe him as stiff, grim, cautious and humorless, without witticisms. Apparently, he showed different parts to different people or in different conditions. He loaned money to his many friends and gave big heartedly to the poor. His generous financial support of cousins, nephews and nieces kept many of his relatives afloat. Regarding his own finances, he saved more than he spent and calculated his expenses to the penny.

Despite supporting slavery, he freed a number of slaves in Pennsylvania that he bought in Washington D.C. He was scrupulously honest according to most people, turned gifts over to the Patent Office and accepted no money, so as not to have any conflict of interest. He walked with an air of dignity and always dressed well.

Buchanan was clearly ambitious and as mentioned, tried four times to be nominated to be president. He wanted to be popular but was private about his personal life. A careful self-promoter, he would shift positions and often maneuvered things strategically to fit his intentions.

His appearance was important. He was imposing and handsome; over 6 feet tall. He cocked his head to the left due to an eye disorder and often closed one eye, as one eye was farsighted and one nearsighted. His general health was good, though one of his eyelids twitched. He drank a lot, though never appeared drunk and it didn't seem to affect his health. Fellow politicians were amazed at how he held his liquor. He could consume 2 or 3 bottles of rye or cognac at one sitting! He liked fancy things.

Buchanan was also quite cautious, conventional, self-restrained, logical, and "wary of the passions in the moment," as described by one observer. Many people observed that he could have a cool attitude inside which was belied by a warm exterior, and could be pessimistic behind a presentation of strength. "Colorless and safe," as described by a political commentator, he was unobjectionable, and cooperative. I think he is likely a Phobic Type 6 who would go with the party line and then freeze when facing decisions, for fear of making a mistake.

Buchanan was conservative, didn't like change and was confounded regarding how to deal with the issues related to slavery. He couldn't wait to get out of the White House. His decision-making process vacillated instead of maintaining a steadying focus and disciplined purpose. Phobic 6s, as I believe Buchanan was, often use Type 3 success building qualities to hide their caution and concerns and Type 9 pacifying qualities to create a warm exterior, even though Type 6 can be warm in its own right. According to biographer George Ticknor Curtis, Buchanan had "strong family affections, engaging social qualities, fidelity to friends and a forgiving temper to those who had hurt him." Loyalty was definitely one of his strong traits, as is true for Type 6.

Buchanan had a very active social life (likely he was a social subtype), worked hard, was calm and pleasant. Some say he was only partially present at times and was possibly distracted by anxiety. He could keep a cool distance, but had an attentive and mannerly demeanor that made it appear he was connecting intimately with whomever he interacted. He could offer clear and logical arguments. Some say he was like a chess player, "cool, calculating, keeping his own counsel, somewhat like Martin Van Buren," quoted from the book *Presidential Temperament*. Buchanan seemed watchful and cautious like a Type 6. Photographs of Buchanan reflect this.

"His cool calculation was rather like the cautious exercise of the ambition of a rather pessimistic Monitor (SJ temperament) whose façade was confident strength, but whose spirit was concern and worry," quoted from the book *Presidential Temperament*. He has been described as timorous, indecisive, "a hopeless ditherer," from the book, *How They Became President.* Basically, he was frozen in indecisiveness and didn't know what to do regarding the slavery issue.

His Myers-Briggs type, I believe, is ISFJ, The Protector. "ISFJs are industrious caretakers, loyal to traditions and organizations. They are practical, compassionate, and caring, and are motivated to provide for others and protect them from the perils of life.

ISFJs are conventional and grounded, and enjoy contributing to established structures of society. They are steady and committed workers with a deep sense of responsibility to others. They focus on fulfilling their duties, particularly when they are taking care of the needs of other people. They want others to know that they are reliable and can be trusted to do what is expected of them. They are conscientious and methodical, and persist until the job is done." truity.com/personality-type/ISFJ

Buchanan was aggressive in his foreign policy, ambitious to gain territory, Cuba being one example, and threatened to attack any who would challenge US interests. He sent federal troops to quell a Mormon "revolt" which was stopped finally by a skilled negotiator, and subsequently stated, "I like the noise of democracy."

Many people blame Buchanan for allowing the Civil War to happen. He refused to surrender Fort Sumter to the Southern interests and later wrote a book justifying that decision. He was a politician with vast experience but wasn't cut out for the presidency it seems, at least during that time in history. He disliked conflict and his efforts to solve the slavery issue failed to quell the anger and passions on either side of the issue. He was a man of detail who carefully balanced his checkbook and was also very generous with others. He died at the age of 77.

Abraham Lincoln, Civil War President, Type 4, INTP, 1861-65

(1809-1865) Abraham Lincoln is our 16th president. Considered by many to be our best president, even though others disagree and would even give him a low rating. Given many opportunities to prevent the Civil War, including a Peace Convention he didn't attend, Lincoln decided to bait the South into firing the first shot effectively starting the war at Fort Sumter in Charleston, South Carolina. Most of his cabinet and many others disagreed with his decision to resupply the Union fort instead of giving the fort up to the South, as he felt that war was inevitable.

The war to keep the union intact was known in the South as the War of Northern Aggression. It led to 650,000-750,000 lives lost, and countless wounded, as well as the vast destruction of Southern cities and homes, which led to bitter hatred between the North and South after the war. Slavery became the main issue as the war progressed but freeing the slaves didn't go well for the former slaves. They faced severe prejudice and violence, and the killing of blacks increased both during and after the war. The Union allowed black soldiers to volunteer to fight, and if they surrendered or were captured, rather than taking them in as prisoners, the Southern army usually executed them.

Lincoln was born in near poverty in a log cabin with a dirt floor. His father was often cruel and his beloved mother died from tainted milk when Abe was nine. His very beloved sister died when Lincoln was in his teens. Both were severe losses. His parents could neither read nor write and were anti-slavery. Fortunately, after his father remarried, Abe's new stepmother created a close bond with him and was highly supportive of his learning and education, adding a library of books for Abe to read. He had only a year of formal schooling, though he read constantly and was considered bookish.

Lincoln's life was filled with hard work, farm chores, reading by candlelight, fighting bullies, wrestling, and building new log cabins while his father continually moved the family from Kentucky to Indiana to Illinois. Abe didn't particularly like farm work, but he did like adventure. He worked on a ferryboat, surveyed, built several flatboats and with a friend, carried produce down the Mississippi to New Orleans. There he witnessed slaves being bought and sold which deeply affected him. He was a postmaster, a storekeeper and held the position of a militia captain during an Indian war in which he saw no action.

Starting at age 25 he won four successive terms as a state legislator, studied law and was admitted to the Illinois bar at age 28. Popular, gaining a reputation as a lawyer and a good politician, he was very ambitious. Lincoln became one of the most well-respected lawyers in the state, representing both commoners and corporations, such as the railroad where he made a great deal of money. He often argued cases before the Illinois Supreme Court.

Known as a teller of jokes and stories, he won votes as well as clients by entertaining others and visiting his constituents. Playing both sides of the race card to gain votes, he was definitely a politician. He could take a stand, even when politically unpopular, as in the case of the Mexican-American War in 1846. His thinking was that it was a war of aggression started by the United States. It was a controversial war opposed by Thoreau, Emerson, the Transcendentalists and a large percentage of the American population. He took a stand against slavery, though he didn't propose to end slavery in the South until the middle of the war. This was mostly a ploy to entice black soldiers to fight for the Union.

Being a U.S. Representative for only one term, Lincoln became popular during the seven debates against Stephen Douglas when he was running for the U.S. Senate in 1858. He publicized the debates, which gained him national recognition. Lincoln won the popular vote in the Senate race but ultimately lost the race because the electors who chose senators, much like the Electoral College today chooses the president, elected his opponent. He joined and then led the new Republican Party, which was against the expansion of slavery to the new western and northern territories. At this point, Lincoln became nationally known.

Even though as a politician he could take different stances to gain votes, he also took solid positions. In his famous house divided speech in 1858, which took place during a Douglas debate, he said that we have to be for slavery or against it, not in-between. His meaning in that speech was misunderstood. The South thought he supported slavery. This led to his presidential win, while the North thought Lincoln would abolish slavery in the South. This was not Lincoln's original position. He took a stronger moral stance for preserving the Union at all costs – even facing and accepting the great loss of lives in the war whether slaves were freed or not.

Initially, Lincoln wasn't a proponent for equality of African Americans, as he perceived them to be inferior. He proposed freedom for them to work and make money, gradually aiming to end slavery. It was not his plan to abolish slavery immediately. Initially Lincoln wasn't an abolitionist but during the Civil War he adopted that position because of the need for black troops (over 200,000 served) to win the war. He also wanted to deprive the South of free slave labor. Lincoln had morals but was very expedient and politically calculating. He always thought about the effect of his decisions.

The Army and Navy were greatly expanded to prepare for war and the draft was started at this time, followed by reactive draft riots. Considered a dictator by some, Lincoln spent government funds without congressional approval. The press was controlled and censured and many newspapers were shut down. All Southern ports were blockaded and trade with the South was prohibited early on; additionally, many Southern cities and homes were burned during the war. Civilians were killed in the process, as well as soldiers. Force and coercion were on his mind, to win the war. To Lincoln, the ends justified the means, and in a state of war it was somewhat understandable.

Lincoln could make decisions independently of his cabinet even though he listened to the cabinet members' opinions. Except for two of its members who agreed with Lincoln, his cabinet wanted federal troops to withdraw from the fort in Charleston, South Carolina to prevent war. Lincoln went against his cabinet in that decision knowing that the South would fire upon the fort if he continued to send provisions. Lincoln was not afraid of conflict and would do what he thought was right or strategic, whether others agreed or not. Many in the country disagreed with Lincoln regarding resupplying Ft. Sumter and there was a large contingent of the populace trying to prevent war.

Within the first few months there was little fighting and bloodshed but after three months when the first summer came, battles became larger with single battles causing many thousands of dead and wounded. Two-thirds of the deaths though in the War were due to disease rather than guns, cannons or bayonets.

Lincoln encouraged Grant to chase the Southern rebels without retreat. Lincoln realized that choosing Grant, who pursued the enemy relentlessly, to head the Army would lead to much more bloodshed and did so as a way to speed the ending of the war. Northern states would fight according to Lincoln "until every drop of blood drawn with the lash, shall be paid with another with the sword." Of course, no one in the beginning of the war realized that it would culminate in the atrocious acts of slaughter that ensued.

In contrast to the awfulness of the war, Lincoln was a man of humor and storytelling. He once observed an older woman garishly dressed in finery and a plumed hat, attempt to cross the street, only to slip and fall in a puddle. "Reminds me of a duck," he said to a friend. "Feathers on her head and down on her behind." Once cornered by a devotee of spiritualism who went on and on about the subject, Lincoln was asked his opinion and said "Well, for those who like that sort of thing, I should think that is just about the sort of thing they would like." He was an avid reader of jokes and storytelling books. On another occasion, the president prefaced a discussion of a draft of The Emancipation Proclamation by reading aloud from a favorite humorist. In response to the disapproval of some members of his cabinet, Mr. Lincoln said: “Gentlemen, why don’t you laugh? With the fearful strain that is upon me night and day, if I did not laugh I should die, and you need this medicine as much as I do.”

Lincoln suffered much loss in his life – three of his four sons did not survive into adulthood – one dying at the White House during the War and one dying at the age of three before his presidency. His mother and sister died young, many close friends were killed during the Civil War, he proposed to a woman who shunned him after a two-year engagement, the first woman he pursued died of a disease, and many close friends died or moved away during his lifetime. Besides his pain of loss, his wife, Mary Todd, was a severe shopaholic who lied about her expenses and would lash out at him if confronted. She had bipolar disorder and was far from loving, especially in the later part of their marriage.

He talked about suicide several times and wrote poetry that reflected his suicidal feelings. On a number of occasions, there were suicide watches placed on Lincoln by friends or neighbors who put aside all his personal sharp objects. For instance, he wouldn’t carry a pocket-knife for fear of hurting himself. He had a sensitive side and wrote a good deal of poetry. He was often melancholy and despairing He was depressed on and off much of his life.

You can read about his depression in the websites below:

http://www.theatlantic.com/magazine/archive/2005/10/lincolns-great-depression/304247/ for Lincoln in general

http://www.abrahamlincolnsclassroom.org/abraham-lincoln-in-depth/abraham-lincolns-stories-and-humor/

Lincoln lost five political campaigns before he became President – the first run for Illinois state representative, once for a run for the US House of Representatives, twice in a run for US Senator, and once in a vice-presidential bid in the election before he won the presidency.

At first, I thought Lincoln was a Type 1 related to his moral stance, with a stress move to Type 4 referenced by his sadness and despair. Of course, anyone with his history might be melancholy and despairing. It was somewhat commonplace to have much loss at that time in history, but many seemed to recover without as much ongoing depression as Lincoln felt. His feelings would often show up in his dreams. Later I changed my opinion.

Lincoln was likely a Type 4 with both a strong 3 wing and also 5 wing though a case could be made for Type 3 with a 4 wing. Both types of 3 and 1 are strong in his personality. The case for Type 4 I think is strongest, as he pondered much on the meaning of life, wrote poetry about loss and death, felt things deeply, suffered tremendously with melancholy and depression and struggled with self-esteem. Here's one of his poems, typical of many he wrote.

My Childhood Home I See Again

My childhood's home I see again,
And sadden with the view;
And still, as memory crowds my brain,
There's pleasure in it too.

O Memory! thou midway world
'Twixt earth and paradise,
Where things decayed and loved ones lost
In dreamy shadows rise,

And, freed from all that's earthly vile,
Seem hallowed, pure, and bright,
Like scenes in some enchanted isle
All bathed in liquid light.

As dusky mountains please the eye
When twilight chases day;

As bugle-tones that, passing by,
In distance die away;

As leaving some grand waterfall,
We, lingering, list its roar--
So memory will hallow all
We've known, but know no more.

Near twenty years have passed away
Since here I bid farewell
To woods and fields, and scenes of play,
And playmates loved so well.

Where many were, but few remain
Of old familiar things;
But seeing them, to mind again
The lost and absent brings.

The friends I left that parting day,
How changed, as time has sped!
Young childhood grown, strong manhood gray,
And half of all are dead.

I hear the loved survivors tell
How nought from death could save,
Till every sound appears a knell,
And every spot a grave.

I range the fields with pensive tread,
And pace the hollow rooms,
And feel (companion of the dead)
I'm living in the tombs.

Lincoln certainly had a lot of Type 1 – driven by a moral code, as well as Type 5 - a mental genius. INTP, which I believe is his Myers-Briggs type, is highly correlated with 5. It would be unusual for an INTP (it's possible Lincoln could be an INFP) to be a 4 but if so, Lincoln had a 5 wing, as well as a 3 wing. I've known many Type 4 men to struggle terribly with their feelings and self-esteem, particularly in a culture like the United States that tends to suppress the sensitive side of men. Lincoln was a very emotional man who tried to keep his feelings and insecurities under wraps.

Lincoln was generally very private about his inner life, though he could confide in, and was particularly close to a few men. He and his wife did talk about politics, as she was politically astute. They were closer in the earlier part of their marriage while raising children. Lincoln didn't confide in his wife except possibly in the first years of marriage, as she tended to be bad at keeping secrets and she could easily go into rage if she heard anything she didn't like. There were stories that she threw a cup of hot coffee at him, witnessed by others, once went after him with a knife and at another time threw a burning log at him. She had a temper!

"INTPs are philosophical innovators, fascinated by logical analysis, systems, and design. They are preoccupied with theory, and search for the universal law behind everything they see. They want to understand the unifying themes of life, in all their complexity.

INTPs are detached, analytical observers who can seem oblivious to the world around them because they are so deeply absorbed in thought. They spend much of their time focused internally: exploring concepts, making connections, and seeking understanding. To the Architect, life is an ongoing inquiry into the mysteries of the universe." www.truity.com/personality-type/INTP

Lincoln has been mistakenly typed as a Type 9 the Peacemaker probably because he wanted to bring the nation together and he wanted to be forgiving to the South after the war. However, he was less a peacemaker in his energy and demeanor, and more a deep feeler and thinker. He was also an achiever who aimed for the top and was a brilliant strategist. He could make firm decisions and didn't need agreement from others as would be true for most 9s.

He had a very strong achievement drive which was likely to compensate for feeling that he had achieved less than his potential. Lincoln had regrets about prior choices, and he was obsessed about becoming famous. He was anxious and pained much of the time, while success driven the whole time. He had too much deep inner turmoil and feeling to be a 3. Of course, he could be a 3 with a strong 4 wing, but I'm still confident he's a Type 4 with a 3 wing, due to his deep and constant inner struggles.

I've known many 4/3s to have this struggle between success and inner fulfillment and longing for a deep relationship with another, as well as to fill a special destiny. 4/3s (4s with a 3 wing) can appear as 1s with strong values, and even appear with a touch of 7 with humor and a manic or hyper energy. This could touch on Lincoln's need for storytelling, humor and jokes so typical of type 7.

4/3s often try to repress the melancholy, pain and depression that can accompany their success drive. The accomplishments of a 4/3 can temporarily block out the pain more easily than the 4 with a 5 wing who is typically more melancholy than a 4/3. In the long run, success itself even for a 4/3 doesn't fulfill the longings of a 4.

In the beginning, secession of the Southern states was considered more of a sin by Lincoln than slavery itself, considering secession from the union nothing short of treason. Loss of life, even though it was very painful for Lincoln to witness, was less important than loss of the Union. His position was: I'll force the Union onto the South because it's "right." His staunch position and the military laws he forced on the civilian populace during the war were the most autocratic this country has ever experienced – basically a military state with over 13,000 jailed who spoke out against the war.

In a civil war encampment and reenactment, I attended several years ago, I talked to a Lincoln re-enactor dressed in full Lincoln garb. When I argued that the war was possibly avoidable, he was very adamant that the Union was more important than lives lost – and worth fighting for. He was strong in his position and there was no point arguing! He didn't seem open to other options and I think he was playing his role well. Lincoln was genuinely open to others' ideas but made his own decisions and was quite independent in that process.

To support the idea of Lincoln's undaunted ambition, his law partner said of him, "His ambition was a little engine that knew no rest." "He handled men remotely, moving them like pieces on a chess board." Lincoln said of himself, "I want to be truly esteemed and want to be worthy of that." Many describe him as ruthless and secretive though on the surface he was friendly, honest and wanted respect. 4/3s are often mistyped as success-driven 3s, as that's what shows on the surface, but underneath there is a cauldron of feelings, longings, a search for depth and a desire for love, understanding and acceptance.

Lincoln at times was severely depressed, which speaks of his Type 4. "I am now the most miserable man living. If what I feel were equally distributed to the whole human family, there would not be one cheerful face on the earth. Whether I shall ever be better I cannot tell; I awfully forebode I shall not. To remain as I am being impossible; I must die or be better, it appears to me." When asked for an autograph by a young woman he once wrote, "To Rosa, you are young and I am older: You are hopeful, I am not. Enjoy life, ere it grows colder. Pluck the roses ere they rot." He was a reader of Shakespeare.

Despite this, he worked diligently to improve himself and worked hard to become a better person. He envisioned himself as someone who would change the world. His humor, storytelling and focus on purpose in life kept him going. He was often criticized and had many enemies particularly during the Civil War.

He said his life was in God's hands if there was an assassination attempt. There were several; once receiving a bullet through his top hat while riding along on his horse that missed his head by inches. There were many foiled plots, and a whole file drawer of threats. Despite that, he had many friends, advanced to the top seat of power, and was also greatly praised for his character, speeches and sacrifices. Nothing however seemed to have sustained him for long before feeling forlorn.

Lincoln openly cried many times during the war. Close friends were killed in action and he was devastated. He anguished over the death of his young son who died at the White House during the war and had to deal with his wife's depression, rage and moods. He was despondent, anxious and aged deeply in the four years of war. He pardoned a number of soldiers who were destined to die by hanging because of desertion or cowardice, due to personal pleas of mothers. Others he condemned to die.

Lincoln was an intellect and is the only US President to have a patent (even though Jefferson invented many things without a patent). His invention was a series of inflatable bellows attached to a steamboat that would cause the steamboat to rise in low water. That circumvented people on the boat from having to take out gear to raise the boat's bottom in the water. He also tried to invent a steam plow.

He spent a year studying war strategies in the Library of Congress most every day and personally hired every general in the US Army during the war. He went to the war office next to the White House as many as four times a day to read telegraph messages on how battles were going and talked to generals about war strategy. He visited an active battle scene, risking his life, being an easy target at 6 feet 4 inches. He barely escaped being shot, with men around him being wounded. Lincoln frequently visited battle encampments, parades, wounded soldiers and he even lived at The Old Soldiers Home in the summer. His energy was totally focused on winning the war.

There has been much speculation about whether Lincoln was gay or bisexual as he slept in the same bed as a roommate and best friend for four years before he married Mary. However, it was common for men to sleep together for warmth or to conserve space or to save money but both men had enough resources to have separate rooms or beds if they wanted. His law partner slept in the same room too in a separate bed for two of those four years. Lincoln loved men and had very close friendships, not uncommon, and this behavior was probably considered more normal then than it would be today without being thought gay.

He often slept with an army captain when he visited the Old Soldiers home when his wife was away. Neither of these circumstances were hidden. He had another former roommate when he was younger with whom he slept. Some people wondered about him regarding his sexual preferences, but most took it in stride as fitting in the cultural norms. Kids growing up almost always slept together and it was very common in inns and boardinghouses for men to sleep two, three or four to a bed. Women would do the same with women. Close male to male or female to female friendships were common without people making assumptions of a relationship being romantic or sexual.

Lincoln was devastated when his four-year roommate moved out and got married. He pledged eternal love, even though he supported his friend being married. They were close friends the rest of their lives and their letters reveal a deep emotionally intimate relationship. It was a different time and in some ways, less homophobic than today. Marriage could be scary, as it was for Lincoln, as he married late in life. His friend and he both wrote about their fear of marriage, fear and concerns about having sex with their spouses, having children and the responsibilities that involved. His strong emotions and inner turmoil reflect his 4ness.

Lincoln could share his personal struggles and feelings but only with people he highly trusted. Most men, such as his law partner of many years, said Lincoln shared almost nothing of his personal struggles. Speaking as a psychotherapist who has worked with a number of male 4s, they search to find people they can share their personal feelings and insecurities with, as the inner turmoil is intense and the rejection and shame of being misunderstood is equally intense.

As was somewhat common, Lincoln had been with prostitutes earlier in his life, fathered four children with his wife and had been deeply in love with two women before he met Mary Todd, whose engagement he broke off before the marriage, then reconsidered and decided to marry her. Going back and forth regarding relationship decisions is not uncommon of type 4. It was also expected that one marries to fit into society and it was even more expected to do so if you were a politician. He certainly had much anxiety about marriage and in his particular marriage with Mary, he had just cause! She was also a Type 4 and 4/4 relationships can be explosive and pose a significant risk, though with maturity could be a heavenly match with mutual passion and understanding.

Separate from war responsibilities during his administration, Lincoln accomplished a lot. He added abolitionists to the Supreme Court, freed slaves in secessionist states with the Emancipation Proclamation and eventually all slaves with the 13th amendment, started the first federal income tax program, initiated the Department of Agriculture, started a national banking system, created a standardized federal paper money, supported the development of a transcontinental railroad, implemented two international tariffs, started the Homestead Act to give away land in the West, and proclaimed Thanksgiving as a national day of blessing.

Lincoln was a man of contrast, depth, courage, brilliance, commitment, humor and despair. No wonder he is universally read about, inspiring and at the same time an enigma in many ways. As an INTP in the Myers-Briggs with also a strong feeling component, he was private, intellectual, interested in theory, concepts and strategy, and was also somewhat remote, though friendly.

He was practical and extremely ambitious, "I have the taste of president in my mouth," he said before his nomination at the Republican Convention. He wanted the nomination badly and had over 100 photographs taken of him by famous photographer Matthew Brady in order to pick the right photo portrait to distribute nationally. His photographs had much to do with him winning the presidency two times. He was very much behind the scenes in planning how to get votes to be nominated. The success drive and accomplished goals of a 4/3 were able to quell some of the painful inner turmoil.

The campaign that highlighted his rail splitting abilities was somewhat a lie, as he hated rail splitting and only did as little as possible. He was a consummate politician and was able to customize his speeches to fit the political leanings of each audience. Lincoln was always adamant about not spreading slavery beyond the South and aimed eventually to abolish slavery during the war. "If I could keep the union together without freeing a single slave I would do that and if I could keep the union together by freeing all the slaves I would do that."

The movie "Lincoln" portrayed by Daniel Day Lewis is fairly accurate and portrays Lincoln as a shrewd politician. He was a genius at calculating the right timing for his decisions. He was a man of decision and action contrary to the erroneous belief that he was indecisive. He thought about his decisions thoroughly and confronted conflict directly. He was imaginative, could be humble and was able to adapt to the situation at hand, as when he quickly became a military strategist during the War. As mentioned, he read many books on war strategy that he checked out from the Library of Congress.

A genius at the use of words, he was verbally succinct with poetic punch, which he knew would be most effective. The Gettysburg Address and the Emancipation Proclamation are the best examples of translating the nation's reality into a moral purpose with transformative meaning. His speeches reflect the depth of a Type 4 that focused on creating meaning and value from sacrifice and loss. He could look beyond the immediate details of his life to see the purpose of his present time, in relationship to the future and history. He was destined to fulfill that purpose to keep the country together as a whole and transform the nation into one that was closer to a democracy, though tenuous in nature.

Everyone knows about Lincoln's death at Ford's Theater. It was the first presidential assassination and a tragedy for the nation as he would have tried to be more protective of former slaves had he survived. His successor Andrew Johnson was a racist. Lincoln's focus in the South was not on revenge but on finding ways to include the white South in the healing process, while simultaneously helping newly freed slaves. Congress wanted to punish the white South. Johnson was lenient on the Southern whites being a Southern white himself, as likely Lincoln would have been also, but Johnson did little for the newly freed blacks and supported repressive laws against the former slaves.

Unfortunately, the Civil War by no means solved the black/white divide. Racism and the aftermath of slavery was simply transferred to new repressive structures though it did abolish the inhuman concept of people owning other people. Killing of blacks by whites increased after the war. The war's aftermath changed the economic structure of the South.

Had John Wilkes Booth not killed Lincoln, there's a chance he would have been assassinated by someone else as there were other plots against him and many in the South hated him. Some speculate that he had cancer or something called Marfan Syndrome, a genetic connective tissue disorder which causes tallness and long limbs, which would likely have ended his life early. Lincoln always felt he would die earlier than expected.

Many books and interpretations of Lincoln exist. He's been idealized but he was a real person with flaws and an ego drive who had the moral courage to act on his vision of keeping the country together. He sacrificed his life for that vision. Lincoln was a man of integrity, vision, brilliance, cleverness, depth, humor and forbearance. Despite his personal pain and inner struggles, he acted outwardly for a larger vision, without giving in to his inner demons.

Andrew Johnson, Reconstruction, Type 1, ESTJ, 1865-1869

(1808-1875) Andrew Johnson, the 17th president, grew up under impoverished conditions in a Raleigh, North Carolina log cabin. His father, who worked as a bank janitor and hotel porter, died while trying to save two of his employers from drowning when Andrew was three years old. His mother remarried.

At age 14, Andrew, along with his brother, were apprenticed to a tailor. Running away at age 16 from the apprenticeship, Johnson became a successful tailor in another state. With no formal education, at age 18 he met 16-year-old Eliza McCardle, who taught him to read and write. She also encouraged him to invest in real estate and farmlands to make money. The following year they were married and as a couple remained close friends for fifty years, even though she was ill with tuberculosis for decades.

Johnson soon entered politics in Tennessee and became an alderman, mayor, state legislator, governor twice, U.S. Representative and Senator. He fought for the common man and loved giving stump speeches. Johnson was for states' rights and owned a few slaves, yet hated the rich Southern plantation owners.

The following quotations by Johnson attest to his down to earth directness. "If I am shot at, I want no man to be in the way of the bullet." "Slavery exists. It is black in the South and white in the North." "It's a damn poor mind that can think of only one way to spell a word."

As a Type 1 with strong 8 tendencies, his language was direct. He was known for his quick temper and gruffness, yet he had a capacity for humility and was easy to understand. I still wonder whether he was an 8 as I first typed him; he was outspoken, angry, direct, strong, opinionated, independent, and had belligerent traits. 1s and 8s can both share these tendencies. However, I believe his desire for conservation, thrift, organization, honesty and focus on moderation makes him a Type 1.

Being a 1, Johnson was conservative with money and his frugality was manifested in a tight federal budget. Accountability was his middle name and he advocated for moderation in all things. He opposed corruption, which was rampant after the war. He had a caregiving side and protected the innocent and poor against the rich "bad guys." He was likely an ESTJ in the Myers-Briggs, though possibly could have been an ISTJ.

"ESTJs command a situation, with the sense that they know how things should go and are ready to take charge to make sure that it happens. They are task-oriented and put work before play. Confident and tough-minded, the ESTJ appears almost always to be in control. ESTJs appreciate structure and often begin to organize as soon as they enter a room. They want to establish the ground rules and make sure everyone does what they're supposed to." www.truity.com/personality-type/ESTJ

Johnson felt that secession of the Southern states was a crime and fought to keep Tennessee in the Union. His wife and two daughters had to leave the state when Tennessee joined the Confederacy. His property confiscated, he was hung in effigy. Johnson placed a pistol on top of the lectern when he gave Unionist speeches, as he was threatened often during the Civil War and was once taken off a train and beaten up by a mob. Eager to respond to hecklers, he often engaged in shouting matches.

Andrew Johnson was the only US Senator from the South not to resign his position when the Southern states seceded and was highly praised by the North for staying with the Union. After the Union captured Nashville and a large part of the state in the second year of the war, he became Tennessee's Military Governor appointed by Lincoln. As Military Governor, Johnson arrested anyone critical of the federal government, closed newspapers and took over the railroads. Eventually supporting emancipation, he freed the slaves he owned.

Johnson thought that blacks were inferior to whites. His desire to free the slaves was more to punish the Southern plantation owners and limit the resources of the South, particularly during the war. Later he pardoned most of the Confederate leaders, contrary to the wishes of Northern congressman.

Some considered Johnson to be kind and friendly and he often loaned money to the poor. Growing up poor himself, he tended to support the underdog. Shunning Washington society, he preferred the company of old friends and common folk. In his eyes, rich people were suspect of being corrupt.

Johnson was a gifted orator, a self-improvement junkie as many 1s are (reading grammar books to improve his speaking), and was direct and firm in his convictions. He was a literal, step-by-step, down-to-earth kind of guy. Mr. and Mrs. Johnson were known for impeccable behavior in the White House and took good care of the mansion.

Sporadically his devotion to moderation flagged. He drank too much the night before his vice-presidential inauguration to quell a cold, causing slurred speech during his speech. With a tug of his sleeve by the outgoing vice president, he ended his talk early. Two of his sons died from complications due to drinking and another died in the military, when he fell off a horse. There's debate whether Johnson had a drinking problem. Apparently, he drank sporadically and it didn't present an ongoing problem.

Johnson was the first vice president to become president due to assassination. He was expected to follow in the footsteps of Lincoln regarding Reconstruction of the South, but being a Southern Democrat, not a Northern Republican like Lincoln, he was at odds with Congress for his entire administration. Congress didn't want a strong president like Johnson who was blunt and outspoken. He was defiant and became opposed to and isolated from Congress.

After the Civil War, Northern congressmen sought to punish the white South and gain the favor of black voters. The Freedman's Bureau, established by Congress, worked to integrate newly freed blacks into society by giving them provisions and enforcing voters' rights. Accordingly, Federal troops were sent by Congress to reinforce the new laws, which Johnson opposed.

Congress passed statutes to give black people additional rights but Johnson vetoed them. In addition, Southern states reinstated limitations on the newly freed African Americans such as curfews, unfair and unequal punishments, and economical restrictions which made it impossible for former slaves to become independent. Nonetheless, there were 16 black US Representatives and Senators elected after the war. These electoral achievements were short lived when the Ku Klux Klan, mostly Confederate veterans, started to punish, threaten and murder black citizens, often by lynching. Johnson's attitudes contributed to holding back the advancement of civil rights.

Johnson went on a speaking tour after he became president in order to gather popular support for his ideas about Reconstruction. This effort backfired and his ideas lost both popular and Congressional support. The House impeached him for refusing to enforce the laws that they passed, for firing the Secretary of War without their permission, and for being at odds with Congress. He maintained his defiance and said (as a true 1) "I know I am right and I am damned if I do not adhere to it." Despite that he remained president with one vote to spare in the Senate and wept with relief that he wasn't removed from office.

Likely, had Lincoln lived, he would have been more moderate and effective, though the South would have resisted any president, especially Lincoln, for trying to include former slaves as equals. Because much of the white Southerners' way of life, land, and homes were destroyed, as well as hundreds of thousands of soldiers killed or wounded, any level of appeasement was unlikely. White Southerners were adamant about keeping former slaves in some form of slavery.

Andrew Johnson's inflexibility, opposition to Congress and obstruction of black progress after the war reflect his low ranking as president, in spite of achievements which include support for states' rights, the purchase of Alaska, and preventing the French from gaining control over Mexico. His leniency toward the white South made things easier in some ways, even though the South disobeyed the laws Congress passed. His greatest trait was his outright honesty but he could be abrasive in how he expressed it.

Interesting additional facts about Johnson:

- When he was Governor of Tennessee and still working as a tailor, Johnson once made a suit of clothes for the Governor of Kentucky.
- His wife was basically an invalid during his presidency.
- His two daughters served as hostesses or First Ladies, even though his wife ran things behind the scenes and made appearances on occasion.
- He relied on and eagerly sought his wife's advice.
- He was the only President to become a senator after his presidency.

Johnson had little ability to compromise, which caused him to be defiant and isolated, particularly from Congress. He had no tolerance for lying and greed and didn't have an effective way to manage his attitude without losing support from potential allies. His prejudice toward rich people limited his efficacy as president but he had popular support from the poor. "I found him kind and helpful," according to one Tennessee neighbor, "especially to the poor young men and he was entirely without condescension."

He rose from rags to riches and was very diligent about everything he did. He was man of maxims, used standard operating procedures and preached a program of moderation and conciliation toward the white South after the Civil War, being a Southerner himself. Had he been more tolerant and fair toward blacks, he would have been rated more highly as President. Johnson died of a stroke in 1875.

Ulysses S. Grant – Union Commander, Type 5, INTJ, 1869-77

(1822-1885) Ulysses S. Grant was the 18th president. Best known for being the General-in-Chief on the Union side during the latter half of the Civil War, he was the first full two-term president in over 30 years, the prior one having been Andrew Jackson. Quiet, shy, and private, he was considered a "butcher" by some, because so many soldiers under his command were killed. Lincoln didn't object to the death toll because Grant, unlike prior generals like McClellan, moved the war toward closure by initiating battles and pursuing the enemy. An interesting side note is that Grant hated the sight of blood and could only eat meat if it was charred! He never hunted, unusual for most boys and men of that era. As a child, he was sickened by working for his father, who was a tanner of hides; a bloody business.

The first son of six children, he was a sensitive child who liked mathematics, art and horses. Even at a very young age he could train horses, especially difficult ones, and neighbors hired him to work with their horses. His love of horses lasted throughout his life and he was considered one of the best horsemen in the Civil War.

Grant's father enrolled him at West Point without first checking to see if he even wanted to go there. Ulysses resisted at first. The name he grew up with was Hiram Ulysses Grant, but the acceptance letter was mistakenly sent to "Ulysses S. Grant." Rather than request a revised letter he enrolled under the new name, which came in handy later when the initials "U.S." Grant came to symbolize his patriotism and dedication to national service.

Grant was an average student; known for his skills of drawing and painting, writing and horsemanship. Many of his fellow students ended up fighting for the South in the Civil War, including James Longstreet who was the best man in Grant's wedding in 1848. Fighting against one's friends and relatives, Confederate or Union, was common. He reignited friendships with many of them after the War.

Before the Civil War, Grant was stationed at lonely Army outposts in the Pacific Northwest, Detroit and New York. He fought valiantly in the Mexican-American War, in spite of his opposition to it. Grant thought it was an unnecessary war and that it had been instigated only for territorial gain.

After the Mexican-American War ended in 1848, he was sent to posts where it was too dangerous or expensive to bring his family. He became very lonely to see his wife Julia and family. Throughout his life he was known for his love, adoration and loyalty to his wife and four children: three sons and a daughter.

He grew weary of military life in isolated outposts, tended to drink too much and in 1854 he resigned from the Army. Some think he was forced to resign because of heavy drinking, which occurred when he was stationed away from his family. He could be depressed for long periods.

From 1854 until the Civil War began in 1861 he ran his father-in-law's farm in Illinois; the work included building a house and cutting and selling timber. Later he tried selling insurance and eventually worked in one of his father's leather goods stores operated by his brother. He wasn't successful in any of those ventures but his father-in-law contributed income to help his growing family.

1861 was a pivotal year in Grant's life, as Lincoln was looking for men with military experience and Grant volunteered to lead a regiment. He was soon promoted to the rank of brigadier general. Grant won important battles and caught the eye of Lincoln who was looking for an effective leader for the Union army. Lincoln appreciated Grant's ability to win battles and the fact that he had an overall strategy to win the war.

Beginning as someone who was unsuccessful in business and had an occasional drinking problem, Grant became the top general in the army and is still considered one of the best military strategists and commanders in American history. Grant "was constantly busy, thinking, planning, writing out clear and concise orders, offering encouragement, issuing commands, almost jaunty in his demeanor," from the book *Presidential Temperament*. He didn't let the enemy retreat and never retraced his army's steps to keep the enemy off guard.

An unassuming man, he disliked the limelight, typical of type 5, avoided public swimming, bathed privately, never cursed and even as a general wore an enlisted man's uniform or rumpled civilian clothes. He had a phenomenally healthy physique and never seemed to get sick. His sons often accompanied him in camp.

Lincoln didn't care if Grant had a drinking problem as he accomplished the goal of winning battles. Grant hammered unmercifully at the enemy never allowing him time to rest. He drove his own men relentlessly but was, for the most part, admired by them, despite heavy casualties. He had a hard edge and smoked as many as 20 cigars a day to relax!

Grant was a master of long-range planning, going into action and pursuing the enemy; it was fine to lose a battle as long as it helped win the war. He was good at anticipating outcomes. In regard to danger, he figured that if a bullet was destined to hit him, it would. His youngest son said, "In my memory of him, and his record, father's uncompromising patriotism, his absolute, self-sacrificing loyalty, stand out as his dominant characteristics; right or wrong, his country came first and he supported it with all that he had. In all my vivid memory of our life together, there is no recollection of one single unkind, unfair, or unjust thing done to me by any one of the family, while the record of their loving acts would cover every day of our association."

His eldest son said, "In private and in public he was a plain, dignified, undemonstrative man, with a quiet, self-controlled manner which never left him, showing consideration in all his actions and words towards others which I have never seen equaled. To me my father was a sacred character. In my recollections of him there is no blur, no shadow. I had the happiness as a child and as a man, of being his constant companion in peace and in war. The admiration I had for him as a boy only deepened with increasing years. It must have been the same with all others who saw him and knew him as well as I did. During the years following his return from California, we lived upon my Grandfather Dent's farm. He raised crops successfully and spent his evenings with his family. I, being the oldest, was permitted to accompany him about the farm, and he began to teach me, at an early age, to ride and to swim. I can see myself now, a chubby little chap, sitting on the back of one of the farm horses and holding on for dear life, my father urging me to be brave. He would not tolerate timidity in his small boy, and a display of it meant an unhappy hour for him, and me also."

Bruce Catton, the noted Grant biographer, once remarked that Ulysses S. Grant's daughter, Nellie (1855-1922), had a "particularly secure place in his heart." She was his only daughter, and was surrounded by affection and attention. Grant was openly demonstrative with Nellie and showed her a quiet consideration that was conspicuous. His fatherly devotion to her was touching to all who observed it. He had a number of nicknames for her, including "Missy" and "Martha Rebecca." In letters he wrote to Julia, his wife, he sometimes referred to Nellie using these different pet names.

Go to http://www.granthomepage.com/nellie_grant.htm for more writings about him from his children.

Grant was a shoo-in as president after Andrew Johnson. Grant was an honest man, but was too loyal to a number of friends and cabinet members who were corrupt. His two administrations were noted for scandals related to gold, whiskey, railroad kickbacks and money allocated to Indian affairs. He had a hard time firing incompetent or corrupt people and tended to trust more than he should have. Possibly his reticence or shyness kept him from firing people. Grant was concerned that his military expertise did not adequately prepare him for politics and the presidency.

As a Type 5 with strong 4 and 6 wings, Grant had the ability to step back and not take things personally. He could be protective and loyal with his love of family and country like a type 6 but could also express feeling through his art, closeness to animals and his familial devotion. Being loyal, he remained too long with people who should have been fired. He's been typed often as a 6, but I think knowledge seeking and privacy were more important motivators than security. He didn't seem to have the anxious tendencies of a 6 but seemed cool and calm, which would more describe a 5.

When Grant worked for his brother in the leather goods store, he was often in the back of the store reading, unaware of customers. Sometimes he forgot the price of goods. Running a store was too mundane for him. Being a Type 5, he needed a job that would enable him to think and use information that interested him like battle strategies, horses, math or art!

He tended to be awkward in his body and somewhat shy if his role wasn't clear. He loved to learn and study and felt out of place otherwise. He turned out to be an excellent writer, as is often true of 5s, when he wrote his autobiography toward the end of his life. In it he included clear notes about war strategies that he gave to his fellow commanders, never long or verbose, just to the point.

Spending time smoking cigars and reading at the Willard Hotel, which was close to the White House while he was president, Grant fell prey to being influenced by unscrupulous lobbyists. He had a gullible side in addition to having a high need for privacy. He was known for loaning or giving money to friends or even complete strangers and not keeping track of who owed him money.

Although confident as a general in the military where the chain of command was clear, he had a much harder time as president supervising and demanding accountability where the relationship rules were murkier. He wasn't into image or impression making and certainly wasn't a self-preservation subtype. Grant was likely a sexual subtype who deeply loved his family, friends and the nation. He didn't have many close friends other than his wife. Social subtype 6s can more easily handle public attention.

Grant wasn't blessed with social graces and tended not to dress well, often true of 5s, but his wife helped him with both of these shortcomings. His interest lay in the complexity of strategy; he believed in authority, his own or that of others and trusted both his gut and his analytical ability to make good decisions. He had a very strong Type 8 side with which he was able to dictate orders in war, but was less effective in doing so as president. He tended to make lone decisions without much counsel from his aides, though he did possess the ability to listen when he found it necessary.

Grant continued post-war Reconstruction from the Andrew Johnson years by sending Federal troops to Southern states in an attempt to protect the voting rights of black men and to secure economic progress for them. It was an impossible task, with prejudice running high against former slaves coming from both the South and North. Grant fought alongside blacks in the War and he felt they were owed equality. He wanted white businesses to thrive and also progress for the black population but those two realities were at odds with white citizens fighting change at every step.

Slavery ended but the plight of blacks continued. Many former slaves became tenant farmers in constant debt to white owners who threatened them if they spoke up or tried to become independent. Grant was criticized for promoting the interests of both races. He was one of the first presidents who believed in racial equality.

Inflation grew rapidly when greenback dollars were introduced to finance the War. Over-speculation in railroads and the Franco-Prussian war in Europe, caused a financial panic in 1873 that lasted for years. Grant tried to improve Indian relations and promoted programs to help Indians become farmers but, without good land to do it, it was an impossible venture. Most government agents who interacted with Indians were corrupt. Violence toward Indians and ongoing occupation of Indian lands continued to insure the United States would remain a white society. Other races were tolerated only to fill low paying jobs or to satisfy the military's requirement for soldiers. There were a number of black soldiers in the Calvary.

During Grant's administrations, the U.S. supported a rebellion in Cuba, tried to buy Cuba from Spain, tried to annex the Dominican Republic (then Santa Domingo) and settled claims against England after they sent armaments to the South during the War to support their cotton interests. A court of arbitration consisting of American, British and Canadian negotiators decided to give the US 15 million dollars for claims against England and settled boundary and fishing disputes with Canada.

After leaving office, Grant and his wife took a well-earned, two-year good will world tour to meet world leaders, artists, writers and royalty. Upon their return, Grant was received with such renewed popularity that he decided to attempt to be nominated for a third term. Enough anti-Grant sentiment was still prevalent to prevent that from happening.

Grant lost all his money in an investment involving his son that turned out to be a scam. His propensity toward loyalty and his naivete in trusting people once again worked against him. A type 6 would tend to be more questioning and cautious.

Julia, Grant's wife, was warmer than he was: charming, affectionate, more extroverted and idealistic. She liked the dramatic but not overly so. She was an excellent First Lady, loved the limelight and was disappointed that Grant didn't serve a third term. She was his emotional center. They were excellent parents and loved sharing that role.

Ulysses and Julia were often caught talking and holding hands affectionately. She was slightly cross-eyed and considered getting an operation to correct that, though he insisted that she not get the corrected surgery, as he loved her exactly the way she was. At balls while he was an army officer, he trusted her to dance with other officers, as Grant didn't like to dance.

To regain his footing when retired and to provide for his wife and family, he began writing magazine articles about the Civil War, which eventually turned into his autobiography. It was in the nick of time, as Grant realized he was dying of throat and tongue cancer due to his excessive cigar smoking. Mark Twain, Grant's friend, published the autobiography after Grant's death. It became a best seller and provided his family with income for a generation. His book is considered one of the best books about the Civil War. Grant was loyal to the end, to his family and country. Sexual subtype 5s like Grant can be as loyal as 6s.

His legacy includes fighting for African-American and Native American rights more than any other 19th century president, even though his efforts had little effect. His honesty and integrity were seldom questioned though many took advantage of his overly trusting nature. Certainly not a self-preservation subtype, he was little concerned or savvy about money. He didn't know how to play the political game well and he apologized to the American people for not having had political experience before he became President.

Grant used terse language, written or spoken, and his comments were dry, controlled and self-effacing. Upon approaching and feeling afraid of his first encounter with a Confederate enemy army, he said in his autobiography, "I had not the moral courage to halt and consider what to do. I kept right on," quoted from the book, *Presidential Temperament* by Choiniere and Keirsey. He was a man of few words. He hated small talk and gossip, as is true for many type 5s. People didn't know that he was very well read and widely knowledgeable. He was seen as impractical, irresponsible and a dreamer in his youth and didn't find the right niche in life until he became a general in the Union Army.

Grant's mother was serious, grim and undemonstrative but his father was proud of Ulysses and pushed him to become a student at West Point. Most children made fun of Grant because of his shyness, which continued at West Point. For the most part, Ulysses didn't like regimen, stiff clothes, marches (he didn't feel coordinated marching was beneficial) and military tradition and training. Those are considerations more important to an SJ or Guardian temperament in the Myers-Briggs. He found much of it pointless. He much preferred military strategy, map reading, mathematics, art and horsemanship, things he could do alone, as is true for 5s. He enjoyed rational thinking and planning, more reminiscent of an NT or Rational temperament. I believe he is an INTJ in the Myers-Briggs.

INTJ, called the Architect cynical but idealistic, quoted from:
www.16personalities.com/intj-personality

"With a natural thirst for knowledge that shows itself early in life, INTJs are often given the title of "bookworm" as children. While this may be intended as an insult by their peers, they more than likely identify with it and are even proud of it, greatly enjoying their broad and deep body of knowledge. INTJs enjoy sharing what they know as well, confident in their mastery of their chosen subjects, but owing to their Intuitive (N) and Judging (J) traits, they prefer to design and execute a brilliant plan within their field rather than share opinions on "uninteresting" distractions like gossip."

Grant's leadership traits include honesty, creativity, modesty, loyalty, dogged determination, the force of action, strength of character, and faith in keeping the Union together. As an INTJ, he was a long range strategic planner, planning beyond any single battle while Union Commander. He loved solving problems and was only successful in life when there were problems to solve. Most of the low-level jobs he did before the Civil War didn't fit his nature.

The presidency didn't allow Grant to use his best traits the way the war did. His ability to detach as a type 5, helped him with many decisions. As President, however, people's greed and inconsistencies were a major challenge for a fact-focused 5. He would rather go to the nearby Willard Hotel, smoke cigars and read a book.

Rutherford B. Hayes, Type 1, ESTJ, Prayer and Hymns, 1877-1881

(1822-1893) Our 19th President Rutherford B. Hayes was one of the most honest presidents, even though the process of the election that got him there was questionable. After four months of wrangling, during which three states couldn't figure out which candidate had the most votes, a partisan commission gave the presidency to Hayes, who was behind by over 200,000 votes. In exchange, Rutherford's Republican party agreed to withdraw Federal troops from Louisiana and South Carolina, the last two states still protecting black men and women. Reconstruction was then officially over and Southern blacks were left to fend for themselves against the bitter discrimination of the post-Civil War South.

Hayes was born on a farm in Ohio. His father, who managed the farm and also owned a whiskey distillery, unfortunately died before Rutherford was born. At the time of his father's death Hayes' mother was also in mourning over the recent loss of her daughter. At the age of two, Rud, as he was affectionately called, lost another sibling, his nine-year-old brother, in an ice skating accident. Frail as a child, Rud became stronger as he grew up and was especially close to his sister Fanny who enjoyed reading Shakespeare to him. His mother was religious, energetic, protective and loving. Both Rud's mother and Fanny, helped him learn to read and write.

Hayes' uncle, who lived in a nearby town, was a successful businessman and surrogate father to Rutherford and Fanny; he provided critical financial support for the family, and by leasing the farm and taking in two boarders the family managed to survive. Rutherford attended the local public school and later two private academies. He attended Kenyon College in Ohio where he was valedictorian of his graduating class and then went on to Harvard Law School where he was again at the top of his class.

Hayes' law practice started out slowly, but he gradually built a reputation as a criminal lawyer. Joining a number of professional organizations including a literary club, The International Order of Odd Fellows and the Sons of Temperance, he became known as a charming, engaging and honest man.

After a long courtship, he married Lucy Ware Webb. Both mothers were delighted with the match. His wife was a conscientious Methodist and a teetotaler who didn't dance. She was a vehement abolitionist like her parents. Rutherford was a moderate drinker and, with Lucy's influence, became a committed abolitionist himself. He soon developed a reputation for defending runaway slaves. Lucy was a well-educated woman and has the distinction of being the first First Lady to graduate from college. Their 36-year marriage was happy and prosperous; they had eight children, five of whom grew to adulthood.

In 1856, Hayes' beloved sister Fanny died from complications of childbirth, which deeply affected him. He soothed his grief through his work and attention to his own children. Soon the Civil War started and Rutherford was determined to join the fight for the Northern Cause.

This desire resulted in an officer's commission by the governor. He fought for four years during which time he was wounded five times and had four horses shot from under him! (Over 1,000,000 horses and mules were killed in the Civil War). Known for his bravery and leadership, he fought in over 50 battles. During the war, he was elected a US Representative but waited until the war was over to serve. "An officer fit for duty who at this crisis would abandon his post to electioneer for a seat in Congress, ought to be scalped. You may feel perfectly sure I shall do no such thing." His beliefs were strong in doing the right thing as a Type 1. Rightness was more important than expediency or personal advancement.

Elected governor of Ohio three times, his third term was unfinished when he ran for President. After winning the election, Hayes tried to assuage the South by investing in the reconstruction of Southern infrastructure and appointing Southern politicians to high-level positions in the government. He transformed the system of procuring civil service positions by political appointment to one of earning positions by merit. He fired corrupt civil service employees and power brokers like Chester Arthur, the chief of the New York Port Authority, who later became President.

Hayes promoted equality and voting rights for African Americans. The Southern states retaliated by passing their own laws prohibiting black people from voting, despite the 14th Amendment, which gave black people citizenship, and the 15th Amendment, which gave them the right to vote. Severe racism still ruled the Southern states. The North decided they didn't want to have another war fought over how the South treated blacks.

Hayes did virtually nothing to stop the onslaught of the murder of the American Indians and the forced relocation from their homelands to much poorer lands, typically far away. The story the government spun was that the intention was to make Indians into farmers thereby converting them into good productive Americans, which was simply a cover-up to take their lands. There were continued massacres of whole Indian villages of men, women and children by the U.S. Army, a major blight on America's legacy.

Indians were marched or transported to reservations and stripped of their heritage. They were forced to speak English and act like white people, under the threat of punishment. Indian children had their heads shorn and were forced to attend reservation schools. The history of tribes, tribal symbols and dances were disallowed. Alcoholism was rampant and alcohol abuse and fighting between tribes was actively instigated by the government. By 1877 when Hayes was President, not one tribe was still living in their native homeland.

Many Chinese were imported to build railroads at slave wages but when the building was near completion, Congress decided to ban all Chinese from coming to the United States. Hayes vetoed that bill and a compromise was reached which allowed some Chinese to enter. Hayes had better intentions toward racial integration than almost any other president, except for Grant, but most of the American public and Congress didn't want racial equality, so it was impossible to enforce laws protecting minorities.

Hayes, influenced by his wife who attended regular church services, encouraged daily prayer and hymn singing with his family and cabinet. Alcohol, profanity and tobacco were not allowed. His wife was nicknamed Lemonade Lucy, and despite the social restrictions, was well liked. She was respected and popular, a very social and gracious hostess, and was considered a major contributor to Hayes' success. Hayes was thought of as fair, honest and reliable. He promised a one-term presidency, thinking it was the right thing to do at the time, particularly with a contested election. He could very well have won a second term as the economy and business improved, and he came close to paying off the U.S. debt.

Hayes was a Type 1, doing what he thought was right, following through with promises, and refraining from doing things for political gain and power. There's a version of Type 1 I call the Positive 1; aligned with positivity as the right attitude to live. He researched his decisions, followed his conscience and got feedback from people he respected, so when he made decisions, he seldom had regrets. He was able to smile, similarly to a Type 7, which is the growth type for 1, because he lived up to his own standards, and was naturally sociable.

He is likely an ESTJ in the Myers-Briggs, which is a match for 1. His extraversion and introversion are close so he possibly could be an ISTJ. "ESTJs are conventional, factual, and grounded in reality. For the ESTJ, the proof is in the past: what has worked and what has been done before. They value evidence over conjecture, and trust their personal experience. ESTJs look for rules to follow and standards to meet, and often take a leadership role in helping other people meet expectations as well. They concern themselves with maintaining the social order and keeping others in line." www.truity.com/personality-type/ESTJ

As a reformer and perfectionist, he was considered by some friends to be colorless and stuffy but also decent, solid, impeccable, deliberate, good-natured and determined. He was so upright that many claimed he never sowed any wild oats. His many diary entries reflected his Type 1 need for self-improvement. He chose to read material that was "useful, instructive and solid." Other diary entries include, "Trifling remarks, boyish conduct, etc. are among my crying sins. Mend, mend." Toward the end of his life, he wrote, "In avoidance of the appearance of evil, I am not sure that I have not unnecessarily deprived myself and others of innocent enjoyment."

Though he tried to be outgoing and pleasant, he wasn't a back-slapping kind of fellow. One nickname he had was "Granny Hayes." Manifesting qualities of the Reformer 1, he was serious minded, dutiful, reliable and well liked, as was his wife who was much the same, though Lucy was warmer and more gracious.

He was asked to run for president in the first place because of his clean record and integrity rather than any seeking of the office on his part. He said he enjoyed his military service, which increased his political value as a war veteran, more than he enjoyed the presidency. Unfortunately, being elected while losing the popular vote was used as a weapon against him his entire administration and he had resistance from Congress. His administration was honorable and uncorrupted as is true for most Type 1 presidents.

After the presidency, he devoted his life to public education and prison reform. He was a trustee of three universities in Ohio and was president of the Slater Fund, which provided funds for Christian education of southern African Americans. He was a social reformer. Well-mannered and well liked, a good conversationalist and positive in perspective, he did his best to include others. He could be compared today to humanitarian Jimmy Carter during his retirement.

"Hayes was never a solitary, a boy of moods," wrote biographer H.J. Eckenrode. "He had no seasons of exaltation followed by depression. All his life he liked society and shone in it in a modest way – not sparkling, not brilliant, but pleasing, satisfying. He had a gift of friendship and most of those he loved in youth he loved in age. As a young man, however, Hayes went through a period of great inner tension, which he himself attributed to a fear that he would one day lose his mind, as some relatives on both sides of his family had done. Overcoming this fear, he matured into a relaxed, easy-going fellow and a keen observer of human nature.

He genuinely loved people and was interested in their thoughts and problems. When travelling by train, he invariably sat in the smoking car, eager to strike up a conversation. He had a remarkable memory for the names and faces of the most casual acquaintances. As a politician, he respected the opposition and welcomed constructive criticism. Although not regarded as a great orator in his day, he delivered well-planned, reasoned addresses in a clear, pleasant voice." Quoted from the website *presidentialham.com*.

Hayes was a man of independent spirit who admired John Adams, a fellow Type 1, as another independent president. He had a fondness for political life, was an idealist yet very practical and down to earth, was very respected, a military hero, made the first telephone call to Alexander Graham Bell and was the first President to travel to the west coast by railroad.

James Garfield, Preacher/Scholar – Type 7, ESFP, 1881

(1831-1881) The 20th President was only in office four months before he was shot and eventually died 80 days later. He remained positive and hopeful throughout his ordeal until he succumbed. His assassination was unfortunate, as he was a strong man yet an adaptable, honest person who would have been a great president. Garfield's profile is similar to that of his predecessor, Rutherford Hayes; raised in Ohio, a Union general in the Civil War, college graduate, professor and a Republican who supported civil rights. They both promoted civil service reform, attempting to do away with the patronage system of awarding jobs to those who supported their election. He was shot and killed by someone who was insane and felt he deserved a political job that he was incapable of doing.

Born in a log cabin on a rural farm in Ohio in 1831, Garfield was the last of the log cabin presidents. He, along with Andrew Johnson was among the poorest of all the presidents and was the youngest of three children who survived to adulthood. His father was a farmer who was known to be an excellent wrestler. He died when James was an infant from the aftereffects of fighting a forest fire to protect his land. His widowed mother, now having no other source of income, was near penniless. She, with the help of James and his two older brothers, worked the farm to survive.

James, like his father, grew up to be a farmer and a good wrestler but dreamed of being a sailor rather than a farmer. He was an avid reader of adventure novels and a dreamer like many type 7s. At the age of 16 he ran away from home and worked towing canal boats for a short while until he fell overboard and almost drowned. He believed he was miraculously saved to pursue a life making a difference in the world. Recovering from malaria, which he had contracted at his canal job, he returned home to be nursed back to health by his mother who gave him her life savings of $17 to attend school.

The family attended the Disciples of Christ Church and at 18 Garfield had a religious conversion experience that served as a strong foundation for the rest of his life; he became an itinerant minister. There were no rules in the Disciples of Christ Church about who could preach, though Garfield was eventually ordained. He was the only Preacher President, and his religion, like Hayes' before him, was the cornerstone of his life.

After studying in local schools, he worked as a carpenter and part-time teacher at an academy, all the while continuing to travel and preach. He then attended what is now called Hiram College in Ohio. Working as a janitor to pay his tuition and board, within two years, he became a professor of mathematics, ancient languages and literature. "I am resolved to make a mark in the world. There is some of that slumbering thunder in my soul and it shall come out." He continued his studies at Williams College in Williamstown, Massachusetts, wanting to have a New England education. Garfield graduated with honors, and then returned to Hiram College to teach classics. The following year, at age 26, he became president of the college and remained in that position for four years!

Garfield married a former student, Lucretia Rudolph who was a teacher at the college, and the daughter of one of the founders of Hiram College. They eventually had seven children, five of whom survived, and all of them became prosperous and successful.

Lucretia and James seemed to be opposite in personality; she was thoughtful and shy, though strong and intellectual, and he was outgoing, ambitious, dashing, charismatic and opinionated. He enjoyed hunting, fishing, billiards and dating before he married, and was known as somewhat of a womanizer. It was, for him, a difficult decision to settle down and get married and it took a long time to adjust; not unusual for many 7s who love options and freedom. In time, he decided to make a mark in politics rather than academia, even though he taught English, history, and geology, as well as Latin and Greek, and seemed to enjoy it. He was also fluent in German. He was a constant learner.

As a Type 7 he had many interests. He taught numerous subjects at Hiram, was positive and loved adventure. Despite his many successes, Garfield had occasional painful self-doubt and anxiety arising from his early years. This characteristic indicates he may have had a 6 wing. The 6 wing Type 7 is more relational, concerning themselves about what others think of them, and altering their behavior a bit to please others. He also had an 8 wing, with an independent air and a habit of being outspoken.

I first typed him as an 8 (partially due to a PBS American Experience documentary on James Garfield that portrayed him as an 8) but my research reveals him to have been a Type 7. His strong characteristics of 6, 7 and 8 persuaded me to type him as a 7 with side wings. He also seemed to have a strong connection to Type 1 with a clear focus on morality and truth telling. This could have been because of his upbringing, his religious beliefs and the marriage to his upright wife Lucretia. His photographs reflect his serious side. 1 is the stress type for 7.

The following quote from the website, myersbriggs.org/my-mbti-personality-type/mbti-basics/the-16-mbti-types.htm, describes ESFP's well, a natural correlation with Type 7. "Outgoing, friendly, and accepting. Exuberant lovers of life, people, and material comforts. Enjoy working with others to make things happen. Bring common sense and a realistic approach to their work, and make work fun. Flexible and spontaneous, adapt readily to new people and environments. Learn best by trying a new skill with other people."

Garfield was a charismatic orator as 7s can be, spellbinding his audiences. He was strong and athletic, had abundant energy and was very handsome at six feet tall. He practiced dueling skills daily, not uncommon for men, but he was probably more adept at speaking than potential dueling. He portrayed his youth as "wild, chaotic and unrestrained." Being a man of action, Garfield became a college president by his mid-20s. He always sought adventure, which is classic for 7, as well as 8. He was a man of abundant energy and ambition who saw politics as an outlet for his exuberance. Garfield became bored if he felt his life was restrained.

Garfield was adept at oratory and politics and also wrote poetry, loved the classics and could dazzle his friends by writing Latin with one hand and Greek with the other at same time! He loved to entertain and show off as well as to constantly learn. He believed an educated populace was important.

He loved his wife's well-balanced mind, her logic and preciseness but it took him a long time to accept the state of marriage. He was easily bored, plus he felt a bit pressured into marriage. 7s try new things to avoid boredom but are can be afraid of long-term commitments. Lucretia really loved him and, particularly after their children were born, he felt good about their marriage. He became a doting father, a teacher and a moral instructor for the children, as both parents continued their focus on The Disciples of Christ Church.

On an impulse (not unusual for a 7), he bought a farm and became a gentleman farmer for a period. His wife was more of a long-range planner and became a political consultant and advisor to her husband, guiding him on his political path. While he could be a bit scattered, as 7s can be, she could hold a clearer vision and was a good judge of people. As one observer wrote, "Lucretia had a strength of unswerving absolute rectitude her husband has not and never will have."

Garfield was the youngest member of the Ohio legislature in 1859. He studied law on his own and passed the Ohio Bar in 1861, just in time to organize and lead a company of volunteers who fought valiantly in the Civil War, rising to the rank of major general. Lincoln requested that he return to Congress, even though he was renowned as the youngest brigadier general in the army and was glamorized by the public for his gallantry. He was known for his courage and leadership.

During the war, he had an affair with a female reporter. Lucretia took the high road given his honesty with her about it, and it seemed to be the start of a much closer relationship between them. Lucretia continued to be the strong foundation for her husband and was well respected by everyone.

In Congress, he could turn with the tides of opinions when power changed. He was more action oriented than reliable for consistent political beliefs. He was a pleaser and tended to avoid conflict when he could, not unusual for a 7, particularly one with a 6 wing.

Garfield became a US Representative in 1863 with Lincoln's persuasion. Lincoln insisted he had plenty of generals in the army but needed good men in Congress; avid abolitionists like Garfield who said, "I am inclined to believe that the sin of slavery is one of which it may be said that without the shedding of blood there is no remission." He thought it was right to force the seceding Southern states to rejoin the Union, confiscating Southern owned land in the North and executing or punishing Confederate leaders! Fortunately, that didn't happen to the degree he wished. He became more moderate as he aged.

He believed in money backed by gold which was also favored by banks, didn't like cooperative farm programs, which he thought of as "communism in disguise," and opposed labor unions. He fought an eight-hour work day for federal workers, believed that federal troops should be used to break up strikes, and was against federally funded relief projects during economic depressions. He served as Minority Leader of the House of Representatives during the Hayes administration.

Garfield tried to ride the middle of the Republican Party with one wing progressive (more his inclination) and the other side stalwart but a bit more corrupt. He served eight two-year terms as a US Representative from Ohio, never lost an election and was considered incorruptible, highly intelligent and was well liked.

Garfield's desire to create a bridge between the two factions of the Republican Party, the Stalwarts and the Half-Breeds, led to his nomination as a dark horse candidate in the 1880 election, totally to his surprise. 7s create a bridge more often than 8s who tend to be more outspoken. During the convention, he wrote to his wife, "I would gladly exchange this turmoil of the convention for the smaller and sweeter turmoil of the farm. Don't fail to write me every day. Each word from you will be a light in this wilderness." He accepted the nomination and was elected by only 10,000 popular votes, though he had more electoral votes. This was the first president whose mother was able to attend the inauguration, as well as to outlive him.

He was only President for four months before being shot, and he had little time to do more than dole out appointments. His main legislative agenda was for civil service reform, which was passed into law; this became his legacy. After being shot he lingered near death for almost three months, even though initially it looked as if he might recover. He did remain conscious during most of that time and felt he was going to recover. His courage was amazing.

The daily newspapers reported his condition in the headlines each day, which put the country on edge, with most everyone praying for his recovery. He likely died more from infection, with doctors probing with unclean hands for the bullet near his spine. In an attempt to recuperate, he was moved to a seaside resort house on the shores of New Jersey in which 300 men built a one-half mile railway to get him to the front of the house. He was well loved.

The nation mourned for the leader who was trying to bring the country together as a just, fair and honest president. His wife, Lucretia, lived on to the age of 86. One of the sons became the president of Williams College, a professor of politics at Princeton and was Woodrow Wilson's fuel administrator. Another son became Secretary of the Interior under Teddy Roosevelt and another son was an architect in Cleveland. Garfield and Lucretia's only daughter married a prominent banker and was active in civic affairs in New York and also Pasadena, California.

Some interesting facts: Garfield was our first left-handed president. One of the sons used to ride his bicycle in the halls in the White House and down the stairs! Garfield's mother was the first president's mother to move into the White House. Garfield had to make 80,000 political appointments, compared with 2000 today. His wife Lucretia contracted malaria – (not unusual for White House inhabitants as it was near a swamp) but she recovered. He said "If I thought her return to perfect health could be insured by my resigning the Presidency, I would not hesitate a moment about doing it." In 1881, there were three presidents—Hayes, Garfield and Chester Arthur. Garfield is the only President who was a US Representative, US Senator Elect and US President at the same time. Of course, he gave up his Representative and US Senate seats to become President.

Garfield was a preacher, scholar, soldier, politician and president, not unusual for a jack-of-all trades type 7. He was honest and respected, a leader on his own terms, overcame childhood poverty, was fair and just, extremely bright, admitted his weaknesses and learned from his mistakes. It's very unfortunate that he died before his time.

"Even though a pugnacious youth, he matured into a good-natured, amiable, gregarious fellow. Extremely tactile, he liked to hug and stroke friends and characteristically slung his arms around the shoulders of whomever he was talking to. He was a gifted orator, among the most popular and persuasive of his day. He was very ambitious but did little to promote his own fortunes. "I so much despise a man who blows his own horn," he commented, "that I go to the extreme of not demanding what is justly my due. To refrain from self-aggrandizement became the guiding principle of his life." Quoted from presidentialham.com

"He was convinced he was destiny's child," biographer Alan Peskin has written, "marked out for some special purpose. Secured in his faith, he placed his career in the hands of his destiny, preferring to drift with the tide of fortune rather than take the initiative and oppose it." As a young adult, he experienced a prolonged period of mental depression, a period he referred to as a period of darkness. Similarly, after his election but before the inauguration, he was overcome by a sense of foreboding. He complained of severe headaches. He began having nightmares of being naked and lost. Throughout his life, his self-confidence was fragile." presidentialham.com.

Despite his challenges, he was an honest, adventurous man of many talents and skills, who had the ability to learn and mature during his life and the presidency. He was friendly and welcoming, acknowledging his fears and still managing to remain positive and productive.

Chester Arthur – Type 8, ESFP, "My private life is nobody's damn business," 1881-1885

(1829-1886) The election of our 21st President came as a surprise, as he had previously served only in civil service positions and never held a government job. He was the fourth Vice President to attain the Presidency because of the death or assassination of his predecessor (James Garfield). A man of party politics and the spoils system, he did well as president. He unexpectedly carried forward some of Garfield's policies. This was surprising since they were on opposing sides of most issues and were for all intents and purposes political enemies, even though they belonged to the same party.

As president, Arthur passed the Pendleton Reform Act, strengthening civil service by basing job acquisitions on examinations and merit rather than political affiliation and reward. He fortified the Navy building modern steel ships and governed during a time of prosperity. There was even a surplus of government funds!

Arthur was the first-born son and fifth child in a family of eight children, six of which were girls. His Irish born father was a Baptist preacher who moved the family frequently from town to town in Vermont and New York because of parishioners' reactions to his abolitionist views. Estimates vary but only 2 to 10 percent of northerners were abolitionists. His mother was from Vermont and although he attended local schools, Arthur was taught to read and write mostly by his mother.

He attended Union College in New York where he became president of the debate society, was known for his pranks, and did well academically. He became a full-time teacher, went to law school and was involved in politics even from a young age. As a young student, he joined a campaign against boys who opposed his favored political candidate and wore a green jacket to support an Irish political faction. He was a prankster as many 8s are, once throwing the school bell into the Erie Canal. His goals were clear – wanting to be a high paid lawyer in Manhattan, a gentleman and a public servant. He loved money and power, not unusual for Type 8.

He became a very successful lawyer in New York City, and was particularly focused on cases involving freeing slaves. One case involved freeing eight black slaves who had crossed into New York State, a free state whose laws gave freedom to any slave crossing into New York, and he also helped win a case concerning a black woman who sat in the white section of a streetcar. This led to desegregation of streetcars in New York City well over 100 years before Rosa Parks' historic case in Alabama! He also worked with wealthy clients and loved living in luxury from the high fees he charged. He liked the life of high society but also defended the abused and downtrodden.

Arthur married in 1859. He continued his law practice, entered Republican politics and became a Judge Advocate General for a brigade of the New York Militia. This led to his appointment as Quartermaster General of New York during the early part of the Civil War; responsible for housing and outfitting the troops. As the assignment was a political appointment, he lost it when the governorship changed hands. His first-born child died at the age of three, a tragic and painful loss. Two other children survived to adulthood.

Gaining favored positions before the presidency, Arthur was appointed as Collector of Taxes for the Port of New York Harbor, a very powerful position. He collected kickbacks of salaries, which were called "assessments," from customs house employees to support the Republican Party. It was considered legal but there were many shady practices in the customs office that he had to turn a blind eye.

Upon Garfield's shooting and hoped-for recovery, Arthur took a low profile. Guiteau, Hayes' assassin, proclaimed when he shot him, "I am a Stalwart and Arthur will be President." Arthur didn't want to be implicated in the assassination and there was no evidence that he had anything to do with the plot. The crazed Guiteau assumed Arthur would give him a government post. Instead, he was tried and hanged!

Arthur, considered a dandy, was well dressed, appreciating fine food and drink. When he was president it was said that he owned over 80 sets of pants! 8s can be self-indulgent with the things they like. He held elaborate dinners and social functions at the White House, and the White House became a favored social destination during his Presidency.

He had cartloads of old stuff from the White House taken onto the lawn to be sold at auction, including clothing that belonged to John Quincy Adams and Abraham Lincoln as well as items that harkened back as far as John Adams. The White House was refurbished by Louis Tiffany, son of the famous glassmaker, and Arthur delayed his occupancy until its completion months later. He also wanted Mrs. Garfield to have time to move out after the death of her husband

Arthur's wife died of pneumonia a year and a half before he took office. She caught a cold while waiting for a carriage ride after a benefit which progressed and subsequently became a deadly pneumonia. He grieved deeply and felt guilty, as his political drive and late-night dinners with cronies kept him away from his wife, who complained of his not spending time with her and the children. He had a stained-glass Tiffany window made in her honor at St. John's Episcopal Cathedral that he could see lit up at night from the White House. Her memory was honored with fresh flowers placed below her White House portrait each day. He never remarried although he had many proposals. His sister Mary became acting First Lady during his administration.

As President, he took a 180 degree turn in attitude in order to support civil service reform. He had been thoroughly entrenched in the spoils system and involved with a good deal of corruption in his former position. He disavowed his former boss, Roscoe Conkling, who had run the New York Port Authority and profited illegally.

Besides supporting civil service reform, he vetoed legislation designed to exclude Chinese immigrants. His veto was overridden which set back Chinese immigration for 60 years and was only overturned in 1943. A compromise bill was passed to exclude the Chinese for 10 years instead of the 20 that Congress proposed, though future Congresses extended it. Arthur was burned in effigy for trying to protect Chinese and Japanese workers who strengthened the economy in his opinion. White workers disagreed with him. He was pro-immigration and advocated for minorities which was to his credit, though he did little to help American Indians. Mark Twain said of his presidency, "It would be hard to better Chester Arthur's administration."

Arthur tried to have the government surplus (largely gained because of high tariffs on imported goods) be reduced and also attempted to lower taxes to benefit farmers and the middle class but Congress would have nothing to do with it. Instead of a 20 percent reduction of tariffs, Congress made a tiny tariff reduction of 1.5 percent. Arthur was a good administrator as a result of his experience running the New York Port and being in charge of Union supplies for New York in the Civil War. Even though as President he was purported to work only from 10 to 4 each day and knock off the rest of the day, he was noted for his efficiency and honesty.

Arthur is stereotyped sometimes as lazy; sounding like a Type 9, enjoying eating and going on fishing trips, relaxing and taking a nap each day. In reality, he often would stay up until 2am and go on walks around Washington in the middle of the night with friends – no wonder he needed a nap!

Arthur was a Type 8 with a strong 9 wing. He was indulgent like an 8 (both 8s and 9s can have that feature) but he was known as The Gentleman Boss. He could take charge and still be amiable, congenial, inclusive and loyal, though he definitely had enemies and could confront people fairly easily. "I may be President but my private life is nobody's damn business." A number of presidents have that 8/9 or 9/8 mix and it's a challenge to ferret out the dominant type.

I think he is an ESFP like Garfield before him. If not, he would be an ESTP with a strong feeling component. "ESFPs are vivacious entertainers who charm and engage those around them. They are spontaneous, energetic, and fun-loving, and take pleasure in the things around them: food, clothes, nature, animals, and especially people. ESFPs are typically warm and talkative and have a contagious enthusiasm for life. They like to be in the middle of the action and the center of attention. They have a playful, open sense of humor, and like to draw out other people and help them have a good time." www.truity.com/personality-type/ESFP.

Arthur was a big man of 225 pounds although he was trim in his youth. He was easygoing but could hold his own if needed, as 8s can do more easily than 9s. He was a good storyteller, a man of grace and polish and was also tender hearted, romantic and loyal. A fastidious dresser, he was nicknamed Elegant Arthur.

He discovered during his administration that he had an incurable kidney disease, which he kept private during his administration. He died from that disease within 20 months of leaving the White House. He had all his public and private papers burned 2 days before he died leading to some speculation as to what he might have wanted to keep hidden from the world.

Grover Cleveland – Type 8, ESTJ, Guardian President, 1885-1889, 1893-1897

(1837-1908) Grover Cleveland was our 22nd and 24th President, the only President to have won two non-consecutive presidencies. Known for honesty and corruption busting, he didn't offer a clear agenda of legislation but rather was a watchdog of Congress. He was known for vetoing bills. Within a relatively short period of time he moved from being a lawyer, to Assistant District Attorney, to being a Sheriff, to Mayor of Buffalo, to Governor of New York, then to President. The country was ready for someone who was above graft and political favoritism.

Cleveland was popular with the public who was open to his directness, toughness, honesty, above board dealings and ridding the government of corrupt politicians. In being accused of fathering a child out of wedlock while he was single, he admitted that he probably was the father, even though his law partner may just as well have fathered the child as he romanced the woman in question too! The child's name included the first and middle name of the law partner and Cleveland's last name. The public, forgave him for admitting his mistake and appreciated his honesty, as it often does if mistakes are revealed and owned.

Cleveland was born in the middle of a pack of nine children. His father was a Presbyterian minister, and even though he had a Yale education, the family was often impoverished. His father died when Grover was 16, forcing him to work to support the family, instead of pursuing his dreams of going to college.

After being a lawyer, and then an assistant district attorney, during the Civil War he bought his way out of serving in the Army by paying someone $300 to fight in his stead. That was totally legal, though he would later be criticized for it during his political career. He was known for memorizing his legal prosecution statements by heart, and he did this when he delivered his inaugural addresses. He had an excellent memory!

Cleveland was a big man of 250 pounds and at times his weight increased to 280 pounds. He loved to eat, drink beer, hunt, fish, and hang out with his buddies. He named his rifle Death and Destruction. He seldom travelled, read fiction or listened to music. He was a Type 8, not afraid to speak his mind, easily contested what he thought was wrong and was a no-nonsense kind of guy. Even though Cleveland won the popular vote, he lost the middle election between his two terms as president because he didn't play the political game. He usually took a position instead of riding the fence. Doing his best not to play partisan politics, he let the chips fall with the positions he took.

Cleveland was an ESTJ.

"ESTJs are conventional, factual, and grounded in reality. For the ESTJ, the proof is in the past: what has worked and what has been done before. They value evidence over conjecture, and trust their personal experience. ESTJs look for rules to follow and standards to meet, and often take a leadership role in helping other people meet expectations as well. They concern themselves with maintaining the social order and keeping others in line.

ESTJs often take on a project manager role at home as well as at work, and excel at setting goals, making decisions, and organizing resources to accomplish a task. The ESTJ wants to achieve efficient productivity and typically believes this is best accomplished when people, structures and systems are well organized." www.truity.com/personality-type/ESTJ

Cleveland was a 47-year-old bachelor when he became president. When his law partner died in a carriage incident, he became legal guardian of the then fatherless eleven-year-old daughter. Initially shocking the nation, he courted her when she was 21 and they married! The public thought he was courting the mother but it was the daughter he was seeing! By the way, the mother approved of the marriage, even though there was a 27-year age gap.

The nation then witnessed the first wedding of a sitting president to take place in the White House, as well as later witnessing the first birth in the White House, her name being Baby Ruth. Yes, the renowned candy bar comes from her name, though some stories say it was named for the famous baseball star Babe Ruth. Cleveland and his wife had five children and she became one of the most cherished of first ladies. She was young, beautiful, very intelligent and a great hostess.

Cleveland was a hard worker, sometimes working to two or three in the morning when he was president. Before being president, as mayor of Buffalo, he exposed corruption in the municipal services (sewer, transportation and street cleaning). As mayor and governor, he fought Tammany Hall, the corrupt political machine in New York.

8s and 1s are partial to fighting corruption. He was known for vetoing pork barrel appropriations or any legislation favoring special interests. He didn't believe in relief for the poor. During the Depression of 1893, in his second administration, he offered no assistance to the unemployed and he vetoed a bill offering drought assistance to farmers. During that time in history, relief for the indigent was not considered a duty of the federal government. Individuals were pretty much on their own and aid was usually forthcoming from one's relatives or relief societies if it was needed.

He was frugal himself, paying for his own expenses, not using the presidential yacht. Not liking fancy food, he preferred pickled herring, Swiss cheese and pork chops. He was known for cussing (not unusual for some 8s) and preferred direct talk rather than political niceness. His opinions were strong as he had the strong energy of an 8 with a 7 wing.

Cleveland was the first Democratic president since James Buchanan, who was the president elected before Abe Lincoln, the first of many Republican presidents until Cleveland took office. The Republican candidate for Cleveland's first presidential run was known for being corrupt and even Republican party members voted instead for Cleveland who had a reputation for honesty. His focus was on efficiency, hiring people of merit, having a tight budget and insuring that Congress didn't overspend. He vetoed many bills he saw as fraudulent or wasteful, such as Civil War pensions. He became a watchdog for inefficiency or anything that smacked of special interest influence or corruption.

Though honest, he had to use party affiliations, party organization and patronage to win elections, even though he would later oppose the groups that elected him. He stood in opposition to temperance, which helped in the German, Irish and Eastern European vote, as immigration was heavy in the 1880s. He opposed integration of schools in New York and basically opposed integration anywhere, believing blacks were inferior to whites.

He supported Jim Crow laws, which limited access to equal rights and voting for black men in the South, thus assuring white political dominance, the support of Democrats and the Southern vote. He believed the federal government should not interfere in social causes, though he did marshal federal troops to block railroad strikes, causing a number of deaths. He did so in spite of the Illinois governor's opposition to the intervention.

Condemning prejudice against the Chinese, he did nothing to stop it and Chinese people were prevented from going home to visit relatives in China. Essentially if they left the

United States they would lose their citizenship. Chinese immigration had already been eliminated during that time. He blamed the Chinese and Japanese for not assimilating quickly enough into "American" culture. Likewise, with American Indians; he did everything possible to pressure Indians to forget their tribal culture while enrolled in the American education system, using English as their primary language, assuming private property rights (which Indians didn't have anyway) and stamping out Indian traditions. A few Indians were given private property while the remaining lands went to public domain, and reservation acreage continued to shrink in great proportion.

America was a land of opportunity if you were white and behaved according to "American" ideals. This, in many ways, created a land of conformity, dominated by the rich. Private minority businesses were allowed to thrive if they found a way to manage and grow in spite of prejudice, had support from their cultural community or white backing. Big business thrived. The Morgans, Rockefellers, Carnegies and Vanderbilts did well.

During an economic depression in 1893, which lasted for four years, labor unions and unrest increase during Cleveland's second presidency. Much of the depression was caused by unwise decisions during Harrison's presidency between the two Cleveland terms. Thousands of marchers walked to the Capitol demanding the President create relief jobs, but Cleveland would not budge. He didn't think it was the federal government's responsibility to resolve the problem. Labor strikes increased. The Democrats lost the next election after the Panic of 1893, which was until then the worst depression the country had endured (the later depression during the 1930s was worse). Cleveland had to borrow money from J.P. Morgan to keep the country afloat!

Regarding foreign policy Cleveland was against entangling alliances and didn't want to expand US territory, though he did intervene in a boundary dispute between Venezuela and England, invoking the Monroe Doctrine and even threatening war with Britain! He also threatened Germany regarding a dispute about Samoa in which Germany tried to create a puppet monarchy. The United States had a naval base on the island. Many unresolved foreign policy issues were left to McKinley, the next president.

Women's clubs and suffragette movements increased. Cleveland didn't support the women's vote but spoke neither for nor against it. He valued women's support and traditional roles. His own wife was traditional and conformed to her husband's wishes. Their marriage appeared very loving and she was a deeply admired First Lady, one of the most loved First Ladies in presidential history. Millions of items were reproduced with her image or that of the Presidential couple together – scarves, bottles and postcards. He disliked all the hoopla but she was graceful about receiving the attention.

Subsequent to the end of his Presidency, Cleveland and his wife and children retired to a spacious house in Princeton, New Jersey where he was honored. Cleveland played the stock market, practiced law, sat on company boards, wrote political essays and was a trustee of Princeton University. His eldest daughter died at the age of 12, which greatly grieved and aged him. He died at the age of 71 and Frances, his wife, lived on until 1947 to the age of 83.

An interesting fact is that Cleveland had a secret medical operation in his second term to remove a malignant tumor in his mouth, in which part of his jaw was replaced with a rubber implant. He had to relearn some of his speech patterns. He did this without the public knowing and it wasn't revealed until after his death!

As an 8 with features of 1, Cleveland was a man of power and directness and was unafraid to veto anything that wasn't honest, thrifty and above-board. He was beyond political corruption but hardly did anything to help the poor, disadvantaged or minorities. He tended to be inflexible in his beliefs and supported the rights of big business and the development of the wealth. His biographer said of Cleveland, "His intimates were struck by the gulf which separated his exuberant, jovial Cleveland of occasional hours of carefree banter, and the stern, unbending Cleveland of work and responsibility, whose life seemed hung round a pall of duty."

Benjamin Harrison, Integrity and Duty, Type 1, ISTJ, 1889-93

(1833-1901) Our 23rd President Benjamin Harrison was the grandson of William Henry Harrison, the 9th President, the only grandfather-grandson presidents. The Harrison family tree dates back to 1630 in America.

Upon Harrison's death, Grover Cleveland said of him, "Always sagacious, fearless, and firm, never feeble or foolish, with a wisdom of speech and a wisdom to act born of a true heart, his life was a glorification of simplicity, straightforwardness, and truthfulness. Never false himself, he was the implacable foe of falsity in others. He had a great soul and loved his country. Taking together his Soldier, Senatorial, and Presidential record, Benjamin Harrison stands in the highest rank of American statesmen."

As a Type 1, Harrison was disciplined, dispassionate, proper, methodical, detailed and overworked. He had difficulty delegating authority to others. He was a man of routine who rose early after sleeping six hours, worked hard and ate three meals a day. He tended to be rather serious, although he was able to relax and be playful with his grandchildren.

He felt pressure to be successful from the tradition of success and respectability of his Harrison ancestors. From within the structure of the presidency, he said, “Life is barren.” For the most part, he disliked being the president but was driven by a sense of duty.

He was born in 1833 in Ohio to a family known for political activism. His father was a prosperous farmer who also served as a Congressman and his great grandfather had been a governor and was a signatory, of the Declaration of Independence. Born of seven siblings, he was privately tutored as a child. Growing up on a farm, he tended livestock, hunted, fished and cut wood. His grandfather, former President William Henry Harrison, lived nearby and Benjamin spent hours reading, his favorite activity, in the library.

After attending a two-year preparatory school, he went on to graduate from college near the top of his class. Benjamin married his college sweetheart, the daughter of his science professor, when he was 20. His wife, Caroline Lavinia Scott, was a year older than he. Near the end of his life, after his wife died, he remarried; this time to the niece of his deceased wife, who was nearly 30 years younger than he was. His children became estranged because they disapproved of that second marriage.

Harrison studied law in Ohio. Soon after his first marriage, he received an inheritance from a relative and moved to Indianapolis, Indiana where he practiced law for six years. He then entered politics and joined the new Republican Party. Campaigning for their political nominees, he became City Attorney, then Secretary to the Republican State Central Committee, and he campaigned for Abraham Lincoln in the Presidential election of 1860.

Known as a loyal party member, Harrison was on an upward trajectory in politics. He soon was the state reporter for the Indiana Supreme Court and became an officer in the Civil War, eventually attaining the rank of Brigadier General. Lincoln requested that he organize a regiment, which he did partly to uphold the honor of his family. He didn’t especially like being a soldier but did his duty well, distinguishing himself. According to Sherman, Harrison served with "foresight, discipline and a fighting spirit."

Harrison lost a nomination to be governor, then four years later got the nomination, ran for governor and lost. He was active in supporting the candidacy of Rutherford B. Hayes and James Garfield for President. He held his first national office as Senator from Indiana from 1881-87 and supported the same issues that he later acted on as President -- limited civil service reform, wilderness conservation, building a strong US Navy and Merchant Marines, high protective tariffs to help US industries, liberal Civil War pensions and statehood for both North and South Dakota.

Harrison ran the presidential election campaign from his porch in Indianapolis. In one publicity stunt, hundreds of drummers from 11 states came to visit and perform. The party organizers financed travel for thousands of people to meet Harrison hoping to secure their votes. Harrison lost the popular vote but won the Electoral College vote, which secured the election for him. This was the third time in US history that a President won an election because of the Electoral College vote rather than by the vote of the people.

Against Harrison's will, his campaign managers advertised that his grandfather was the former President and they carried on the log cabin heritage theme even though he never actually lived in a log cabin. The campaigners fashioned a large ball filled with political watchwords, such as "Keep the ball rolling," just as they had done with his grandfather. Even though he accomplished a lot as president, he was ridiculed because of his stature (he was 5'6", the second shortest president) and according to many, didn't fill the shoes of his grandfather or other presidents.

As President, Harrison greatly expanded forest reserves; he loved the outdoors and visited Yellowstone three times. He passed the Forest Reserve Act in 1891, which set aside land for parks in most western states, including Alaska, and established Yosemite National Park as well as two others. Trying to protect seals from slaughter in the seal fur industry, he lost an international court case against Great Britain and Canada. Type 1s, like Harrison, often advocate for good causes. Six new states entered the Union during his term as president.

Harrison's wife Caroline was an excellent First Lady. Her father was a Presbyterian minister and the First Couple shared their religion as a central part of their relationship. She took on the task of overhauling the White House with new plumbing and the first electric lights, though neither of them trusted using the switches, and war was waged against the rats and rodents by letting loose ferrets in the White House!

Caroline designed a custom set of dishes and established a china collection with examples of patterns used in previous administrations. She founded the National Society of the Daughters of the American Revolution. Dying of tuberculosis a few weeks before the presidential election in her husband's bid for a second term, he was deeply saddened by the sudden loss of his wife, which took all the steam out of campaigning. Their daughter stepped in as First Lady to complete the term.

Immigration increased exponentially during his administration and Ellis Island opened as a port of entry. The population of poor people swelled in cities like New York City, with immigrants crowding into tenement apartments. The McKinley Tariff was passed to encourage US industry to prosper and limit foreign trade. Instead it backfired, causing US products to cost more, because of industry monopoly and greed in setting high prices.

Reciprocal trade agreements were made with friendly countries, mostly in Central and South America, which lowered tariffs for those countries. There was even a government surplus due to high tariffs, which went largely to Civil War veterans. The system was abused when young women, even teenagers, married older vets to insure their lifelong security through the inheritance of their husbands' pensions when they died!

The Sherman Anti-Trust Law was passed in 1890, the first major legislation, still on the books, to limit monopolies. It wasn't enforced well but managed to set a standard that Teddy Roosevelt and Taft as President later enforced. Harrison claimed to support aid to education for blacks in the South and tried unsuccessfully to increase voter's rights in the South for blacks.

The Sherman Silver Act was passed which established silver as a standard for paper money. This was an attempt to increase the money supply and help farming interests in the West. In 1890, in the Battle of Wounded Knee, the US Army massacred over 150 American Indian men, women and children. Harrison said he wanted to help the Indians but white giveaway land grabs in Oklahoma and the Dakotas foretold the end of Indian ownership of their original homelands. The American frontier was gone. Western lands were turned into ranches and farmlands. Mines were opened, railroads traversed the land, communications were opened up as telegraph companies thrived, and dams and irrigation canals were constructed along with vacation resorts for the well to do.

In foreign affairs Harrison convened the Pan-American Conference to increase trade, set up a protectorate of the Samoan Islands with Britain and made Frederick Douglas ambassador to Haiti; the first black man to hold high office in America. Harrison almost went to war with Chile over the mistreatment of American sailors and built a much larger armored Navy, setting the stage for the United States to be a world imperialistic power. He pushed for the annexation of Hawaii as well as a canal in Central America, all to take place after his term as President was over.

Although considered stiff and formal in public, criticized for not looking people in the eye and sometimes even labeled “the human iceberg,” he was more relaxed with friends and family. Someone said, “for God’s sake, be human.” Harrison said, “I tried it and I’ll never try it again.” Type 1s, like Harrison, can be perceived as icy but often they are warmer inside. Trying to do what’s right can be serious business.

His extraverted wife balanced his more reserved personality. He loved to play with his grandchildren and there’s a favorite story of his grandkids and he, with top hat and cane, running down Pennsylvania Avenue trying to capture their runaway pet goat. He had a whole menagerie of farm animals on the White House lawn for his grandkids. Thank God, they could bring out his fun 7 side, the growth type for 1s. He worked hard but took time off to visit friends and go on hunting trips.

”The household was run methodically, with meals served at their appointed time. Breakfast was followed by prayers led by the president. An hour in the afternoon was reserved for a brisk walk or drive. On Washington's streets, Harrison was often seen conversing with citizens who accosted him. The Harrisons remained regular churchgoers; the president engaged no business on Sunday and left his mail unopened.

Mrs. Harrison, a lively presence, decorated hundreds of porcelain dishes the proceeds of whose sales were donated to charities; engaged a professor of French to instruct the wives and daughters of cabinet families and others, and presided with charm and grace at White House functions. The Harrisons conveyed an easy informality, a relief to many after the stiffness of the Cleveland years. The Harrisons restored dancing at the white house." Quoted from www.presidentialprofiles.com

As mentioned, Harrison ran for a second term and lost, his enthusiasm severely dampened by the fact that his wife died only weeks before the election. He apparently was weeping most all the time and was actually relieved that he lost the election. He remarried four years later and had another daughter in addition to the two he had with his first wife. In retirement, he practiced law, gave lectures, wrote books about government and spent much time playing with his daughter. "For 60 years of my life I was driven by work. I want hereafter to be driving myself." He died at the age of 67 of pneumonia.

Harrison, who was known as a great public speaker, was private, quiet and reserved in small groups. He was often deep in thought and could walk past people without recognizing them. He could appear cold and unfriendly but was actually a warm, kind-hearted person, just not a backslapping politician.

Harrison was an introvert, a Type 1 with a 9 wing. Honesty was very important to him and he was consistent in his beliefs and actions. He was very religious and a weekly church-goer, praying out loud, teaching Sunday school and upholding traditions. He was loyal to his party and family, was a man of routine and a pillar of strength. Being true to his values was most important to him. Quite possibly he had the concealed weakness that many 1s have, a hedonistic aspect, atypically displayed by marrying someone 30 years his junior; the same as John Tyler, the 10th President, and another type 1, did years before.

As an ISTJ in the Myers-Briggs, he was steady and reliable, a man of his word who was detailed, structured and lived a life of disciplined routine. He believed in tradition and duty, carrying on in the name of his ancestors. He perpetuated the military and political service tradition of the Harrison family.

William McKinley – Well-Liked, Spanish-American War, Type 2, ESFJ, 1897-1901

(1843-1901) William McKinley became the next President, number 25, another native son of Ohio and the last president to fight in the Civil War. He was the first “modern” Chief Executive – using the telephone and national wire services. The nation's top newspapers run by William Hearst and Joseph Pulitzer, recorded film of his speeches. He lobbied Congress, spoke directly to audiences nationwide and was very tuned into and on good terms with the public media. He expanded America’s colonial influence to Cuba, Puerto

Rico, the Philippines, Hawaii, Wake Island and Guam in the Spanish-American War. McKinley was the fifth president to die in office and the third to be assassinated.

As a youth, he attended public schools, played Army games with friends and went fishing, hunting, swimming, ice-skating and horseback riding. In school, he was known as an excellent public speaker. McKinley attended a Methodist supported school before attending college where he stayed for only one semester, dropping out due to illness and lack of finances. He was planning to become a Methodist minister. His mother was devout; teaching him to pray and be honest, respectful and courteous to all people. His father ran an iron foundry and demonstrated the virtue of a life of hard work.

Joining the military, he spent most of his time in the commissary, delivering supplies to the troops and eventually achieved the rank of major in the Civil War. He served all four years in the war without being shot or falling to illness. He fought in combat at times even though he didn't have to, as he was the commissary sergeant, or chief cook, serving soldiers hot meals while under fire. Already his Type 2 giving characteristics were in play. Nothing's better for a 2 than cooking and serving food. He served militarily under Rutherford B. Hayes, the future president, his mentor who later helped forward his political career. After the war, he attended law school, the classic course for entering politics.

He was known for his kindness and was "warm and gracious as a summer breeze," from *Presidential Temperament*. He was charming, tactful, very personal and had a moral focus. "He had such a good heart that the right thing to do always occurred to him," commented Howard Taft. When discharged from his regiment at the end of the Civil War, it is said of him that, "he was the only man in the regiment who had completed his hitch without ever having uttered a profanity, gotten drunk, or lost his virginity," from the book, *Presidential Courage*. He was considered mild-mannered, gentle and responsive.

His first post was as a county prosecutor. Then, he served a dozen years as a US Representative and became famous as the author of the McKinley Tariff, which backfired leading to higher domestic prices on goods. This caused the loss of his bid for reelection to the House of Representatives. Despite that, two years later he ran for Governor of Ohio and served for two terms, becoming famous for setting up arbitration boards to settle disputes between management and labor. While sympathetic to laborers, he called out the National Guard when violence occurred with the United Mine Workers.

The McKinley presidential campaign, supported by big business, spent five times as much money as his opponent William Jennings Bryan, who did a three-month long speaking tour of the country aimed at garnering the vote of the common man. The rich magnates of Morgan in banking, Rockefeller in oil and Carnegie in steel contributed large sums of money. McKinley ran a front porch campaign in Canton, Ohio and won by a large majority. Partially due to his wife being an invalid, he stayed at home rather than campaigning elsewhere. Campaign managers would transport thousands of people to his house to meet him! Others campaigned for him across the country. McKinley always imagined he would be President someday. I guess it helps to believe in yourself!

McKinley remained loyal to his wife throughout their marriage in spite of her ongoing depression and epilepsy. Within four years of their marriage, his wife Ida lost her mother, both of their daughters and favorite grandfather and grandmother. During that time, a blunt trauma to her head and back possibly created her epilepsy. Her physical and mental health declined, never to return. As First Lady, she knitted thousands of pairs of slippers to give away to friends and for charity auctions.

As a Type 2 Giver, McKinley nursed and pampered his wife while still advancing his career, which added to his popularity. He certainly had an eye and ear toward his public image, as he likely had a strong 3 wing, as well as a 1 wing with a focus on morality and doing what he thought right. His giving nature and symbolic gestures are indicative of a 2.

He was especially attentive to his wife. McKinley would massage her head often to alleviate her stress and, when he was governor of Ohio, he would wave at her from across the street with his handkerchief at an appointed time of the day. She lived across the street, and he would only smoke his cigars when he was away from her, as she didn't like cigar smoke. She would sit next to him at state dinners and he would cover her face with a handkerchief delicately (he always had a handkerchief ever ready as a Type 2) if she had a seizure and if she became too ill, he would take her to a special room and spend time with her until she recovered. He often fed her, soothed her and nursed her, reading poetry and speaking to her lovingly. It sounds like this arrangement worked well for both of them.

As President, he focused more on foreign relations than domestic affairs. His biggest notoriety occurred in 1898 when he reluctantly engaged in a war with Spain. The USS Maine blew up in Havana harbor and initially Spain was blamed for the incident. This turned out to be a false accusation. There's actually a good deal of evidence to support the idea that a mechanical error was the cause of the engine blast that killed over 250 Americans. The United States was looking for a reason to enter the war and expand US territories.

Teddy Roosevelt, Under Secretary of the Navy at the time, strongly pushed for war and collected a bunch of friends, horses and supplies, and took a boat to Cuba, which he personally financed. They made Calvary charges under the name of Rough Riders; the most important charge was made on San Juan Hill in an effort to right wrong as well as to gain fame and prestige. Many people thought Teddy was crazy! It worked though for his tough guy image and propelled both himself and McKinley forward politically.

Meanwhile the US Navy easily destroyed the Spanish fleet in the Atlantic and Pacific and the United States gained four territories in the process. Guam and the Philippines gave the US military bases to help gain influence in Asia and China. Island bases for military operations were increased soon again when McKinley annexed Hawaii.

McKinley initiated plans to build the Panama Canal, which was carried out later by Teddy Roosevelt. He sent troops to China to put down the Boxer Rebellion and also to Nicaragua to protect American property rights. McKinley put the entire world on alert that America would intervene in other countries if he deemed it necessary. He set the stage for Roosevelt to bully the world and take over other nations' sovereignty.

McKinley spent his evenings playing cards with his wife or personal secretary, taking walks or carriage rides or answering letters. Smoking a cigar and drinking a glass of whiskey were his relaxing activities before going to bed. McKinley loved dressing up and talking to people and always had a pink carnation in his lapel which he would often give to people. 2s love to give special gifts. He was religious and prayed before any important decision; he was very hesitant about going to war with Spain. McKinley's later Vice president, Teddy Roosevelt said of him, "he has no more backbone than a chocolate éclair."

McKinley had a calm demeanor and was efficient in his use of time. He fed the media what he wanted them to publish and they liked him because he stayed in touch and had an engaging manner and personal demeanor. He was a very popular president and greatly increased the power of the executive department. During the Spanish-American War, he used funds as needed without congressional approval. 2s give a lot but also have a lot of personal power and love to impress others.

He was the first major imperialistic president, competing with Europe and Japan for colonial possessions, markets and influence. The Spanish-American War set the precedent for military intervention in Latin American from then to now. After the Spanish-American War ended, over 200,000 Filipinos were killed by the American military in their drive for independence from the United States, just as they had tried to become independent from Spain. The United States has a history of freeing a country from an oppressor and then becoming the next oppressor or setting up a puppet government to run the country. The United States military massacred whole villages of Filipino people. We weren't really freeing them from Spanish rule – just changing the ruler. Our underlying motive for supporting the Filipinos and other island people like in Cuba in their fight for "independence," was to take over their country. Resistance to our "influence" and rule was instantly put down, and death or imprisonment was the punishment.

Government employees and bureaucracies increased dramatically during McKinley's presidency. There were increased taxes - inheritance, excise and a stamp tax on public documents (that's what started our Revolutionary War). America was becoming the strongest industrial power on earth and McKinley knew he needed reciprocal trade agreements and occasional military force to coerce countries such as China to trade with us. That's why the United States put down the Boxer Rebellion in China – to force China to trade with us. Type 2s can have an aggressive side to get what they want, particularly when they have a 3 wing.

Countries becoming independent of their imperial colonizers, the idea of which was supported by the US in theory, posed a potential threat if they didn't conform to the political will of the United States. That fear set the precedent for the continued use of military force by the United States toward countries that "disobeyed". McKinley used the excuse that we needed to "Christianize" countries who were not as "civilized." Therefore, the use of missionaries was encouraged in Hawaii and the Philippines to help those who were less civilized. America either controlled, "Christianized" or massacred rebellious people in its territories. The paradigm was to do away with native cultures like that of the Philippines and replace it with our "civilized American" culture. Some missionaries were helpful and giving, probably balancing some of the destruction from our military and governmental policies.

McKinley was very tuned into public image, conscious of what people wanted to hear, and had the technical means to carry out policies and make his motivations sound better than they actually were. His natural smiling politeness covered up his less than genteel motives. "He had a way of handling men so that they thought his ideas were their own," quoted from his War Secretary. He was cheerful, optimistic, open and friendly, common for 2s. Being a Type 2, McKinley took care of his wife, nursing and often feeding her. That added to his public image as a sweet man thus belying some of his cold- hearted decisions regarding foreign policy.

The White House was also a source of propaganda from which McKinley enhanced the United States' reputation as a successful world power. All the while he struggled a bit with his conscience and religious beliefs, which ran absolutely contrary to his actions. He was a 2 with a 3 wing - giving, warm, engaging, courteous and charming but still very success driven. He wanted to win. He certainly had a lot of qualities of 1 also – service oriented, moral and doing what he thought was right.

His religious focus gave him type 1 undertones. He was meticulous, believing that everyone needed a purpose and he believed in destiny. In spite of hating the memory of the Civil War he felt the United States had a manifest destiny to rule the world, even if lots of people died in the process. He was also competing with Europe to conquer other countries. Type 2 is a good fit for ESFJ.

"ESFJs are conscientious helpers, sensitive to the needs of others and energetically dedicated to their responsibilities. They are highly attuned to their emotional environment and attentive to both the feelings of others and the perception others have of them. ESFJs like a sense of harmony and cooperation around them, and are eager to please and provide.

ESFJs value loyalty and tradition, and usually make their family and friends their top priority. They are generous with their time, effort, and emotions. They often take on the concerns of others as if they were their own, and will attempt to put their significant organizational talents to use to bring order to other people's lives." www.truity.com/personality-type/ESFJ

McKinley did a six-week tour of the country at the end of his first presidency and easily won the 2nd election to be president but within months was assassinated by an immigrant who felt he was oppressing the poor to benefit the rich. McKinley was shot at the World Exposition in Buffalo, New York and had just given the carnation in his lapel to a little girl. He told his aides to be careful about how they would inform his wife. People began beating the shooter and McKinley, still conscious, told his protectors not to hurt him. He was a loving 2 to the very end!

He was well respected and was successful in many of the goals that he set out to accomplish. He died at the age of 58. McKinley's wife, Ida, only recently recovered from a nearly fatal case of blood poisoning, visited his coffin daily for 30 months before it was finally interred in a receiving vault at West Lawn Cemetery in Canton, Ohio. There it was held until his monument was completed 6 years later. His wife died at age 60 and is buried with him at the McKinley Memorial.

"McKinley was more than popular," according to historian Margaret Leach, "he was beloved. Even his political opponents were attracted to the peculiar sweetness of his personality." (Sweetness is a term generally only ascribed to 2s or 9s). His biographer stated, "His uniform courtesy and fairness commanded the admiration of Democrats as well as Republicans. The general public found him free from vanity or affectation

Teddy Roosevelt – Type 8, ESTP, Domestic Reformer and Imperialist President, 1901-1909

(1858-1919) Our 26th President, Teddy Roosevelt was a classic Type 8, the Powerhouse - 8s are generally easy to type. "Speak softly and carry a big stick." From my perspective, as an 8, Roosevelt actually meant, "Speak harshly and carry a big stick and whack the guy in front of the stick." Roosevelt is a classic Type 8 with a 7 wing filled with energy galore. He bellowed like a 'bull moose,' thus his nickname and the political party's nickname. Whatever Teddy wanted, he made it happen. He probably broke more constitutional rules than any other president, other than Andrew Jackson and possibly Donald Trump.

Teddy was quite a Renaissance man, publishing over 40 books from bird watching to naval history. He was a deputy sheriff, a police commissioner, led troops in battle, went on many hunting expeditions and was an excellent horseman and cowboy. He was naturally bellicose, loved to fight, and in one instance continued delivering a speech after he was shot and bleeding with a bullet in his chest! As a man of contrast, he was tender with animals and he was willing to hunt and kill them. He had the strength and staying power of a type 8 and had the adventures and accomplishments to prove it.

Teddy Roosevelt would be an ESTP in the Myers-Briggs. "ESTPs are energetic thrill seekers who are at their best when putting out fires, whether literal or metaphorical. They bring a sense of dynamic energy to their interactions with others and the world around them. They assess situations quickly and move adeptly to respond to immediate problems with practical solutions. Active and playful, ESTPs are often the life of the party and have a good sense of humor. They use their keen powers of observation to assess their audience and adapt quickly to keep interactions exciting. Although they typically appear very social, they are rarely sensitive; the ESTP prefers to keep things fast-paced and silly rather than emotional or serious." www.truity.com/personality-type/ESTP

Roosevelt was a Representative in the New York State Legislature, a member of the US Civil Service Commission, President of New York City Board of Police Commissioners, Assistant Secretary of the Navy, Governor of New York, Vice President and then President of the United States. He was one of the physically strongest presidents, yet as a child he was weak and asthmatic. As he grew Roosevelt bolstered his strength by weight training and boxing. He boxed many opponents throughout his life, especially as an undergrad at Harvard, where he came close to winning the lightweight championship title. When he was President, he boxed a professional boxer, and as a result lost his sight in one eye. He kept his injury and the resulting disability a secret, being unable to admit weakness, classic for Type 8/7s.

Throughout Roosevelt's life he was haunted by his father's image. He pushed Teddy and never allowed him to show weakness. Because he recognized his child had physical limitations, he pushed him to exercise constantly, stand up to bullies and to never give up. His father died when Teddy was 20 but he lived on forever in Teddy's mind. He wanted to make his father proud both when he was alive and also after his death.

His famous charge up San Juan Hill was accomplished on foot and the ensuing battle was hand-to-hand combat. Teddy bragged, "I killed a Spaniard with my bare hands like a jackrabbit." The Rough Riders were rough but should have been called the Rough Runners! He gave up his job as Assistant Secretary of the Navy to have the honor of gathering a bunch of cronies from his cowboy days and his Ivy League athlete friends to go to war. They outnumbered the enemy 15 to 1 in his charge up the hill, plus they were trained by a career soldier, as none of them had ever seen combat.

Most people thought he had lost his marbles when he went to Cuba to fight, but after the war this escapade added to his tough image. His rough and tumble fighting reputation helped him be chosen as Vice President, mostly because many Republican politicians hoped that as VP he would become obscure seeing as he had a lot of political enemies who didn't want him in power. Little did they know McKinley would be assassinated and Teddy could never be obscure!

Everything he did, he did big. He typically ate a dozen eggs for breakfast, climbed the Matterhorn after graduation from Harvard, built a tennis court at the White House and played as many as 90 games in a day! He studied martial arts, boxed on and off all his life and ran long jogs, particularly with dignitaries who couldn't keep up with him. 8s are very physical and love to win while the 7 wing adds a positive perspective.

He was vulnerable on rare occasions. His mother and his first wife Alice Hathaway Lee died the same day, Valentine's Day, in 1884 in the same house and his grief was unbearable. His wife's death occurred as the result of complications incurred when giving birth to their first child. He put his newborn in the custody of his aunt and went to the Badlands to become a cowboy. He could cowboy with the roughest among them, despite his spectacles, and belying his Harvard education and wealth. He became a rancher and a naturalist in North Dakota, as well as a deputy sheriff, loving the outdoors and his two-year stay in the West. It became the focal point for his desire to conserve land for national parks. He never mentioned his first wife Alice again, even in his autobiography. Apparently, it was just too painful to revisit.

He then married Edith Carow, whom he had known as a child in New York City, and they had five children. Teddy was always in motion and was the first president to ride in an automobile, airplane and submarine, as well as to travel outside the United States to Panama to oversee the building of "his" Canal.

His action-packed life often led to accidents – he was hurled through a glass window on a boat in the Gulf of Mexico, twice suffered a broken arm, once during a fox hunt and another while playing at stick-fighting, and he landed in a wheelchair for several weeks when his carriage collided with a trolley in Pittsfield, Massachusetts. His secret service agent was killed and others were injured during that incident. 8s can have accidents as they take big risks!

Some interesting facts: There are two different stories about how the Teddy Bear got its name. The first one says he saved a bear cub when he was on a hunting trip and the press loved it. Another story says a guide tied up an old bear for Teddy to shoot and he refused, needing more sport than that. Someone else shot the bear. I like the first story better! The press loved him.

As a young child, Teddy watched the Lincoln funeral procession from the window of his New York City residence. Roosevelt had a near perfect memory and was known to quote obscure poetry he had read years earlier. He wrote over 150,000 letters in his life and he only lived to be 60! It's amazing what he accomplished. He dropped out of Columbia Law School, as he was ready to start his political life and didn't care to finish his education.

Aside from his aggressive nature, he had a peaceful side. He won the Nobel Peace Prize in 1906 after successfully negotiating a peace treaty, in Portsmouth, New Hampshire, that ended the war between Japan and Russia. He also settled a dispute between France and Germany over dividing Morocco.

Roosevelt accomplished a great deal while he was President. He built the Panama Canal using bribes and force, nearly instigating war between Columbia and Panama. He needed Columbia's permission to land in order to go through Panama. He encouraged Panama to become independent of Columbia, which only happened through payoffs and the US Navy sending a fleet to prevent Columbia from attacking Panama. The Canal took 10 years to build and Panama did become "independent," and also became a military staging area for the Unites States.

Later the US Navy did a worldwide tour of its ships to showcase its strength, in case anyone didn't notice, and six different times Roosevelt used this gunboat philosophy to persuade other countries to do what he wanted. Type 8 people, particularly 8/7s, often love to show off their power. He doubled the size of the Navy. His threats prevented war in this case. He was, however, actually sad that war didn't erupt during his presidency.

He confronted the German Kaiser who was threatening to invade Venezuela because of money it owed to Germany. The German fleet blockaded Venezuela and was sinking their boats. Roosevelt, who was eager to show off his Navy's prowess, had ships nearby ready to uphold the Monroe Doctrine, which prohibited European influence in Central and South America. The US Naval presence helped Germany arbitrate with Venezuela at The Hague. Roosevelt sent the ships without Congressional approval, which he often circumvented anyway. Like many 8s, he was either loved or hated but for the most part Roosevelt was a popular President. He could have easily sought a third term and won but had promised to end his Presidency at the end of the second term and he honored that promise. He went on an African safari instead of running for president again!

Roosevelt was generally a supporter of big business but he wanted to set precedents that would impose limits on the powers of big business. In 1902 the US Justice Department filed suit and won against a railroad conglomerate headed by JP Morgan, a magnate who occasionally bailed out the US Government when it found itself in difficult financial straits. This sent a shock wave throughout the business world. Teddy created several laws to regulate the railroad industries, due to their abuses of favors and kickbacks that led to monopolies and higher prices to consumers.

The Square Deal was a program based on the institution of arbitration commissions created by Roosevelt to force management and labor to arbitrate when strikes occurred. He believed the government should intervene when necessary to create social and economic justice between management and labor, consumer and business, and development and conservation. It was the precursor to Franklin Delano Roosevelt's New Deal, as well as Woodrow Wilson's New Freedom and Truman's Fair Deal. Roosevelt used his presidential authority to issue executive orders creating 150 new national forests, five national parks, 18 national monuments, and 51 wildlife refuges.

Roosevelt used the power of the media appealing directly to the American people and circumventing political parties and machines. His forceful personality and strong opinions made good copy for the press. Newspapers loved him!

Investigative journalism became more commonplace, exposing political party excesses. Both parties were guilty of and vulnerable to exposure of abuses. For instance, the writing of Upon Sinclair's *The Jungle* exposed the terrible conditions of the meat packing industry and Roosevelt helped pass the Meat Inspection Act and the Pure Food and Drug Act of 1906. This endeared him to the public and to those corporations that favored government regulation as a means of achieving national consumer standards.

His relationship with the black population was muddled. He believed generally that the black race was inferior even though he declared that some individual African Americans were superior to some whites. He invited Booker T. Washington to dine with him at the White House, which enraged many in the South. He did little to try to change discrimination in the South regarding voting or equal rights. In one case, he gave three Army companies of 160 black soldiers all dishonorable discharges because there was an uncorroborated belief that one of them killed a white soldier in a shooting spree. There was no trial or evidence to support the allegations.

In foreign affairs, the Roosevelt Corollary was created to solve a problem that occurred as a result of Latin American countries borrowing money from European nations. Those same European nations felt that they were entitled to collect their unpaid debts by sending their Navy to Latin America and waging war against countries that failed to pay back their loans on time. That violated the Monroe Doctrine. Roosevelt committed to United States intervention; the US would act as the world's policeman with regard to Latin American economic issues and internal affairs, as well as with European nations' business with Latin America. That set the stage for American intervention in Latin American affairs from then to the present time.

Roosevelt loved his family life with Edith, which included six children, one of which was from his first marriage. At the White House the children reigned supreme, with ponies riding in elevators and climbing stairs, snakes crawling around and water balloons dropping on the heads of guests. At their summer house in Oyster Bay, New York there were obstacle courses, hikes, ocean swims and stories about ghosts and the Wild West. His boys boxed and his girls ran. He was affectionate with his children and much praise was given for courage and aggressiveness. Weakness wasn't tolerated. His wife took it all in stride and seemed to enjoy life with her grown up boy at heart.

During Roosevelt's Presidency, women increased their numbers in the workforce, the country became increasingly urban, voter participation decreased as party politics diminished and laws forbidding non-citizens to vote, increased. The South's prejudice got worse as most blacks couldn't vote due to poll taxes, property qualifications and unfair literacy tests. Poor or illiterate whites were also eliminated from the polls. 1300 black men were lynched or burned alive in the South or Midwest between 1900 and 1910. Women though, were organizing to demand voters' rights, which didn't happen until 1920 nationally, but in five states women had been enfranchised for state elections between 1910 and 1912—Wyoming, California, Kansas, Arizona and Oregon.

Roosevelt felt he had a responsibility to ensure that government would create reform for the people at large. He created a progressive movement to support welfare legislation, government regulation and land conservation. In theory, he believed in making society fair and equitable economically for all Americans. His two terms were the foundation for the New Frontier of Kennedy and The Great Society of Lyndon Johnson. Party politics diminished and the power of the individual president increased. People voted for the individual when they voted for Roosevelt rather than for his party. The power of the

Executive Branch continued to increase because of Roosevelt's influence. His progressive attitude was not extended to other countries however.

After serving his two terms as President, Roosevelt accompanied a scientific expedition to the Amazon in 1913-14, sponsored by the American Museum of Natural History. He caught a tropical fever after sustaining an injury to his leg that happened while he was trying to rescue his canoe in the rapids. He lost 50 pounds from the deteriorating infection and nearly died. Since Roosevelt was so ill that he couldn't walk and had to be carried by stretcher, he asked his companions to leave him to die. They refused so he insisted the expedition continue, carrying him on a stretcher, instead of disbanding to seek better medical attention!

Due to a prior injury in a car accident and the bullet that stayed in his chest from the assassination attempt, his health declined. Despite that, he insisted on forming an expeditionary force to fight in World War I. That effort was refuted by President Woodrow Wilson. Roosevelt died at the age of 60 in 1919, having accomplished so much in his years.

Teddy is credited with strengthening the power of the Presidency. He passed legislation that was the precursor of the modern welfare state, set in motion legislation aimed at big business, known as Trust Busting, and initiated leadership in the land conservation movement. He was the main promulgator of American imperialism. He was one of our most courageous and action-driven presidents. Certainly, he was a powerful force for change; completing everything he set out to do. Many loved his boldness and his outspokenness, as well as his fight against corporate greed and the annexing of territories outside the continental United States.

William Howard Taft, Type 9, ISFJ, Supreme Court Justice, 1909-1913

(1857-1930) Our next and 27th President was William Howard Taft, personally chosen by Theodore Roosevelt as his replacement. Taft had been Secretary of War during Roosevelt's last term, during which he oversaw the building of the Panama Canal and set up a protectorate in Cuba. As his mentor, Roosevelt expected Taft to follow in his political footsteps by supporting the policies he had created during his presidency; it didn't turn out that way. Taft didn't want to be President. He was persuaded to run for office by his wife, by Roosevelt and also by his party. Taft felt more comfortable in the Judiciary Department and later fulfilled his lifelong dream of becoming the Chief Justice of the Supreme Court, which was much more to his liking and ability. He was considered to be much better suited to an administrative position, being a detail person and legal summarizer, than a politician or initiator of legislation. He was the sixth President to come from Ohio even though his political background was strongly rooted in New England.

His father had been Ulysses S. Grant's Secretary of War and Attorney General as well as the Ambassador to Hungary and Russia under Chester Arthur. His ancestor, Lydia Chain Taft, is credited with being the first woman to cast a vote in an American election (she did so in 1756). Another of Taft's ancestors served as a soldier in the Revolutionary War. He owned a tavern in his civilian life and was known to have welcomed George Washington as a guest in his home.

Taft's father was sensible, kind, gentle, and highly "Victorian" -- a man who kept his emotions under control, supported women's rights and encouraged his wife to be independent. His mother was the energetic, curious and adventurous Louisa Taft who organized a local and statewide movement to add kindergarten education to the public schools, started an art association, book clubs, German and French language clubs and traveled widely with her husband on his diplomatic missions. Taft's parents exposed him and his seven siblings (including two half-brothers from his father's first marriage) to a wealth of experience and progressive ideas.

William lived in fear of not meeting his parents' expectations. No matter how well he performed, he was anxious about obtaining their approval. For instance, when he graduated from high school second in his class, he chose to address his fellow students on the subject of women's suffrage, telling the audience about the philosophy of his progressive parents.

Taft's excessive weight, according to some scholars, stemmed from the internal anxiety he generated when he attempted to push himself beyond his own desires in order to meet his parents' expectations. Type 9s are often more anxious than they appear outwardly as they try to pacify others or live up to what they perceive as others' expectations. He had a strong 8 wing, as well as a Type 1 wing and a strong Type 6 stress point. I perceive him as a Type 9 with an 8 wing.

Taft was an excellent student who graduated from an elite private high school and then went to Yale, where he graduated second in his class. He went on to Cincinnati Law School, became a lawyer and was soon appointed to a judgeship. His parents, especially his father, were demanding. They encouraged him to excel and become and well known. He was married when he was 29 to an ambitious woman, Helen Louise Herron, who hoped for him to become President. He held important judicial positions and became Solicitor General from 1887 to 1900, which was the fulfillment of his passion in a career choice.

Under President McKinley, after the Spanish American War ended and the US had established Military rule in the Philippines, he was invited to be Governor General of the islands. He felt pushed into that position by his politically ambitious wife. McKinley added to the pressure by promising to appoint him to the Supreme Court if he would accept the position in the Philippines. Actually, McKinley and Roosevelt both offered him the Supreme Court position but Taft, once committed, wanted to finish the job in the Philippines. His character demanded he complete projects he began and he wanted to ensure that the Philippines were more peaceful when he left than they had been when he arrived.

Type 9, The Peacemaker, Taft restored the islands, which had nearly been destroyed under brutal US military rule, to a civilian government, which in time was accepted by the Filipino population. He helped create a Constitution as well as an efficient form of government for the islands, established a civil service system, a judicial system, English-language public schools, a transportation network, and health care facilities. Taft distributed this land by way of low-cost mortgages to tens of thousands of Filipino peasants, and built roads and infrastructure for the islands. He was an efficient administrator and excelled at everything he began.

By the time he left the Philippines, he had pacified most of the islands and the country was much better off than it had been prior to his administration. The Philippines were nearly destroyed by the US Military, which massacred thousands of people and even entire villages when the people rebelled against the US takeover. Type 9s who are engaged in life like Taft, are able to create harmony and balance in the most difficult of situations. They understand that force used in these situations almost never works in the long run.

Taft even as a child was obese, but that didn't keep him from being an all-around athlete. He played second base and was a power hitter in baseball, took dance lessons, loved riding horses, enjoyed playing tennis and became the Heavyweight Wrestling Champion at Yale. He was a friendly, warm, open, cheerful, amiable person who was easy to get along with, and was known to have an infectious chuckle. An introvert by nature, he appeared outwardly to be an extravert; having the social skills to mix with many different kinds of people; he was nonetheless a quiet person. He was naturally reclusive, tended to forget names and rarely remembered to wave to crowds when they cheered.

Taft was an ISFJ, which is not uncommon for a type 9 to be, as ISFJs are the friendliest of the introverts and often appear to be extraverted. The energy is more laid-back, receptive and connecting rather than active, aggressive or highly engaging, except on occasion. He had a difficult time saying no. Even as head of the Supreme Court, he said, "I would not think of opposing the views of my brethren if there is a majority against my own," a common sentiment for a Type 9 and often for ISFJ.

As president, he became an avid golf player and was the first President to throw the starting pitch for the Washington Nationals' baseball season. He enjoyed fishing, having dinner with his buddies out of doors, and taking trips in nature. His preferred small groups over large gatherings or crowds. He was very down to earth as a sensing type in the Myers-Brigg. He, was feeling oriented and sought harmony as a feeling type and, as a judging type, had the capacity for decisiveness.

Being President of the United States however was not his cup of tea and he was more anxious, lonely and depressed during his term of office than he was at any other time in his life. Under stress, Type 9s revert to Type 6 and can become quite anxious. He said he felt "like a fish out of water." His weight skyrocketed to 350 pounds and a special bathtub had to be built in the White House to accommodate him!

Like his protégé Teddy Roosevelt, he would often eat a dozen eggs, a pound of bacon and a stack of pancakes for breakfast! His weight probably contributed to his tendency to doze off at inappropriate times during state dinners and funerals. He even fell asleep at a parade in his honor, as well as in the middle of conversations with people! He often fell asleep next to his wife in the car while being driven by their chauffeur. She nicknamed him "Sleeping Beauty."

His wife Helen, also called Nellie, visited the White House as a girl of 16 to attend the celebration of the Silver Wedding anniversary of Rutherford B. Hayes and his wife, who were close friends of Nellie's father. She determined then that she would live in the White House someday. She met her future husband at a bobsledding party two years later, but it took Taft seven years of courting and three proposals before she gave in and married him. Eventually she fulfilled her dream of becoming First Lady.

She was the main influence that brought Taft to the White House as President, being that he was personally quite satisfied in the judiciary. Unfortunately, her lifelong dream had only come true for a short time when Helen had a stroke. Within weeks of her husband's Inauguration she was stricken. The stroke damaged the part of her brain that governs speech and she had to learn how to speak all over again. After recuperation and speech therapy, she was finally able to fulfill many of her roles and also be an informal political advisor to her husband.

Helen was a remarkable woman. After she recovered from the stroke, she had thousands of cherry trees planted in Washington, D.C. and inaugurated public outdoor music concerts. She ran the White House Staff, replacing the white ushers who greeted guests with black ushers – a prestigious job for a black man at that time; it was a bit scandalous to have black ushers but it was actually considered to be a progressive move. Helen also invited divorced women to the White House as guests (they had previously been denied access), as well as all members of Congress. Helen's daughter helped her, as the First Lady was still recovering her speech.

Nellie was amazing. As horse drawn carriages were replaced by automobiles, she rode with her husband in the inauguration parade for the first time in history, did much to improve working and sanitation conditions in federal buildings, attended many plays, and supported the arts and women's right to vote. The list is endless regarding her work for positive change in peoples' lives.

During Teddy Roosevelt's reign as President, Taft and Roosevelt were very close friends, but they were opposites on many levels. His former closeness with Roosevelt evaporated when Taft became President, as Roosevelt felt that Taft wasn't following through with many of the policies that Roosevelt initiated. Taft was also a progressive but he was considerably more conservative than his former mentor.

Taft's spirits returned when he left the Presidency and became a professor at Yale Law School. He ultimately became Chief Justice of the Supreme Court, which was his lifelong dream. He lost 100 pounds once he returned to the profession that he loved! Fame is less important to a Type 9 than the comfort of doing what they like.

As president, he did plan to carry out Roosevelt's progressive policies but his focus was more on creating an effective administration than legislative initiation. Yet he strengthened the Interstate Commerce Commission to regulate rate hikes for railroads and expanded it to include the regulation of telegraphs, telephone and radio. He improved the Civil Service, placing postmasters and civilians who worked for the Navy under its the protection. He enacted the National Income Tax Amendment to the Constitution, and instituted the direct election of senators. Prior to this, US Senators had been elected by state legislation. He consolidated the executive budget under one umbrella, thereby instituting more efficiency and better accounting.

Taft's administration brought many anti-trust lawsuits, to court (100 in all) many more than in Roosevelt's administration, including suits against the Standard Oil Company and the New Jersey American Tobacco Company, which were begun during Roosevelt's time in office. The Taft Administration won a lawsuit against the American Sugar Refining Companies for setting unfair prices. Roosevelt broke ties with Taft when he tried to break up the US Steel monopoly, as Roosevelt felt the economy needed a monopoly in that business.

It pained Taft greatly, particularly in the 1912 election, when Taft and Roosevelt were competitors and Roosevelt called him names in public like, "Taft's a fathead with the brains of a guinea pig". This caused Taft to break down and cry; they had been especially close friends most of their lives and Taft was deeply hurt. 9s can be quite sensitive and are averse to conflict but are able to fight when necessary.

Taft fought back and got the nomination from the Republican Party. Roosevelt felt that it should have gone to himself. Ironically, Taft was personally conflicted about winning the nomination and was relieved when he lost the election! The Bull Moose, Roosevelt, created his own party and ran against Taft, splitting the Republican vote and therefore losing to the Democrat Woodrow Wilson. Wilson wouldn't have won without their squabble! Type 8s and 9s are often drawn to each other's differences in order to learn from each other; the 8 needing to learn to be less abrasive and more negotiable and the 9 to be more assertive, but it's a challenge.

Taft was very committed to increasing foreign trade. He fostered a program called "dollar diplomacy" to encourage investments in Central and South America, the Caribbean and the Far East, selling heavy industrial goods and military hardware. This set the precedent for selling arms to foreign countries in order to bolster the US economy and then engaging our military to fight wars either for or against the very countries to whom we were selling the arms! 9s can go along with others' agenda initially to establish a feeling of agreement, even if it goes against peace in the long run!

Even though not as aggressive in foreign affairs as Roosevelt, Taft sent 2700 Marines into Nicaragua to support the US backed government in their fight with rebels, and intervened in Cuba and the Dominican Republic. He proposed that US bankers support railroad construction in other countries such as China, but negative feedback stopped that measure. Even though he didn't exercise as much presidential authority as Roosevelt, Taft was in favor of Presidents having more executive authority.

Subsequent to the end of his Presidential term, he taught at Yale Law School until he was appointed Chief Justice of the Supreme Court by Warren Harding and at that point said,

"I don't remember that I ever was President." He served until his death and wrote over 253 decisions, mostly conservative and aimed at limiting governmental power.

Taft died in 1930 at the age of 71 of high blood pressure and heart complications. His funeral was broadcast on the radio. He is buried at Arlington National Cemetery, the only president until John F. Kennedy to be given that honor. His wife lived another 13 years and wrote a memoir of being First Lady, the first to do so. One of their sons, Robert became a highly distinguished US Senator called "Mr. Republican" and their daughter Helen received a PhD in history from Yale and became a history professor, dean and acting president of Bryn Mawr College.

Taft was a happy man when he was doing what he wanted, placidly quiet when he was engaged in activities that fit his nature; being a judge and an administrator or while fishing with his buddies, creating harmony when he could. Even though he wasn't cut out to be President, he did a decent job. As a Type 9 with both wings (8 and 1) but a stronger 8 wing, he was a nice guy and a good-natured leader; able to be tough when necessary. Taft teaches us that we'll do best using our native strengths and doing what we love.

Other traits he possessed included affection and loyalty to friends, generosity, honesty, reliability, fairness, integrity, good-naturedness with benevolent intentions, and kindness. He could be strong and decisive when he needed to be and had the ability to handle much detail, administer efficiently and show appreciation to others.

Woodrow Wilson, The PhD Idealist, Type 1, INTJ, 1913-21

(1856-1924) Woodrow Wilson was President number 28. He was deeply admired by Harry S. Truman, another Type 1. Wilson was a true Southerner, growing up in Virginia, Georgia, North Carolina and South Carolina. When he was eight years old, he witnessed Jefferson Davis, the Confederate President, in handcuffs being escorted by Union soldiers to a Union prison. From the blueprint of that memory, he, forever after, had a Southern leaning viewpoint. Wilson was born in 1856, five years after the Civil War began. His father was a Presbyterian minister who believed in the Southern cause and the justification of slavery. Wilson naturally inherited those beliefs and fostered bigotry in his heart until his death. The Integration of Federal offices, which had been established during the Lincoln administration, was set back during Wilson's two administrations, and segregation, including laws forbidding interracial marriage, was reinstated in the Capitol. Interracial marriage remained illegal in most states until 1967, when a Supreme Court decision outlawed anti-miscegenation state laws.

Due to the disruption of life in the South during the Civil War Wilson's education was conducted by his father and former soldiers, who set up temporary schools to fill the gap left by the destruction of schools during the war. Wilson probably had dyslexia; he couldn't read until after the age of 10. His father patiently taught him to read and write, debate, and taught him how to persuade people to his beliefs. He was mostly a loner as a child with few friends except for those he made while playing baseball. A detailed book of rules about baseball was amongst his first writings. Learning shorthand at the age of 16 gave him the ability to take notes quickly on everything he studied.

As a child, Woodrow was often in the company of his parents and other adults, not unusual for a Type 1 child. Looking back as an adult, he said that he was a mama's boy. He briefly attended college at age 16 but soon dropped out. Later he attended Princeton University and graduated with a major in history. He was known as a debater, often arguing for the righteousness of the Southern cause and getting angry when people didn't agree with his ideas and positions. He was editor of the school newspaper, acted in plays, was president of the baseball association, and sang in the glee club and in a quartet. A natural leader, he envisioned himself as a senator. He even made a business card saying as much. After college, he studied law at the University of Virginia but dropped out. He practiced law for a year but realized it wasn't his calling.

Wilson worked hard at what he set out to accomplish, and dreamed of becoming well known and changing the world. His father told him he was chosen by God to make the world a better place where justice and goodness would reign. Throughout his life, he felt guided by God and justified everything he did as God's will. It's not unusual for a Type 1 to feel driven by a moral purpose.

He was serious, forthright and thorough in everything he did as most type 1s are. Many people saw him as rigid, a cold fish, a non-compromiser, a brilliant intellectual, and more focused on his ideas and ideals than reality. He became both an excellent writer and a great speaker, authoring many books.

At the age of 28, Wilson married Ellen Louise Axson, who was an accomplished painter and connoisseur of literature. She so excelled as an artist that her paintings were hung in museums and galleries. Like so many women of her age who gave up their careers, she let go of dreams of running an art school and becoming a well-known artist, to marry and have a family. She, like Woodrow, was the child of a Presbyterian minister. Woodrow pursued her as intensely as he pursued everything, writing a love letter to Ellen almost every day. "I tremble with deep excitement when I think of you." Wilson was passionate in everything he did, not unusual for a Type 1. This internal passion was exactly the opposite of his external appearance, which was often perceived as cold and distant.

Ten months after the wedding the couple had a child and, with yet another on its way, Wilson decided to get a PhD in order to support his family via a career in academia. He entered John Hopkins University where he majored in political science. His PhD thesis was published nationally and engendered glowing reviews of his philosophy on how power and politics should work together, how to wield power that affected people optimally and how the presidency should be strengthened. His dissertation led to him being hired by Princeton as a professor, the position he held for many years before becoming the University's President. He was the most sought-after professor on campus, with students often giving him a standing ovation after a lecture. Wilson is the only US President to have earned a PhD.

Being deeply affected by books of photographs that came out in the 1890s depicting the horrors of tenement housing, squalor, poverty, and inequality brought on by the kings of business, he determined to fix the situation by speaking and writing about injustice. He spoke to many crowds, political clubs and civic organizations and his articles on progressive reform were published in newspapers and magazines such as *Harper's Weekly.*

As President of Princeton for eight years, he reformed many of its policies. He got in trouble when he tried to change the fraternity system and privileged special eating clubs.

He lost his battle, because of objections made by wealthy parents who sustained the college as donors. He perceived that college was too much a playground for the entitled wealthy class and he detested the "restless, rich, empty-headed people. They and their kind are the worst people," he wrote.

At one point, while he was college president, the stress of conflict affected his health and he became almost blind in one eye when his blood pressure skyrocketed. A trip to England helped him to relax. Even on vacation he walked 14 miles a day to strengthen his blood flow. 1s can work hard just to relax! Fortunately, his sight returned but he was always prone to hypertension and piercing headaches, and his arteries were already hardening. The stress of such effort and attempting to be perfect was hard on his body.

As a Type 1 Perfectionist and Reformer he was always pushing, overworking and being resentful if people didn't see the rightness of his ideas and policies. He wasn't prone to compromise and giving in. He was convinced God was guiding him and he didn't want to disappoint.

In the Myers-Briggs I believe he was an INTJ.

"INTJs are analytical problem-solvers, eager to improve systems and processes with their innovative ideas. They have a talent for seeing possibilities for improvement, whether at work, at home, or in themselves.

Often intellectual, INTJs enjoy logical reasoning and complex problem solving. They approach life by analyzing the theory behind what they see, and are typically focused inward on their own thoughtful study of the world around them. INTJs are drawn to logical systems and are much less comfortable with the unpredictable nature of other people and their emotions. They are typically independent and selective about their relationships, preferring to associate with people who they find intellectually stimulating." www.truity.com/personality-type/INTJ

To rest and recuperate from the stress of being president of a college, he visited Bermuda. During that trip, he began an affair with a woman whom he continued to visit. She was vivacious, danced, smoked, and drank and was friends with Mark Twain. He lost his self-consciousness with her and felt happy. Her "dark side" appealed to Wilson. His wife put an end to the relationship, even though she allowed that they could be friends. Wilson himself eventually put an end to it when he saw that an attempted friendship was impossible. His wife Ellen discovered the love letters he had written to his lover and she forgave him. 1s can rebel against the pressure to live up to high standards and act out against the stricture of long term discipline.

Ellen admitted that living with Woodrow wasn't easy. He was very dependent on women, particularly her, to be upbeat for him in his challenging political life, as well as to help with his physical illnesses. This was not an easy task for Ellen as she also took care of her surviving brother and sister; one of her brothers drowned along with his two children, which set up a course of long term grief-stricken depression for Ellen. To add to her burden, Wilson's father moved in with the couple for a while before he died. Ellen also took care of their three daughters who they both deeply loved. Her life was as stressful as her husband's!

When she was a child, Ellen's father committed suicide, which was attributed to manic-depression, and her surviving brother inherited the condition. She put on a comforting front for her husband, but the stress took its toll. Woodrow wanted a lively companion, but Ellen had a hard time fulfilling that role for him. She even went out of her way to invite talkative, lively women to White House parties to engage him!

Because of his crowd-pleasing speeches and articles, Wilson was selected by the Democratic Party to run for Governor of New Jersey. He accepted. The political bosses assumed they could tell Wilson what to do when he was elected. Instead, he created four reform bills, all of which passed. The legislation he sponsored was focused on corruption, election reform, corporate regulation and the creation of worker's compensation. He denounced political bosses, bankers and corrupt corporate heads. Social subtype 1s, like Wilson, want to reform society. He almost certainly had sexual subtype traits also; expecting too much from his wife and harboring intense romantic desires.

After two years as a successful governor, he had enough popular support to be nominated to run for President. He did so with the backing of William Jennings Bryant, a prominent

Democrat who had himself run for president three times and lost. Ellen set up a private dinner with Bryant and her husband who were at that time politically at odds, encouraging them to work together, and it worked! She was fiercely loyal to Woodrow and he always listened to her advice, political or otherwise.

Wilson, who was nominated by the Democrats on the 46th ballot, ran against Taft and Teddy Roosevelt, as well as Eugene Debs, the Socialist candidate, and won. Taft and Teddy split the vote that caused the academic, intellectual, cerebral Wilson, with 42 percent of the vote, to win. The election of 1912 was one of the most exciting in history. The outspoken Roosevelt was even shot during one of his campaign speeches and yet was able to continue his speech. Taft was happy to lose the election and ran mostly to counter Roosevelt in their feud with each other. Wilson was only the second Democrat to win the Presidency from 1860 until 1932 and he won only because of the Roosevelt/Taft feud, which split the Democratic vote.

Wilson believed he'd been chosen by God to be President, even though he was reminded, by his party that it was their hard work, including a number of payoffs, that had done the job, not God! As president, Wilson toughened anti-trust laws, protected labor unions, reined in big business, created a lasting income tax which made it easier for everyday Americans to get loans, legislated for an eight-hour work day, banned child labor and tried to make government more accountable and open. He became a modern president, creating a welfare state. The Democrats became the party of reform, the position the Republicans had previously held. Even though he was initially hesitant to support women's suffrage, they finally won the right to vote during his second administration.

Though many African Americans voted for him, Wilson did nothing to improve their lot. He in fact increased segregation, bigotry and laws aimed at limiting the freedom of black people, never getting past his Southern upbringing. He did nothing to curtail the burgeoning membership in the Ku Klux Klan, which swelled after he publicly approved of an early American film called, *The Klansman* as well as *The Birth of a Nation*, which supported segregationist philosophy. There's some question as to whether Wilson supported the film, but he certainly supported its ideas and loved sharing the film with friends. He was friendly toward Jewish people and appointed Louis Brandeis to the Supreme Court; the first Jewish man to become a Supreme Court Justice.

His foreign policy was questionable. In order to protect US sailors and quell civil unrest in Veracruz he invaded Mexico. He tried to eliminate Pancho Villa, who had killed Americans across the northern Mexican border. Pancho Villa escaped, but soldiers on both sides were killed for years in the ongoing pursuit of him This might have led to another war with Mexico had World War I not erupted! The US also invaded and occupied other Latin American countries such as Haiti and the Dominican Republic.

Wilson was seen as a Yankee Imperialist despite his ideas of peace. He knew very little about foreign policy in the beginning of his presidency given that the political theory he had written about for years was almost exclusively about domestic policy. His progressive domestic ideas were obviously limited to whites. A moralist and idealist in theory, Wilson, in practice, had many contradictory ideas about freedom and the inclusion of others.

The War in Europe started in 1914, the same year his wife died of kidney disease. He was devastated by Ellen's death, as well as by the beginning of the war, which he had attempted to prevent. A severe depression ensued after these events, which included memory loss and confused thinking for a while. Ellen had been his mainstay for 30 years and he seemed helpless without her. He fought feelings of loneliness and desolation.

His pain was soon assuaged when he fell in love with Edith Bolling Galt and started seeing her secretly on chauffeured limousine drives in the country and along the Potomac. He sent love letters to her on days they spent apart. Within three months he proposed though Edith waited a while to accept. Edith was an independent woman who had her own electric car, travelled to Europe and was outspoken. The papers caught on and ran an unfortunate headline declaring, "The President has been entering Edith regularly" meaning to say of course, "The President has been entertaining Edith regularly". The second edition corrected the mistake but it's clear that the passionate Wilson didn't do well without a woman in his life.

Wilson's second election was won on the slogan, "He kept us out of war." Teddy Roosevelt severely criticized Wilson for being a coward and traitor but Wilson was determined to keep the United States out of the war. When the British ocean liner, Lusitania, with 128 US citizens aboard, was sunk by a German submarine, pressure mounted. Wilson, still reluctant to declare war, acquiesced when Germany stated it planned to go on sinking American ships and then a dispatch was discovered that uncovered Germany's attempt to ally with Mexico in order to take over part of the Southwestern United States. He then encouraged Congress to declare war, and in 1917, the measure was easily passed and Congress declared War on Germany.

Wilson talked about a "world safe for democracy" and that "doing what is right is more precious than peace." He created a moral crusade with patriotic fervor; it's typical for Type 1s to couch their ideas with a moral argument for what is right. In spite of his progressive humanitarian beliefs and freedom loving ideals, Wilson passed the Espionage and Sedition Act in 1917. It closed down papers and jailed thousands of people, including suspicious immigrants and pacifists who spoke out against the war or the reinstated draft. This law forbade the use of "disloyal, profane, scurrilous or abusive language" about the government during the war. As with John Adams and Abraham Lincoln, civil liberties were suspended. German books and music were banned and Eugene Debs, the socialist and political rival of Wilson, was sentenced to 10 years in jail. Speaking against your neighbors suspected of anti-patriotism was encouraged. It's interesting that a so-called peacemaker who ran on the platform of not entering war, outlawed basic American freedoms.

Sending over four million soldiers to Europe was the instrumental action that clinched victory for the Allies during World War 1. Wilson wanted to create a world where war, especially a world war, would never again occur, "a war to end all wars." He developed a fourteen-point plan to prevent a future war, stop the spread of imperialism and create an international organization dedicated to maintaining world peace and providing a forum for resolving international disputes called The League of Nations. The League would be charged with discouraging secret treaties that caused nations to join war efforts and also to create a way to not overly punish Germany. He feared punitive retaliation against Germany would create another war. His foresight was correct as in many ways World War II was an extension of World War 1!

His blinding headaches increased with all the stress. Golf became a remedy for him although Edith and his personal doctor easily beat him! He even played in winter and had all his golf balls painted red so they could be found in the snow.

He traveled twice to Europe, the first sitting President to do so, to gather support from world leaders for his 14 Points of Peace and the Treaty that ended World War I in Versailles. The leaders in Europe, the French and English prime ministers in particular, would at first have nothing to do with the 14 Points of Peace. They wanted to punish the Germans and limit the power of a potential League of Nations, though they did eventually vote for it. The US Senate though rejected both the Treaty of Versailles and the League of Nations!

Wilson worked tirelessly in Europe and the United States to try to gain the acceptance of his ideas for the Treaty and League but his own passionate and uncompromising character didn't help. He had a personal vendetta against the Majority Leader of the Senate, Henry Cabot Lodge, who was probably a Type 1 as well, and their mutual vitriol killed the deal. Lodge wanted to protect America's interest and refused to enter into European agreements that might entangle us in another European war. Wilson wanted to create a world order to prevent future wars. Wilson eventually won a Noble Peace Prize for his efforts.

Giving up on persuading the Senate to endorse a League of Nations, Wilson embarked on a US rail tour with the intention of appealing directly to the people. A third of the way through his 10,000-mile tour he was forced to return home by blinding headaches and a near stroke. Shortly after he got home he actually did have a stroke. The after effects of the stroke caused an enduring paralysis on one side, and Wilson was basically bedridden for the last 17 months of his Presidential term. During this time Edith made most of the Presidential decisions.

His wife Edith, a type 8, could pull it off. Her concern was that Wilson would be declared unfit to run the country and his power would be turned over to the Vice President. When a few US senators decided to visit him to determine whether Wilson was still in command of his mental faculties enough to make informed decisions and was physically well enough to serve as President, Edith and the doctor formulated a plan.

She and the doctor created the image of a well-enough Wilson, his paralyzed arm concealed by sheets in a darkened room. It worked. The stroke was successfully covered up and never known about until years later! It's the only time in American history that the president really wasn't able to be president for any length of time. Edith was in actuality the first acting female president! The 25th Amendment to the Constitution passed in 1967. It addressed the situation that occurs when a president is incapacitated while in office and a vice president takes over the Oval Office. It took a while for Congress to resolve this issue.

After two terms, Wilson retired to a Washington D.C. home where he watched old newsreels of his former days and listened to baseball games on the radio. His daughters, grandchildren and friends visited him until he died at age 67. Edith lived on until the age of 89 and she died in the 1960s.

Wilson's Type 1ness led to positive social reform but it was also the cause of great personal distress; the emotional and psychological ramifications of unrelenting stress, which came from his uncompromising nature and the resentment that arose when people didn't agree with him. He was very dependent on women to help him keep a positive outlook on life. His view of the world was idealistic; devoid of the limits and complexities of reality. Even though the Senate didn't ratify the League of Nations, his positive vision of a peaceful world paved the way for the League of Nations to eventually become The United Nations. His progressive ideas escalated the tradition of Teddy Roosevelt and set the stage for the progressive ideology and programs of Franklin Delano Roosevelt.

Warren Harding – Type 6, ESFP, "Can't say no," 1921-1923

(1865-1923) Becoming the 29th president and the 7th born in Ohio, Warren Harding won the election on a platform of "return to normalcy" after years of the progressive politics of Teddy Roosevelt and Woodrow Wilson. Harding was more conservative than his predecessors in that he supported big business, suspended many anti-trust laws and held office during a time of prosperity. At the end of his term in 1923 the unemployment rate was only two per cent. People were tired of the pain and sacrifices they made during World War I. The years of his presidency from 1921 to 1923 were relatively calm and prosperous in comparison to the previous years of war.

Born on a farm near Corsica, Ohio in 1865 at the end of the Civil War, Warren Harding was the firstborn of eight offspring born to Phoebe Dickerson and George Tryon Harding, both of whom were doctors. His mother, one of the very first female medical doctors, was predominantly a midwife and assistant to her husband, who was also a farmer, veterinarian, owner of a newspaper and a business broker.

In 1875, Harding's father bought a failing newspaper, and moved his family to Marion, Ohio. After school, ten-year-old Harding swept the floor, cleaned the printing press, and learned to set type. He also lived a typical farm life that included chores and swimming in the local pond. He learned to play the cornet as well as practically every wind instrument in the local village band. He attended a one-room schoolhouse as most kids did at that time.

Fourteen-year-old Harding attended his father's alma mater, Ohio Central College where he studied Latin, math, science, and philosophy. He excelled at writing, speaking and debating and founded the school newspaper, which he named the *Spectator*. He received a Bachelor of Science degree in 1882 at the age of 17 but didn't yet know what career path he wanted to follow.

In May of 1884, his father, Tryon, bought another newspaper that happened to be failing, called the *Marion Star*, and made his son its editor. Harding loved to cover human-interest stories as well as Republican politics. When his father was forced to sell the *Marion Star* in order to pay a debt, Harding and two friends bought the business. One partner soon lost interest and sold his share to Harding and the other lost his share to Harding in a poker game, but stayed on as a reporter. At the age of 19, Warren Harding was the editor and owner of the *Marion Star*.

The owner of the paper's competitor was the man who would one day be Harding's father-in-law. He vehemently opposed the match between Harding and his daughter, Florence, and when they married he refused to speak to her or his son-in-law for seven years! Florence pursued Warren more than he ever pursued her. Having money from her father, she was divorced and had a ten-year-old son. She was also 30, five years older than Warren himself when they married. The Marion Star thrived with Florence's input as its business manager. She supported Warren's successes, recognized his acumen and enthusiasm for politics, and encouraged him to pursue it.

Florence was Warren's opposite; defiant, a non-conformist, in charge and strong. She took over the management of her husband's business affairs. He was her ticket to success. She wanted power while Warren was more truly more interested in the pleasure that power brought. He wanted good times and popularity.

As a phobic Type 6 with a 7 wing, and a social subtype, Harding was amiable, generously spirited, felt overly loyal to his supporters, but was also insecure. His photographs are illuminating as they show him to be an anxious Type 6. He also had qualities of a 9, his likely secondary type. Warren was easygoing, friendly, cheerful and avoided all conflict. The social Type 6, particularly if extraverted, can project a quality of warmth very much like that of a Type 9. He remembered people's names and was loyal to his political party. This loyalty is a strong characteristic of a phobic Type 6; there were even occasions when he abstained from voting to avoid the discomfort he anticipated at the thought of displeasing anyone in his political party.

Type 3 is the stress type for Type 6. This means that in stressful situations a Type 6 will display successful Type 3 characteristics to present a good image while they hide and protect their underlying fear and anxiety.

Harding was an accomplished speaker, enjoyed meeting people, loved to travel and had patience and persistence. These qualities were important in his business as well as in politics and contributed greatly to his success. At one point, he sold insurance. Good looking and a natural people pleaser, he was a born politician. He abhorred being criticized, avoided taking a strong stand and disliked serious discussions. One writer said, "If I had known him as a traveling salesman, a vaudeville actor, a nightclub entertainer, or a restaurant keeper, I should have liked him very much." Being a politician, Harding did his best to hold his cards close to his chest.

He liked people, had a relaxed managerial style and got along with practically everyone. He refused to malign his political opponents and focused on his own positive traits when he campaigned. He was humble, aware of his limitations and sought approval, not trying to be top dog. His likeability got him to the presidency. Because of his inability to say no, his father said of him, "that it was good that he wasn't born a girl, as if he were, he would be in the family way all the time."

In the Myers-Briggs system, Harding was likely an ESFP. "ESFPs are vivacious entertainers who charm and engage those around them. They are spontaneous, energetic, fun loving, and take pleasure in the things around them: food, clothes, nature, animals, and especially people. ESFPs are typically warm and talkative and have a contagious enthusiasm for life. They like to be in the middle of the action and the center of attention. They have a playful, open sense of humor, and like to draw out other people and help them have a good time." www.truity.com/personality-type/ESFP

He was elected twice to be Senator of Ohio, as well as Lieutenant Governor, then later US Senator. He gave the nomination speech at the Republican Convention in 1912 and then did so again as Chairman of the National Republican Convention in 1916. Known for going along with the party bosses, he missed more vote counts than he attended to avoid disapproval, especially on controversial issues like the women's vote. He wasn't one to stir up conflict. Being attractive and in good shape, tall and a "natty" dresser, as well as an easygoing extravert, he got along with practically everyone. A smooth talker, he won votes fairly easily.

Even though he appeared calm and debonair on the outside, Harding dealt with a great deal of internal stress. Once he had a nervous breakdown and was hospitalized for several weeks to recuperate. Five other times he was secretly admitted to a Michigan sanatorium for brief rests and was able somehow to keep those hospital visits private. Often worried, anxious, frozen and unable to act, he had hypertension, diabetes and other stress related illnesses.

The secure type for 6 is 9, which is likely how he managed to keep up the appearance of being at ease. To enjoy life and also to calm his nerves, he played poker at least twice a week (once he lost all the White House china), smoked, drank whiskey, played golf, and fished. As already mentioned, the stress type of 6 is 3; project an image of success to cover up the anxiety. He probably had a 7 wing because he had many interests, a positive outward demeanor and many friends. This wing type is called The Buddy.

Alice Roosevelt Longworth, the daughter of Teddy Roosevelt, once described the scene that she encountered at one of Harding's card games, "the air was heavy with tobacco smoke, trays with bottles containing every imaginable brand of whiskey, cards and poker chips ready at hand — a general atmosphere of waistcoat unbuttoned, feet on the desk, and spittoons alongside." This was during Prohibition and the President bought lots of alcohol in the guise of "medical supplies." Obviously, prohibition didn't work too well and the boss certainly didn't set a good example! He wanted a "return to normalcy" i.e., a return to the old days and a sense of rural nostalgia.

Another way that Harding managed his stress was by engaging in two long-term affairs. One was with a neighbor, Carrie Phillips. Carrie and her husband, who had once been a close friend of Harding, were paid off with hush money and a "free" worldwide tour. Harding's affair with Carrie began while Florence, his wife, was recuperating from a kidney operation. It lasted for 15 years.

The paramour of his second affair, thirty years his junior, was given a job by Harding that was close enough so that visiting him at the White House was easy and it's said that they liked to dally in the closets! She eventually wrote a book after Harding's death, detailing their long-term affair and illegitimate child whom Harding helped support. As President, he would visit the Gayety Burlesque Theater, where he had a private box from which he could see the girls onstage without himself being seen. Reports of many dalliances exist through letters. He had a bad habit of sending letters to his lovers, which created strong evidence against him. Harding's wife seemed to know of these affairs, tolerated them and tried to cover them up.

He got away from the White House when he could to go on a weekend jaunt or go camping, which he did once with Henry Ford and Thomas Edison. Unfortunately, eight movie cameras followed them along with radio interviewers. Despite his anxiety, Harding was a popular president, as the economy was good.

Harding was not overly confident. He enjoyed the newspaper business but found politics, and especially the presidency, more stressful than he could deal with. He said to his wife after winning the presidential election, "God help me, for I need it." After serving a while, he stated, "I am not fit for the office and should never have been here. The presidency is hell." He was good at mediating conflict for others but not for making decisions that might engender conflict.

To campaign for president, instead of traveling, he gave stump speeches on his porch in Ohio and over 600,000 people attended. Newsreels and photo ops became the normal venue of providing campaign coverage to the public, in addition to hearing election results on the radio. Movie stars, singers, live music and famous entertainers such as Al Jolson, provided the excitement. The strategy worked, as Harding won by an overwhelming majority with over 60 percent of the popular vote but he was all too soon overwhelmed with the responsibility of the office. Since this was the first election that included the women's vote and Harding supported the Suffragettes, he got great support from them.

He had competent men in his cabinet, like Secretary of Commerce Herbert Hoover who had been in charge of hunger relief in Europe after the war, Charles Evan Hughes as Secretary of State, who was given the power to do pretty much what he wanted, and Andrew Mellon as Treasury Secretary, one of the wealthiest men in the world.

Also in his Cabinet were friends and old poker buddies from Ohio. They were often referred to as the Ohio Gang, and some of them were, as was later revealed, crooks. The Chief of the Veteran's Bureau took bribes and kickbacks for construction projects he secured for his friends, and sold alcohol during Prohibition. When Harding found out, he grabbed his friend by the throat and shook him in anger. He eventually ended up in jail. Harding said, "I have no trouble with my enemies. It's my damn friends that keep me walking the floor at night."

The Secretary of the Department of the Interior illegally sold the leasing rights to secret federal oil reserves in Wyoming (The Teapot Dome Scandal) as well as in California, which he used as bribes. He was the first US Cabinet member to go to jail. Other Cabinet Members were also found out to be involved in bribery. This discovery led to firings, a few suicides and generally was a bad reflection on Harding's reputation, even though there's no evidence proving that he was involved in any way. Much of the corruption that occurred during his administration was discovered after Harding died. Loyalty to his friends got in Harding's way; blind loyalty is a Phobic Type 6 quality.

Harding did accomplish some important things during his administration. He negotiated an arms reduction agreement between important naval powers, secured the participation of nine countries in an open-door trade agreement with China that guaranteed that country's safety, reduced the dollar amount of loan repayment from Germany regarding war debt, reduced federal spending and softened anti-trust laws. He was favorable to reduced business taxes and encouraged foreign trade benefits for the United States with international trade. He gave his Secretary of State, Secretary of the Treasury and Secretary of Commerce the power to do what they saw fit. Harding had a hard time saying no to his friends and apparently never fired anyone in his life!

He signed a law to present a unified federal government budget to Congress, in which receipts and outlays from federal funds and the Social Security Trust Fund were consolidated. He created the General Accounting Office to audit government expenditures, gave money to help with farm expenditures and credit, and was progressive on civil rights issues. Harding criticized the poor treatment of African Americans, even though during his administration Ku Klux Klan membership increased exponentially. Cutting taxes and reducing federal expenditures made him a popular president. He helped free many of the people that were imprisoned as a result of Woodrow Wilson's Sedition Act, including Eugene Debs, a socialist labor leader imprisoned for antiwar activism, who Harding invited to the White House.

He encouraged people to enjoy themselves and set forth a good example of how to do it! It was the beginning of the Roaring 20s. With Prohibition, alcohol seemed to flow even more freely, young people began to "date" (which was a new word), sexuality was a little looser (which he contributed to) and some of the old values were waning. People were using radios and advertising made Listerine, General Foods and Betty Crocker household words. The Harding years introduced "welfare capitalism" with benefit programs like insurance, pensions, cheap lunches in company cafeterias, and paid vacations, all introduced by business to entice workers to leave or refrain from joining labor unions.

The Hardings took a six-week railway tour of the United States that included Canada and Alaska, to connect with the public, soften the talk of scandal within his White House staff and create an air of prosperity. On his return while the train was stopped in San Francisco, he died of a heart attack. One doctor thought it was food poisoning and there was even speculation that his wife poisoned him, though there was no evidence to prove it. He was the sixth president to die in office. His wife died a year later. He has been ranked poorly as a president even though he was in power during a time of prosperity. His distaste for the office itself and the scandals surrounding his presidency overshadowed his accomplishments.

His strengths included an ability to compromise, honesty in sharing personal feelings and insecurities, loyalty to friends, his choice of some cabinet members who were very competent (and who continued into the Coolidge administration), along with his good public image, reassuring words, and smooth appearance. As mentioned, he did enact some very effective legislation. On the other hand, he craved acceptance and found it difficult to take a firm stand on issues. There were many skeletons in Harding's closet and he was self-indulgent. He was a bit too insecure, yet he had the courage to admit his fears.

Calvin Coolidge – Type 1, ISTJ, Silent Cal, 1923-1929

(1872-1933) The 30th President was Calvin Coolidge, often called "Silent Cal." He believed the best government is the one that governs least, and in that way, he was the forerunner of the philosophy of the modern conservative movement. The conservative president, Ronald Reagan, emulated him, and rehung Calvin's portrait in his office.

Coolidge believed in non-interference of government, and was a strong supporter of the interests of business, even referring to business as a "sanctuary in which to worship." Needless to say, he advocated for minimal governmental regulation. He decreased the federal budget from year to year, which would be unheard of today. President from 1923 to 1929 during the roaring 20s, his life exemplified the opposite of that era's pursuit of pleasure and excess. Instead, he believed in living a life of frugality, reserve, honesty and reason, with just a bit of enjoyment, but not to excess.

Becoming president upon Harding's unexpected death in 1923, he retained his main cabinet appointments of Mellon, Hoover and Hughes. Coolidge helped prosecute members of Harding's corrupt Ohio Gang. He sustained most of Harding's policies, but the two presidents were, in fact, quite different from one another. Whereas Harding was extraverted and prone to excess, Coolidge was a reserved and a quiet introvert. He was able to make decisions with less anxiety than Harding, vetoed bills more easily and got to the point in seconds, that is, when he actually spoke! Apparently, he would invite congressmen to the White House for breakfast, listen and never say a word but would respond later with some action in relation to what had been said at breakfast.

Despite his reticence, he was an avid hand shaker. He was the last president to greet the public at the White House and he would sometimes shake thousands of hands in one day. Calvin held more press conferences than any other president now or since and would dress up in costumes for picture taking! His silent exterior disguised a much more entertaining and engaging personality beneath. Coolidge was a Type 1 with a strong connection to his secure fun side of Type 7. Because of his silence and privacy, common characteristics of an introvert, he could easily be mistaken for a Type 5.

Calvin grew up in Vermont and some say his taciturn nature was attributable to the harsh winter climate and reserved Yankee culture. His stern father held various political positions in his hometown. These included: justice of the peace, tax collector, constable, Vermont House Representative, and state senator. His father was silent, thrifty, prosperous and honest and modeled these exemplary behaviors for his son.

In addition to his political involvement Calvin's father supported the family by farming and running the general store. As a boy Calvin would do farm chores and tend the store.

He loved working on the farm and learning from his father. Their relationship was close and he sought advice from his father throughout his life. He was devastated at the age of 12 when his sweet, sensitive mom passed away and, some years later, he lost his sister as well. His father remarried and Calvin grew close to his stepmother. As an adult he often returned home to visit and work.

The only president to be born on July 4th, he was scared and awkward around newcomers as a boy. He loved to join in when other farm boys played pranks but was basically reliable and trustworthy and did his chores early in the morning. Coolidge attended local schools until he moved to Massachusetts to study at Amherst College. At school he blossomed as a public speaker known for his dry wit and humor. He joined a fraternity as a senior, something he wanted earlier but had been denied; it took time for others to get to know him and see his strengths. Self-promotion went against the grain. A loyal alumnus throughout his life, Coolidge made friends at Amherst and maintained lifelong connections with those who supported his political career.

Encouraged by his father to stay in the Northampton area after college, Coolidge rose in rank politically, becoming a lawyer, Northampton City Councilor, county clerk, local Republican leader, Northampton Mayor, head of the state senate, lieutenant governor and then Governor of Massachusetts. As governor, he broke a policeman's strike in Boston that set his reputation as a conservative. He said "there is no right to strike against the public safety by anyone, anywhere, anytime." In his entire political life, he only lost one election – when he ran for a seat on the school board.

As Governor of Massachusetts, Coolidge pursued a fairly progressive agenda for the times. He supported a cost-of-living pay increase for public employees, limiting the workweek for women and children to 48 hours, and placing limits on outdoor advertising - measures welcomed by reformers in both parties. He also restructured and consolidated departments in the Commonwealth's government, which supported the progressive ideal of efficiency along with the conservative idea of small government.

Coolidge was a Type 1 with a 9 wing - tidy, moral, consistent, principled and philosophical. Lean, thin-lipped with his mouth turned down at the corners, he wasn't a backslapping kind of guy. He smiled occasionally but you needed your camera ready if you wanted to remember the image since it didn't happen very often. Once, a woman sitting next to him at dinner said she had placed a bet with a friend that she could make him say more than two words and he said, "You lose." He was the first president to speak in front of a moving camera and he read from a script.

His ISTJ personality in the Myers-Briggs fit his 1ness. "ISTJs have a serious, conservative air about them. They want to know and follow the rules of the game, and typically seek out predictable surroundings where they understand their role. You may find the ISTJ doing something useful even in social situations (for instance, organizing coats and hats at a party) as they're often more comfortable taking charge of a task than they are chatting up strangers. When given something to do, they are highly dependable, and follow it through to the end." www.truity.com/personality-type/ISTJ

His daily routine didn't vary and he could always clearly tell you what he believed in. His speeches were not flowery, but to the point and short. He also had a prankish side, for instance, buzzing for his bodyguards and then hiding under the White House desk where they couldn't find him. Posing for pictures wearing a cowboy outfit or an Indian headdress, he had a Type 7 fun aspect to balance his seriousness and silence.

Resting took precedence and he took a long nap after lunch and went to bed fairly early, even on nights when he hosted state dinners. After he took the oath of office to be president, given by his father in the middle of the night at his Vermont childhood house, he immediately went back to sleep. He knew how to relax, as he sat on the White House porch in his rocking chair smoking a cigar after dinner. Even though he took time to rest, most people say he worked hard.

He could be surly with a bad temper and even Coolidge himself said he was hard to get along with. Believing in privacy, he felt one got into less trouble by keeping silent. He stated, "I don't get into trouble for what I don't say." As was mentioned earlier, it's easy to think he might be a type 5 because of his silence, but rightness and structure were more important than learning was to him, which would be the hallmark characteristic of a Type 5. He liked a clearly defined life that was organized and simple.

As a 1, his beliefs were strong and he was not prone to changing them. Being an introvert, he planned what he wanted to say. Although he held more press conferences than prior presidents, he would write out the questions for the reporters to ask beforehand and was taciturn in his responses.

He ran on a campaign slogan in 1924 of "Keep Cool with Coolidge." It was a difficult time to run again as he and his wife suffered the tragic loss of one of their sons who died of blood poisoning. He had acquired a blister on his foot while playing tennis on the White House court. Their other son grew up to become a railroad executive and donated the buildings that became the President Coolidge Historic Site in Plymouth, Vermont.

A fairly popular president, people liked Coolidge's old-time values and trusted them; perhaps too much, as the Great Depression happened soon after his term ended, probably due in part to his decisions. People bought stocks on a small margin of the actual cost and his laissez faire support of business, with little or no regulation, might have contributed to the crash. He didn't purchase stocks himself and thought it was foolish to buy on margin but he didn't create legislation to prevent it. Very few people, even economists, predicted what was to happen, though Herbert Hoover, his Commerce chief, foresaw the possibility of a crash.

Coolidge was credited for slashing the budget, most people paid low or no taxes, businesses were doing well and people were purchasing cars, homes and new electric appliances. Credit was easy to get. Jazz, singing stars and flappers were the rage, speakeasies were everywhere and unemployment was low. People liked the security of an unflappable president.

His view of his office was to avoid harm rather than support new legislation and to enforce the law rather than change it. Cabinet members were in charge of their departments and would only be talked to if something went wrong. H. L. Mencken describes his presidential style, "Coolidge's ideal day would be the one in which nothing happens." Since the economy was going well, few people criticized the president. Coolidge summarized his term as "minimum government regulations, tax cuts, balanced budgets, low interest rates and cheap foreign policy."

Department budgets were constantly diminished. Unfortunately, there were no government programs to help those in need. Small farms often failed because large agribusiness success caused overproduction of food, bringing down prices. The poor, racial minorities and the elderly remained in need of assistance. Foreign countries in debt couldn't buy our products. Low interest rates that increased speculation such as that of the Florida land boom, buying stocks on margins as low as 10 percent and a lack of government intervention, set up the dynamics that contributed to the market crash of 1929. In foreign policy, Coolidge negotiated when there were disagreements rather than sending troops to invade other countries and there was only one intervention in Latin America.

Coolidge spoke out against racial prejudice and the many lynchings of black men as well as some women, mostly in the South. But he was silent on the issue of the Ku Klux Klan whose membership increased to five million people during his tenure! There was even a major march of thousands of Ku Klux Klan members wearing robes walking down Pennsylvania Avenue in Washington, D.C. White Supremacy, decreasing quotas for immigration and prejudice in general seemed to be on the rise. Coolidge signed an Indian Citizens Act in 1924 that gave American citizenship to all American Indians while retaining some support for tribal rites and rituals, but prejudice and restrictions continued.

Even though he could have easily won a campaign for reelection, Coolidge retired to Northampton, Massachusetts, wrote books and articles and took it easy. He continued to work in the insurance industry and was a trustee for the National Geographic Society. In fact, as he admitted in his autobiography, he was never one who loved power or fame and was ready to be "relieved of the pretensions and delusions of public life." 1s are more focused on what's right than on they are on pretensions.

As a child, Coolidge almost died of tuberculosis. It is possible that he realized his health was not in prime shape, and decided to leave Washington, as he died at age 60 in 1933. After the presidency was over, he said "I'm no longer for these times."

His wife Grace lived on until the age of 78 in Northampton. She was the first First Lady to graduate from a coed college, was an educator for the deaf and was close friends with Helen Keller. Grace was warm, at ease, friendly, graceful as her name implies and very popular; a real balance to Cal's cool demeanor. She and her husband's first "meeting" was unusual. Watering her garden, she noticed Coolidge through the open window of a nearby house, in his long underwear, shaving and wearing a top hat. She burst out laughing at the sight and he happened to notice her! He definitely had a fun and playful side.

A visit to his hometown in the hills surrounding Plymouth, Vermont, is well worth it. Coolidge returned to his home to visit throughout his lifetime. His birthplace, country store, church, farm and barns, set in a bucolic environment, give a strong picture of the foundation of his steady, honest and hard-working life.

Herbert Hoover – Type 5, INTJ, Food Relief, Administrator, Depression-Era President, 1929-1933

(1874-1964) President number 31 was Herbert Hoover, a confident, opinionated, determined, action-oriented, very smart man who was quiet and reserved; he hated to be criticized. He was a multimillionaire by the age of 40, having made his fortune in the mining industry. His was a rags-to-riches story, typical of Type 5s who have a secondary Type 8, Hoover's growth type. He possessed the success drive of a Type 3, as do 8s. In many ways, Hoover appears to actually be an 8; but, upon closer inspection, it's clear that his primary drive was toward learning rather than power, which identifies him as a 5. He also had a tendency to be detached, which solidifies the argument that he was a true Type 5. As a 5, his wing was 6, skeptical, questioning and research-oriented. He had the core characteristics of Type 5; a strong desire for privacy, solitude and independence.

Born in Iowa, his father was a blacksmith who sold farm equipment and his mother was a teacher and women's advocate. He was the first president born west of the Mississippi River. Unfortunately orphaned by the age of nine, Hoover was raised by his aunt and uncle in Oregon. He made money as a child weeding vegetables, working on farms killing potato bugs, delivering papers, and later managing a laundry. Growing up in the Quaker religion, he was responsive to humanitarian concerns. This became a focal point of his life, and is what he is best remembered for.

Determined to make something of his life, he was in the first graduating class at Stanford University, where he majored in geology, and where he met the only female geology major; she later became his wife. Her name was Lou Henry and she eventually became fluent in five languages. While at Stanford, Hoover organized a group called the Barbarians as a way to include those rejected by the snobbish fraternity men. This rendered him so popular that he was elected as student treasurer on campus, the first non-fraternity man to be elected to an office at Stanford.

Hoover was fascinated by and wanted to learn about everything. He was especially interested in the social sciences and wanted to solve the glaring problems of society. Other interests of his were in the fields of economics, engineering and metallurgy. He was bold and innovative in trying new approaches, technologies and methods of problem solving. What was important to him was becoming competent, mastering skills and gaining expertise in whatever he pursued. He disliked being around inefficient people and hated incompetence. These traits are typical of Type 5s, and combined with his type 8 traits, he had no trouble letting people know when they failed to meet his standards.

Hoover was an organizational genius and served as the head of many public agencies and international relief efforts. He was skillful, energetic, brilliant; a strategic thinker who could plan very complex undertakings. Hoover's presentation was austere, with little sense of humor or playfulness. He disliked being in crowds or public speaking and hated small talk, as is true of most 5s. He was a natural leader and hated wasting time. He preferred being left alone to plan or administer a program. Although he was showered with public acclaim it was far less important to him than his desire to work. His speeches were considered dry, dreary and academic.

Hoover loved to strategize and study. When he socialized, his objective was always to learn something new or meet interesting people. "An evening's guests might count an eminent statesman or financier, but it was likely to include a prospector fresh from the Klondike, a writer or painter, a railroad man from India or a Quaker acquaintance from back home. Always there was lively talk and the friction of clashing views," from the book, *Herbert Hoover*.

Despite his leadership qualities, he was shy, and as mentioned, didn't like public speaking, crowds, social manners or niceties. Being rational and matter-of-fact, he sought to solve problems by the use of reason. He recognized the value of self-restraint, calm and patience and had no tolerance for lying, greed or incompetence.

As a Type 5, he was an intellectual one-man think tank, disliked being disturbed, and wanted to solve problems. An INTJ in the Myers-Briggs correlates well with Type 5.

"It's lonely at the top, and being one of the rarest and most strategically capable personality types, INTJs know this all too well. INTJs form just two percent of the population, and women of this personality type are especially rare, forming just 0.8% of the population – it is often a challenge for them to find like-minded individuals who are able to keep up with their relentless intellectualism and chess-like maneuvering. People with the INTJ personality type are imaginative yet decisive, ambitious yet private; curious, but they do not squander their energy." www.16personalities.com/intj-personality

After college, he was hired as a mining engineer by a British mining company and travelled internationally to evaluate mines for purchase. He administered, ran and reformed mines in Australia, Russia, China and many other countries. Until age 40 he travelled around the world, owned a silver mine in Burma, and collected royalties from a major textbook he wrote on mining engineering. From his mining operations and his book, he had learned how to make money. He thought that a person wasn't worth much if he didn't make a million by age 40. Similarly, Bill Gates and Howard Hughes, both 5s, are examples of other 5s with the ability to make money; both also gifted with a genius level mentality.

His wife partnered with him in the mining industry and even accompanied him to China during the Boxer Rebellion, where they both risked their lives to protect the people who worked for them. Their home was riddled with bullets, and Lou's bike tire was shot out while she was riding! During the Boxer Rebellion, Hoover engineered and built earthen dams around the mine he worked as protection from rebels.

At the outbreak of World War 1, Hoover helped 120,000 Americans who were stranded in Europe return to the United States. During the war he administered the food relief program for Belgium, which had been overrun by Germany. He was the National Food Administrator during WW1, helping US citizens ration food so the government could send more to the soldiers. After the war, he was appointed head of European relief and rehabilitation, saving thousands of lives. Praised worldwide, he was considered a savior, even though the British prime minister said of Hoover, "Tact is not one of his many great qualities." He was nominated for the Nobel Peace Prize five times for his humanitarian efforts.

An excellent administrator, Hoover was chosen to be Secretary of Commerce under both Presidents Harding and Coolidge. One of his outstanding achievements was his administration of relief during the Mississippi Flood of 1927 in which 500,000 people were rendered homeless. He was highly praised by both presidents and the American public. He proved he was at his best when quick and decisive action was necessary.

Being nominated for president was a natural next step, and there was little opposition. He had never run for public office, as all of his political positions had been appointments. Used to success and praise, most everything he attempted turned to gold. He also promoted and created laws for the aviation industry, public health for children and child welfare in general, the use of radio airwaves, civil liberties and public education.

Hoover was hardworking, often putting in 14 - 18-hour days, self-reliant, blunt, direct and impatient. He's unusual for a 5, but I've seen many 5s who are very assertive like 8s (I call them 5/8s). He tended to be impersonal, at times rude, and expected a lot from others.

Hoover was very efficient, focused on long-range planning as well as details of immediate concern and was not very open to feedback. He trusted his skills and thought government should run like an efficient business. His speeches were considered dull and were read mostly word for word, seldom while looking up. Being a Type 5, ideas were more important than people skills.

He famously said while campaigning, "We in America today are nearer to the final triumph over poverty than ever before in the history of any land," but a year later the stock market crash of 1929 struck, proving him wrong! The "chicken in every pot and two cars in every garage," campaign slogan he ran on, turned out to be false. This was the first time in his life he experienced anything close to failure and his health declined. He became highly distressed and withdrawn, even going so far as saying that no one was starving in the country, which was anything but true.

Like most presidents before him, Hoover didn't believe government should interfere in helping the poor or in giving direct financial relief to farmers and people in general. His core beliefs were about rugged individualism and hard work, which had worked for him and many other Americans. Hoover's programs supported business and balancing the budget, hoping that money would trickle down to the poor.

In contrast to the poor, Hoover and his wife ate lavishly, and a famous movie clip was shown in theaters of Hoover feeding his dog a T-bone steak at the White House. Most of his meals were seven-course affairs, which didn't go over too well with the public, many of whom were starving. Unemployment reached 25 percent and many people lived in shantytowns and tent cities. There was a proliferation of breadlines, soup kitchens and people on the streets holding signs begging for work.

Hoover created public-work projects during the Depression, and he encouraged businesses not to fire anyone. He met with business leaders frequently and passed new banking legislation making it easier for people to get loans, but nothing seemed to work. He believed that volunteerism, and relief organizations like the Red Cross should be able to fix the problems, but this only helped in limited ways.

Thinking the economy and the market would correct itself in time, his hair turned white while waiting for that day, and he lost weight and became melancholy. He had been successful in most endeavors he had undertaken in life, and this was the first time his strategies didn't seem to work. He was blamed for the economic debacle, even though like many presidents, he happened to be in the wrong place at the wrong time. Historians today believe he did a lot to forestall the crash from being even worse. He thought there should be a mental solution to everything, but people needed food more than they needed ideas. He was bitter about his defeat to Franklin Roosevelt who took more action.

A high-tariff law was passed which turned out to be unhelpful; European nations couldn't afford US made products, thus limiting international trade. The Depression spread worldwide and while most suffered, some greedy bankers and brokers walked away with large fortunes. Hoover tried to preach optimism, but his personality, even in good times, was rather stiff and dour; his encouragement didn't seem believable. People got tired of his promises and good intentions.

Things escalated dramatically when 20,000 World War I vets marched on Washington from all over the country to demand a bonus they had been promised that wasn't due to be paid out for another twelve years. Congress refused the request. Many marchers returned home with a free transportation ticket given to them by Congress, but some remained in their Washington D.C. tent city with their families. The tent city was eventually burned out. Some people were shot and killed by an overly aggressive General Douglas McArthur, whose federal troops attacked men and even children with bayonets. No inhabitants of the tent city fired any shots. Hoover was blamed for the violence and then roundly voted out of office at the end of his term.

His wife Lou mediated some of Hoover's difficult qualities. She was adventuresome, and as a child, went on many camping and hunting expeditions, rode horses and tinkered with taxidermy. She loved rock climbing and archery, played baseball and was skilled at basketball. An expert in metallurgy like Hoover, she was an equal partner admired by her husband. She gave public addresses over the radio, allowed pregnant women to be in receiving lines at the White House, a first, and she and her husband spoke Chinese to each other when they wanted a private conversation!

They had two sons, one a mining engineer who became Undersecretary of State from 1954 to 1956 under Eisenhower, and the other a banker who ran the Hoover Institute, a public policy think tank at Stanford University. Both Hoover and his wife were active and goal directed. Hoover had proposed to Lou by telegram when he was working in China; she accepted and moved there to work with him. As First Lady, she became President of the Girl Scouts worldwide and helped in many humanitarian causes; equal in many ways to Eleanor Roosevelt.

Despite his reputation for being hard working, rather cold and aloof Hoover was able to warm up and relax when he was on vacation. He and Lou enjoyed travelling to Florida and the Caribbean, and they had a vacation home in the Blue Ridge Mountains of Virginia.

Fishing was his favorite hobby and, always the engineer he carried rocks and built dams in the river to increase the odds of catching fish.

In later life, he was appointed by President Truman to head food-relief programs during and after World War II in Europe, and later was appointed by President Eisenhower to help reorganize the US Executive Branch Departments. His legacy is that of a humanitarian administrator of food relief around the world. He outlived his wife by 20 years, the reverse of most presidents.

Some interesting facts about Hoover: He was the first president to appear on television, as well as the first one to have a phone placed directly on his desk. He received 87 honorary degrees, had many schools, streets, two asteroids and a dam named after him. He founded The American Child Health Organization to research children's health issues and was the first Quaker President. Because of his Quaker principles he refused to repeat the oath of office, but did a presidential affirmation in its place. As President, he had the staff every morning play Hoover ball, a combination of volleyball and tennis played with a four-pound volleyball tossed over a net!

He was a leader who was dispassionate but brilliant, focused on reason, new ideas, restraint, independence, hard work, continual learning, and a strong ability to create organization, good planning and humanitarianism.

Franklin Delano Roosevelt, Type 7, ESTP, Social Security and the New Deal, Longest Presidency, 1933-1945

(1882-1945) FDR, Franklin Delano Roosevelt was president number 32, the only president to have held more than two terms. Born into wealth, he was particularly aware of the poor; his wife Eleanor was his personal educator about social justice and welfare. His own disability gave him empathy for those who suffered. Becoming president during The Depression of the 1930s, he created the greatest social legislation in American history. Social Security helped the old, the unemployed, the poor and the sick. He believed that it was the government's responsibility, as well as that of individuals, to insure freedom for all citizens.

Guarantees were created to make life safer, particularly during a time of insecurity. His optimism and smiling face, despite his own personal challenges, kept the nation going.

Being a positive Type 7 with an 8 wing personality, allowed people to trust in his good intentions. Admitting that many of his programs were experiments, he had the courage to act, in order to create social change that was backed by great ideas and a clear vision of what the United States could be. "It's common sense to take a method and try it. If it fails, try something else."

7s correlate well with ESTP, a common type for presidents.

"The first thing you notice about the ESTP is likely to be their energy. They're often chatting, joking, and flirting with friends and strangers alike. They enjoy engaging playfully with others and amusing everyone around them with their irreverent sense of humor. They tend to keep people on their toes, never quite knowing what the ESTP will poke fun at next. ESTPs are unabashedly gregarious with people, but their interest in individuals may not last long; they are more likely to work a room, having a laugh with everyone, than they are to engage in depth with any one person." www.truity.com/personality-type/ESTP

An only child of an overprotective mother, Roosevelt was personally tutored and had the luxury of European travel with his parents. In addition, he was showered with attention from his nanny and the Roosevelt family network. He lived in a world of privilege and self-importance. Teddy Roosevelt was Franklin's cousin and his family name was very well known, having endured for generations. Life became challenging when at the age of 14 he entered Groton, a private boy's school in Massachusetts, where athletics was a cultural staple. Sporting activities were not one of his strengths so Franklin didn't fit in at his new school. The headmaster, understanding the dilemma, encouraged him to consider the idea of public service, which had more appeal for him and helped set a new course for his endeavors.

Roosevelt attended Harvard and was only an average student, but enjoyed fraternity life and being editor of the school's newspaper. He became engaged to his fifth cousin Eleanor while in college. He enrolled in Columbia Law School, didn't finish and yet passed the New York bar and became a corporate lawyer. He soon realized however that law was not his calling, and politics was a better fit.

Franklin won a state senate seat, then was appointed Assistant Secretary of the Navy and lost bids for the US Senate and Vice President. Learning the ins and outs of the political landscape, he was gaining the skills and expertise necessary to win national recognition. He imitated his fifth cousin Teddy Roosevelt in many ways – being the Assistant Secretary of the Navy, wearing the same type glasses, going on hunting trips and publicizing them, and being outspoken. He was happy to follow the blueprint of TR.

Despite the agony of realizing he had polio at age 39, with the encouragement of Eleanor and others, he was able to overcome his initial major depression and maintain a positive outlook even though he would never walk again. Learning to walk on iron crutches, with years of physical therapy, he was able to face his pain and limitations. His is an example of the highest level of a Type 7, the Optimist.

After a stint as New York governor, Roosevelt saw an opportunity to run for President. He saw that his commitment to government intervention in the economy provided a way to win the hearts of the people. His upbeat, charming personality and promises of relief, recovery and reform were the ticket to win the presidency from Herbert Hoover, who was almost universally blamed for the Depression. Roosevelt faced the greatest American crisis since the Civil War in having to deal with the Depression.

His "New Deal" created many new programs to regulate banks, support farm prices, employ young men, regulate wages and prices, restore public faith in banks, regulate the stock market, subsidize mortgages and provide relief to the unemployed. This countered the American philosophy of individualism, and many criticized Roosevelt as being a socialist and communist. The Supreme Court ruled that several of the New Deal programs were unconstitutional. Even though Roosevelt didn't solve everything, unemployment decreased and the economy improved.

"We have nothing to fear but fear itself" was the message of his weekly fireside radio chats. Newsreels about Roosevelt were constant, and it was the beginning of the march toward the age of presidential media. He gave people hope, and his forceful, engaging personality inspired trust in a brighter future for many. Newness, hope and positive actions are the cornerstone for type 7s.

He was a clever politician; he could, on one hand, support Americans' isolationism at the start of WWII, but in his planning, build an "arsenal for democracy," realizing it was unlikely he could keep the United States out of war. There's some evidence that Roosevelt knew in advance of the likelihood that Japan would bomb Pearl Harbor and allowed it by not preparing the fleet in Hawaii, as an excuse to ensure we would go to war. Roosevelt then introduced the Four Freedoms including freedom of speech, freedom of worship, freedom from fear and freedom from want. Freedom is a key word for 7s. A master of words and highly repeatable phrases, his positive message rang in everyone's ears.

Roosevelt was smiling, gregarious, outgoing, robust, encouraging, and warm hearted; all Type 7 traits. The former presidents Coolidge and Hoover didn't come close to his charisma, passion and personal engagement. Hoover, his predecessor, had confidence but was intellectual and dour, and Coolidge was avoidant. The country needed Roosevelt to bring them out of the doldrums. His personality was so strong it overcame any public concern about his disability.

Many people knew of his paraplegia, but publicity about him emphasized his courage in overcoming it. A Time magazine and New Yorker article in 1934 showed pictures of his wheelchair and described his medical condition, but focused on his strength and ability to get around. Other than that, photos almost always left out Roosevelt's wheelchair, and secret service agents would rip out people's film if they took pictures of him in sitting in it. Mostly his disability was disguised or downplayed, but it was obvious to many that he needed help and had braces. His sons often walked with him, propping up his arms.

Roosevelt was witty and he effectively used anecdotes and metaphors, as his gift of language was remarkable. This is typical for 7s. He held many press conferences and had a good relationship with the press, as well as being a master at utilizing the radio to reach the public. His ability to emphasize, and then pause to show strength, conviction and emotion was masterful. He spoke on the radio often and his speeches were rebroadcast so everyone could hear them; his voice communicated a message of comfort and reassurance. The slogans he used fed the public: "Together we cannot fail," "Happy days are here again," "I have a New Deal for the American people."

At least a dozen speechwriters were hired throughout his term as president to polish his speeches. Archibald MacLeish, poet and playwright, as well as Pulitzer Prize winner Robert E. Sherwood, were hired to write for him. As many as twelve drafts of important speeches would be written and then continually revised while the writers stayed up half the night fueled by coffee, Coke, bourbon, and sandwiches. Roosevelt was actively involved, and he wrote most of the best lines.

Roosevelt and his speechwriters used the simplest language that common people would understand, referring to himself as "I" and the American People as "you." There was often a common enemy: "The few men who might thwart our great common purpose by seeking selfish advantage," "The professional economist who insists that things must run their course and that human agencies can have no influence on economic ills," "The chiselers in every walk of life, and those in industry who are guilty of unfair practices," "The isolationists, the cowards, the hoarders, the pessimists." He certainly believed that honesty, clarifying the enemy and positive thinking would get people out of the mood of poverty and greed of others. Roosevelt had the ability to ad-lib during his speeches; he would add or subtract words and phrases that seemed more likely to engage his audience. Quoted and paraphrased from the book, *The Fireside Chats*, edited by Russell D. Buhite and David W. Levy.

His wife Eleanor served the longest reign as First Lady, and set standards that were almost impossible to uphold. She pioneered and modeled a new level of activism. Growing up shy, she took speech lessons and hired coaches during the White House years to become a proficient public speaker. The Roosevelt partnership was mainly a political one; after five children and Franklin's long-term affair with his secretary, the romance of their early relationship had dwindled.

Eleanor's growing independence, her increased leadership managing her disabled husband, and her risk taking to protect everyone's welfare - particularly labor, children, families and African Americans, set the stage for everyone in the Roosevelt's sphere to feel more protected. "The future is literally in our hands to mold as we like. But we cannot wait until tomorrow. Tomorrow is now," she said.

She held 348 press conferences and had her own radio show and newspaper column. Her support continued when she was appointed by Harry S. Truman and John F. Kennedy to represent the United States as part of the US delegation to the United Nations, and she helped draft the Universal Declaration of Human Rights. She was gracious, though hurt, when her husband died in Warm Springs, Georgia where he was getting treatments and soaking and swimming in mineral baths with Lucie Mercer, who he was still seeing as a romantic partner.

Roosevelt's policies set the stage for the modern presidency and certainly have been a major model for the Democratic Party. Roosevelt was a man of courage, action, optimism and spunk. He didn't mind experimenting to figure out what would work. He moved the country toward more equality, security and trust in the government than it had known before. He was a shining example of a Type 7 who could face pain and difficulty and still be positive.

His positive childhood at Hyde Park was the anchor that supported him throughout his life. When asked how he managed going to bed at night knowing he would never walk again, he said, "I coast down the hill knowing every curve in the snow on my sled and I walk slowly uphill," just as he did in his childhood. He was a man of deep determination that carried him through the vulnerability of needing to be carried upstairs and into cars, saw him through the struggles of managing the Depression and World War II and bolstered him to face the criticism of many, even though he did have a great deal of popular support. He was the king of progressive politics.

Harry S. Truman, Type 1, ISTJ, The Buck Stops Here, 1945-53

(1884-1972) Harry S. Truman was president number 33. He was born in Missouri, and as a child he spent his time reading history books and literature, playing the piano and dreaming of becoming a concert pianist, as well as a soldier. Having poor eyesight made a West Point commission impossible, and his family's financial condition prevented him from attending college.

For the most part Harry worked on the family farm, which he detested, until he was 30. After one semester at a business college and having taken some law courses, he held jobs as a bank clerk, worked in a mailroom and in a construction company, working hard at everything he did. Truman was a lifelong learner and avid reader.

Having met in Sunday school when his future wife Bess was five and he was six, they reconnected in their teens and began writing letters to each other. After one proposal rejection, Bess consented to marry him when he was 35, the longest courtship of any president! Five years later their only child Mary Margaret was born.

At the age of 30, after his father's death, Harry tried to earn a living as owner of a small mining company and oil business, but it didn't work out. World War 1 had erupted during that time and his National Guard unit was deployed to France. He became a top-notch soldier and was promoted to the rank of captain; leading a successful artillery unit. In an important event, he ordered his men back as they started to run from the battle and was able to enforce his command as they stood their ground. Being an officer built his self-confidence and he was deeply respected by his men.

Returning home from the war, Truman and an Army buddy opened a men's haberdashery selling socks, underwear, ties and accessories. After two years they were operating at a loss, due in part to an economic downturn in 1920. He was asked by the Democratic Party to run for a county judgeship, which he won, then lost another term, then won again becoming presiding judge for eight years during the Depression. As judge, he was also the county commissioner, overseeing road and other construction projects and was in charge of county finances. Truman was a Type 1, which is often a good fit for a judge. He was known for honesty, efficiency and integrity.

Truman was elected to the US Senate by the same political machine that got him the judgeship. As a senator he headed the Truman committee, a watchdog for defense spending, and worked on legislation in the transportation and airline industry, which won him a second term in the Senate. He supported the buildup of armaments before World War II as well as the selective service when the war started. "We are facing a bunch of thugs, and the only theory a thug understands is a gun and a bayonet." 1s often like to keep it black and white.

He was chosen as the vice-presidential candidate in Roosevelt's 4th term. Because of his clean record he secured the approval of Southern Democrats. Little did he know that, after only 82 days in office Roosevelt would die, and that he would inherit the most powerful office in the world. Unfortunately, Roosevelt wasn't close to Truman and neglected to fill him in on decisions, such as the Manhattan Project to build an atomic bomb. Truman had to make the important decision to drop atomic bombs on Japan, which ended the war and set the stage for the modern atomic era. He never regretted his decision, even though many important people were against the atomic bomb being dropped, including Eisenhower, the Allied Commander.

Truman perpetuated Roosevelt's New Deal agenda and struggled with the relationship with Russia during and after the war. That difficult relationship turned into the Cold War. He took steps to get support from his Democratic base of blacks, urban dwellers and unions, narrowly winning the 1948 election to remain in office. The Republican-controlled Congress fought him. Truman embarked on a railroad tour campaigning across the country; this made the difference when he severely criticized Congress and his opponent Dewey, who had been expected to win. Dewey mistakenly assumed he would win without much work. Newspapers headlined Dewey as winning before the electoral votes were in.

Truman made inroads with civil rights, particularly when he integrated the military in 1948, which set the stage for the civil rights legislation of the 60s. He protected New Deal gains and was president during the beginning of a recovering economy that lasted for 20 years. It was a time during which Americans reverted to some of the financial gains of the 1920s with increased home buying and purchasing of cars, gadgets and new technologies. He oversaw the end of WW II, the start of the United Nations, the Nuremburg Trials, the Cold War, the creation of NATO, the Korean War and the building of the hydrogen bomb.

After World War II, Truman was committed to and was highly praised for his pivotal role in the economic reconstruction of Europe and culturally with the Marshall Plan, strengthening US ties to Europe, and saving thousands of lives. He was considered a strong, honest leader even though his ratings went down when the Korean War began in 1950. Deciding not to run for another term, he retired to his home in Independence, Missouri and led a relatively quiet life. Harry Truman died at the age of 88. He was considered the guy next door, a man you could trust.

According to historian and writer David McCullough, he had many of the traits of his ancestors who were of Scotch-Irish descent, "he could be narrow, clannish, short-tempered, and stubborn to a fault. But he could also be intensely loyal and courageous and deeply patriotic. He was one of us, Americans said, just as they also said, "To err is Truman." He was, as his pal Harry Vaughan once said, "one tough son-of-a-bitch of a man...and that," said Vaughan, "was part of the secret of understanding him." He could take it, as he had been through so much. There's an old line, "Courage is having done it before."

In the Democratic Convention of 1948, according to David McCullough, "Truman, in a white linen suit, walked out into the floodlights and did just what he did in the Vosges Mountains when he told his soldiers not to run. He gave them hell. He told them, in effect, to soldier up -- and that they were going to win. It was astounding. He brought the whole hall to its feet. He brought them up cheering. Old-hand reporters, even the most diehard liberals who had so little hope for him, agreed it was one of the greatest moments they had ever witnessed in American politics."

McCullough continues, "Now he did make mistakes. He was not without flaw. He could be intemperate, profane, touchy, too quick with simplistic answers. In private conversation, he could use racial and religious slurs, old habits of the mouth. In many ways, his part of Missouri was more like the Old South than the Middle West.... Yet here is the man who initiated the first civil rights message ever and ordered the armed services desegregated.... When friends and advisers warned him that he was certain to lose the election in 1948 if he persisted with his civil rights program, he said if he lost for that, it would be a good cause. Principle mattered more than his own political hide. His courage was the courage of his convictions." Everything described about him is about the best traits of 1 – honesty, strength, determination, responsibility, hard work and doing what's right.

According to McCullough, "No president ever campaigned so hard or so far. Truman was sixty-four years old. Younger men who were with him through it all would describe the time on the train as one of the worst ordeals of their lives. The roadbed was rough and Truman would get the train up to 80 miles an hour at night. The food was awful, the work unrelenting. One of them told me, "It's one thing to work that hard and to stay the course when you think you're going to win, but it's quite another thing when you know you're going to lose. The only reason they were there, they all said, was Harry Truman." The poll-takers, the political reporters, the pundits, all the sundry prognosticators, and professional politicians--it didn't matter what they said, what they thought. Only the people decide, Truman was reminding the country. "Here I am, here's what I stand for--here's what I'm going to do if you keep me in the job. You decide."

“To really understand Truman,” wrote his daughter, “you must grasp the importance of humility.” He didn’t brag about himself or claim credit in public. It was against his principles. “But,” Margaret Truman said, “the practice of humility never meant that dad downgraded his worth, his accomplishments, in his own mind.” He was confident about his judgments and acted boldly and decisively. Once he made a decision he forgot about it and moved on. He was earnest, incorruptible and blunt. He could blow off steam in public. He was not moody or prone to depression.” According to President Truman, “If you can’t stand the heat, get out of the kitchen.” “The buck stops here.” He used simple, straightforward sentences in his speeches. He had some type 8 in him (likely 8 was his secondary type), but he was definitely a type 1. Many 1s are ISTJs though we have had a number of ISTJ, type 3s as president, such as Washington and Monroe.

“ISTJs are quiet, serious, earn success by thoroughness and dependability. Practical, matter-of-fact, realistic, and responsible. Decide logically what should be done and work toward it steadily, regardless of distractions. Take pleasure in making everything orderly and organized - their work, their home, their life. Value traditions and loyalty.” www.myersbriggs.org/my-mbti-personality-type/mbti-basics/the-16-mbti-types.htm

Truman could make unpopular decisions and be ok, not concerned what people thought, as popularity wasn’t important to him. He fired General MacArthur, even though it was very unpopular with the public. The right decision was what was important. He berated the Ku Klux Klan, “as a bunch of cheap, un-American fakers.” He was unafraid of criticism and saw it as a healthy part of the American process. Truman said, "If the people couldn't blow off steam they might explode. Half the fun of being a citizen in this country comes from complaining about the way we run our government.” He was very down to earth and easy to understand.

"Worrying never does you any good. So I've never worried about things much. The only thing that I ever do worry about is to be sure that where I'm responsible, the job is properly done." Dean Acheson, Truman's Secretary of State, wrote that his chief was totally without what he called, "that most enfeebling of emotions, regret." He had strongly defined values and saw things in black or white, right or wrong. There was always a better, right decision and once he made it, that was it. He tended to like or dislike you and had a hard time with grays and in-betweens. "I never gave anybody hell...I just told the truth, and they thought it was hell." He lacked charisma, but had strength, strong definition, and conviction.

In a Chicago Tribune article, it stated, "brash though he was, Truman was also a man of enduring humility, who in the White House, continued to recite a childhood prayer asking God to make him 'truthful, honest and honorable in all things: and to give him the ability to be charitable, forgiving and patient with his fellowmen.'"

Truman was a man of routine, which is not usual for a type 1. As president, he awoke at 5 a.m., took a two-mile walk wearing a suit and tie, had a rubdown, a bourbon, a light breakfast, worked, had lunch with his wife Bess, took a short nap, worked, had a mid-afternoon swim with his glasses on, had a cocktail and ate dinner with Bess, and sometimes worked at night; but if things were light, he'd watch a movie or listen to music. Once or twice a week, he'd play poker with his male friends at a private house. He vacationed at the Naval Base in Key West, Florida.

During the Truman years, women started working more outside the house both during and after the war, suburban communities were expanding, anti-communism and the red scare and McCarthyism were on the rise, many blacks moved north, civil rights legislation was being passed and Jackie Robinson integrated baseball and became rookie of the year.

After his presidency ended, Truman lived another 19 years in Independence, Missouri writing his memoirs, receiving guests, talking to school groups, being visited by scholars, reading, and commenting about the presidencies of Eisenhower whom he disliked, Kennedy and Johnson, whom he did like. He wasn't a fan of Nixon. He died in his late 80s, and his wife Bess lived to 97, the longest lived First Lady to date.

Truman was a man who could sleep at night, due to the fact that he had a clear conscience, because he was doing what he thought was right. He could definitely make decisions and was a man you could count on.

Dwight Eisenhower – Type 1, INTJ, General, Planner and Peacemaker, 1953-1961

(1890-1969) The 34th president was Dwight Eisenhower, a Type 1. Because he was a well-known general you might imagine him to have been a warmonger not a peacemaker, but at their best, generals command to achieve the goal of peace. And that is exactly what Eisenhower embodied, the best traits of a warrior. He was known to bridge between warring factions, and in his case, especially between warring leaders on the same Allied side in World War II. He could manage difficult egos and utilize the strengths of each one. He fired Patton, the Army commander who slapped a soldier, but rehired him when the timing was right. He was able to negotiate differences and conflicts and strike the right balance between those holding opposing points of view. With a strong 9 wing that softened his perfectionism, he led with peace in mind and tempered his innate hot headedness.

Eisenhower presented like a Type 9, but really was a Type 1. He was a long-range planner, very disciplined, serious, ethical, workaholic, competent and had brilliant organization skills. He had a broad grin, was patient and was able to play a leisurely game of golf; qualities that might seem 9ish. In fact, that appearance concealed a person who was never lazy or passive. He worked tirelessly and didn't much like praise. His work and the result of it were enough reward, as is true for 1s.

So many people who fight for peace are typed as 9s, when the manner in which they fight for peace is more important in the typing process. For instance, Type 1s can focus on peace as a goal as much as 9s, but 9s are peaceful by nature. 9s have a peaceful approach most all the time until people push them or fight them.

Eisenhower had a wide grin and friendly smile that he used to diffuse any situation, but he was also ambitious, strong, competitive and sternly disciplined. He had strong parents who modeled a disciplined life for him. British Field Marshall Montgomery said of him, "He has the power of drawing the hearts of men toward him as a magnet attracts the bit of metal. He merely has to smile at you, and you trust him at once."

People often trust more conscious 1s like Eisenhower because of their competence and commitment. His diplomatic but strong nature engendered trust. According to an essay by Stephen Ambrose, "By 1952, the year Eisenhower entered into politics at age sixty-two, his character, as formed by heredity and experience, was set in cement. It included qualities of love, honesty, faithfulness, responsibility, modesty, generosity, duty, and leadership, along with a hatred of war. These were bedrock."

Born in Texas to a relatively poor family, he spent most of his youth in the small town of Abilene, Kansas. His father was a mechanic in a creamery and his mother was a Mennonite pacifist who was greatly distressed when her son obtained an appointment to West Point. As a child, Eisenhower did family chores, hunted and fished, played football and read military history. He was also a prankster, played cards, smoked and made average grades. After graduating from West Point in the middle of his class with fellow student Douglas

MacArthur, he was given various military assignments, espoused theories about the better use of tanks, and married Mamie Doud.

He rose in the ranks as an officer and became an aide to both Pershing and MacArthur, both well-known generals. His posts included bases in Texas, Maryland, Kansas, Panama and the Philippines. He was loyal to his commanders even when he disagreed with their policies, such as when MacArthur burned the Bonus Marchers encampment in Washington, D.C. during the Depression. Loyalty is a strong trait of 1s.

Before World War II Eisenhower played an important role in massive training exercises that were held in Louisiana where over 400,000 soldiers participated. Known for his keen ability for strategic planning, he was promoted to brigadier general. Moving to Washington, D.C. days after the attack on Pearl Harbor to do war planning, he was highly praised by George Marshall, the Army Chief of Staff who rarely spoke words of praise. Eisenhower was promoted to lead command invasions of North Africa, Sicily, then Italy, before finally being promoted to Supreme Commander of the Allied Invasion of Western Europe. He was in charge of the D-Day invasion.

His successful contribution during WW II led to his being honored in celebrations in Washington, D.C., London, Paris and Moscow. Controversy ensued around decisions he made allowing the Soviet Army to enter Germany at the end of the war, relieving Patton as the military governor of Bavaria after the war, and returning Soviet citizens who had been in the US occupied zone to Russia. He made decisions based on prior agreements of what he considered as the most desirable outcome for all concerned parties. He certainly faced many conflicts.

He opposed the dropping of the atomic bomb. At the end of 1945, he returned to Washington, D.C. to become the Army Chief of Staff and prepare the Army for the ensuing Cold War with Russia. In 1948, he became the president of Columbia University though he would return to Washington D.C. at times to be the informal chair of The Joint Chiefs of Staff. In 1950 when the Korean War broke out, he donned his uniform again to become the NATO Commander of Europe. He was a natural born leader, as is often the case for 1s.

Eisenhower tended to be evasive in press conferences even though he was able to be clear in private conversations. He chose not to "engage in personalities" and refrained from the temptation to criticize or mention adversaries by name. He knew how to appeal to a wide range of people and tried not to make enemies, though it took effort and focus. With his clean-cut image, he could be humble. His style was certainly different than Truman and Roosevelt who were more outspoken and abrasive. Eisenhower was more contained.

Committed to maintaining harmony during the war, he had no tolerance for bickering or internal rivalry among his generals. His maturity, his Type 1 nature to do what was right and his Type 9 wing all combined to guide his decision-making toward the highest good for the all concerned. He had the authority from General Marshall, FDR and Churchill to relieve anyone in command who created disharmony and he exercised that authority on several occasions. He was decisive when needed. Unassuming mostly due to his introversion, he could be a real risk-taker when necessary. He was charming, confident, amiable and sociable with troops; tolerant and eager to appease, though he could be very opinionated. A stabilizing force, Eisenhower was generally even-tempered, though he could flare up in anger at times. He was the solid rock everyone needed.

From George Marshall, Army Chief of Staff, "Although I did not know Eisenhower well, he came highly recommended by Douglas MacArthur. I asked General Mark Clark, whom I respected, to give me ten names as possible candidates to be my assistant in the War Department. He gave me Eisenhower with nine dittos." Eisenhower impressed Marshall with his personal charm and geniality, critical character traits that were sorely needed in keeping the Allies working together as a team. 1s who are mature, like Eisenhower, often develop the personal qualities that are right for the situation at hand.

"Eisenhower wanted to like people," says biographer Peter Lyon, "and he wanted people to like him. He was distressed when it failed to happen so. His need for friendly rapport was one reason for his reluctance to speak ill of anyone." Probably that need came from a childhood incident when he was forbidden to go out with older boys on Halloween and he beat his knuckles on a tree. After his mother nursed his hand, he made a vow not to show hatred. He rather showed a happy optimistic personality. He also was a bit superstitious and always carried three lucky coins in his pocket. 1s often work hard to be positive.

Eisenhower said, "I adopted a policy of circulating through the whole force to the full limit imposed by my physical considerations. I did my best to meet everyone from the general to private with a smile a pat on the back and definite interest in his problems." He treated everyone equally and encouraged his leaders to get to know their men.

Said Lyons, "He talked with and shook the hands of the paratroopers of 101st Airborne and stood on the roof of the nearby headquarters to salute each plane that took off to France. As the planes soared into the night sky, he thought of the dangers of those brave men would soon be facing, and tears filled his eyes." The pain of men's deaths affected him deeply. He knew his decisions had a big effect on individual men and their families.

For a decade, he worked 12 to 14-hour days seven days a week, drinking many cups of coffee and smoking up to four packs of cigarettes a day and yet he remained optimistic and wanted to be an example for his men. Camaraderie and caring were his trademarks. He didn't want the officers to get special treatment. Eisenhower wrote many articles about leadership and the qualities most important to successfully lead men and bring out their best. His values were clear and he wrote often about those standards. You know where 1s stand with their values.

Eisenhower, the five-star general, was one of the 11 presidents who ran on a war record. His campaign slogan was "I Like Ike." As President, he oversaw the ceasefire of the Korean War, managed the early stages of The Cold War by threatening to use nuclear weapons if necessary, and started the space race with Russia. He authorized the use of secret anti-communist operations, including assassinations that led to the overthrow of governments in Iran in 1953 and Guatemala in 1954. Supporting the South Vietnamese government against communism, his decisions led to the US intervention in Vietnam.

On the home front, he created the federal interstate highway system, strengthened the social security system, created the Department of Health, Education and Welfare, helped combat Joseph McCarthy who was behind the paranoid monitoring and jailing of "communists," and strengthened civil rights in the military. He only partially enforced desegregation of schools brought on by the controversial Supreme Court decision in 1954 of Brown vs. The Board of Education. Sending federal troops to protect black students integrating schools in Little Rock, Arkansas, he signed civil rights legislation in 1957 and 1960 to protect black voters.

Eisenhower tried to create a détente with Russia by advocating an "open skies" policy to monitor each other's installations. Soviet relations remained relatively cordial throughout his two terms as president, including a summit meeting with Nikita Khrushchev, but hopes of harmony were dashed when the Russians shot down a US spy plane over Russia. In his farewell address in 1961, he warned of the "military-industrial complex," and how big business and the military were unduly influencing American government.

His two terms in office were accompanied by relative prosperity and his approval ratings were high. Eisenhower oversaw the building of our nuclear arsenal even while he talked with Khrushchev about limiting the US arsenal. Eisenhower was deceptive; talking about creating and enforcing peace while simultaneously building our missile supply and sending secret U2 planes over Russia to spy.

After his presidency, he retired to his farm in Gettysburg, Pennsylvania, wrote his memoirs and books, painted, raised Angus cattle, spent time with Mamie, gave advice to John F. Kennedy and LBJ, and travelled, once to Normandy to film a documentary about D-Day. He spoke his final words while holding Mamie's hand while looking at his son John and his grandson, "I want to go. God take me." He died in 1969 at the age of 78. His son graduated from West Point and had a military career, once serving as his father's military aide and later becoming known as a military historian.

Eisenhower's presidency took place during suburban expansion, proliferation of the bored housewife syndrome (even though more and more women were attending college and working), the baby boom, younger marriages with more children, continued movement of blacks northward and the threat of nuclear war.

Eisenhower's leadership qualities included: peaceful strength, self-discipline, the ability to negotiate and make personal connections, strength of character, excellent planning and going over details many times to prevent errors, self-management and self-improvement, listening well, hard work, perseverance, decisiveness, and courage - all traits of a conscious Type 1. He said, "You don't lead by hitting people over the head. Leadership is a matter of persuasion and conciliation, education and patience. It's a long, slow, tough work."

The following is paraphrased from the chapter about Eisenhower from the book *Presidential Temperament*, Eisenhower's patience was a learned characteristic, not a native trait. His mind was brilliant and he always had to restrain his temper. Sloppy work was never tolerated. He chose words carefully, as he knew the power of words and their effect. We are lucky he worked so diligently on his personality development. He was always aware that his actions could have potential negative consequences. These are all traits of the higher qualities of Type 1.

As an INTJ, he was organized, a long-range realistic planner, controlled, systematic in his organizational structure and the development of his support staff, and he had clear lines of authority. He was rational in his approach, goals and writing, and very comprehensive with plans that would affect outcomes for the future. He was truly a man to admire.

John Fitzgerald Kennedy, Type 7, ESTP, Overcoming Obstacles, Camelot, 1961-1963

(1917-1963) John F. Kennedy (also called Jack) was president number 35. He was born into wealth and privilege to a family steeped in politics. His maternal grandfather, John Francis "Honey Fitz" Fitzgerald, was the mayor of Boston for two terms and head of the Democratic Party in Massachusetts in the early part of the 20th century. Educated at New England's finest prep schools, John's father Joseph Kennedy Sr. was a multi-millionaire who made his money in stocks, banking, film production and liquor sales. His maternal grandfather and four of his uncles were state senators.

Kennedy was born in Brookline, Massachusetts. The family moved to the Bronx when he was 10. Jack's father, Joseph Kennedy, Sr., was appointed Ambassador to England by then

President Franklin D. Roosevelt. Attending Harvard like his father and his older brother Joe Jr., Jack spent part of his student years living in England. He came from a large family that included three brothers and five sisters. Joe Kennedy raised all his children to be competitive, successful, verbal jousters, who were winning athletes. Sympathy for a competitor's woes and thoughts of losing completely out of the question!

John was active in campus politics and competed on the swim team as he was unable to play football due to a bad back. Visits to England during his Harvard years provided Kennedy with opportunities to observe political dynamics, and it was there that he became interested in social conditions and the problems of social unrest stemming from the extremes of the right and left political factions. Traveling throughout Europe, Eastern Europe and Poland, he witnessed firsthand the conditions that he came to understand were responsible for the rise of Hitler.

His father favored appeasement with Hitler while John's thinking favored preparing the country for war. At a young age John's interest in foreign relations led him to write his first book, *Why England Slept*, as his senior thesis at Harvard. The book explained why England tried appeasement during the 1930s with Germany. Along with his foreign policy ideas, the book set the stage for John's political career. His father Joe stumbled to the end of his political career by favoring appeasement, which was antithetical to FDR's hidden agenda to go to war.

John was sickly as a child and was often in the hospital or sick ward in schools he attended with conditions related to a bad back and also what is now called irritable bowel syndrome and Addison's disease, a condition caused by adrenal failure. The back condition was a combination of a congenital predisposition that was aggravated by injuries he suffered while playing sports. One leg was almost an inch shorter than the other, which made matters worse. In his childhood, he also had scarlet fever, diphtheria, appendicitis, whooping cough, asthma and pneumonia.

John suffered great physical pain throughout his life but despite that, he was almost always cheerful, optimistic, positive and smiling, all traits of Type 7, the Optimist. Despite many operations and times when he was near death and given last rites, Kennedy joked, remained active and was adventurous. He continued the family legacy of public service and making a positive difference in the world. As a matter of fact, he was given last rites three times due to serious infections and expected death, before the fourth final last rite.

In one operation doctors fused his spine; unfortunately, the fusion didn't alleviate pain. He wore a back brace for most of his life, often used crutches when he was out of the public eye and took pain killers, amphetamines and steroids on a daily basis monitored by doctors, one nicknamed Dr. Feelgood. Despite his pain and periods of recuperations, he was charming, seldom stayed down for long, and being a Type 7, his smile was infectious and his grin was famous. Similar to FDR, another Type 7, he bore his pain well and kept busy. He often thought his life would be short as a result of his medical conditions so he worked extremely hard to create a positive legacy. His courage and stamina are to be praised.

7s are amazing in their ability to stay focused on the positive more than on negativity or pain. They see what they have more than what they lack. They look at options for themselves, seek out ways to create the best possible outcomes and tend to keep themselves stimulated and in constant action.

Joe Kennedy, John's father was a Type 8, the Boss. He pushed his children to be successful and kept his family in the public eye. Jack served in the Navy during WW II despite the fact that he couldn't pass the medical exam. His father got him medically qualified anyway. Jack was a PT boat captain in the South Pacific. In one horrific incident, during the middle of the night, an enemy destroyer rammed and split his boat in half. Two of his men died in the initial hit.

Kennedy's remaining crew clung to the remains of the boat for 12 hours and then Kennedy and the others swam miles to an island while holding an injured mate, collapsing on the beach. Another version of this story claims some of his crew made a makeshift raft and swam, pulling the raft to the island. The survivors lived off coconut water and rainwater before their rescue a week later. Kennedy scrawled a message on a coconut husk, which was taken by a native to another safe island, asking someone to launch a boat rescue. Kennedy kept the survival coconut on his White House desk.

Receiving the Navy Marine Corps Medal and Purple Heart for his bravery, his experience and story added to his political clout. Unfortunately, his brother Joe Jr., who served in the

Navy, was killed in a dangerous special bomber mission. As the oldest surviving son, the responsibility to further the family legacy now fell to John; he was to propel forward the mission that his father initiated. John had not necessarily expected to enter politics or aim for the White House, though he probably would have gone in that direction even without Joe Jr.'s death. In his younger years, John thought he would write or teach as his primary focus.

His father's wealth gave John the ability to travel to countries on fact-finding missions to interview locals and learn how others lived. Kennedy wanted to understand different countries' political structures, as well as meet world leaders. His story is similar to the Siddhartha or Buddha story. He grew up rich and wanted to see the world of those who are poor. He wanted to understand the suffering of others, and learn to relate to the world without the comfort of his privileged condition.

As mentioned above Kennedy's personal story included a great deal of physical suffering. In spite of his pain, he managed to be active and employed people to clean up his messy rooms, the results of his affairs and to handle his finances. His favorite sister Kathleen, nicknamed "Kick", died at age of 28 in a plane crash while Kennedy was young. His brother, Joe, Jr., also died in a plane crash, so despite being born with the proverbial silver spoon in his mouth, he learned much about loss and pain through his own life experiences. He didn't deny pain but didn't dwell on it either.

Kennedy also knew about enjoying the hedonistic aspects of life. Following in the footsteps of his father he was a womanizer, who had numerous lovers throughout his life and during his marriage, including his time at the White House. He enjoyed yachts, travel, special attention and having whatever he wanted. 7s love pleasure, fun, action, travel and stimulation.

He had vision and could be patient with political decisions, stepping back to analyze and make independent decisions. During the Cuban Missile Crisis, almost all his advisors recommended going to war with Russia and Cuba but Kennedy had the vision to wait it out and have a good outcome. He learned from the disastrous Bay of Pigs invasion to always be cautious and never blindly trust his CIA and military advisors. He was loyal to his family and trusted their advice more; Bobby his brother, Sargent Shriver his brother-in-law, his brother Edward (Ted) and many relatives. He promised his father he would appoint Bobby to his cabinet if he won the presidency, against the advice of many. It was an Irish clan running the government!

Before the presidency, he served six years in the US House and eight years in the Senate. He was often absent during votes due to his travels, surgery, being debilitated by physical pain or campaigning. As a tireless campaigner, he gave speeches, shook hands, and in his early campaigns, went house to house to meet and greet people on the street. He created alliances with political bigwigs. His smile and relaxed positive charm won people over. Kennedy was popular even in the face of obstacles, like being Catholic and not being in the favor of party bosses who tended to promote cronies based on length of time in the party and a voting record that supported their interests.

He was the most eligible bachelor in America. As an aspiring president, Kennedy knew that being married would greatly enhance his chances of winning. In 1953, he married Jacqueline Bouvier, also very eligible and beautiful. She was born of wealthy parents who were divorced and had been a newspaper photographer before her marriage to Jack. Later in life she became a book editor.

Jackie coached her husband to enhance and develop his already winning charm and public speaking presence. Even though she was shy and private, she campaigned for her husband. Jacqueline as a Type 4, The Depth Seeker, wanted more personal privacy for herself and the children and Jack wanted and enjoyed lots of publicity, as is typical of many 7s. As First Lady, she was graceful and poised, tried to tolerate the pain of her husband's affairs, redecorated the White House, orchestrated a famous White House tour that was televised, and raised two children. Subsequent to Kennedy's assassination she was a single mother for five years. In 1968 she married the Greek shipping magnate, Aristotle Onassis. She died of cancer in 1994.

Kennedy's medical condition, like that of FDR, was almost entirely denied and hidden from the public. Even when Lyndon Johnson ran against him for the Democratic presidential nomination and exposed his Addison's disease, the Kennedy machine wholly denied it. Although Johnson was in many ways Kennedy's nemesis, he was also an essential political ally. It was the solely the need to win the state of Texas that forced him to tap Johnson as his running mate.

The Kennedy clan was politically savvy. It had the clout to win as well as money to buy votes that propelled Jack forward to take the presidency from Nixon. Jack was very telegenic, winning the first ever recorded television debates; he charmed the audience with a great display of calm and confidence. Nixon appeared nervous, sweaty and anxious. Many who listened on the radio thought Nixon won the debate but the TV audience who watched it thought Kennedy won by a landslide. 7s tend to be charming, positive and energetic, winning approval for their positivity.

Despite the promise of the Camelot court of young attractive people, which included many of his advisors, Kennedy's first year in office was somewhat disastrous because of the Bay of Pigs invasion debacle to oust Castro. Jack was depressed for a long time about the needless death of the Cuban dissidents who fought in the Bay of Pigs. That incident forever changed his perspective on trusting military advisors and the misguided information they provided.

After this, Kennedy had a meeting with Nikita Khrushchev that ended in a stalemate when the Russian denied sending missiles to Cuba. Khruschev did so in spite of former pledges in which he agreed to refrain from sending arms to Cuba.

The gradual buildup of "advisors" going to Vietnam to combat the spread of communism proved to be another very difficult set of circumstances, with the leader of South Vietnam being assassinated in a coup d'état. The United States didn't seem to have a clear purpose other than to stop the spread of communism and combat Russia and China. His foreign policy decisions generally seemed to have been a failure, although in 1963 a nuclear arms reduction and test ban treaty were signed with Russia.

Things looked better for the US concerning its goals in the space race when Alan Shepard manned a flight in 1961 and John Glenn followed in 1962. Technological advances in the US competitive drive against Russia encouraged Kennedy to announce a goal of going to the moon by the end of the decade. It's unfortunate he wasn't alive to see the fulfillment of that goal.

Some advances in civil rights were made during the Kennedy administration. He sent federal troops to Alabama and Mississippi to support and protect black integrating students who were in danger from threats made by white mobs. A number of civil rights marches erupted in violence when racist locals and police started beating, using fire hoses and unleashing attack dogs on black and white anti-segregationists. Kennedy intervened when four black children died in a church bombing in Birmingham, Alabama.

Kennedy's initial contact with Martin Luther King was positive and King's March on Washington and the "I Have a Dream" speech occurred during his administration. Kennedy was very concerned about losing the Southern white vote because he supported blacks' rights, yet he wanted to retain the black vote. There's a question whether he actually supported civil rights as a choice of moral conscience or whether he did it for the black vote. Probably it was both. Nonetheless, there were inroads made that led to Johnson's Civil Rights Act of 1964.

Kennedy proposed legislation regarding federal aid to education, medical aid to the elderly, mass transit, and he formed a Department of Urban Affairs and Economic Development for Appalachia. He managed an increase in minimum wage and the economic development of the Appalachian region, even though his other programs were denied funding.

Just before his death, he proposed a civil rights bill that became law after his assassination. The Peace Corps was created during his administration and he initiated the planning for the war on poverty. Kennedy was the first Catholic president and he hired many Jews for top-level positions in his cabinet, seats on the Supreme Court and as advisors. When he ran for president and knew of Anti-Catholic sentiment, he said, "I'm not the Catholic candidate for president. I'm the Democratic candidate for president." He made many references to America being a country that fought prejudice. He knew how to appeal to the higher moral principles of the people and motivate them to act on those.

People loved Kennedy's youthfulness. He was the youngest elected president at age 43; Teddy Roosevelt was 42 when he inherited the White House position after the McKinley assassination. His beautiful wife Jacqueline and the two young children, Carolyn and John, Jr., who were photographed running around to the delight of national magazine readers, added greatly to Kennedy's popularity. Two other children died; one was a stillbirth and another lived for only two days.

People questioned his brother Robert's appointment as his attorney general. In 1967 a law was passed preventing a relative from being directly supervised by the president. His brother Edward became a US senator in 1962. Robert continued on in politics after Jack's assassination and was himself assassinated in 1968 while running for president. Bobby as a type 6, was totally loyal during Jack's presidency and turned out to be a very competent attorney general in spite of the fact that he wasn't a lawyer.

Not everyone succumbed to the Kennedy charm. "Kennedy controlled every person who came in contact with him. He was a Brueghel in the sense that he created a world of his own, but instead of squeezing oil paint, he squeezed people to create his own personal world. He was at the center of all he surveyed. He enjoyed using people, and setting them against each other for his own amusement. He lived life as a race against boredom," quoted from an essay by Richard Reeves.

Kennedy was controlling in a charming way though he could be ruthless, had a temper and could use people and then drop or toss them away. He had a number of enemies as was evidenced by his assassination on November 22, 1963. The question of the assassin and the mystery of the people behind the plot have never been solved satisfactorily. Suggestions concerning the perpetrators include the Mafia, connections related to Cuba, Russia, the CIA or other US government officials. The Warren Commission was set up by Lyndon Johnson to investigate the assassination and it concluded that the assassin acted alone and there was no conspiracy. Most people don't believe the lone assassin story. He might have been assassinated anyway as there were five other planned and bungled assassination plots in Chicago, Miami, Tampa, Los Angeles and Nashville against Kennedy beyond the successful one in Dallas.

Kennedy was highly competitive and probably had Type 3 as his secondary type. He was also witty and charismatic, loved to engage with people and was an excellent speaker. Having Type 7 as his dominant type, he was almost always positive, active, engaged and smiling. He changed the nature of politics in which one had to work your way up and be next in line to win the party's nomination to be president. He had an urgency to win the presidency due to his expectation of an early death from his many medical problems.

Quotes by Jack include:

“We choose to go to the moon in this decade and other things not because they are easy but because they are hard.”

“Ask not what my country can do for you but what you can do for your country.”

“We are passing the torch to a new generation.”

Some interesting additional facts about Kennedy: His book *Profiles in Courage* about the history of courageous US Senators, was given a Pulitzer Prize in 1957. He had a secret taping system in the White House that he used mostly for the sake of writing a book about his presidency. He suggested a joint mission to the moon with the Soviets. Kennedy is the only president to win a Purple Heart and he was the first president to dance with a black woman at an inaugural ball.

Kennedy was a James Bond fanatic and wrote a plot about Lyndon Baines Johnson throwing a coup d’état against the president! He was the only president whose grandmother lived longer than he did. The film, *7 Days in May* starring Burt Lancaster and Kirk Douglas and authorized by John Kennedy, is a movie about the peace and military factions in his cabinet, particularly the Joint Chiefs of Staff plotting an overthrow of the government for signing the Nuclear armament treaty.

I believe John Kennedy was an ESTP in the Myers-Briggs System.

www.paladinexec.com/personality_comparison/ESTP/

“Leadership Style: Instantaneous, spontaneous decision-makers comfortable with taking risks, ESTPs are skilled tacticians who view obstacles and rules simply as impediments around which to maneuver. In leadership positions, they function admirably in chaotic environments, keep followers focused on present realities, and provide optimism and a "can-do" attitude.

Conflict Resolution: Assertive and direct ESTPs meet conflict head-on. They welcome others' contributions in a nonjudgmental manner, maintain an open-minded approach, and accept compromise in an effort to move toward finding resolution.

Communication Style: Active, engaging, and results oriented, ESTPs do not sit idle and discuss issues for long periods of time. Unwavering and to the point, they communicate present realities with energy, enthusiasm, acting quickly without taking the time to explain their actions. ESTPs persuade through logical analysis while stressing the need for precise and immediate action. They are persuaded by straightforward common-sense solutions to short-term problems based on practical information.

Career Satisfaction: Motivated by a need for action, ESTPs rely and trust what their senses tell them about the world around them. In order for work to be meaningful to them, it must involve constant use of their senses to experience their environment in a variety of ways."

Kennedy was a man of charisma, positivity, tolerance for pain, a learner, and a man of action, inspiration and leadership. He transformed himself from his special upbringing to be able to include the poor in his vision for more freedom and the awareness of others' suffering. He encouraged everyone to live their vision, to include and welcome differences and to give and sacrifice for others.

Lyndon Baines Johnson – Type 8, ESTP, Powerhouse – Civil Rights and Vietnam, 1963-1968

(1908-1973) President number 36 was Lyndon Baines Johnson who vowed to continue the legacy of John F. Kennedy on civil rights and to end poverty. Johnson had a genuine interest in fighting for peoples' rights and being an advocate to empower and change the lot of the downtrodden. He counted himself as being among the disenfranchised when he was growing up. He did more for social security, domestic justice and racial equality than any president other than FDR. From the age of 12 on he had a lifelong dream to be not only the president but also the greatest president.

Johnson was born into a poor family in Texas. From a stock of early Texas settlers, his ancestors were cattlemen, cotton farmers, and Confederate soldiers. He was the oldest of five children. His mother was reserved and genteel and his father was a talker and a dreamer who served five terms in the Texas legislature, while trying to carve out a living as a farmer. His father was in debt most of his life.

Johnson particularly wanted to change a system in which the price of cotton could drop from 40 cents a bushel to 6 cents only to impoverish people whose livelihood depended on it, as happened to his family. Growing up impoverished, like all those around him, he vowed to help the poor when he became a man. He graduated first in his class of six students in a one-room high school to which he rode three miles each way on a mule.

Attending Southwest Texas State Teachers College only to find himself doing poorly, he dropped out. Drifting for a while, he bought a car with five friends and ended up in California doing odd jobs, working briefly in a cousin's law office, and getting into trouble fighting, drinking and finally getting arrested. Hitchhiking back to Texas, he worked on road crews along the way back and went back to Southwest Texas State Teachers College.

In college, he excelled more in extracurricular activities such as journalism, debating and student government than he did at his academic studies. He was assigned as a student teacher to a school of Hispanic students and excelled in his teaching role. He engendered hope and pride in his students and encouraged them in their achievements. With excellent references, he graduated from college at the beginning of the Depression and soon realized politics was more a fit for his extraverted personality. His volunteer work in politics set the stage for his growing political career.

Johnson helped a political friend of his father win an election and then was hired as a political aide in Washington, D.C. He worked tirelessly attending to every detail of his job. When he moved back to Texas, he met Lady Bird Taylor and within three months they were married. Lady Bird got her name from her nanny who described her as a baby saying, "she was as pretty as a bird." Shy, but genuine, charming and a gracious hostess, she was a balance to Lyndon's boisterous, hyperactive nature.

Johnson, with the help of the Texas politician and future Speaker of the House Sam Rayburn, won an appointment as the Texas director of a youth employment program under FDR's social programs. When a local congressman died, he ran for the vacant office and won, with the help of funds from his wife, who owned the local radio station and some real estate. He was proud of the fact that as a member of the US House of Representatives, he brought dams, federal housing projects and especially, electricity to his district. He said that was the proudest moment of his entire life. Johnson typically worked 12 hours a day, seven days a week.

He served six terms as a House Representative and finally won a Senate seat, quickly rose in power to become majority leader and aimed for an eventual presidency. Known for the Johnson treatment, a combination of his 6'2" towering figure standing over shorter senators, speaking softly, cajoling, flattering, berating, bribing or whatever he had to do to win a vote, he often got what he wanted. He befriended the power figures, got on the right committees and powered his way through.

From 1940 to 1942 Johnson was appointed by FDR to the Naval Reserve as a Lieutenant Commander, working on ways to improve manpower and production issues that were slowing the building of aircraft for the war. He travelled extensively in the US and South Pacific and even flew on several combat missions as an observer. Before boarding one plane he had to use the restroom and upon returning, he had to board another plane as the initial one had taken off. It was incredibly good luck, as that first plane was shot down!

He had a heart attack when he was 50 that caused him to stop smoking, lose weight and delegate more. He was a severe workaholic and the stress of overworking contributed to the heart attack. He was an ally of Eisenhower, supported any civil rights legislation, was behind the space race, was a key player in new legislation and was considered the power man in the Senate. He was obsessed with his place in history.

Johnson had his heart set on winning the Democratic presidential nomination of 1960 but the Kennedy machine was more sophisticated than his. He felt he was owed the nomination from his years in Congress but decided to take Kennedy's offer as Vice President. Even though he was relegated to the outside, he had some power, as he headed the space program, was given a key role in military policy, and headed the President's Committee for Equal Employment Opportunity. Overall though, he was frustrated as Kennedy's advisors didn't seek his advice and he wanted to have more of a key role in foreign affairs.

Lyndon was a larger than life character. As a classic Type 8, he was always direct, in your face and could easily intimidate or befriend you as he saw fit. He made friends as well as enemies with equal ease. Not an intellectual, he was nonetheless smart, cunning, clever, power driven, knew what people wanted, knew how to get his way, and also knew how to make deals to create a win/win. Many arms were twisted by him.

He was brazen, bullying, and crass, loved dirty jokes, pulled dogs' ears and once showed his belly button to the public after an operation. He had the bold direction and earthiness of an 8 with a 7 wing. His secondary type may have been 3 as he was cunning, clever and was known to spin the truth to his advantage at times, though getting results and holding power were more important than image or impressions. Longing for grandeur, like Johnson, can be equally true for 3s or 8s. He held a strong physical body of boldness, recognizable as an 8 more than 3.

He was the classic ESTP. "ESTPs are energetic thrill seekers who are at their best when putting out fires, whether literal or metaphorical. They bring a sense of dynamic energy to their interactions with others and the world around them. They assess situations quickly and move adeptly to respond to immediate problems with practical solutions.

Active and playful, ESTPs are often the life of the party and have a good sense of humor. They use their keen powers of observation to assess their audience and adapt quickly to keep interactions exciting. Although they typically appear very social, they are rarely sensitive; the ESTP prefers to keep things fast-paced and silly rather than emotional or serious." www.truity.com/personality-type/ESTP

As president, he was unconventional, holding meetings in his bedroom or the White House swimming pool in the buff, sometimes still talking while he was in the bathroom, as is true for some extraverted 8s who have little concern for public sensitivities. He believed in his Great Society with freedom and justice for all. He was responsible for a new voting rights act, Medicare and Medicaid, federal aid to education, environmental protection laws, food stamps, Head Start, National Public Radio, the Public Broadcasting System, consumer protection laws, the Civil Rights Act, and the war on poverty. He cut the poverty rate by half.

The War in Vietnam was another issue. He trusted his advisors and even though he sent over 100,000 troops, no progress was made in “winning the war.” It pained him to have protesters within shouting range of the White House saying, “How many more sons have you killed today?” He wanted to be liked and his thrust for the war ran counter to his need to protect society from the bad guys. He couldn’t stand being seen as one of them and the protests decimated his desire to run another term. He died four years after he retired. Politics had been his entire world of interest in which to play out his personality and beliefs.

The article below gives the best explanation of Johnson’s psychological makeup:

Excerpted from an essay by Robert Dallek*:*

www.pbs.org/newshour/spc/character/essays/johnson.html to see the entire article

“Johnson was much loved and greatly hated -- not just liked and disliked but adored by some and despised by others. Some people remember him as kind, generous, compassionate, considerate, decent, and devoted to advancing the wellbeing of the least advantaged among us. Others describe him as cruel, dictatorial, grandiose, and even vicious.”

“Johnson was a man possessed by inner demons. From early in his childhood, he manifested character traits that shaped his behavior throughout his life. As a boy and a man, he suffered from a sense of emptiness: he couldn't stand to be alone; he needed constant companionship, attention, affection, and approval. He had insatiable appetites: for work, women, food, drink, conversation, and material possessions. They were all in the service of filling himself up -- of giving himself a sort of validity or sense of self-worth.”

“Johnson's neediness translated into a number of traits that had a large impact on his political actions. He had a compulsion to be the best, to outdo everybody, to eclipse all his predecessors in the White House and become the greatest president in American history. As journalist Nicholas Lemann says, Johnson "wanted to set world records in politics, as a star athlete would in sports. 'Get those coonskins up on the wall,' he would tell people around him."

“As a senator, he had to be top dog, and drove himself to become Majority Leader. He turned a post with limited influence into the most powerful position in the Senate, from which he directed the passage of significant laws affecting labor, the elderly, housing, civil rights, defense, and space exploration. As Majority Leader, he was thrilled to be the first legislator in Washington with a car phone. When Everett Dirksen, Republican Minority Leader and a friendly rival, also acquired one, he telephoned Johnson's limo to say that he was calling from his new car phone. "Can you hold on a minute, Ev?" Johnson asked. "My other phone is ringing." 8s often like to compete and be on top.”

“The same neediness that made Johnson so eager for personal grandeur contributed to his desire to help the least advantaged. Throughout his life, he identified with poor folks who had neither the material possessions nor the social regard held by and accorded to the most affluent members of society.”

“The Vietnam war brought out the worst in Johnson. His failure to deal effectively with the conflict partly rested on his character flaws: his grandiosity that could overcome every obstacle and his impulse to view criticism of his policies as personal attacks which he would overcome by increasing his efforts to make his policies succeed. Johnson fought in Vietnam for many reasons. He genuinely believed it essential to hold the line in Vietnam against Communist advance. Otherwise, the United States would face the loss of all of Southeast Asia to a hostile ideology. He also believed that a failure to stop the Viet Cong and North Vietnamese in South Vietnam would embolden Moscow and Peking and raise the likelihood of another larger, possibly nuclear, war.”

Johnson was a political genius who put everything into what he did. A chain smoker before his heart attack at 50, he was always in motion and action. He cared about the poor and wanted to empower them and wanted to be seen as the man who ended poverty and racism. He won the largest popular vote as president until then in 1964. He lacked restraint and was a larger than life character who was overly controlling as well as optimistic. For him moderation didn’t exist. Some people have typed him as a Type 3, which might be his secondary type, but he was a Type 8; a power-driven, overconfident bully, who fought for the good causes in his heart. His poverty-stricken background coupled with his personal drive, ambition and desire to change the world helped millions of his constituents.

Richard M. Nixon – Type 6, INTJ, Watch Out for Enemies, 1969-1974

(1913-1994) Nixon was president number 37, a man obsessed with whether you were his friend or foe. He was something of a loner, very secretive and suspicious and was always protecting his dream of hoped for grandeur. Ambitious, with a desperate need to prove he was worthy of the job, he had to be in control of everything and when he was president, became more and more paranoid about those he felt were against him. He was afraid that people were out to bring him down. His cabinet was made up of men who would go along with his beliefs; openness and trust were nowhere in the picture, but for a favored few, and even then, they were closely watched. Nixon ran foreign policy with special advisor Henry Kissinger, bypassing his secretary of state and secretary of war.

In his campaign for president in 1968, he promised the American public that he would end the war, but he privately promised the South Vietnamese that he would continue bombing Cambodia and invading Laos. Of course his duplicity was discovered but Nixon actually thought he could keep his dealings secret! When it did get in the papers, Nixon blew his top and did everything he could, including wiretapping the suspected whistle blowers' phones, to trace the leak.

He made many secret agreements with the help of Kissinger between South Vietnam, North Vietnam, China and Russia and it was impossible to know or trust what he was doing. Even his most important officials were kept in the dark. Meanwhile, he was secretly taping everyone in his office, authorizing wiretapping of reporters, break-ins of the Black Panthers strongholds and cache of weapons, secret infiltrations of peace marches and student organizations and the overthrow of the Chilean government. Secrecy, duplicity and denial were his trademarks, as can be true for some Counterphobic Type 6s.

He tried to cover up the stealing of documents and wiretapping of phones at the National Democratic Headquarters office regarding his reelection campaign of 1972; this became known as Watergate. Nixon denied any connection to the "plumbers," the men who perpetrated the break in, though eventually the truth and his cover up were discovered. To avoid impeachment, he resigned, the first resignation of a US president.

Nixon grew up in a small town in California of Quaker parents. His father was argumentative and many people who knew him portrayed him as a violent bully. His mother was known to be even-tempered, strict and not particularly warm. His father ran a grocery store and gas station and Richard spent many hours behind the counter selling goods and buying produce for the store, starting as early as 4am each morning. Harsh financial problems were ever present.

Nixon had four brothers, two of whom died of tuberculosis, causing great pain for Nixon. His mother had to devote most of her attention to her sick sons. Nixon grew up insecure, withdrawn and emotionally repressed. He did well in school, winning debates and school elections, and securing leading roles in dramatic productions, yet despite his many achievements, he wasn't popular and didn't have close friends in his life.

He felt solitary, alone and socially awkward and seemed to have a difficult time enjoying his successes. His fiercely competitive nature caused ongoing tension for him. He graduated from Whittier College and Duke University Law School second and third in his class. Nixon became a practicing attorney and in his spare time he was active in community-theater where he met his future wife. During World War II, he was a naval officer with administrative roles, seeing no combat.

As president, Nixon avoided cocktail parties and business breakfasts. He was an introvert, but he tried to appear extraverted. Press pictures seemed staged and he generally had a negative experience with the press and hated press conferences. He preferred to make decisions in private after reviewing memos and documents, working in his den at the Old Executive Offices next to the West Wing of the White House. He wanted to rule the world through paper and ideas (he had a strong 5 wing) and if he met with people at all, he preferred the meeting to be one to one. He actually preferred to use intermediaries, such as John Ehrlichman, Bob Haldeman and Henry Kissinger, who became collectively known as the Prussians.

He disliked chit-chat and had no use for most interaction with people, which also speaks of his strong 5 wing. Kissinger said, "Nixon didn't enjoy people. I don't understand why he went into politics. Isolation had become almost a spiritual necessity to this withdrawn, tormented man."

In school and in life, Nixon achieved through hard work, grim determination, good grades and by being fearfully studious. He seldom smiled and he spent his Saturday nights in the library when he was a student. He devoured history books, was moved by world leaders such as Woodrow Wilson, Churchill and Lincoln. He was determined "to leave behind his footprints on the sands of time," a quote from Henry Wadsworth Longfellow inscribed on a portrait of Lincoln given to Richard by his grandmother on his 13th birthday. He was driven by an insatiable desire to be famous and remarkable.

He was known as mean-spirited and attacked people any way he could – the dirtier the better, true of some Counterphobic 6s who can challenge and find the dirt in people to protect against their own negative qualities. They can win through finding enemies. His smear campaigns in running for US congressman in 1946 and senator in 1950 implied that his opposition candidates were Communists – both untrue, but he won on the implications. One of the first women who ran for Senate against Nixon was, according to Nixon, "pink down to her panties." She called him "Tricky Dick" and it became his nickname after that.

He was ruthless in just about everything he did and even though he was hated by many people, his communist accusations got him elected Vice President during both of Eisenhower's administrations. Tricky Dick was a master at gaining trust by instilling fear. There's some evidence to support connections to the Mob though that is speculative. Dwight Eisenhower, his boss said, "This man will never be president. The people don't like him." "Nixon is shifty, a goddamn liar and people know it," stated Harry Truman. "If I've done nothing for this country, I've saved them from Dick Nixon," said Kennedy. The list goes on and on.

He had a lighter side, at times playing piano and singing old tunes and he could play the clarinet, saxophone, accordion and violin. He enjoyed listening to classical music. He loved to bowl and had a bowling alley built in the White House, loved to read and was a huge football fan.

As a Counterphobic 6 with a 5 wing, he strengthened his name early in politics by questioning Alger Hiss, a top state department head who was a Harvard graduate and according to Nixon, was probably a Soviet agent. Nixon nailed him on a perjury charge. He envisioned himself as the protector of Middle America and held a grudge against rich snobs, elitists and "those who have everything who sit on their fat butts." Nixon was always looking out for enemies.

As an INTJ he possessed the classic gifts of innovative long-term planning and strategy, living in his head, and, being a Type 6, he was also very good at noticing and analyzing details. He lacked the feeling component of creating a natural sense of harmony and often made decisions without collaborating with important members of his team. He became isolated in his process.

He particularly disliked and had a vendetta for East Coast intellectuals. Losing to Kennedy in an extremely narrow defeat in 1960, as well as losing a bid for the California governorship, further solidified his hatred. He felt "kicked around by the press" and said he was quitting politics, which turned out to be far from the truth.

His insatiable drive to be famous propelled him forward. He made a comeback by campaigning for other Republican candidates, traveling overseas to talk to leaders in other countries, positioning himself to be the spokesman for "silent, law-abiding Americans." He bid for the 1968 nomination and election, promising the nation the end of the War in Vietnam and a return to lawfulness after many anti-Vietnam protests spiraled out of control into bitter violence.

He projected the image of a dignified statesman and demanded that everyone call him "Mr. President." He wanted to be seen as unifier of the country. The stress point of Type 6 is Type 3 who likes to create an image of success at the expense of truth, as was true in Nixon's case. The political demonstrations pained him. Treating his campaign as all-out war against McCarthy, he told the American public he wanted peace but secretly told South Vietnam to ignore Lyndon Johnson's desire to have peace talks. His Machiavellian tactics worked; he won the race with the electoral votes of 49 of the 50 states and over 60 percent of the popular vote, but his victory set the stage for his eventual downfall. His lying, deceit and the perspective he held of politics, which was being at war with his enemies, i.e., the liberals, the press and the Democrats, kept him in a state of anxious hyper-vigilance. He was wholly unable to enjoy his own success.

When at last Nixon, the outsider, finally became the insider he envisioned himself as world peacemaker, possibly to live up to the Quaker ideals of his background. Unfortunately, the tactics he used to get to the prized White House were anything but peaceful. He temporarily fooled the public but the seeds of his destruction were already sown.

The heart of Nixon's political ideology rested in his relationship with National Security Advisor Henry Kissinger. It was an odd match between a reclusive paranoid person who held a grudge against the world and a Jewish intellectual socialite who dated movie stars. In reality Kissinger was probably like Nixon underneath, an anxious loner at heart who was obsessed with his image and his place in history.

Both were deeply suspicious and Kissinger is likely a Type 6 also. Natural conspirators, secrecy was the key to their vision of success, but being unable to get outside feedback or create trusted alliances, isolated them. Their illusions of grandeur were not to be shared with others. They worked well together for a while but eventually their relationship with each other unraveled. Once friends, they became fearful enemies. One of them had to win and it was eventually Kissinger, who became Secretary of State in the second administration. He took credit for creating détente with Russia and China and ending the Vietnam War. Kissinger was more skillful at creating a positive public image, although it eventually backfired on him too.

What was important to Nixon was having secure information, no press releases, but rather the use of threats and strategies. Nixon lacked the ability to make personal connections. The plan was for Nixon and Kissinger to settle the Vietnam War on their own without regard to ethics, honesty or public scrutiny. It was a dark period in American politics which included recording real or imagined enemies' conversations, wiretapping their phones, liberal use of slush funds to pay off people, creating lists of names to prosecute, secret talks with the Vietnamese and Russia, security measures and increasing isolation for the president.

Nixon attempted to force the communists to come to the negotiating table through incessant bombing of Vietcong camps in Cambodia. That strategy failed and instead reinvigorated the Vietcong will to fight even harder. American demonstrators increased their protest marches. Lying Tricky Dick was finally seen for what he truly was; not really concerned for individual Americans but only for his greedy desire for power and being a hero.

When the secret bombing in Cambodia came to light, the press and public were infuriated, but Nixon just dug in more. He had a "friends and enemies" list consisting of political commentators, liberals and students. Members of the press were increasingly added to it. Nixon was becoming more and more unbalanced.

His office became a bunker, his aides were sent as spies, intrigue was the name of the game and Nixon was drinking more and more to the point of slurring inebriation. In May 1970 four students were shot dead at Kent State in Ohio, in the midst of a peace protest that disintegrated into violence. Nixon felt besieged when thousands of demonstrators marched to Washington. He couldn't sleep and he confronted protestors in person, telling them that peace the way they wanted it was an illusion.

He created a giant chess game in his head to strategize how to use the fear Russia and China had for each other to stop the war. He visited both China and Russia, the first president to do so in 25 years, to create a détente that would lead to a peace accord regarding Vietnam and he finally succeeded!

Nixon and Kissinger disagreed on the process, but their diplomatic strategy with Russia and China tempered the Cold War. Nixon's international visits and the vision of an end to the Vietnam War paid off with another reelection win, with 60 percent of the popular vote going to Nixon. Despite his win, Nixon couldn't relax; Kissinger was getting too much credit and trumpeting his successes. Kissinger compared himself to a wild-west hero, leaving Nixon out of the picture.

Many of his personality traits were negative but actually Nixon accomplished a lot and in many ways had a positive influence on the world. The following below comes from The Nixon Foundation that lists his accomplishments. www.nixonfoundation.org

"In his domestic policy, he ended the draft, moving the military to an all-volunteer force, he founded the Environmental Protection Agency and oversaw the passage of the Clean Air Act, the Clean Water Act and the Mammal Marine Protection Act. By appointing four Supreme Court justices, he ushered in an era of judicial restraint. He dedicated $100 million to begin the War on Cancer, which created a national cancer center.

He signed into law Title IX of the Education Amendments Act of 1972 preventing gender bias at colleges and universities receiving federal aid, opening the door for women in collegiate sports. He initiated and oversaw the peaceful desegregation of southern schools. We welcomed the astronauts of Apollo 11 safely home from the moon, oversaw the 26th Amendment to lower the voting age to 18, and he broke the back of organized crime, authorizing joint work between the FBI and the Special Task Forces, resulting in 2500 convictions. He ended the forced assimilation of American Indians, returned sacred lands and became the first American President to give American Indians the right to tribal self-determination.

On the foreign front, he participated in the Strategic Arms Limitation Talks (SALT) with Soviet Secretary General Brezhnev in 1972 as part of the effort to temper the Cold War through diplomatic détente. He signed the Anti-Ballistic Missile (ABM) Treaty, helping to calm US-Soviet tensions by limiting the threat of nuclear weapons. He was the first President to visit the People's Republic of China, where he issued the Shanghai Communique, announcing a desire for open, normalized relations, which brought a billion people out of isolation.

He signed the Paris Peace Accord ending US involvement in the Vietnam War. He established a new relationship with the Middle East, eliminating Soviet dominance in the region and paving the way toward regional peace. He brought home POWs from Vietnam, initiated Project Independence to set a timetable to end reliance on foreign oil, avoided a second Cuban Missile Crisis involving the Soviets and supported Israel with massive aid in the 1973 Yom Kippur War."

Upon retirement, he wrote ten bestselling books on domestic and foreign policy, wrote The Memoirs of Richard Nixon, advised Carter, Reagan and Bush on foreign policy and met with world leaders. His reputation grew and there was change in perception to include his many accomplishments, beyond his limitations. He lived in California, New York City and New Jersey and he and his wife Pat spent much of their time with their family. He gave many public talks, particularly about foreign policy, and on a trip to China and other countries he was warmly welcomed, with some world leaders thinking the Watergate Affair was overrated and should not have been his downfall. He died in 1994 and many world leaders and dignitaries attended his funeral.

Nixon is an example of a great man who was unable to feel secure in himself or his accomplishments. As mentioned, 6s go to 3 when stressed in an attempt to be successful, look good, and hide their fears. Nixon would have done better had he found the support he needed to accept his fears and trust the right people, without continually having to prove his worth, cover up so much and go into isolation.

He tended to see the worst side of people, looked at strategies more than personal connection, and was myopic regarding his own weaknesses, rather blaming others for his difficulties. Despite his weaknesses, Nixon accomplished much that was positive in his political lifetime.

Gerald Ford, Type 9, ESFJ, Devotion and Balance, 1974-77

(1913-2006) Gerald Ford was president number 38. When it was discovered that Richard Nixon's Vice President, Spiro Agnew, had accepted bribes and avoided paying taxes he resigned and the vice presidency was offered to Ford. Ford then became President after President Nixon resigned to avoid being impeached following the Watergate Scandal. Ford was appointed Vice President and then became President for being exactly the opposite of Nixon – Ford was honest, above board, trustworthy and had no political enemies.

Congress knew when it offered the vice presidency to Ford that he was likely to succeed Nixon, who was already being investigated for his involvement in Watergate. After serving 25 years in the House of Representatives and as Republican Minority Speaker of the House, Ford was reliable and consistent. Both Democrats and Republicans agreed on Ford as the only vice-presidential candidate to be offered the position, as he was the most likely person who would be approved quickly by Congress.

Gerald (his birth name was Lesley) Ford's early childhood was more than interesting. His mother, who was strong and resourceful, birthed her son when she was 21. Realizing on her honeymoon that her new husband was physically abusive, a liar and a drunk, she decided to divorce him and never moved in with him, quite a bold step in 1913. It was a decision even her husband's parents supported! Nonetheless she was already pregnant. A few days after Gerald's birth, his father came into the room with a butcher knife, threatening to kill the mother as well as the child and nurse. The police had to be called to restrain him and protect the mother and newborn son. What a way for Gerard Ford to start his life!

The following year, his mother met and married a responsible and loving man, Gerald Ford, Sr. Lesley didn't learn of his birth father's existence until he was in his late teens. He had been called Gerald after his mother married Gerald Ford, Sr. and his name was legally changed to Gerald Ford, Jr. after college. The message from his stepfather (whom he thought was his biological father) was "work hard, be honest, and come to dinner on time." His mother was a strict disciplinarian who, when Gerry got angry, would require him to recite a long poem. It seemed to be an effective method to temper his anger, which she felt was inherited from his biological father.

Gerald was named most popular in his high school class, made good grades and loved history and government. He was a football star, which smoothed his entrance into the University of Michigan. He also was academically successful in college and was named the most valuable football player at the University of Michigan. He could have become a professional football player and was offered positions with both the Green Bay Packers and the Detroit Lions! He turned down both offers because the teams only paid $200 per game at that point in time.

Gerald went to Yale Law School instead, where he became assistant football coach, as well as a boxing coach. His classmates at Yale included the future Supreme Court Justice, Potter Stewart, Secretary of State, Cyrus Vance, and Peace Corps Director, Sargent Shriver. After graduation he made extra money working as a male model!

Ford began a law practice in Michigan and only months later enlisted in the Navy to serve in World War II. He became a naval officer on an aircraft carrier, which saw combat during the war. Once he was almost washed overboard during a typhoon. Being in the Navy gave him a new perspective allowing him to see that the United States should take the stage as a world leader and emerge from its isolation. Upon his return from the war Ford resumed his law practice and met his future wife, Elizabeth Ann "Betty" Bloomer who was a dancer and worked as a fashion coordinator for a department store.

Ford served 12 consecutive terms in the US Congress as a Representative. He was anti-Communist and was known to work with both parties. He was in the middle between the Republican extremes – the left of Nelson Rockefeller and the right of very conservative Barry Goldwater. In Congress, Ford's conservatism, warm personality and willingness to accommodate opponents gave rise to his Republican leadership. As House leader, he opposed most of President Lyndon Johnson's Great Society legislation and urged the president to push the Vietnam War more vigorously. When Ford's friend and colleague Richard Nixon became President in 1969, Ford hoped for greater cooperation between Republicans in Congress and the Nixon White House, though that never came to pass.

By all accounts Ford was considerate, honest and friendly. He listened to what you had to say, was direct but gentle, and he had few enemies. "He never tried to outsmart anyone," observed Bud Vestal, a Grand Rapids reporter, "but if from intellectual hubris a tormentor gave him a chance, he would out dumb him, swiftly and deadpan. It would take days before the attacker to realize he'd been had." He was mocked unmercifully, especially by Saturday Night Live comedian Chevy Chase, for being clumsy and for having the misfortune of tripping and falling down when he was president. The irony is that he was naturally more coordinated than most people given his athletic youth and ongoing participation in golf and swimming. He was fit and trim as a result of his active lifestyle and was a stylish and sporty dresser as well.

As a Type 9, Peacemaker, Ford talked about brotherly love and the golden rule to help heal the wounds of Watergate. One month after he became president, he pardoned Richard Nixon. Two-thirds of the populace were shocked and wanted to put Nixon on trial. They assumed Ford must have cut a deal with Nixon, which was not true. Ford wanted an end to the incessant controversy about Nixon so he could move on with his agenda and thought Americans needed to focus their attention on other matters to regain the country's mental balance and health. He lost credibility though because much of the nation wanted revenge for Nixon's misdeeds rather than brotherly love!

President Ford had to deal with many economic problems, an energy oil crisis and a mostly Democratic Congress, that wanted to regain power it had lost during the Nixon years. He worked hard to maintain détente with the Soviet Union and was instrumental in the signing of the Helsinki Accords, agreements that eased the tensions of the Cold War. He presided over the evacuation of Saigon when North Vietnam invaded South Vietnam. The U.S. had to close their embassy and get U.S. personnel and some of the South Vietnamese citizens out of the country. Congress refused appropriations of any more funds for South Vietnam during this process.

Traits of Ford included an amazing ability to remember names; he personally addressed hundreds of people. Very gregarious, he often phoned or met with fellow congressmen and had the personal touch, in addition to having great ideas. He was persuasive but in a gentle way, very different from Johnson or Nixon. He would also ask questions about family members by name.

Ford had adversaries but no enemies, as 9s try to do. He could disagree without being disagreeable, even with those who had opposing ideas and agendas. He would often give out his home phone number. He met with many world leaders, all of which praised him, and he attended the first G6 world summit meeting. They have continued to meet to this day, with the top leaders of industrialized countries.

Ford was straightforward and unassuming and was described as the "least neurotic" president in the last generation of presidents. 9s tend to be that way – unassuming and less complicated. He's probably the least psychoanalyzed of all the presidents because he didn't seem to have any dirt in his background or personal quirks! Being a conservative, he didn't promote bold programs but instead, he cut government spending. He was sometimes described as a do-nothing or boring President but alternatively he was praised for settling the country's turmoil. He was the steady calm after the turbulence of Watergate, Vietnam, and divisive national protest. The Nation celebrated its two hundredth anniversary in that calm. He was perfect for his time. His marriage was stable and he had four children who seemed all-American.

Sports were a major outlet for Ford. In high school and college, he played football, basketball, tennis and ran track. When he was president he swam every day, and had a new outdoor pool installed at the White House. He went on ski vacations with his family and played tennis and golf. One time, jumping on a trampoline with his daughter he got a black eye. He was the first president to have earned the distinction of being an Eagle Scout. Setting the precedent for his children, he was truly all-American.

He was a pro at self-effacing humor and would laugh at himself, not unusual for a Type 9. At his inaugural address, he joked saying "he was a Ford, not a Lincoln." After leaving office he wrote a book, "*Humor and the Presidency*" about how presidents have used humor in politics. During a political debate with Carter, he said, "there was no Soviet domination in Eastern Europe," which was incorrect and cost his political reputation dearly. He meant to say that Eastern Europeans didn't accept Soviet domination. When asked what he was going to do when he retired, he said he was going to teach for the University of Michigan but that he wouldn't be teaching European history! After the collapse of the Soviet Union in 1991, he said he had been correct but was just 15 years early.

Ford was an ESFJ – a loyal guardian who was consistent, warm, friendly, personal, hardworking, conscientious and honest. His geniality and sensitivity made it difficult for him to be tough with or fire people who worked for him as he looked for the best in them and had a personal touch. He would give people a second chance and had a hard time being dismissive. He was a family man who placed a very high value on his relationship with his wife and children.

www.myersbriggs.org/my-mbti-personality-type/mbti-basics/the-16-mbtitypes.htm

"ESFJ - Warmhearted, conscientious, and cooperative. Want harmony in their environment, work with determination to establish it. Like to work with others to complete tasks accurately and on time. Loyal, follow through even in small matters. Notice what others need in their day-by-day lives and try to provide it. Want to be appreciated for who they are and for what they contribute."

He believed in long-term goals unlike most politicians who act or legislate for the short term to win an election. Ford chose to do what was right economically to solve problems in the long run, even though it cost him the election with Carter. Presidents since Ford have followed many of the economic policies he established, economics being his strong suit.

At his first press conference, when asked about a code of ethics for the executive branch, Ford replied, "The code of ethics that will be followed, will be the example that I set." His character did set an example.

His wife, Betty Ford, studied modern dance at Bennington College in Vermont and decided to make a career of dance. She performed with the Martha Graham Concert group in New York City while supporting herself as a fashion model. She organized a dance group of her own and taught dance to handicapped children. Her first marriage ended in divorce after five years.

She met Gerald Ford while he was on a modeling job. Gerald and Betty were soon wed and lived in Washington, D.C. for over 30 years. She expressed herself with confidence, humor and forthrightness and she was open in talking about her breast cancer surgery in 1974. She frankly shared her views, such as her support for the Equal Rights Amendment for Women. From her later home in California she bravely talked about her dependency on drugs and alcohol and established the Betty Ford Treatment Center. They were a good match and were role models of a stable, forward thinking couple.

Gerard Ford was a Type 9 with an 8 wing and had the qualities to prove it – honesty, simplicity, what you see is what you get, guilelessness (though he was politically astute), warmth, friendliness, a tendency to include others and accept people as they are.

Jimmy Carter, Type 3, ISTJ, Humanitarian Post President, 1977-1981

(1924-) President number 39 was Jimmy Carter. Many people assess that Carter has been a better post president than president. He has built houses for the homeless, eradicated worm disease in millions of people in Africa, monitored free elections in many countries, negotiated peace with many countries as a freelance ambassador promoting human rights, and has written many books about power, politics and peace.

Carter was the first president born in a hospital, not in the family home which was without electricity or running water. He was named after his father who had a peanut farm, warehouse and store in Plains, Georgia. In the 1920s his mother reached across racial barriers and counseled poor African American women on health issues. By the age of 10,

Jimmy would stack produce from the farm and carry it by mule driven wagon to the store in town to sell. By the time he was 13 he had saved enough money to buy five houses at rock bottom Depression prices which he rented to needy families! He was an ambitious child. He sold peanuts in five-cent bags and saved his money. His father was stern but proud of Jimmy and his mother highly encouraged him to read. Growing up Baptist, he was religious and attended church and Sunday school.

After graduating at the top of his small class in high school, he applied to the Naval Academy and was accepted. Influenced by pictures, stories and letters sent by his uncle, who was in the Navy, he wanted to visit exotic lands. Upon graduating near the top of his class at Annapolis, he was stationed aboard the first experimental submarine and then went on to serve in submarines for seven years. Influenced by his upbringing about racial equality, he refused to attend an exclusive party for white officers only. Carter served under the tough Admiral Rickover whom he deeply admired, not minding hard work and discipline.

Originally, I thought of Carter as a Type 1. He has always been moralistic, industrious, improvement-driven, self-disciplined and also a bit self-righteous. He is a positive thinker who intends to have inner peace. Being very religious, he has been a Sunday school teacher and has been active in his church his entire life. He has been a major supporter and advocate for equal rights for African Americans since an early age. He recently quit the Southern Baptist church due to its decision to discontinue having women as pastors. I still debate whether he is a 1.

Then I thought Carter might be a Type 2 with a strong 1 wing. He has that constant smile and is very giving with a warm, affectionate, personal touch. He is able to lead at times with an apparent warm, persuasive, vivacious quality and generosity like many 2s.

Then I considered Type 9 as he has often been typed. Carter was as much a religious leader at times as a political one, and he believed in the promise of peace as a motivator more than using the threat of war. This is a very strong Type 9 aspect. Carter, however, doesn't have the avoidance behavior of a Type 9 and he isn't laid-back at all. He's driven. Similar to George Washington, who was a Type 3, I think Carter tries to hide his ambitious nature.

On inauguration day, Carter and Rosalyn walked on Pennsylvania Avenue rather than riding in the car. He chose a business suit for the inauguration activities instead of a tux. When it came time to address the nation on television about conserving gas and electricity he wore a cardigan sweater, engendering an air of informality and modeling an attitude of discipline, rather than extravagance. He wanted to connect to people and not be superior or distant, and also model the values of restraint. I can see how he could be taken for a 9 or 1, as he includes himself in others' suffering, with a focus of peace. He seems however to expend effort to create those images, i.e., they don't feel totally natural.

Then I reconsidered which type was dominant and none fit exactly. Many 1s are peacemakers because it's the right thing to do but the manner in which they do it often has a righteous and moral tone. 2s have a personal drive to help and connect to people and be acknowledged. 9s tend to be peaceful and avoid conflict in a general sense. Carter could stand his ground and do things in a more independent way than a 9, who likes to have agreement from others, and Carter was more concerned about his image more than a 9 would be. Type 1s and 2s are more focused and intense than 9s, less distracted and less persuaded to go along with others.

Type 3, as I finally decided Carter is, can alter to be like any type, in order to create a win. Type 3s can alter their behavior to portray the image they need at any given time – and I'm convinced that Carter is a Type 3 – that is, to have the best characteristics of 9, 1 and 2. I think his focus is on success and winning, starting with his strong focus on being an entrepreneur in childhood. His current reality is peacemaking, negotiation, and service to the world, which reflects his maturity as a person and as a 3 with the higher traits of 9. He also has developed the higher side of 6, to include others in his team and not have to be the star.

Some of the personality description of Carter comes from reading the book *Presidential Temperament*, a major resource book that has descriptions of each president's characteristics related to some of the Myers-Brigg's traits. Like George Washington and James Monroe, Carter is a 3 who is an ISTJ (very Type 1 like).

"ISTJ - Quiet, serious, earn success by thoroughness and dependability. Practical, matter-of-fact, realistic, and responsible. Decide logically what should be done and work toward it steadily, regardless of distractions. Takes pleasure in making everything orderly and organized - their work, their home, their life. Value traditions and loyalty." www.myersbriggs.org/my-mbti-personality-type/mbti-basics/the-16-mbti-types.htm

Carter is a serious Christian. He attends church every Sunday. He's the only president to use the world "love" in a Christian sense in virtually every campaign and political speech he gave. His political ideology is a moral and personal one and he's very clear about the difference between right and wrong. His secondary type apparently is 1, but he has a 2 wing, as well as traits of 4.

If there had been a moral crisis during his office tenure, he would likely have been elected for a second term. If the major issue in the late 70s had been the morality of the Vietnam War or integration as it was in the 60s and early 70s, he would have been the perfect president. Instead, the overriding domestic issues of his era were financial, managerial and problems of dealing with vested interests.

Type 3 is driven by a need to succeed and win. Carter was extremely ambitious and used the moral drive of a Type 1 to focus on right action, and the charm of a Type 2, a winning smile combined with the ability to connect personally and a desire to be of service to his constituents as well as the country. Both of these were strong characteristics of his mother. According to Carter, at an early age he wanted "to be the best," which alludes to a Type 3 persona, although Type 1s can have the same aspiration.

To further solidify the case for Carter being a 3, he hated losing at anything he attempted. He wanted to hit a home run every time at bat, win every debate he participated in, attend the Naval Academy and have that open doors to prestige for him. He announced to friends in his youth that he wanted to be governor of Georgia. He was intensely competitive and strove to get ahead. His introverted personality made it more difficult. Introverted 3s often have a harder row to hoe; they have to behave as an extravert would in order to gain the support needed to be president. Modern presidents have had to be more extraverted than earlier ones, who were promoted by others rather than have to campaign and make their own political speeches.

Carter was a man of contrast – warm and friendly on the one hand and cold, calculating and rejecting on the other. He would gather a wealth of facts and claimed to be interested in a broader perspective but wasn't able to easily verbalize what that was. Carter has an amazing ability to remember facts, but as a politician had a difficult time putting them into a practical use. "He had a penchant for isolated facts and standard operating procedures rather than for interrelated concepts and strategic intentions," according to *Presidential Temperament*.

He could seem stiff and reserved but at other times gracious and open. Photos of Carter show a winning smile that seemed staged, with a brow that was furrowed with eyes distant and not connecting.

As a strong Type 3 Achiever, he had a tendency for hyperbole; as one writer said, he had a way of exaggerating his strengths, but with facts that weren't true. He claimed to have understood Tolstoy's War and Peace by the time he was 12 years old, that he was a nuclear physicist, that he had been a finalist for the prestigious Rhodes scholarship and that he had served in two world wars. There is some truth in a few of these statements but when it came right down to it, they were proven to be false. These statements were likely concocted and exaggerated to magnify his winning image.

Many have said that Carter's warmth toward others could be turned on or off like a spigot, while others said that he could seem like a phony. 3s can be said to be fickle as they alter behaviors from one moment to the next to create a "win." It seemed as if "morality, helping, caring and belonging are things that he could bring about by proclamation by following the rules and by exhorting others to do likewise," according to *Presidential Temperament*. It was hard for Carter to put things into context beyond following rules and achieving.

For instance, Carter wanted cabinet meetings open to the press to create an image of honesty and openness; however, such openness was at odds with the privacy needed to engage in in-depth discussion regarding matters that could be damaging if made public. It seemed the image of how he wanted to be seen got in the way of properly carrying out his duties. He quickly abandoned the idea of open cabinet meetings when it became clear that it inhibited the members' ability to conduct frank discussions.

Carter had few close friends as president (not true today). He was especially close to Rosalyn, his wife, who often attended cabinet meetings and whose advice he held in esteem; however, he tended to mistrust others and usually chose to make difficult decisions unilaterally. He trusted his individual interpretation of facts without seeming to need any further understanding of the big picture beyond his own and without considering multiple points of view.

It seemed at times that his rural religious background, his need to be right, and his image were more important than his overall effectiveness. Critics gradually perceived him as too narrowly focused, ineffective, apolitical and insufficiently inclusive and alliance-driven, and he became too isolated. It's as if he hid behind a facade of morality and helpfulness (though genuine from his perspective) and wasn't getting enough feedback to be effective in the real world.

Long before his presidency, after serving for seven years in the Navy, while he was still in his 20s, Carter returned to farming which offered less financial security. The racial dynamics in Georgia were tense. The 1954 Supreme Court decision to end segregation was deeply resented in Plains, Georgia as well as most of the South. The White Citizens Council in Plains was created to maintain the status quo of white supremacy, and Carter was the only business owner in Plains who refused to join. His business was boycotted as a result, but he stood his ground, and the boycott was eventually lifted.

Carter ran and won a seat on the county board of education and then was elected to two terms in the state senate. He won an election after he demanded a vote recount, in which was discovered fraudulent votes by his opponent. He was always known as a man of integrity, reforming wasteful government and going after laws discouraging the African American vote. He earned a reputation as a tough and independent man.

Carter ran for governor and lost to the racist Lester Maddox, but ran again four years later and won, deciding in the meantime to create alliances with Lester Maddox and some of the segregationists. He learned to be more political, and to appear somewhat as a segregationist to be able to win -- even being called a "racist" peanut farmer by a major newspaper.

Once in office as governor of Georgia, he switched his stance and called for an end to segregation, increased black staff on his payroll by 25 percent, consolidated hundreds of state agencies down to 25, thus eliminating waste, while promoting environmental awareness and funding for education. His "holier than thou" attitude as some saw it, kept him isolated from more potential allies. As governor, he was checking the political landscape for a possible presidential run in 1976. Type 3s can more easily switch positions to fit the perception of how they want to appear effective. Think of Bill Clinton, Mitt Romney and John Kerry as 3s.

Carter was elected president, partially due to the fact that he was perceived as being an outsider, not part of national politics with its inevitable scandals. Even though his party, the Democratic Party, was in charge of both the Senate and House at the time, Carter didn't seem to know how to play the political game, and Congress refused to pass many of his bills. The economy was struggling due to inflation from overspending by prior administrations. There was an energy shortage resulting from an Arab oil embargo and angry drivers had to wait in long lines at the gas pump.

As president, Carter had to deal with the energy crisis, the War between Afghanistan and Russia, and a hostage crisis in Iran. As had been the case with Ford, Congress exerted more power over Carter than it had over Nixon or Johnson, both of whom were more dominant as executives. Despite the lack of support from Congress and a lack of national experience, Carter dealt with these problems with courage, steadfastness and idealism.

People wanted Carter to succeed after the Nixon fiasco and Ford's short tenure, but the already established inflation made things challenging. Carter started out by pardoning draft resisters from the Vietnam War, killing the B-1 bomber project, and trying to create a consumer protection bill. He vetoed "pork barrel" bills from Congress that he considered wasteful and corrupt and his outspokenness created friction with Congress. His focus was on saving money, and he went so far as to limit Congressional get-together breakfasts to sweet rolls instead of full breakfasts. The breakfasts were later reinstated due to Congressional complaints. He retired the presidential yacht and limousine and was driven in a smaller car.

He appointed minorities and women to key posts, increased environmental protections, and promoted research of environmental alternatives. Carter created a Department of Energy and also a Department of Education. Deeply promoting human rights in his relations with foreign counties, he withheld foreign aid to any country that was unjust in dealing with foreigners or even its own citizens. He was more focused on human rights for all citizens of the world than any other president.

Carter arranged for Panama to gain its rights to the Panama Canal, causing much opposition in Congress. He continued positive relations with China and organized and supported international protests such as the boycott the 1980 summer Olympics in Moscow, after the Soviet Union invaded Afghanistan.

Carter is a complex character. He can be alternately shy and self-confident, compassionate and tender but also judgmental and critical. The press had a hard time with President Carter, as he could seem aloof, condescending, and impersonal with reporters. They saw him at times as too moralistic, arrogant and also not politically savvy.

Carter was a strong believer in peaceful dissent and was in accord with the statements written in the United Nations 1948 Declaration of Human Rights, which were foundational for the modern human rights movement. He had a strong and very genuine moral drive that may have concealed some of his discomfort at being seen with traits of Type 3, driven by success.

The President and his advisors denounced human rights violations by the Soviet Union, its Eastern European satellites and North Korea and he spoke out against the human rights practices of the governments of Chile, Nicaragua, El Salvador and Uganda. Carter was attacked by conservatives for criticizing US allies. In time, Carter backed off his criticism of the Soviet Union to support arms control talks.

Carter was criticized as weak for what was perceived as giving away our rights to protect Americans in the Panama Canal Zone even though both FDR and Kissinger had previously negotiated a treaty giving all rights back to the Panamanians. Carter had better luck with the Middle East in helping negotiate a peace treaty between Israel and Egypt in the Camp David Accords. Begin of Israel and Sadat in Egypt received the Nobel Peace Prize in 1979, in large part due to Carter's achievement in helping with the Peace Accord -- possibly his greatest achievement as President.

Carter is an introvert though he can appear to be an extravert, seeming comfortable meeting people and being assertive and self-confident. He can seem like a feeling type with his genuine compassion toward others' suffering. He dressed as a "man of the people" and had a jovial smile with prominent white teeth. Because he is an introvert, it requires work for him to be and look extraverted.

Carter and his wife Rosalyn worked together as a team. She was one of the few First Ladies who attended cabinet meetings and major briefings. Representing the President at ceremonial occasions, she served as the president's personal emissary to Latin American countries. She was a skillful speaker and a hardworking mother of four children, three of whom were adults by the time Carter assumed residency at the White House. Carter was criticized for giving too much power to her as his representative.

The Carter's young daughter Amy lived in the executive mansion. Sometimes she was invited to sit at executive dinners, though often would read a book, possibly not being good company for a politician, staff or visiting emissary. While raising her daughter, Rosalyn focused national attention on performing arts and invited well-known artists to the White House. She took a strong interest in mental health, the elderly and building community life. She wrote an autobiography, *First Lady from Plains*, and has been the director of the Carter Center, managing an active mental health program and working on human rights, conflict resolution and childhood immunization programs. Rosalyn's warm personality lent Carter the appearance of being warmer than he actually was.

Some people consider Carter to be the greatest former U.S. president. The Carter Center at Emory College in Atlanta, Georgia is dedicated to issues of human rights worldwide. Habitat for Humanity International builds houses for underprivileged people and Carter in earlier times was active holding beams and hammering nails in the building.

Carter falls into the same tendency as the Type 3 ISTJ tradition of some of our founding fathers such as Washington and Monroe. Carter is a man of great self-development. He demonstrates an ability to change and an ongoing commitment to civil rights and women's rights. He is a man of integrity and strong support for humanitarian concerns. He has been an active leader for fair elections worldwide, protecting citizens against their governments, and speaking out about abuses by the U.S. government. Certainly, he is not only an achiever, but also a man of sacrifice, commitment, hard work and inclusion of all peoples.

Ronald Reagan, Type 9, ENFJ, Movie Actor, 1981-1989

(1911-2004) President number 40, was Ronald Reagan, a former movie star and a man who set the standard for modern conservatism. As president, he believed in deregulation, private enterprise, strong business support and "trickle-down" theory, the idea that wealth will trickle down to the poor. The theory is anything but new and has been discredited as inaccurate.

Even though he was once a liberal Democrat who supported FDR and Truman, Reagan switched to the Republican Party, and put a stop to the liberal trend in politics. Reagan was so left wing in the early part of his life that at one point in the 1930s he applied to join the Communist Party (many of his friends had joined) but he was rejected for not being able to carry on an intelligent conversation for five minutes! The Communist Party in the Depression era of the 1930s was much more accepted than it was in later years and was known to help the unemployed, poor, homeless and oppressed.

Quite apart from his earlier philosophy, when he was president, Reagan said, "We are a nation that has a government – not the other way around. And this makes us special among the nations of the Earth. Our government has no power except that granted it by the people. It is time to check and reverse the growth of government, which shows signs of having grown beyond the consent of the governed. It is my intention to curb the size and influence of the Federal establishment... It is to make it work – work with us, not over us; to stand by our side, not ride on our back. Government can and must provide opportunity, not smother it; foster productivity, not stifle it."

Nice in theory, but in practice, Reagan didn't reduce government but expanded it and got the US into debt, even though initially the economy improved. Taxes were cut and the military budget was greatly expanded in the belief that a strong military deterrent would cause enemy nations to back down. It worked with the Soviet Union.

At the time Reagan was the oldest president at 69 to be sworn in until Donald Trump at 70. He still had a youthful appearance, smiled often, and projected a positive confidence. People needed that optimism after the economic downturn during the Carter years. Reagan was an extravert, genial, likeable, dynamic and engaging in public. He was the "great communicator" and inspiring speaker, with anecdotes and pithy statements that appealed to what many wanted to hear. He seemed more interested in engaging the audience with simple, repeatable ideas (true for many type 9s) rather than in curious exploration and deep understanding. He called himself a "citizen politician."

Reagan didn't actually have many close friends, but could be the life of the party. He was somewhat emotionally detached in private and seemed most comfortable being in front of an audience, possibly stemming back to his days as a movie star and the adoration of the public. He spent much of his time with his wife Nancy, who managed many of his activities and planned his schedule, often based on the astrological readings of Joan Quigley, whom Nancy completely trusted. Type 9s, The Peacemakers, are often managed by others, as 9s tend to go along with their spouses or those who take charge of their lives. 9s don't want to risk too much conflict with important people and sometimes would rather let others make decisions for them. He was strongly guided by his Type 2 wife, Nancy.

Much of the next four paragraphs, including this one, are paraphrased or quoted from a National Review article entitled, "Why Ronald Reagan's Example is Still Relevant Today"

Reagan always spoke to his audiences as "we," a united America. He didn't like divisiveness, as is true for 9s. Let's be together of one mind with peace and comfort for all. Reagan preached the values of family, faith, neighborhood, work, peace and freedom. "We" were the citizens connected by the same love for America. When Reagan stated, 'We are Americans!' it was his voice of optimism declaring that in this land we have greater potential than anywhere else in the world to be creative, heroic and to excel to build a great nation. Reagan likely had a strong secondary type of 7, the Optimist.

"Reagan emboldened America. He set forth a daring vision and policies that told the world America is back, and once again, we will be doing great things. His goal was not just to heal our economy, but to make America the growth, jobs, and investment leader of the world. Accordingly, he cut taxes deeply and equally for everyone, eventually dropping the top rate all the way from 70 percent to 28 percent, while providing enterprises strong incentives to compete and restoring a dollar as good as gold. He fought hard against ever expanding, encroaching bureaucracy, reduced non-defense spending, and eliminated subsidies and price controls, all of which provoked howls of protest. Reagan's critics never stopped insisting he would fail disastrously."

"Finally, Reagan protected America. He not only called our enemies what they were — evil — he rallied the free world and worked secretly with Pope John Paul II to roll back the Soviets. His policy was crystal clear: "We win, they lose." From day one, he pursued peace through strength by rearming America, conventionally and strategically, from top to bottom."

"When his work was done, he sought no praise, and gave all credit to God and to the American people, whom he loved more than anything else on earth, except Nancy." Mother Theresa was quoted, "In this man, greatness and simplicity are one."

"Quiet on the set," says Reagan from one of his films, a former movie actor of 53 mostly B-films. His analogies were often movies, and he and Nancy usually watched a movie a day on television or in the movie room at the White House. Reagan's flag-draped, conservative rhetoric had a popular appeal that almost seemed out of a 1930's movie. His message was patriotic, simple, love of country and family and appealed to the hearts of many Americans.

Reagan was affable, cheerful and optimistic. This came through even when in an assassination attempt he was seriously wounded only 10 weeks after his first inauguration. Generally, 9s are optimistic though they can take on the range of all emotions. In the hospital after being shot in an assassination attempt, he said, "I hope the doctors are Republicans." This assassination attempt and his recovery finally broke the legendary curse of Indian Chief Tecumseh who said that in every 20-year election from 1840, every US president would die in office. In reality from 1840 to 1980 that is exactly what happened. Every president who won the election in 1840, 1860, 1880, 1900, 1920, 1940, and 1960 died in office or was assassinated or incapacitated in the case of Wilson!

According to the New York Times, "His aw-shucks manner" (note this is true for many 9s particularly with 8 wings) and "charming good looks disarm those who from a distance think of him as a far-right fanatic." He was described as private, aloof and reluctant to reveal much personal information. His staff saw him as often passive, disengaged from day to day operations, timid at asserting authority, unable to confront and at times lacking the ability to understand basic issues. 9s are often passive or passive-aggressive, disengaged, timid and afraid to directly confront people. He was more confrontive in public speeches.

Reagan's impatience with detail and willingness to delegate authority were often criticized. He left much to be handled by others, and as a 9, did not assume authority or take on the I'm-responsible position. As mentioned, his schedule could suddenly change due to relying on Nancy's astrologer. This shocked many of his staff with concern about decisions dictated by astrological alignment. He was certainly a Type 9, dependent on his wife Nancy, somewhat disengaged but still personable, popular to the audience but not as assertive or decisive as needed in specific situations. He seemed to prefer the comfort of movies to reality.

Whether he was feeding squirrels, having a weekly Mexican lunch with Vice President Bush, eating Jelly Beans or laughing at himself, he had a good time. He was great at humor and loved dirty jokes. Ron could make America smile and laugh. The only professional actor to become president, he could tell endless tales of his Hollywood days. 9s often like to talk about days gone by, want to feel good and don't like to face contradictory or difficult realities. There's a dip in a positive, fantasy world.

Reagan grew up in Illinois with a father who moved his family often while looking for better sales jobs, mostly selling shoes. Used to moving, Ronald didn't maintain many close friendships but played with his older brother Neil and was close to his parents. His father was gregarious, a dreamer who was burdened by alcohol abuse. His parents were Democrats and his mother was active in the Disciples of Christ Church. During the Depression, both parents worked for FDR's Works Project Administration (WPA), his father as a local director.

Ronald's parents were into equality for all – and against religious or racial intolerance. His father refused to let his children see the movie *Birth of a Nation,* which advocated for the Ku Klux Klan. Ronald took after his mother, a genuine do-gooder who visited prisons, poorhouses and hospitals to help and visit those in need. She organized drama recitals that featured her sons and also worked as a seamstress and sales clerk. She was known by all to be a compassionate and generous woman. Ronald always had fond memories of her.

In high school, Reagan played football and basketball, became president of the student body, acted in school plays and wrote for the yearbook. He was the all-American boy with a Type 3 drive, the secure type balance for Type 9. (Refer to the last chapter of the book for further explanation about secure type). For six summers he was a lifeguard on a dangerous river, and said he saved 77 people from drowning. In college, he was an average C student, majoring in economics. His extracurricular activities included: football, swimming and debate club. In addition, he was a reporter for the school paper, edited the yearbook, and was president of the student council.

Admitted on a partial football scholarship, in college he made extra money washing dishes and being a lifeguard and swimming coach. In 1940, he was the recipient of the "Most Nearly Perfect Male Figure" award by the University of California. He posed for art students who sculpted his nearly perfect human physique.

After college, he got a job using his great voice as a radio sportscaster and making commercials. Within a few years, he was making a good salary as a sportscaster for the Chicago Cubs and Big Ten football. Reagan met a movie scout while covering spring training for the Chicago Cubs and was hired to replace a rising young actor who was killed in a car accident. They even looked alike. After completing a screen test, he was hired by Warner Brothers. This job launched a 20-year acting career.

His breakthrough movie was "Knute Rockne - All American," about a football player who was terminally ill; from this role Reagan got his nickname, "The Gipper." He was known for his ability to memorize lines quickly. He played mostly in light comedies and action films and during this time he learned a great deal about staging films. He used those skills to his advantage in his subsequent political campaigns. Reagan almost always played good guy characters in films, certainly a preference as a Type 9. It would be hard for a 9 to play the bad guy part, as 9s naturally gravitate toward goodness. During WWII, while serving in the military, he narrated training films and appeared in patriotic war movies like "Jap Zero," "For God and Country," and performed in a musical, "This is The Army," which raised money for wartime charities.

Reagan remained a Democrat until the age of 50, when he changed his party affiliation to Republican. This change of affiliation was likely related to his increased wealth and higher tax bracket. He had a growing sense during years when he worked for General Electric that the federal government was stifling economic growth and individual freedom. His income was growing and, being influenced by new wealthy friends, he wanted to protect it. In his lifetime shift from being relatively poor to being rich, his politics changed.

Supporting Barry Goldwater started his political career. As the corporate spokesman for General Electric, Reagan had developed a basic identity, including many stories filled with statistics, which became his foundation. He delivered magnetic speeches filled with humor and charm. He argued that government restrictions and taxation were causing the erosion of individual freedom. He felt that the Soviet Union was dominating the world and the United States was not doing enough to stop it. After Goldwater lost, Reagan became the new standard bearer for conservative Republicans.

He decided to run for governor of California in 1966. He won and was reelected in 1970. His support came from a group of wealthy Southern Californians and he was encouraged by his wife Nancy. Despite his beliefs, he agreed to a record tax increase to solve an inherited budget deficit. Reagan restored order to a number of college campuses in disarray from protests, worked with Democrats to achieve welfare reform and property tax relief, and protected the rivers of the state's northern coast.

As president, his economic strategies led to a boom in the 80s followed by deficits in the 90s. There was a growing gap between the rich and the poor. Reagan was more of a philosopher and idea generator than an economist. Indeed, although he majored in economics in school, he earned only a C grade. He was generally admired, not for being an intellectual, but for his optimism, patriotism and encouragement.

He was reelected for a second term as president in a gigantic landslide against Democrat Walter Mondale, on a slogan of continued domestic prosperity. He used the tried and true old saw of waving the flag and celebrating American virtues, but had a blind spot when it came to the reality of the country and his own failings. Important issues of AIDS, women's rights and homelessness were pretty much ignored during his administrations. Some Type 9s can focus on positive images and simple slogans rather than the hard issues and conflicts around such problems as poverty, discrimination and violence. 9s can also go along with the status quo or expectations of those in their immediate circle. They want to be liked and Reagan's desire for acceptance was satisfied by his friends' and party's support.

Many other 9s would have more empathy and compassion toward the poor, disadvantaged and victims of discrimination. Reagan didn't want to use government for social change. He likely wanted distance from his less than well-to-do childhood.

He criticized the "evil empire" of the Soviet Union, and took credit for ending the Cold War by causing the Soviet Union to falter. He is famous for his proclamation, "Mr. Gorbachev, tear down that wall" (the Berlin Wall) and for his Star Wars missile defense system. SDI, Strategic Defense Initiative, was developed to intercept missiles in space by creating a "shield" of protection. Reagan's inspiration for SDI came to him when he saw the famous sci-fi film, *The Day the Earth Stood Still*.

He held four summit meetings with Russian Prime Minister Gorbachev that led to limiting the use of nuclear weapons. The Russian budget couldn't keep up with the United States' military prowess and Gorbachev backed off, contributing to the demise of the Soviet

Union. Gorbachev and Reagan were fairly chummy and shared a mutual admiration for each other, so even Russia fell under the spell of Reagan's charm.

"I don't know if I could do this job if I weren't an actor," said Reagan. His acting career and television hosting gave him the background to play the part. Twice Reagan had been president of the Screen Actors Guild. He hosted the weekly TV show General Electric Theater and introduced Death Valley Days, a popular television show. As already stated, 9s have little problem repeating the same speech over and over and tend to like the comfort of repetition. All of this served as a backdrop to his unique leadership qualities as president.

Reagan was a long-term fan of John Wayne and modeled himself after the actor's behavior asking himself "What would the Duke do?" when he needed to make a decision. They were allies; Wayne supported Reagan politically, excerpt when it came to Reagan's criticism of Carter for returning the Panama Canal to Panama. John Wayne's first wife was Panamanian and Wayne knew more about the Panama Canal than Reagan.

Reagan was so wrapped up in watching movies (some 9s can certainly escape into movies, books, food – anything to avoid conflict and the pain of reality) that he would use them as an excuse to avoid reading important presidential briefings, saying things like, "The Sound of Music was on last night and I couldn't miss it." Ronald and Nancy watched hundreds of movies at the White House, one a night on average, such as The Jazz Singer, Superman II, Chariots of Fire, On Golden Pond, E.T., Top Gun, The Karate Kid, Butch Cassidy, The Color Purple, Terms of Endearment, King Lear, Cabaret and Moonstruck. He liked action oriented, popular and inspirational movies.

Though appearing strong, Reagan had flaws. Cabinet members disagree on this point, but likely he fell asleep (9s can easily be sleepy and drift off) at cabinet meetings. He would doodle and make drawings to stay awake. He tended to have a lax management style, which might have been the problem during the Iran-Contra Affair. The US was secretly selling arms to Iran in exchange for hostages in Lebanon and then funding anti-communist Nicaraguan rebels with the money. He claimed he didn't have knowledge of the deal, which might have been the case, as he wasn't aware of everything that went on in his administration, especially in the National Security Council. He avoided criminal charges by accepting responsibility for the "mistake." 9s can sometimes be forgetful or have foggy memories but can apologize more easily than other types – anything for harmony.

Possibly his memory was fading at that point, as it's argued he had early stage Alzheimer's in his second administration. His hearing and speech started to falter. His subordinates took much of the blame for Iran-Contra. His growing struggle with prostate cancer and Alzheimer's affected him and he seemed more and more removed from reality and was forgetting people's names.

Some interesting additional facts about Reagan: Twice he reported seeing a UFO outside his private plane that others witnessed also. Another time, he and Nancy saw a UFO on the way to a party. He switched to jelly beans -- his favorite flavor licorice, as a substitute for pipe smoking. Reagan was partially deaf in one ear due to a gun that went off close by in a movie set. He's the only president to have been divorced - his first marriage was to actress Jane Wyman. Reagan nominated five Supreme Court justices.

In the Myers-Briggs I believe he is our first NF president, being an ENFJ, very idealistic, visionary and supporting positive values. He loved positive feelings, optimism and everyone feeling good. "ENFJs are idealist organizers, driven to implement their vision of what is best for humanity. They often act as catalysts for human growth because of their ability to see potential in other people and their charisma in persuading others to their ideas. They are focused on values and vision, and are passionate about the possibilities for people.

ENFJs are typically energetic and driven, and often have a lot on their plates. They are tuned into the needs of others and acutely aware of human suffering; however, they also tend to be optimistic and forward-thinking, intuitively seeing opportunity for improvement. They feel responsible for making the world a better place." www.truity.com/personality-type/ENFJ. In Reagan's case, it seems he was more compassionate when he was younger, poorer and empathized with the negative effects of social injustice.

Reagan was a Type 9 with an 8 wing, wanting comfort, not much detail, loved a positive, simple view of life and disliked the complexities of decision-making. He was an actor at heart; charming, a bit detached from reality and didn't particularly want to see the suffering of others. He would go on stage and engage, and then wanted to be left alone to watch the movies to get a breather from reality. He fulfilled the image many people wanted to see of optimism, inspiration and calm. Reagan likely had a secondary or strong aspect of Type 7, the Optimist, to promote the idea that conditions are more positive than they really are. He was reassuring to many who needed relief from the conflicts of society.

George Herbert Walker Bush, Type 6, ISFJ, Create Coalitions, 1989-93

(1924-) George Herbert Walker Bush was president number 41, the first sitting Vice President 1981-1989 to win the presidency by election since Martin van Buren in 1836. There only two other sitting Vice Presidents to do so were John Adams and Thomas Jefferson. Besides John and John Quincy Adams nearly two hundred years earlier, he and his son, George W. Bush were the only other father and son to become Presidents. George Bush, Sr. was elected to two terms in the US House of Representatives and was appointed US Ambassador to the United Nations, Chairman of the Republican Party, Envoy to China and Director of the CIA. He lost two campaign bids for the US Senate.

Born in 1924 in Milton, Massachusetts, his father, Prescott Bush, was a wealthy investment banker and held a seat in the US Senate for 11 years as the representative from Connecticut. Prescott Bush was a liberal politician who supported civil rights, the

United Negro College Fund, Planned Parenthood, healthcare, the environment, labor unions and higher education. He was anti-communist but opposed the scare tactics of Joseph McCarthy. Bush's grandfather, Samuel Bush, made a fortune in Ohio's railroads.

As a child, George was nicknamed "have-half" as he tended to share things with others. He was very dependable doing household chores and cleaning up. His tendency was to be kind, cheerful and generous. As someone in the Bush family stated, "if Bush were running for sainthood he'd make it unopposed." His early life was stable and disciplined as well as relatively happy. His father read from the Bible every day before breakfast and the family attended church regularly. In contrast to this idyllic portrait of happiness and stability, George's father used a belt to administer corporal discipline to the children and Bush remembers his father as being "pretty scary." George was an avid sports fan and played tennis and baseball when he was young.

The family moved to Greenwich, Connecticut shortly after he was born and the Bush family has had a vacation home in Kennebunkport, Maine for over four generations. Bush was raised among wealthy people who devoted their lives to public service. He was taught noblesse oblige; give something back, whether in business, public service or the military. Public service was stressed in his family. As an example, his father was the Greenwich town meeting moderator.

George had the privileges of the wealthy, being chauffeured around in limousines and attending Phillips Academy, a private boarding school in Andover, Massachusetts. He was captain of the baseball and soccer team, member of the varsity basketball team, president of his fraternity and senior class president. He wrote for the school newspaper and was on the editorial board, a member of a religious organization, a deputy housemaster and of service in many other ways. The guiding principles of kindness, courtesy, honesty and thrift were constantly instilled in him by the family. His father modeled public service and his mother, Dorothy Walker Bush, having a competitive nature, taught him about winning. His mother was an active golfer and played tennis and baseball as well. His maternal grandmother won trophies playing golf. Bush's maternal great-grandfather established the Walker Cup, a famous American and British amateur golf tournament. The competitive spirit was important but good sportsmanship was stressed as just as important. When George came home to "brag" about winning three goals in soccer, his mother asked how the team did, rather than how he had done, to encourage him not to brag and to be a team player.

Bush graduated from high school on his 18th birthday, and on that same day enlisted in the Navy. Rebelling against the will of his father to join the service at that time, he went on to became the youngest fighter pilot ever in the Navy, engaging in 58 combat missions in WW II. At one point his plane was shot down after accomplishing his bombing mission, the target of which was a radio station on a Japanese island. He parachuted into the water where he inflated a life raft and, hours later, was rescued by a submarine whose mission was to rescue the crew of downed planes. Two members of his crew perished on that mission, and this has haunted George his entire life. He was awarded many medals for his brave service.

He met Barbara Pierce at a Christmas dance when he was 17 and she was 16 and it was love at first sight according to Barbara. "He was the handsomest human being I ever saw, and maybe the nicest and most relaxed," says Barbara Bush. They married while he was on leave from the Navy and they had six children, one of whom died of leukemia at the age of three. That loss encouraged and inspired Bush to pass the Americans With Disabilities Act while he was president.

After finishing his naval duty, he attended Yale University in an accelerated program and graduated in 2 ½ years. He played first base as captain of the baseball team and played in two college world series where he met Babe Ruth. On behalf of Yale, Bush received the original manuscript of Babe's Ruth's autobiography. Bush was a strong swimmer, golfer and tennis player, volunteered for the United Negro College Fund, and was a member of the exclusive Skull and Bones Society, in which his son George W. Bush, as well as several presidents and high ranking political figures, have been members. Graduating Phi Beta Kappa, he majored in economics.

He could have stayed in New England where the peoples' values were more aligned with those of his father, but he wanted to strike out on his own. After graduation, he moved his family to Midland, Texas, and began working in sales. He worked his way up the corporate ladder to eventually become president of an oil equipment company, making his first million in the process. He was known for his strong ability to connect with people, a strong handshake and for knowing everyone by name. His sense of the importance of public service continued to play an important role in his life and he campaigned for better hospitals, schools and museums in Midland, Texas. The family moved to Houston and during his political life, the family moved 29 times! It was a blessing to have the stability of their vacation home in Kennebunkport.

Like many phobic 6s, Bush is loyal and tends to be deferential as he demonstrated in the eight years he served as Reagan's Vice President. When he became President, he then had the power to be more resolute, independent, and determined, as he demonstrated during the Persian Gulf War. He also had the backing of international allies. This is typical for the phobic Type 6 who would rather have alliances and support than forge on alone.

In rehearsing for his public appearances during the first Iraq war, he would get choked up thinking about the civilian casualties the US was causing in Iraq. He would, however, eliminate anything that might make him look weak from his speeches. He was very diplomatic with other world leaders in keeping the allies together. Bush had a fairly good relationship with the press, particularly during the first Iraq war and sometimes held impromptu news conferences. More comfortable in small groups than large audiences, he was able to relax when he was with friends.

Friends often described him as warm, witty, friendly, polite, and unpretentious but also flighty and even jumpy at times. In childhood as mentioned, his mother emphasized the importance of humility, modesty and downplaying one's accomplishments. He learned to navigate the world without bragging or bringing undue attention to himself, which probably cost him dearly as an adult when he ran for president the second time in 1992. He incorrectly assumed his achievements should speak for themselves during his second presidential campaign. He was wrong about that and it cost him the election.

He had awkward gestures that seemed disconnected from his body when he was nervous, even though he was an excellent sportsman and proficient in golf, boating, tennis and horseback riding. He tended to worry but calmed down when things went well. He was known for making disconnected statements, Bushisms, that were hard to understand.

"For seven and a half years I've worked alongside President Reagan. We've had triumphs. Made some mistakes. We've had some sex...uh...setbacks." —in 1988

"We're enjoying sluggish times, and not enjoying them very much." —in 1992

"I just am not one who – who flamboyantly believes in throwing a lot of words around." —in 1990

"Please don't ask me to do that which I've just said I'm not going to do, because you're burning up time. The meter is running through the sand on you, and I am now filibustering." —in 1989

"If you're worried about caribou, take a look at the arguments that were used about the pipeline. They'd say the caribou would be extinct. You've got to shake them away with a stick. They're all making love lying up against the pipeline and you got thousands of caribou up there." —speaking in 1991 about the Alaskan pipeline

"It's no exaggeration to say the undecideds could go one way or another." —George Bush Sr., in 1988

"I put confidence in the American people, in their ability to sort through what is fair and what is unfair, what is ugly and what is unugly." –in 1989

"I stand for anti-bigotry, anti-Semitism, and anti-racism" in 1988

"Remember Lincoln going to his knees in times of trial and the Civil War and that stuff, you can't be. And we are blessed. So don't feel sorry for – don't cry for me, Argentina."

From his biographer, Timothy Naftali, "He was an emotive, an emotional leader, much more emotional than people thought. He cried quite readily. One thing that made George Bush a less appealing candidate was that he refused to show his emotions. That's not what a man did -- a man of his generation and of his upbringing. And so the public saw a slightly awkward man who didn't seem quite ready to share his true self with them. When you got to know him, the human side, the emotional side was there. It came out."

Bush struggled with wanting to be honest versus using manipulation, negative campaigning and "lies" to gain votes. Like most politicians who want to change things, you generally don't win elections if you're totally honest or nice. Much of the public is geared for conflict when it comes time for an election and if a candidate doesn't wage war against his opponent, some people don't trust him or just think he's weak.

In many ways, Bush created the new Republican Party in the South by converting Southern Democrats, once the white racist party, into new Southern Republicans with an agenda that was racist and segregationist. The new Democratic Party was becoming more civil rights oriented and more inclusive of blacks and legislation that called for equality for minorities, and the Republicans needed to distinguish themselves in their bid for southern votes.

A few years before the civil rights movement gained national attention, Bush's hometown of Houston, Texas became the regional center for registering new Republicans in the South, which included John Birch Society members and segregationists, who had no interest in civil rights. Bush was becoming known as a major opponent of Johnson's civil rights legislation and voted against it.

After visiting Vietnam and developing a closer connection with black soldiers Bush became more personally aware that they were dying for their country just as white soldiers were and he made a 180-degree turn in his attitude; he became an advocate for civil rights and specifically fought to eliminate discrimination in housing. His constituents were appalled and he even got death threats via letters and phone calls.

Bush called a meeting with his political donors and supporters and shared his personal conversion to a position of wanting to insure equal rights for African Americans in America and many supporters were converted by his honesty and heart-felt feelings regarding black veterans. He said it was the most important political experience in his career. Bush helped move part of the new Republican Party constituents to the middle of the political road.

Bush was appointed by Nixon to be Chairman of the Republican Party; Nixon was aware of Bush's loyal character and exploited that loyalty to his own advantage. He sent Bush around the country to give speeches in support of his policies and the Republican Party. Bush took it on faith that Nixon had nothing to do with Watergate. It was an enormous blow to Bush when he came to understand that Nixon lied. Bush deftly maneuvered the situation to encourage Nixon to resign without belittling him, in spite of the fact that he was angry that Nixon used him.

Bush was an excellent diplomat. This became apparent when he was president; he did everything he could to restrain himself from gloating and doing a jig when Gorbachev dissolved the Soviet Union and its eastern satellites and tore down the Berlin Wall. Many people including Congressmen wanted Bush to lord the triumph of the US "winning" over Russia but Bush was reserved. He didn't want to be arrogant about winning, as that could have created a backlash in Moscow. He sacrificed his own political interest for what was best for America's image in the world, as can be true of 6s who are thinking about the big picture result of their decisions rather than their own need for glory.

Bush did more than anyone to end the Cold War diplomatically without backlash from the defeated. He learned from the lesson of Germany and the ending of both world wars to treat a defeated country with equanimity and compassion. By treating both East and West Germany well at the tearing down of the Wall, there were no extra negative repercussions.

Likewise, Bush supported Reagan's ongoing positive image even though many of Bush's economic woes were caused by Reagan's overspending. He didn't blame Reagan and took the rap when his campaign slogan, "read my lips, no new taxes" couldn't be sustained. Bush ultimately felt he had to raise taxes to bail out the failed savings and loan scandal to the tune of 150 billion dollars, which was primarily created by Reagan, but also partially created by his own son Neil who was doing illegal activities related to savings and loans banks. Bush's Clean Air Act and anti-pollution program, the comprehensive Americans With Disabilities Act, the Desert Storm war in Iraq and Kuwait, all cost money.

Iraq invaded Kuwait, a US ally, in 1990 and Bush spent five months deciding what to do in response. Saddam Hussein in Iraq felt that America had promised to stay out of in inter-Arab conflicts. When America attacked Iraq to move forces out of Kuwait with the backing of 26 allied countries, Saddam held his ground instead of backing down.

The United States was even more concerned that Saddam might invade Saudi Arabia and steal their oil reserves, so America stationed troops there also. American losses in Iraq were 148 killed but over 10,000 Iraqi soldiers were killed. Additionally, thousands of civilians were killed in the bombing, and thousands more died because of sanctions and the devastation following it, which ultimately destroyed the infrastructure of the entire country. Us bombs were tipped with uranium and plutonium, causing thousands more to die from the effects radiation poisoning and cancer.

Kurds and Shiite Muslims, encouraged by Bush to rebel against Saddam right after the war, thought they would be supported by what they believed were promises from President Bush that the American Army would fight with them against Saddam. Instead, the Kurds and Shiite rebels were gassed and killed by Saddam without US support or intervention. We may have won the war quickly in the eyes of many people but Iraq was devastated, as it would be again by his son. Bush, Sr. was less approved of when the US invaded Panama. This cost the lives of 500 Panamanians in addition to the bombing and destruction of entire villages just to capture Manuel Noriega, the President and drug lord of Panama.

Stateside, Bush's support for programs like the Americans With Disabilities Act and the Clean Air Act, were driven by his father's liberal influence, contrary to the conservative image that Bush tried to portray.

Bush was good at making friends and creating alliances between world leaders, making many connections when he was at the United Nations, as an envoy to China, in the CIA or as Vice President travelling abroad. Reagan in his laissez faire management style let Bush guide foreign policy when he was vice president.

Bush made many phone calls to check in with friends and leaders as can be true for a social subtype 6, meeting many in person, giving speeches and sending personal thank-you notes to leaders at home and abroad. He had a personal touch and was much warmer and more charming in person than he was onstage, where he was stiff and quite serious. Bush was an introvert attempting to look like an extravert.

Presidential historian Robert Dallek points out, "Bush seemed less ready to address the more pressing domestic issues troubling the country at the end of the eighties – crime, drugs, massive government debts and deficits, bank failure, faltering education system, homelessness, increased poverty and racial divisions." His strength was perceived from his foreign policy decisions. He was often considered to be out of touch with the average American.

Bush had an image problem. He wasn't considered to be tough enough, especially in that he was thought of as a lapdog to Reagan when he was vice president. He was mocked because of his speech gaffs and known to switch positions too readily for people to trust him.

Reagan was funnier than Bush and also had a tough image. They both touted family values. Reagan was tough in his movie roles playing a fighter pilot but Bush actually was a wartime fighter pilot as well as a sports figure in college. He continued to play competitive sports all his life and managed to have a happier family than Reagan whose children often fought with him. Reagan's son, Ron, is a liberal political commentator opposing many of the policies his father supported. Bush is a family man who is genuinely loved by his family. He spends as much time with them as possible, and is especially loved by his daughter and his political sons Jeb, former Governor of Florida and presidential candidate, and George W, though he and George W have been known to quarrel at times.

George Herbert Walker Bush struggled with his conscience many times. For instance, he didn't like the confrontational smear tactics used by his campaign manager Lee Atwood when he ran against Michael Dukakis for president. Bush talked about wanting "a kinder and gentler nation," but that wouldn't win him the election or give him the clout needed to win allies, according to Atwood. George Sr. preferred talking about himself, his policies and his own record in a self-deprecating manner rather than attacking others, unless it was a clear enemy like Saddam Hussein. Bush seemed to lack a clear vision of what needed to be done and was criticized for being too straight-laced.

Bush's qualities and actions that relate to his being an Enneagram Type 6 include his sometimes-nervous disposition, loyalty to others even when it sabotaged his own needs, his self-restraint, cool headedness and planning abilities such as taking the time to create alliances before attacking Saddam Hussein and Iraq. He tended, as president, to be careful, thoughtful and methodical in his work. In contrast, but consistent with a Type 6, is his tendency to have sudden jolts of radical change in his normal behavior; on the first day of his presidency he kicked all the workers out of the White House with orders to leave before sundown. Normally he was warm and friendly. Wanting to separate himself from Reagan probably encouraged that action.

Below ISFJ description which I believe fits Bush, is taken from:
https://www.16personalities.com/isfj-personality

ISFJ PERSONALITY ("THE DEFENDER")

"The ISFJ personality type is quite unique, as many of their qualities defy the definition of their individual traits. Though possessing the Feeling (F) trait, ISFJs have excellent analytical abilities; though Introverted (I), they have well-developed people skills and robust social relationships; and though they are a Judging (J) type, ISFJs are often receptive to change and new ideas. As with so many things, people with the ISFJ personality type are more than the sum of their parts, and it is the way they use these strengths that defines who they are.

ISFJs are true altruists, meeting kindness with kindness-in-excess and engaging the work and people they believe in with enthusiasm and generosity.

There's hardly a better type to make up such a large proportion of the population, nearly 13%. Combining the best of tradition and the desire to do good, ISFJs are found in lines of work with a sense of history behind them, such as medicine, academics and charitable social work.

ISFJ personalities (especially Turbulent ones) are often meticulous to the point of perfectionism, and though they procrastinate, they can always be relied on to get the job done on time. ISFJs take their responsibilities personally, consistently going above and beyond, doing everything they can to exceed expectations and delight others, at work and at home.

The challenge for ISFJs is ensuring that what they do is noticed. They have a tendency to underplay their accomplishments, and while their kindness is often respected, more cynical and selfish people are likely to take advantage of ISFJs' dedication and humbleness by pushing work onto them and then taking the credit. ISFJs need to know when to say no and stand up for themselves if they are to maintain their confidence and enthusiasm.

Naturally social, an odd quality for Introverts, ISFJs utilize excellent memories not to retain data and trivia, but to remember people, and details about their lives. When it comes to gift-giving, ISFJs have no equal, using their imagination and natural sensitivity to express their generosity in ways that touch the hearts of their recipients. While this is certainly true of their coworkers, whom people with the ISFJ personality type often consider their personal friends, it is in family that their expressions of affection fully bloom.

ISFJ personalities are a wonderful group, rarely sitting idle while a worthy cause remains unfinished. ISFJs' ability to connect with others on an intimate level is unrivaled among Introverts, and the joy they experience in using those connections to maintain a supportive, happy family is a gift for everyone involved. They may never be truly comfortable in the spotlight, and may feel guilty taking due credit for team efforts, but if they can ensure that their efforts are recognized, ISFJs are likely to feel a level of satisfaction in what they do that many other personality types can only dream of."

As mentioned, Bush expected people to be naturally loyal to him because of his political record (an expectation 6s often have). He then declined to put in the necessary extra effort to create a winning image that would have convinced the voters to reelect him. He was at the pinnacle of his career after the Iraq invasion in 1990 when his approval rating was at an all-time high of 89 percent, the highest that any president had ever reached. Unfortunately for Bush, the economy began wavering soon afterward and people were swayed over to vote for Clinton who promised a better economy. Just before Bush left the White House, the economy strengthened and Clinton got some of the credit for the economic policies that had been created by Bush.

Bush retired to his home in Houston Texas, and spends time in Kennebunkport, Maine as well. He stays in touch with politics through his sons George W and Jeb. He parachuted out of a plane with a parachute buddy helper on his 80th, 85th, and 90th birthdays and appeared at the Superbowl in 2017! He's sat on various boards, volunteered at church and teamed up with Bill Clinton in various worldwide relief efforts. Bush has written a number of books on politics and is known for his ability to create coalition and his expertise in team building, loyalty to country and family, and an ability to be flexible as he encounters new information. Being of service has always been very important.

Bill Clinton, Type 3, ESFP, Come Back Kid, 1993-2001

(1946-) President number 42 was Bill Clinton whose early life was one of hardship and tragedy. His father, a travelling salesman, died in a car crash before he was born and his mother could barely make ends meet. She decided to go to nursing school in New Orleans to improve her finances and left Bill in the care of her parents. When Bill was 4 she returned home to Hope, Arkansas where she married an alcoholic violent man, and Bill eventually had to stand up to him to protect her. Once his stepfather fired a gun during a family fight and was thrown into jail.

Most people in Hot Springs, Arkansas where Bill moved to when he was 6 years old, knew nothing about his upbringing. Despite the difficulties he faced at home, Bill Clinton did well in school. He was an honors student, was elected to many class and club offices, and joined the Boy Scouts. He played the saxophone, won music contests, attended music camp in the summer, sang in his Baptist church choir, and loved gospel music. On the other hand, he attended some of the city's gambling facilities and many of its well-known spas. Hot Springs was known as a city of gambling, graft, corruption, drugs, illegal dealings, sex and fun.

Bill planned to be President of the United States early in his youth, which was highly encouraged by his mother. At age 10 he watched the entire Democratic and Republican Conventions on television. In 1963 he attended Boys Nation, a national forum that conducts civic training and leadership run by the American Legion for select high school youth. There he was elected to visit Washington, DC and at the White House he met President Kennedy. The occasion of meeting and shaking hands with Kennedy fueled his political ambitions. Bill was offered many academic and music scholarships and decided to attend Georgetown University in Washington, DC to be near the seat of power. Majoring in international affairs and political science, he became an intern for Senator Fulbright, the chairman of the Senate Foreign Relations Committee.

Clinton was a top college student and won a Rhodes Scholarship to Oxford University in England for two years. Heavily influenced by the civil rights movement and the anti-Vietnam war movement, he returned to the US to attend Yale Law School with a political career in mind. There he met Hillary Rodham, and they became the perfect political couple with the same ambitions. It was love and politics at first sight.

Clinton then taught at the University of Arkansas Law School, married Hillary and ran for Congress, but lost. He was soon elected Arkansas State Attorney General for two years, then ran for governor and won. He was 32, at that time the youngest governor ever elected. He was shrewd, sociable, bright and knew how to make connections. Some of the alliances Clinton made were with shady powerful figures, probably not that unusual in Little Rock. He had all the characteristics of the Type 3 Go-Getter and his extraverted nature, typical of 3s, helped create alliances to move him in the directions he wanted.

He determined he could transform one of the poorest states in the nation by raising taxes on drivers licenses to generate the funds needed to improve the highways. The strategy failed, and his arrogance, irritated the populace. Losing the next election, he stepped back and did some soul searching to learn from his mistakes. Clinton was elected again two years later, and was governor for five more terms; he learned how to listen to his constituents. He became one of the most talked about governors in the US, headed up the National Governor's Association and helped steer the Democratic Leadership Council, a group of business leaders and moderate Democrats who focused on shaping national policy.

As governor, he pushed for welfare reform, legislating that welfare recipients had to join the workforce after a designated period of time on the welfare rolls. He supported educational reform by having all teachers take a competency test, starting a national debate. He promoted affirmative action and hired minorities in political offices. He based many of his choices on public opinion polls and created sales campaigns using television, leaflets and phone banks to pressure lawmakers and encourage voting. As a Type 3 Achiever he knew how to market himself. He emerged as a leading reform governor in the country and encouraged the Democratic party not to use race as a dividing issue, as the Republicans tended to do. He was positioning himself for a presidential bid and Hillary helped in every way she could.

Clinton had a philosophy that was pragmatic, moderate and centrist. He felt that the government should support free enterprise and if that wasn't enough, it should help individuals to work and be responsible. He gave a nominating speech for Michael Dukakis at the Democratic Convention that turned out to be long and boring. He apologized for the speech on the Johnny Carson show, poking fun at himself and seemed to be forgiven by the national audience. Nicknamed the "comeback kid," he seemed to always land on his feet.

In 1992, he was ready to enter the presidential race as a more moderate candidate than most in the Democratic party. Hillary was his closest political advisor and he ran on a platform of investing money in schools and job training, overhauling the health care system, protecting women's right to choose, and improving the economy. As the third youngest president at age 46, he replaced 12 years of Republican presidential leadership.

He loved policy, details and how government worked. The Clinton/Gore ticket was the first all-Southern Presidential ticket since Andrew Jackson in 1828.

Hillary took on more responsibilities than any First Lady since Eleanor Roosevelt. Besides heading up the health care reform initiative, she traveled extensively on behalf of her husband, advocated for the rights of children, occasionally sat in on cabinet meetings and wrote a weekly newspaper column. She tried to protect the privacy of their daughter, Chelsea, and supported her husband during the scandals of his presidency. Many in Congress and the public felt nervous about her power; she is, however, the only First Lady to seek and win an elected office.

In the first two years of office, Bill Clinton appointed many women and people of color to high positions. Some of these included Secretary of State Madeleine Albright and Attorney General Janet Reno. He appointed five Afro-Americans as department heads in 1993. He signed into law the Family and Medical Leave Act and the Brady Handgun Violence Prevention Act. The economy started to recover and with the Cold War over, Clinton felt he could ease up on military funding and devote more attention to the economy.

He sent troops to Haiti to restore the democratically elected president to office after a military coup and sent the air force to join NATO in bombing Serbian positions during the Bosnian war. Clinton held a belief that peace around the world would be created by economic stability rather than fighting. He supported NAFTA, an agreement to establish free trade between the United States, Canada and Mexico that has extended to other countries.

Despite initiatives that worked, Bill and his new advisors often took a long time to make decisions. This is one of the reasons why he is often typed as a 9. In my opinion, he is a Type 3 because he devoted so much attention his image and was influenced by public opinion polls. He has a 2 wing with a desire to help and personally connect.

His business dealings are known to have been a bit shady at times and he's cool with those who disagree with his ideas or policies. He's known for womanizing and has had a number of affairs. His inappropriate sexual advances have been corroborated by many women's testimonies. Some refer to Clinton as a sex addict.

Type 9s generally wouldn't be able to manage or even cause the kind of conflict and discomfort that have ensued from his choices. There have been many accusations and investigations against him regarding illicit sex, money laundering and payoffs and real estate scandals. Whether the accusations are true or not, the unhealthier aspects of 3s show up when they leave a trail of deception and cover ups, as is true in this case. 9s tend to be so uncomfortable with the almost inevitable difficulties that arise from dishonest dealings that they walk the straight and narrow to preserve their peaceful lifestyle.

Two investigations stand out in Clinton's past: Whitewater, an investigation regarding a shady real estate deal in which the Clintons made millions, and Travelgate, which occurred when established travel agents in the White House were replaced by a friend of the Clintons who owned a travel company. The former head of travel for the White House was fired on unproven trumped up charges by the Clintons but was later exonerated in court.

There was some questionable evidence that when he was governor of Arkansas, he covered up money obtained from drug dealing. Some of both Hillary and Bill's former employees or friends ended up in jail for crimes. Stories of "enemies" of the Clintons who were threatened or who were reportedly beaten up by thugs working for the Clintons or mysteriously died in questionable circumstances, seemed to trail Bill. Many of these are alleged. Interviews and negative reports of people involved with the Clintons are on record. It could be a "right wing conspiracy," as claimed by Hillary and Bill or a campaign to target the Clintons. However, as already stated, this is a trail of events a Type 9 wouldn't leave behind or even be able to handle.

Clinton is an ESFP in the Myers-Briggs. "ESFPs are vivacious entertainers who charm and engage those around them. They are spontaneous, energetic, and fun-loving, and take pleasure in the things around them: food, clothes, nature, animals, and especially people.

ESFPs are typically warm and talkative and have a contagious enthusiasm for life. They like to be in the middle of the action and the center of attention. They have a playful, open sense of humor, and like to draw out other people and help them have a good time." www.truity.com/personality-type/ESFP

In the first midterm elections both houses of Congress became Republican, as Clinton had much opposition. There were temporary shutdowns of some departments of government due to the Republicans failure to pass budgets, a direct plot to pressure Clinton. That backfired on the Republicans as the American public blamed them instead of Bill.

Clinton easily won re-election against Bob Dole. In the long run, more money in the pockets of average Americans is what wins elections. "It's the economy, stupid" was a phrase coined by James Carville, Clinton's campaign manager. Clinton's corruption charges didn't seem to make a big difference in the election or his approval ratings and were overshadowed by a better economy.

Bill pushed for inclusion of homosexual soldiers in the military ('don't ask, don't tell'), against fierce resistance from his own generals. Many felt he was pushing for change faster than it could be integrated. His legislation placing time limits on receiving welfare payments was popular. The end of the second term, marked the longest economic expansion in US history, low unemployment and a high rate of new jobs. There was even a government budget surplus which Democrats and Republicans debated about how to spend! During his administration, the Bosnian War ended and there was a temporary agreement of limited self-rule for Palestinians.

The crime rate was lowered during the Clinton years, depending on the statistics one uses, and it was reported that this was attributable to Clinton's tough criminal justice laws and his support for the death penalty. He took on the tobacco industry, especially in his attack on cigarette ads aimed at the teenage audience. He was environmentally sensitive, protecting millions of acres of new forest, wetlands and desert, and expanded the Safe Drinking Water Act. During his administration, NATO expanded into Eastern Europe which was approved by Russia. China entered into the World Trade Organization and Clinton helped broker the peace accord in Northern Ireland between Catholics and Protestants.

In the midst of all these positive activities, Clinton was impeached by the House of Representatives for perjury and obstruction of justice concerning his affair with Monica Lewinsky. The Senate exonerated him. The public was divided in its opinion of the decision; some thought this was a personal affair and others thought it sullied the office of the presidency. There were also suspicions of fund raising abuses during his 2nd presidential campaign.

Many people criticize Bill Clinton for decisions he made during his time as President. With self-examination, even he would admit that he should not have locked people up for minor drug offenses. The three-strikes law jailed a person for life if they had two previous drug offenses no matter what the circumstances. The prison population nearly doubled. Minorities were incarcerated in numbers that were disproportionate in the extreme to the number of whites imprisoned for breaking the same laws.

Clinton changed the rules of Welfare, many of which were punitive toward people who didn't work or find a job fast enough. Welfare regulation was transferred to the jurisdiction of individual states, without oversight by the federal government. Many banks were deregulated without proper safety standards. The NAFTA Free Trade Agreement between the US, Canada and Mexico prompted the relocation of jobs outside the United States. This hurt U.S. manufacturers as well as local foreign economies, causing many Mexicans to be paid lower wages and forcing more of them to immigrate to America.

The Defense of Marriage Act severely limited rights for same sex couples, the death penalty was expanded, and the female Surgeon General was fired for openly discussing the idea of educating our youth about masturbation (she was criticized for using that word) as an alternative to sex. The Clintons were criticized for allowing wealthy guests to stay overnight in the Lincoln bedroom in exchange for campaign donations.

Clinton bombed a Sudanese pharmaceutical plant mistakenly thinking it was producing nerve gas. Sanctions were placed on Iraq leading to many thousands of Iraqi deaths and specifically causing the starvation of children, and the government did nothing to stop the Rwandan genocide in Africa. U.S. citizens didn't want to see bad things going on in the world that were related to the U.S. foreign policy. A good economy tended to narcotize many Americans from seeing how others in the world suffered because of United States policies.

Bill's attractive, positive, youthful, energetic look is very characteristic of 3s, particularly those with 2 wings. This charisma drew many people to him. During his presidency, Clinton didn't take a moral stand without checking the "weather" first, that is, checking the polls. 'Slick Willie' is a nickname Clinton was given. It refers to his habit of trying so hard to please others that his behavior bordered on lying to get approval. Clinton is personable, a natural extravert, has a ready handshake and pat on the back for people, can be compassionate and empathetic, but can also be vengeful if challenged too much.

His eight years as president included polarization by the Republicans and anger toward him for supporting Hillary's power as a woman. His two terms showed that a president can be popular despite party opposition, impeachment, sex scandals and disagreements. A good economy tends to overshadow many factors and Americans love a positive attitude in their president as exhibited by both Clinton and Reagan. A smile and an upbeat attitude goes a long way in politics.

Clinton is charming, witty, ambitious, smooth, genial and friendly. The question is whether his charm is a tool he uses to deceive others or even himself. Does he genuinely care about people or is his behavior driven by a desire to please others to satisfy a need for approval? Many of his programs had a positive effect whether they were introduced to enhance his image or not.

In a Time magazine article on Oct 8, 2008 by John Gartner called "Putting Bill Clinton on the Couch," he states that Clinton is hypomanic. It's important to start out with the idea that it's a temperament. It's inborn, it's genetic, it's not an illness. Hypomanic people have tremendous energy. Clinton hardly sleeps. He can campaign for three or four days straight without a break. With this syndrome, you also have immense confidence, and it makes you someone who is very ambitious, hard-working, and creative. There are a lot of positives. At the same time, there are those vulnerabilities. Impulsiveness — not just in the area of sex, but also in eating, and in terms of his temper."

Of his affair with Monica Lewinsky, Gartner says, "What people don't realize, because they've heard all the jokes, you know, cigars and stuff, is that this was a true love affair. There's no question that this was a very psychologically complex relationship. Monica Lewinsky represented something very important to him psychologically. She looked like his mother, Virginia, who had recently died. Clinton kept saying how much she reminded him of his mother. Monica kept saying she felt like she was having a relationship with a lost little boy. This is the President of the United States. She was an intern. Yet she felt maternal in her relationship with him. It was an affair, yes, and he lied about it, yes, but it wasn't just a cheap exploitation."

Bill was similar to Kennedy in that many of his affairs were actual ongoing liaisons, but they both also had one-time flings. Likely his affairs were to bolster his ego, have pleasure and a sense of power, relieve stress or possibly to get back at women, his mother, Hillary, etc. On one hand, he loved women but he certainly used them and could be quite unconscious of the pain he caused, though he would probably repress that. He needed to see himself as positive and it's highly questionable whether he felt guilty. He is known to express anger to anyone who limits him. 3s can become enraged if their positive image is challenged.

Clinton suffers from chronic laryngitis caused by allergies. He's allergic to dust, mold, cats, pollen, certain greenery like Christmas trees and dairy products. He's left handed and slightly hard of hearing. He's 6 feet 2 inches (George Bush Sr. is also 6 feet 2 and left handed) and had a weakness for indulging in junk food until his heart attack.

Some interesting facts about Bill Clinton include: his original last name is Blythe, he is a Leo, and he won 2 Grammy Awards for Best Spoken Word Album. Since his presidency, he has been an activist in the arenas of global warming, fighting childhood obesity, stopping the AIDS epidemic and raising money for flood and tsunami relief. He was generally a popular president and is loved by many today.

We learn from President Clinton how to listen to feedback and change, to lead with a smile, to take risks, to never give up, to market yourself well, to be well-informed and be positive. He came from a difficult background and rose from obscurity by defining clear goals, creating a vision, taking risks and acting on his vision.

George W. Bush, Type 6, ESTJ, 911 and Iraq, 2001-2009

(1946-) George W. Bush was president number 43. Son of George Bush Sr., he is one of only two father-son president combinations, the other being John Adams and John Quincy Adams, the 2nd and 6th presidents. George W. grew up following the traditions established by his wealthy family. He went to Phillips Academy in Andover, MA, then to Yale where he joined The Skull and Bones Society and then on to Harvard's School of Business to get an MBA. He became a pilot, played baseball (was co-owner of the Texas Rangers) and went into the oil business. W, as he is affectionately called, worked for his father's political campaigns, was himself governor of Texas twice, ran for President twice and won, though both elections were contested. He idolized his father and very much followed in his footsteps.

He was the President when the 9/11 attacks took place, during the War in Iraq, general global terror and the 2008 economic debacle that lasted until Obama became President. He was voted at times as very popular and also least popular. He had 90 percent approval ratings after 9/11 and 25 percent at the end of his presidency, which correlated with the financial crisis of 2008.

"Georgie" grew up in Odessa, Texas during his father's political life. His siblings Jeb, Neil, Marvin and Dorothy followed. His sister's death at age 3 (his parents told him days after her death) occurred when he was only 7 and greatly affected his life. He grew closer to his mother and seemed to adopt his mother's bluntness, wit and temper. He attended a public elementary school but switched to a private school when his family moved to Houston.

Bush has many nicknames, among them: Dubya, W, Bush Jr., Junior, Bush II, 43, and Shrub. Like his father, he attended the elite Philips Academy in Andover, Massachusetts. It was a struggle for Bush academically and he stayed up past his 10pm curfew to study and gradually improved his grades after he made a zero on his first paper. W was afraid of his parent's disapproval. However, he got great marks in the social scene and made lots of friends. "I could make friends and make my way no matter where I found myself in life."

His time at the all-male Philips Academy was indicative of the qualities Bush has had though out his life and presidency. On campus he was known for his social engagement, humor, friendliness, loyalty and verbal quips. He became the head cheerleader and was the "stickball commissioner." He created a stickball league with this "rebellious" game of sticks and a tennis ball to counter the traditional athletics on campus. He was known to rebel by ignoring the dress code and choosing clothes disapproved of by the school administration. He hung out with the jocks. Bush was an average academic student and sportsman, but he excelled at creating coalitions, antics and making people laugh. He was a popular man on campus though no one expected him to excel in politics or be highly successful. Any A's he earned were for his social skills. To find out more about his life at Philips Academy: partners.nytimes.com/library/politics/camp/061000wh-bush.html.

At Yale he majored in American and European history and joined a social fraternity. Later he became president of the fraternity. His social status took precedence over his grades, as he was a C student. In playing baseball as a pitcher, he wasn't particularly successful but excelled in rugby. He was engaged for a brief time without it leading to marriage.

1968, the year he graduated from Yale, was a year of turmoil with Martin Luther King and Bobby Kennedy murdered and the conflict in Vietnam at its peak. Joining the National Guard, it was contended that he avoided the draft by that decision, having special privilege from his family to get into the Guard. His political education grew as he helped his father with his political campaigns.

Bush II completed his MBA at Harvard and then entered the Texas oil business with a job hunting for oil drilling sites and negotiating leases with landowners. Starting his own oil company, he learned how to set clear goals and achieve them. Bush was a bachelor at age 30 and was known for partying and drinking. When he met Laura Lane Welch at a barbeque, they started dating and were soon wed. Laura's relaxed and calm nature balanced Bush's high energy and outgoing nature. Initially having a hard time conceiving, within four years of their marriage, they had twin daughters, Barbara and Jenna, named after their grandmothers. The Bushes joined the Methodist Church after their daughters were born and George deepened his Christian faith, especially after a personal visit with the evangelist Billy Graham. He started reading the Bible daily and attending weekly Bible study meetings.

Bush lost his first bid to be a US Representative. Having helped in many political campaigns, including that of Gerard Ford, he helped his father in his run for President. He could have stayed in Washington in a political capacity during his father's administration but decided to resume the running of his business in Texas. His next venture was to purchase the baseball team, the Texas Rangers. There he learned about large-scale management, was instrumental in building a new stadium and made a hefty profit when he sold the team.

After his father was defeated by Bill Clinton in his run for President, the Junior Bush decided to run for Governor of Texas against popular Governor Ann Richards. The campaign was helped by Bush's humor and ability to make fun of himself. On a publicized bird hunt, he was criticized but apologized for accidentally shooting an endangered killdeer. With the help of political strategist Karl Rove, against all odds, Bush won. Governor Richards had called Bush a jerk and a "shrub," playing on his family name of Bush. She emphasized that he was born "with a silver foot in his mouth." Some people disliked her mean-spirited jibes and voted against her and for Bush's humor and ability to keep cool despite his anger.

Bush met weekly with his Democratic Lieutenant Governor and State Speaker of the House, reaching across party lines when he could. He worked to limit the amount of money that could be won in litigation, made efforts to reform education so every child could learn to read, accomplished some tax reform and gave special support for faith-based initiatives. He ran for a second term as Governor of Texas on "compassionate conservatism," small government and support of free enterprise. His brother Jeb also won in the race for Governor of Florida. George Bush prepared to run for President.

Even though Bush lost the presidential election by one half million popular votes, he won the electoral college vote in Florida by a few hundred popular votes and a dispute over "chad" cards, though that was contested, considering his brother was Governor of Florida at the time and might have influenced the outcome. Many Democrats refused to consider Bush a legally elected President. The United States Supreme Court decided the Bush win in Florida, which gave the Presidential election to Bush over Gore.

President Bush worked with religious organizations for educational and community support and supported the No Child Left Behind Act, which set national standards for educational reform based on a skills competency test rather than allowing local autonomy and standards to determine a child's proficiency and readiness for advancement. Teachers, parents and children complained that teachers were forced to teach for the test instead of engaging their students in a more natural and individualized way.

Bush had one of the highest presidential ratings for his response to 9/11, uniting the country against terrorists but had mixed reviews for his invasion of Iraq and Afghanistan. Protests of millions around the world diminished United States' status, particularly when it was discovered there were no "weapons of mass destruction" in Iraq. Bush pushed for more privatization of health care and Medicare and was unsuccessful in his attempt to privatize Social Security.

He appointed two Supreme Court Justices that moved the court to the right. His handling of Hurricane Katrina was highly criticized and the financial debacle in 2008 lowered his ratings even more. A main cause for the failure was an exaggerated bubble in the housing market and the flagrant selling of unqualified, low interest rate mortgages. Deregulation of banks prevented healthy and safe federal financial guidelines. The US economy plummeted to its worse state since the Depression of the 1930s and unemployment skyrocketed.

Bush appeared easygoing and fun. He was voted on by many as best chosen to spend time to have a beer with than Gore. An attendee of one of my couples' communication weekends, was a classmate of Bush at Phillips Academy in Andover. He reported that Bush was a jokester who was the life of the party. His extraverted and humorous nature probably hid more anxiety underneath.

I'm including two articles (first article below) about Bush that highlight some of his traits and behaviors.

Jason Reed / Reuters

By BEN FELLER Associated Press Writer

http://www.nbcnews.com/id/28482517/ns/politics-white_house/t/analysis-bushs-personality-shapes-his-legacy/#.WgdBDWhSyM8 (2 pages) For the entire article go to the website above. It's worth reading

EDITOR'S NOTE: Ben Feller covers the White House for The Associated Press.

WASHINGTON — "President George W. Bush will be judged on what he did. He will also be remembered for what he's like: a fast-moving, phrase-mangling Texan who stays upbeat even though his country is not. For eight years, the nation has been led by a guy who relaxes by clearing brush in scorching heat and taking breakneck bike rides through the woods. He dishes out nicknames to world leaders, and even gave the German chancellor an impromptu, perhaps unwelcome, neck rub. He's annoyed when kept waiting and sticks relentlessly to routine. He stays optimistic in even the most dire circumstances, but readily tears up in public. He has little use for looking within himself, and only lately has done much looking back."

"Bush demands punctuality and disdains inefficiency. Every meeting better have a clear purpose. And it better not repeat what he already knows. He is up early and in the Oval Office by 6:45 a.m. By 9:30 to 10 at night, it's lights out. He likes to be fresh and won't get cheated on his sleep. In sessions with policy experts, Bush tends to ask questions that get right to the nub of a sticky issue. They describe a man who is deeply inquisitive, not blithely incurious as much of the world thinks. When Bush wants answers, guessing isn't advised."

"You can tell the issues that really get Bush going, because he talks about them differently, more passionately: education, AIDS relief, freedom. They happen to be ones that can be viewed more clearly through a moral lens. That's how he sees the world. Bush reads the Bible regularly. Another devotion: exercise. He makes time for a workout at least six days a week, wherever he is. And he goes at it hard, especially on his mountain bike on the weekends, when he pushes Secret Service agents to keep up with him. He is competitive and likes to stay in command."

"Bush can flash a temper and impatience. But if he takes criticism personally — and he gets lots of criticism — he tries not to show it. When former press secretary Scott

McClellan wrote a scathing book about Bush's leadership, the president told his senior aides to let it go. "Find a way to forgive, because that's the way to lead your life," White House press secretary Dana Perino remembers Bush advising her."

"The toughest moments for him come when he meets the grieving families of the troops he sent to war. Or when he meets severely wounded troops in recovery. Many of the hurting tell Bush they want to get back out in active duty. He is moved by the sacrifice. "I do a lot of crying in this job," Bush once acknowledged. He shows consideration to people close to him in little ways. He sends birthday notes to staff members. He remembers little details about their families. When he visits an Army post to thank the troops, he's been known to wander into the kitchen, too, to praise whoever cooked him the French fries."

"The president is a proud dad of two grown daughters, Jenna and Barbara. The public got a tiny glimpse of his softer side when Jenna married Henry Hager in May. Bush said afterward that his little girl married a really good guy. First lady Laura Bush says her husband now has a son."

"Bush is not much for the social scene. He and his wife will go to friends' homes but stay away from restaurants and Washington's other delights. His aides say he doesn't like to cause a security hassle for the public. "I'm a nester," Bush said. Nowhere is that more true than at his beloved, secluded ranch in Crawford, Texas. He has spent more than a year of his presidency there. Bush chops cedar, clears brush and builds mountain bike trails there. The summer heat doesn't bother him so much as enthrall him. He even set up a little competition, true Bush: People who work for him get a coveted T-shirt and bragging rights if they run for three straight miles on days hitting 100 degrees. He relaxes by reading quite a bit, mostly U.S. and world history. He likes the spy-spoofing "Austin Powers" movies. He chills out with his wife. "I will leave the presidency with my head held high," Bush says.

Bush tends to dress conservatively but with a silver buckle, cowboy boots and hat. He dresses more casually for reporters. When he was younger he was often messy and was known to leave his clothes on the floor.

He is a good speaker but like his father, he mangles words with "Bushisms," uses bizarre logic at times that is not understandable. Perhaps he has a form of dyslexia or a similar learning disorder. Bush is lively and outgoing. In his younger years he was the life of the party; he has a quick wit and is good at telling jokes. Until he reached the age of 40 he drank a lot and was something of a playboy. He changed after he married Laura and the birth of his twin daughters had an enormous impact on him. Laura threatened to leave him if he didn't curb his drinking.

A religious conversion experience with Reverend Billy Graham provided the impetus for him to stop drinking. Religion is a major inspiration and guide for his life, and prayer, bible reading and attending church are some of the most important aspects of his life. Bush is intensely loyal and does not allow anyone to speak ill of his father.

Bush's confidence never seemed to flag, even in the downturns in his life. He is punctual, has short meetings, usually five minutes in length, and is a man of total routine that seldom changes from day to day. He doesn't allow for interruptions and one might lose a job if he is overly late. W is competitive in the extreme and has to win in sports and all areas of life. He's fun but not loose or laid back. There's a nervous edge.

Even though he appears like a 7 on the surface and smiles in his photos, he's actually a Counterphobic Type 6 with a strong 7 wing called the "Buddy." His thinking is black and white with no room for the gray areas of life. He challenges people with questions to determine the truth and has a skeptical nature. Trust must be earned and he makes people work hard to get it. He's a very loyal person and expects the same from those around him. He relies on only a few trusted advisors and dislikes ambivalence, preferring clear straightforward information. He uses humor both for connection and to cover his anxiety. He's more serious than he appears.

The following article is from: http://www.politicaltypes.com/bush_type.html

What is George W. Bush's MBTI Type?

"Extraversion or Introversion? The picture that emerges over Bush's life is one of an extravert. As a child, he is portrayed as something of the family clown or entertainer. In his school years, he takes on extraverted roles such as cheerleader and fraternity president. He earns a playboy reputation and demonstrates a bias for action by flying for the Texas Air National Guard.

His personality on the political campaign trail comes across as sociable, active, outgoing and energetic. In contrast, his Democratic opponents--Al Gore and John Kerry--both earned reputations as being too "stiff," "wooden," or "boring."

Bush's tendency to spend significant time at his ranch in Crawford, Texas or at Camp David may at first consideration suggest a preference for Introversion. A closer look at Bush's behavior in these settings, however, further suggests a preference for Extraversion in that a key theme is sociability; in addition to the presence of presidential staff, Bush is known to engender long and active days that often involve friends and family.

Some have commented that Bush's extraverted behaviors may reflect his attempt to live up to parental expectations for achievement (not unusual for a first-born child) or an ongoing Oedipal rivalry with his father. Such perspectives pose interesting questions for political psychology, but do not directly aid a study of Bush's type preferences (unless one is willing to delve more deeply into the psychoanalysis of type development).

Paintings by George Bush (images.gawker.com)

Sensing or Intuition? Sensing and intuition refer to different ways of perceiving. People who prefer sensing generally are described as practical, realistic, and focused on living in the present. Sensing types are seen as emphasizing tradition and experience. People who prefer intuition generally are described as theoretical, imaginative, and oriented to the future. Intuitive types are seen as emphasizing possibilities, originality and the abstract. Given this brief overview, George Bush appears to be a sensing type.

The picture of Bush as a sensing type seems clear if we consider the younger Bush--before he became a politician and thus subject to political spin and image building. In particular, the picture of Bush that emerges from his younger days is one of a person who thrives on living in the moment--whether it be playing sports or partying. Moreover, his college major--history--can be seen as attractive to sensing types in that history emphasizes tradition and experience in terms of concrete, specific people and events. Books that Bush reportedly read during his presidency also seem oriented to historical materials that provide experiences and examples that serve to inform his policy process. Finally, Bush's recent engagement with painting seems to indicate a sensing preference in that the paintings generally represent literal images such as world leaders with whom he worked, his dog Barney, landscapes of his ranch, and so on. To the extent that some of the paintings seem to indicate a critical perspective on the object might be interpreted as the influence of a thinking preference.

Thinking or Feeling? Thinking and feeling refer to how people make decisions or come to conclusions. Thinking types emphasize impersonal and task related criteria whereas feeling types emphasize personal and interpersonal criteria. Thinking types tend to be questioning, critical, and concerned with fairness and equity when making decisions. Feeling types tend to be concerned with ensuring harmony and avoiding conflict with those involved in the process.

Former White House speechwriter David Frum's comments about George Bush suggest Bush demonstrates the traits of a thinking type:

- "He is a tough-minded person. He is not always charming. He can be very brusque and dismissive.'
- 'Well, Bush is not a sweetie in the way that Ronald Reagan was. I mean, he is a very tough and often quite acerbic person. He has a temper. I think that the part of his personality that is least understood is the strength of it.'
- 'He was tart, not sweet. He's quick to anger. He is very skeptical of people. You can see when people talk to him and they say nice things to him, as they do to anyone who's president, that you can see how unimpressed by that he is. In fact, you could often see as someone would compliment him, that that person's stature in the president's eyes [was] dropping moment by moment by moment with every additional helping of whipped cream he tried to serve the president. He didn't seem to be someone who had a lot of illusions about human nature or a very high opinion of it.'

- He was not a gentle taskmaster. People made mistakes. He got angry about it.

Some people may 'type' Bush as a feeling type given Bush's friendliness, sociability, and willingness to share his feelings with others. Moreover, Bush promotes himself as a compassionate (feeling) conservative. Our impression, however, is that Bush's friendliness, willingness to share feelings, and so on reflect his extraversion preferences more so than feeling preferences; moreover, his theme of compassionate conservatism reflects more his evangelical beliefs than his psychological type preferences.

Judging or Perceiving? Judging and perceiving indicate different preferences for dealing with one's environment. Judging types prefer to plan, organize, and control their environment whether at work or at play. Judging types thus prefer an environment characterized by procedures, schedules, goals, and routines. Judging types like to get started early on a task, follow planned procedures, and then complete the task. Judging types are seen as decisive. Perceiving types, on the other hand, prefer an environment that allows for the freedom and spontaneity to let things emerge. Perceiving types thus feel constrained by routine and schedules preferring instead to experience the variety that spontaneous events bring to one's life.

Accounts of Bush's daily regimen as president suggest Judging preferences. For example, the following Associated Press description clearly reflects judging characteristics such as a preference for planned routines and schedules:

So regimented is Bush's lifestyle one can predict his conduct months in advance.

If you want to know what the president will do on Election Day, odds are that he'll get up about 5:30 a.m., push the button on the coffee maker, scan the day's headlines (perhaps more carefully than usual), then study the daily devotional for Nov. 2 laid out in Oswald Chambers' "My Utmost for his Highest." The topic will be authority and independence; the scripture will be John 14:15: "If ye love Me, ye will keep My commandments." Next year, he will switch back to reading the One Year Bible.

On a typical day, Bush heads to the Oval Office by about 7 a.m., toting the 50-to-70 page briefing book on the day's events that was his bedtime reading the night before. He will start his meetings by 8, and carve out time during the day to exercise — on the elliptical trainer, perhaps, if biking is not an option.

Although the above quote suggests Bush prefers judging, there is the possibility that the demands of Bush's work situation as President require such a regimen. However, comparing Bush with his predecessor--Bill Clinton--suggests that a president's personality sets a 'tone' in the White House. In particular, the Clinton White House was rumored to be much less organized and more open to spontaneity and emergent events.

Further evidence that Bush has a preference for judging is reflected in the following quote from Bush about a typical day at the Crawford ranch:

I'm going to have lunch with Secretary of State Rice, talk a little business; Mrs. Bush, talk a little business; we've got a friend from South Texas here, named Katharine Armstrong; take a little nap. I'm reading an Elmore Leonard book right now, knock off a little Elmore Leonard this afternoon; go fishing with my man, Barney; a light dinner and head to the ballgame. I get to bed about 9:30 p.m., wake up about 5 a.m. So it's a perfect day.

This quote suggests Bush, even when on vacation at the Crawford ranch, prefers that his day be planned around a schedule thus reflecting a preference for judging. Further, the manner in which Bush seeks to separate work from play also suggest a preference for judging."

Bush does seem like an ESTJ. He can seem impulsive at times that might mimic ESTP (many type him as an ESTP) but his beliefs are clear and definite. His behavior may seem spontaneous but it's based on well-established beliefs. He likes a predictable future. He isn't an in-the-moment kind of guy in general, preferring a planned day even when he's not in office. Being an extravert, he enjoys people and stimulation but he likes them on his own terms. He's practical and down to earth as sensing types are, and tough minded as thinkers tend to be.

Bush is cautious, evaluates quickly but with forethought, with more of a black or white perspective and he likes things definite. He's a counter phobic 6 who can challenge people with questions and he has a strong 7 wing. He's a fun guy but likes things on his own terms. He is traditional and likes structure and order, though he can be spontaneous. 6s tend to make decisions when they trust that's it's right and that it's the most secure thing to do. He tries to show his 7 side more than his 6 side, but you can detect the anxious and insecure 6ness in his eyes and face. In public, he is warm and funny though he likes to appear strong as well. 6 with 7 wings often are funny and many are comedians. In private his tough side shows up more. He questions until he gets a clear answer. His earlier life reflects much of his 7 side and possibly to counter his father's more serious nature. In truth, they are very similar, though his father, George Herbert Walker Bush is more a Type 6 phobic type.

Barack Obama, Type 9, ENFJ, First Black President, 2009-17

(1961-) President number 44 was Barack Obama. After much reflection, I believe Obama is a Type 9 with a strong 1 wing, social subtype, though people have typed him as a 1, 3 or even a 5. He can be charming and inspiring like a 3; tries to create harmony with his opponents in Congress like a Type 9; is brilliant and scholarly like a 5; and can be righteous and morally driven like a 1.

I first thought Obama was a type 1. He has very clear values, at times uses a preacher's tone of voice, can be definite with strong emphatic words and has a focus on what's morally right. He works hard, compromises to create the best solution for all and sacrifices his own needs for what he considers right, as mature 1s tend to do. He's hard to type because he is emotionally mature and has great qualities of many types, which is actually the case for many 9s, as they alter themselves for the sake of peace and harmony.

Obama is very thorough in his thinking, is a great and inspiring speaker, is extremely intelligent, has a positive vision and thinks before he speaks. His administration had no scandals. He lives according to his values as a good husband, father and promoter of ethical action. He is inclusive of all economic levels, cultures, races and gender.

His background as a community builder is very consistent as a likely social subtype. He is idealistic, objective, ethically oriented and principled. He studied constitutional law in law school, as a 1 might do to have a thorough knowledge of the legal and moral framework of the United States. He can be preachy and talks like a passionate minister; many ministers are 1s. He abides by rules and makes decisions via logical deduction using facts, not by impulse. He has strong inner convictions. In his community organizing work in Chicago, Obama was an advocate for the poor. In spite of strong evidence that might lead to the conclusion that he's a Type 1, I have come to see that Obama is a 9 with a very strong 1 wing. As already mentioned, Type 9s often have strong characteristics of a number of types, as 9s are malleable.

As a Type 9 President, Obama liked to bring people together, promoted a sense of peace and harmony, avoided conflict, resisted quick decision-making, was even-tempered and controlled his anger. Even when the Republican Congress opposed everything he put forward, he generally kept his cool. He weathered racial prejudice and withstood lies told about him, such as those put forth by the birther movement, with equanimity, patience and fortitude.

People sometimes take advantage of the Type 9's tendency toward inclusion and mutuality. He tended to appease the Republican Congress rather than standing up strongly and fighting them. His agreeableness and hope that they would work with him failed to create the mutuality he was hoping for. Later in his administration Obama issued more executive orders. In doing so he bypassed Congress, in particular Republicans who tended to block anything he initiated. Michelle Obama speaks of her husband as loving, open, and steady with no mood swings, typical of 9s.

Obama's speaking style is rational and can be passionate (part of the reason I originally thought he might be a 1), but is also inclusive, respectful and acknowledges all points of view like a 9. He includes plenty of long pauses in his speeches, tends to be reflective, affirms and is openly appreciative of others, very typical of a mature 9. I think he was one of the brightest and most progressive presidents we've ever had.

He's been criticized for being indecisive but in reality, he thinks about decisions very thoroughly. For instance, his decision not to send troops into Syria was based on his experience with Iraq and Afghanistan and the results of those choices. He can act decisively though, as was exhibited with his decision to eliminate Osama bin Laden and the decision to remove troops from Iraq. When he was a Congressman he was one of the few Congressmen who voted against the American invasion of Iraq.

From his book, *Dreams of My Father* (1995), Obama wrote, "of my constant, crippling fear that I didn't belong somehow, that unless I dodged and hid and pretended to be something I wasn't I would forever remain an outsider, with the rest of the world, black and white, always standing in judgment."

Belonging continued to be an issue, however. He started working in poor neighborhoods. "Wandering through tough neighborhoods, my fears were always internal: the old fears of not belonging. The idea of physical assault never occurred to me." This alludes to his strong desire to belong as a social subtype 9.

Enneagram author Elizabeth Wagele wrote of Obama, "Belonging and a sense of community are important to 9-Peace Seekers. Obama struggled between his desire for authenticity and the lure of prestige, as exemplified by the 3-Achiever: his idea of his father, fast cars, beautiful clothes, and so on. Then he decided to go to Chicago and become an organizer to help the poor. Type 9 and its idealistic 1-Perfectionist wing won over type 3. He conquered his waffling and his 6-like fear and made an important decision."

In college he was waffling and wavering. He tended to smoke pot a bit, not sure what direction to take. He was inspired by stories and images of success and wanted to live his life with purpose. He was able to create a vision of educating inner city kids to understand themselves and their environment and have a bigger vision for their lives.

The following is quoted from an article: https://today.law.harvard.edu/obama-first-made-history-at-hls/ The article from Harvard Law Today in November 1 2008 speaks of his mature type 9 qualities while at Harvard Law School.

"Most remarkable, given his complex identity, was how comfortable Obama seemed with himself. Barack's identity, his sense of self was so settled," recalled Cassandra Butts '91, who met him in line at the financial aid office, in an interview with PBS' "Frontline." "He didn't strike us in law school as someone who was searching for himself."

Professor Tribe rarely hired first-year students but recalls being struck by Obama's unusual combination of intelligence, curiosity and maturity. He was so impressed in fact, that he hired Obama March 31, 1989 — for posterity.

Tribe likes to say he had taught about 4,000 students before Obama and another 4,000 since, yet none has impressed him more.

Professor Martha Minow recalls: "He had a kind of eloquence and respect from his peers that was really quite remarkable," Minow says. When he spoke in her class on law and society, "everyone became very attentive and very quiet."

"Student Artur Davis '93 still vividly recalls how much Obama inspired him with a speech he gave during orientation week on striving for excellence and mastery. Davis, now a United States Congressman from Alabama, insists he left that speech by Obama convinced he'd just heard a future Supreme Court justice—or president."

Obama displayed other traits in law school besides eloquence that would define his success as a presidential candidate. "You could see many of his attributes, approach to politics and ability to bring people together back then," says Michael Froman '91, who worked with Obama on the Law Review.

As a campus leader, he successfully navigated the fractious political disputes raging on campus. By 1991, student protestors demanding the school hire more black faculty, had staged a sit-in inside the dean's office and filed a lawsuit alleging discrimination.

Obama spoke at one protest rally, but largely preferred to stay behind the scenes and lead by example, recalls one of the protest leaders, Keith Boykin '92. Obama opted against taking sides in the ideological disputes that often divided the politically polarized Law Review staff, casting himself instead as a mediator and conciliator. That approach earned the enduring respect of Law Review members including those not necessarily inclined to agree with his political views today.

He tended not to enter these debates and disputes but rather bring people together and forge compromises," says Bradford Berenson '91, who was among the relatively small number of conservatives on the Law Review staff."

Obama grew up in Hawaii with a white mother and Kenyan father who met while they were both studying at the University of Hawaii. His father left the family when Barack was 2. His mother married an Indonesian man when Barack was six and they moved to Indonesia. They lived there for four years and Barack attended Catholic and Muslim schools. Concerned for his education, Barack was sent by his mother to his mother's parents to live in Hawaii where he attended a prestigious school from the fifth grade through high school. His mother returned for part of that time to Hawaii to study cultural anthropology and meanwhile divorced her second husband. In high school, Barack was a good student and played varsity basketball. "I was raised as an Indonesian child and a Hawaiian child and as a black child and as a white child," Obama later recalled. "And so, I benefitted from a multiplicity of cultures that all fed me."

In *The Audacity of Hope*, Obama wrote: "As the child of a black man and a white woman, someone who was born in the racial melting pot of Hawaii, with a sister who's half-Indonesian but who's usually mistaken for Mexican or Puerto Rican, and a brother-in-law and niece of Chinese descent, with some blood relatives who resemble Margaret Thatcher and others who could pass for Bernie Mac, so that family get-togethers over Christmas take on the appearance of a UN General Assembly meeting, I've never had the option of restricting my loyalties on the basis of race, or measuring my worth on the basis of tribe."

Barack's mother was politically liberal, admired the civil rights movement of the 50s and 60s and encouraged her son's personal growth by instilling the same values in him. Obama left Hawaii to attend Occidental College in Los Angeles where he studied for two years and then transferred to Columbia University in New York City. His major was political science and he invested his energy deeply in reading about politics and international affairs. After graduating Obama got a job as a community organizer in Chicago's black South Side. He pressured city hall to improve conditions in the mostly black housing projects and found a part of himself in the black community that had been missing for him, having been more a part of white communities in which he had been raised.

Obama then enrolled in Harvard Law School where he became the first African American president of the prestigious Harvard Law Review. With that honor and graduating summa cum laude he received a contract to write *Dreams of My Father: A Story of Race and Inheritance* in 1995, a personal story about his struggle being a black man mostly raised by white society without the benefit of a black father, while trying to find his identity.

He met Michelle LaVaughn Robinson, his future wife, who was a Chicago South Side native as well as a Princeton and Harvard Law School graduate, at the law firm where he worked and where she was his supervisor. He pursued her ardently and they were married after a four-year courtship. They settled in Chicago's racially integrated Hyde Park and had two daughters Malia and Sasha. Helping with black voter registration in 1992, Obama accepted a position as a civil rights lawyer and also a lecturer at the University of Chicago law school.

As an Illinois state senator for eight years and US senator, he helped pass over 300 bills related to helping the poor, children, older people and labor unions, as well as campaign finance reform. He was elected a US Senator in 2004 by an overwhelming majority, highlighting his opposition to the Iraq War, and announced his candidacy for US President in 2007.

Concerning legislation, Obama as President supported health care reform, climate control, immigration reform, gun control and racial equality, issues that a Type 9 would naturally support - more equality and inclusion for all. As our first black president, he encountered the conundrum of leadership; attempting to maintain a neutral stance regarding racial issues despite facing strong racial prejudice himself from a racially fractured populace, as well as contending with severe resistance by conservatives to his more progressive agenda.

The following article speaks of his strong connection to 9 and 1 as part of his leadership characteristics of inclusion, equality for all, fairness and right action.

Leadership Characteristics of President Barack Obama

https://prezi.com/f8x23rmwhcfd/the-leadership-characteristics-of-president-barack-obama/ by Sydnie Cooper on 24 January 2015

To summarize and quote from the above article and highlight Obama's strengths:

"Obama was a community organizer, which helped him to relate on a personal level.

He responded with patience when challenged or besmirched.

Obama helped students by taking action to reduce student loan interest rates.

Despite continuous efforts to block his initiatives and slander his name, President Obama responded with patience and focused on the big picture.

As a U.S. Senator he had the vision that entering the Iraq War was wrong.

As President his first priority was to sign into law the Lilly Ledbetter Fair Pay Act, improving equal pay opportunities for women workers.

To become reelected for a 2nd term, he had the vision to establish a revolutionary grassroots campaign.

He proved to all young people that by dreaming big and working hard, anything is possible.

Though he knew universal healthcare was politically damaging, President Obama took action towards insuring that all Americans have the opportunity to be covered.

Upon taking office, the country faced a bleak financial outlook and President Obama took quick action to establish economic stability.

Even though there was political pressure to engage militarily with Russia, President Obama made the decision to use successful economic pressure.

He also helped students by eliminating bank involvement in new student loans, stopping the profit game.

President Obama is a great motivational speaker and also knows how to have fun. He has a great singing voice!

He really cares and is not afraid to shed a tear publicly.

To motivate and inspire others, he willingly serves in what is considered as servant roles, such as volunteering to cook.

To set the right example for the nation, he demonstrates how to be a great family man, loving his wife and kids.

He regularly speaks with political allies, foes, and world leaders in order to seek diplomatic resolutions to global issues."

President Obama studies the issues in order to make good choices. As a mature Type 9, he is a good listener, hears all sides, and is slow to take risky action. When conflict is very intense, he tunes-in, is prayerful, and accepts responsibility if the outcome is bad. He remains calm through difficulty and allows others to receive credit, when due.

There's a list of 50 of Barack Obama's accomplishments at: washingtonmonthly.com/magazine/marchapril-2012/obamas-top-50-accomplishments/

http://presidentialham.com/u-s-presidents/barack-obama-with-ham/
http://www.spangledwithstars.com/us-presidents/barack-obama.htm

The following paragraph is from the two above websites above: presidentialham.com and spangledwithstars.com:

"Anyone, friend or foe, will attest to Barack Obama's strong, charismatic and powerful personality. Much was made of his laid-back coolness – this was a man not easily ruffled and who stayed focused on what he considered important." There were many who encouraged him to change the tone of his campaign to become vitriolic but he kept it positive. He's been described as "calm, down to earth, scholarly, assured and confident." He pays attention to detail and his nickname is "No Drama Obama" reflecting a careful concern for his presidential image. He is serious but has a great sense of humor. He is open minded and seeks options from people he trusts. He is a visionary who inspires people with confidence." His calmness under pressure, reflective and patient nature speak of his type 9 nature.

As far as his Myers-Briggs type, I believe Obama is an ENFJ but his E and I are close and he could be an INFJ.

ENFJ PERSONALITY – PROTAGONIST

QUOTED FROM WWW.16PERSONALITIES.COM/ENFJ-PERSONALITY

"ENFJs are natural-born leaders, full of passion and charisma. Forming around two percent of the population, they are oftentimes our politicians, our coaches and our teachers, reaching out and inspiring others to achieve and to do good in the world. With a natural confidence that begets influence, ENFJs take a great deal of pride and joy in guiding others to work together to improve themselves and their community.

Firm Believers in the People

People are drawn to strong personalities, and ENFJs radiate authenticity, concern and altruism, unafraid to stand up and speak when they feel something needs to be said. They find it natural and easy to communicate with others, especially in person, and their

Intuitive (N) trait helps people with the ENFJ personality type to reach every mind, be it through facts and logic or raw emotion. ENFJs easily see people's motivations and seemingly disconnected events, and are able to bring these ideas together and communicate them as a common goal with an eloquence that is nothing short of mesmerizing.

The interest ENFJs have in others is genuine, almost to a fault – when they believe in someone, they can become too involved in the other person's problems, place too much trust in them. Luckily, this trust tends to be a self-fulfilling prophecy, as ENFJs' altruism and authenticity inspire those they care about to become better themselves. But if they aren't careful, they can overextend their optimism, sometimes pushing others further than they're ready or willing to go."

As mentioned, Obama could be an INFJ and there's certainly a case to present that he might be an introvert – serious thinking, private, reflective, deep. It's unlikely an INFJ would be president, though many believe he is that type. INFJ below paragraph, truity.com/personality-type/INFJ. "INFJs are guided by a deeply considered set of personal values. They are intensely idealistic, and can clearly imagine a happier and more perfect future. They can become discouraged by the harsh realities of the present, but they are typically motivated and persistent in taking positive action nonetheless. The INFJ feels an intrinsic drive to do what they can to make the world a better place.

INFJs want a meaningful life and deep connections with other people. They do not tend to share themselves freely but appreciate emotional intimacy with a select, committed few. Although their rich inner life can sometimes make them seem mysterious or private to others, they profoundly value authentic connections with people they trust."

Obama was a modern president using the internet to move his message during his presidential campaign, was personal and vulnerable yet could stand up for what is right, and he chose strong people to work under him. He honored his wife Michele who stood for justice, women and children's rights, combatting childhood obesity, advocating for more exercise and healthy eating, promoting the arts, supporting military families, balancing work and career, working in the White House vegetable garden and teaching the importance of growing real food for one's family.

To learn more about Michelle's accomplishments go to: https://blackdoctor.org/483712/job-well-done-first-lady-16-accomplishments-of-michelle-obama/

Obama, a 9 with a strong 1 wing, is a man of maturity, honesty, intelligence, patience, calmness, objectivity, stability, inclusion, diplomacy, vision, depth, forethought and tolerance. With the extra burden of being spotlighted as the first black president, he endured many tests beyond the already extraordinary challenges all U.S. Presidents have to face.

Donald Trump, Type 8, ESTP, Deal Maker, 2017 –

Photo by Bill Bonner

(1946-) Donald Trump, president number 45, is a Type 8 who is impulsive and outspoken, even more so than many 8s. He's direct, black and white in his thought process, seeks attention and instigates controversy. He's often seen as a bully who loves to win at all costs. It appears that he doesn't mind if you don't like him. He never admits fault or apologizes in public. He attacks if he's challenged. Truth is what he says it is; often his statements are not based in fact. Fact checkers who worked during the presidential campaign, as well as throughout Trump's presidency, have stated that much of what he says is exaggerated, inaccurate or a lie. Current statements often collide inconsistently with prior declarations. His America First slogan reflects his egocentric me-first attitude, although he can be generous and is able to create a win-win situation given the right circumstances.

He has a 7 wing, meaning he's animated and outspoken with a spur-of-the-moment speech and action pattern. 8s with 7 wings have the fastest and most decisive energy in the Enneagram. He's a sexual subtype who has to be the dominant male. He tends to use sexually graphic images and allusions and loves to control or put down anyone who is critical or not loyal to him. Loyalty is more important to Trump than accuracy or truth.

His sexually graphic language includes, "she got schlonged," referring to Hillary. "Hillary can't satisfy her husband. What makes you think she can satisfy America?" Referring to Megyn Kelley who questioned Trump during a political debate, "You could see there was blood coming out of her eyes, blood coming out of her wherever." About Princess Diana, "I could have nailed her." Even about his daughter Ivanka, he implied that he would be interested in her if he weren't her father. He loves to belittle women's sexual parts. Go to theenneagraminbusiness.com and see blogs about Trump by Ginger Lapid-Bogda, who writes about the Enneagram, to read about Trump, dominance and sexually graphic images. She has written many Enneagram books, particularly about Enneagram as it relates to business and work.

Trump's childhood in Jamaica Estates in Queens, New York, reflects his life. The fourth of five children born to a millionaire real estate mogul, Donald was driven to school and chauffeured to his appointments by limousine. He lived in a beautiful nine-bedroom house run by a highly disciplined father who worked seven days a week. On Sunday mornings, the children would go to abandoned building sites to pick nails for reuse. Donald was taught by his father to compete and win at all costs, though it already seemed to be in his nature. Trump's father encouraged his sons "to be killers and kings."

Donald was a demanding son, a troublemaker who was violent, disrespectful and disruptive. He allegedly punched his teachers and fellow students if they upset him. Even as a young child he had to be first in line. He tells a story of asking for his brother's building blocks to make a skyscraper and then gluing them together to prevent his brother from reusing them. He loved knocking down others' blocks and he always had to be number 1.

His father sent him to New York Military Academy with the hope of civilizing him, and Donald seemed to thrive in the environment of harsh discipline and abusive hazing. John Gotti, the gangster, and Batista, the former Cuban dictator, also attended the Academy. Trump excelled in athletics, especially baseball. He was voted Ladies' Man in the school yearbook and loved his heroes; the Playboy mogul Hugh Hefner, the fictional James Bond and Clint Eastwood's tough guy movie characters.

Immigration plays a large role in Trump's history. His grandfather, Friedrich Trump, was a German immigrant who moved to New York City in the 1880s. He worked as a barber in his teens, and at 23 he moved to the wilds of Seattle, Washington. He settled in the roughest part of town where he opened a restaurant surrounded by taverns, gaming houses and construction projects. Ultimately the two Italian chefs had a fistfight in the bar, which effectively closed his restaurant.

He then moved on to build the first Trump hotel in a new mining town in Washington State surrounded by saloons and brothels. Friedrich then migrated to the Canadian Rockies during the gold rush. There he sold horse burgers to the miners, which were made from the meat of horses that died transporting goods along Dead Horse Trail. When the gold ran out, Friedrich closed his horse burger business to build and open a two-story hotel.

Just when it was starting to make a profit, the miners left town. He took the entire hotel, sliding it down the mountain and then loaded it on a barge. During the journey the barge encountered rapids, which destroyed the barge and the entire hotel. He then salvaged the remaining wood and rebuilt the hotel on a piece of prime real estate that he didn't own in the town of White Horse. The hotel sold food and drinks in the restaurant downstairs and the services of prostitutes in the upstairs brothel. Gambling tables were at the ready. Three thousand miners visited the hotel every day. The Canadian Mounties eventually closed down his establishment and he decided to move back to Germany, only to find himself deported back to America. His native land didn't want him back because he didn't seek permission to leave in the first place and he had skipped out on his military duty.

While Friedrich was in Germany he procured a wife and upon returning to New York City they had three children including Fred, Trump's father. Friedrich began his new life in America as a barber on Wall St. and then made it big building and selling real estate. Drinking became an issue. Unfortunately, he died at the age of 49 in the 1918 influenza epidemic. Friedrich's wife, Trump's grandmother lived to a ripe old age of 86. The Trump legacy is filled with restlessness, adventure, high-risk behavior and shady deals.

Trump's father, Fred, followed in Friedrich's footsteps building homes and housing projects from the 1930s through the 1960s and pocketed money from government subsidy programs. Senate hearings challenged him regarding his shady money practices but the money he requested and pocketed from the government was declared to be unfair but legal. The national scandal enraged Eisenhower. The Trumps have proven to be geniuses at making deals and sliding through legal loopholes.

Fred started making blueprints and building garages by the time he was 12 and built his first house when he was 17. When another real estate company went bankrupt, Fred, with the backing of his court cronies, took over the properties and mortgages and started his own housing construction company. Having the right connections with important people, he built thousands of houses and apartments and prospered.

Although he was more introverted and quieter than Donald, Trump's father knew how to market himself. In 1939 he hired a barge to float past Coney Island carrying ten-foot tall individual letters that spelled out TRUMP. Fred was accused of discriminating against blacks and Hispanics by the US Justice Department in the early 1970s. A settlement was reached with the company, and young Donald Trump declared it a victory, initiating a pattern that has endured; never admit defeat. Donald spoke privately in an assuming way to the prosecutor saying, "You don't want to live with them either, do you?"

Trump's father Fred met beautiful Mary Anne MacLeod at a dance. She was a Gaelic speaking immigrant from The Isle of Lewis In the Hebrides off Scotland. They were soon married. She had the same strong inner confidence as her husband and transformed her life of service as a domestic maid to one of being driven around New York in a Rolls Royce. She would be decked out in furs and jewelry while collecting quarters from the machines in her laundromats. She gave Fred Trump five children including our current president.

Like his father and grandfather before him, Trump is driven by his determination to win at all costs. Achievement is everything to him and fast deals are the means to winning. Trump tweets instead of using emails. He never reveals weaknesses and admits, "I don't want to reveal fears." "I don't believe in win-lose. I believe in winning."

Trump hardly reads but loves activity and people contact. Receiving compliments for his achievements, having followers, celebrity status and high energy are his trademarks. He is the king of marketing, reality TV and being in control.

He claims never to have had an alcoholic drink; his personal commitment to sobriety was reinforced when his more sensitive, nice guy brother, Fred, died of alcoholism at age 43. His brother was a pilot, then captain of a fishing boat, and then worked on the maintenance crew of Trump Organization buildings. He was, however, unable to fit into the killer/winner pressure generated by his father and brother. In his early 20s Freddy, Jr. began a downward spiral of drinking. Donald holds a belief that people are predestined by their DNA to living life as winner like him or a loser like his brother. Trump admits that he was greatly affected by the suffering and death of his older brother.

Trump's past as a real estate developer and builder is filled with lawsuits, bankruptcies and doing his own thing his own way. He tends to disregard laws, leaving a trail of enemies. Trump tends to say and do whatever he wants. To defend him in lawsuits filed in his early career, Trump hired Roy Cohn, a high-profile lawyer who also represented Joseph McCarthy and Mafia dons. He surrounds himself with coaches who support him at all costs. Laws seem to simply be impediments for Trump to get around.

Trump has had various businesses; building and owning hotels, resorts, golf courses, casinos, an airline and beauty pageants. He sells the branding of his name on many products – real estate, golf club memberships, steaks, wines and other food products, magazines, clothing, mattresses and much more.

Trump had a successful television show for many years, called "The Apprentice", where he loved to eliminate contestants who were competing to win by being able to remain on the show while others were eliminated. The contestants completed business tasks assigned to them by the host, Donald Trump. His famous statement on the show was an enthusiastic, "You're fired!" The appeal of the show was his "truth" speaking, going for or against the establishment as he saw fit, and creating the illusion of advocating for the common person. The show differed from Trump's actual business policies and his present administration's position, which are geared to support corporate America and the rich.

He competes with everyone, and that even included his father, who bought up real estate in Queens. Trump turned his attention to higher class Manhattan real estate and claimed he wanted to own the whole island if he could. He enjoys loudly proclaiming his triumphs. Everything is a contest and he wants to be the winner. He likes a good fight. As he stated, "if you hit me, I'll counter punch."

Trump follows in the footsteps of his dad. He believes in "truthful hyperbole," a term made up by his biographer in *The Art of the Deal*. He takes the position that all publicity is good publicity. Exaggerating the truth to enhance your case is considered part of the game. Repeat something enough and people will believe it. Trump loved the prestige of being chosen to be on the television show, "Life of the Rich and Famous." Being in the news every day and every moment is a dream come true for him.

Trump often uses violent imagery that incites a crowd to action (not unusual for 8s, though many 8s, use violent or aggressive imagery without encouraging action) and his campaign rallies often erupted in physical fights. Trump relished egging on the crowd. His provocations included "throw the bum out," "knock the crap out of him," "I would like to punch him in the face," "he should have been roughed up," "and the audience hit back and that's what we need a little more of," "part of the problem is that nobody wants to hurt anyone anymore," and "if you hurt him I'll defend you in court." These are direct quotes from Boss Trump. Trump makes gestures with his fists as if he's punching someone, as a way to encourage the crowd to punch people who oppose his ideas.

In July of 2017, he sent out a tweet video of a wrestling match with Trump's face superimposed over an actual wrestler's face, holding down his opponent, CNN News, and pummeling them on the face (the CNN logo) with his fist. He hates the news media, particularly the liberal media. He despises weakness and supports strength, even if he hurts former friends or allies or edges into violence. He's not afraid to make fun of anyone, including the disabled, crying babies, strong women or men who oppose him. He is known to insult and make racial and religious slurs about anyone who opposes him.

Trump's record demonstrates the opposite of being on the side of the common person -- he sometimes refuses to pay workers the amount of wages he previously agreed on and by many reports, has stiffed numerous contractors who have worked for him. Many of his employees have written books speaking out against him. The now defunct Trump

University, was a scam and Trump settled three lawsuits for 25 million dollars. Many other lawsuits are still in process. His verbal statements allude to his sexist and racially and religiously biased beliefs. Many white racist groups support him. He has been accused by at least 15 women of sexual groping, and many additional women have accused him of making sexually explicit and inappropriate comments. His sexual misconduct accusations go back well over 30 years.

He speaks and acts against climate change and global warming, is a strong proponent of fossil fuels, supports strengthening the coal industry, is against the Affordable Care Act though he doesn't provide a viable alternative, and is anti-abortion, though he used to claim to be a proponent of abortion. He easily switches policy positions, even claiming that he never held a prior position when video evidence shows otherwise, i.e., supporting Medicaid in campaign speeches and reversing that position after he was elected.

Some people have typed him as a 3, but 3s are more strategic in their planning. They also prefer to be approved of by most people and they attempt to create friends rather than enemies. 3s are also more image-oriented than Donald who prefers a more controversial bad boy image, and seems to relish continual conflict, the hallmark of a less than mature 8. His strategy is to get attention; whether positive or negative doesn't seem to matter.

Donald is blatant in his approach and has a hard time controlling his commentary. He is a physical /earthy body type as 8s usually are; down-to-earth, matter-of-fact, impulsive, in your face and bold, the opposite of intellectual or image oriented. He thinks in extremes, black or white, and dislikes complexity. Fast reactions and controversial tweets are more important to him than strategic planning. 3s and 8s both like to win and 8s are every bit as achievement-oriented as 3s but 3s prefer less controversy and higher ratings from a large audience. They want to please everyone if possible rather than a smaller cadre of loyal fans.

Trump denigrates and mocks anyone he perceives as weak or who opposes his ideas or actions. He sees people as either friends or enemies. His secondary type may be 3, but his negative seeming Type 3 qualities are due to impulsiveness and narcissism, which immature 8s can certainly have as well as 3s. Trump's own political party and his aides have had a hard time managing him, both on the campaign trail and as president. They can be as surprised as anyone else by his actions and statements.

Trump's need for support in his narcissism is more important to him than general approval. "My way or the highway" is his motto. Smooth talking 3s want to please more than 8s. 3s plan in advance and are concerned about and try to avoid failure. Trump may have a lot of 3 characteristics, but he is driven by Type 8 lust for power, control and dominance. He has to be top dog! Both types 3 and 8, when immature, have a me-first attitude hidden behind insecurity, and a need to win at all costs.

8s want autonomy and freedom and are easily oppositional. Immature 8s ignore rules they expect others to follow. They can be rebels, particularly with a 7 wing like Trump. The 8 with a 9 wing seeks out more harmony and are not as outspoken but still strong. Type 3s are not as oppositional as immature 8s. As already stated, they want to be seen in a positive light, they smile more and want everyone to like them. They want as wide an audience as possible. When under stress, 3s and 8s can both veer into deceptive practices. The high energy of conflict can be a turn-on for some 8/7s. Enemies are simply accepted as being "part of the package" for a less than mature 8. They see a dog-eat-dog world and want to lead the pack.

Many in Trump's cabinet are millionaires and billionaires; many are inexperienced politically, shade the truth and make decisions without creating standard coalitions, using commonly accepted practices, or adhering to generally accepted democratic principles. He protects loyal family members who are also on his advisory team. Trump hires and fires people quickly just as he did on his reality TV show. He is the first U.S. President in history with no government or military experience, though as mentioned, he did go to a military school in his youth. His background is entirely business. Trump shows strong signs of compulsive lying, extreme narcissism, strong racial prejudice, sexual misconduct and anti-social behavior. Attention and winning are his priorities more than honesty, inclusion or standard practices. Tradition seems irrelevant unless it happens to fit his present need.

Trump takes revenge against anyone he perceives as opposing him; revenge is a trait of an immature 8. In a Mother Jones article, "At the second presidential debate, GOP nominee Donald Trump went where no major candidate has gone: he vowed that if elected he would prosecute and imprison his opponent. This promise was a pure act of vengeance and drew much scorn. But Trump's supporters, who have long rallied around the "lock her up" meme, embraced his declaration. Days later, Trump expanded on his pledge: He said he would also "throw Clinton's lawyers into the hoosegow," and after the *New York Times* and other media published the accounts of women who said they had been groped, grabbed, and kissed against their will by Trump, the former reality television star threatened payback against his accusers and the press." www.motherjones.com/politics/2016/10/donald-trump-obsessed-with-revenge

So much about Trump is a projection of unconscious parts of himself. He seems to have a vendetta against immigrants yet two of his three wives are immigrants. His grandfather was an immigrant. He actually seems fine with immigrants as long as they're white, supporters, or rich and prefers to admit those into the country who already speak English.

He avoids seeing or showing any weaknesses and he makes fun of anyone who is weak. He attacks other political candidates for some of the same faults he has in himself. He wants to lock up Hillary for what he perceived as illegal actions, not admitting some of his own actions have been illegal or questionable, and he loves to break tradition and even laws. He hides his background and distorts the truth, yet attacks anyone he sees as dishonest or against him.

His first wife Ivana was a female version of himself, tough, likely a Type 8, who made strong business decisions. He seemed to be happy for a while in their power relationship. Donald's parents were pleased with his match. Ivana wanted to share in the decisions and did a great job running things with Donald. Eventually Trump didn't want to stay with a strong wife. Two Type 8s in the same household were too much. He regretted being married to a business partner who wanted to share his power.

While married to Ivana he started dating an actress, TV and film star, Marla Maples from Georgia. Upon discovering his affair, Ivana decided she wanted a divorce. She fought Trump's pre-nuptial agreement, and their fight was publicized in tabloids nationwide. Trump's parents were mortified, especially his mother. To cope with the stress Trump bought an airline shuttle, the sixth largest yacht in the world and a football team. He also purchased the estate of Mar-a-Lago in Florida for his new girlfriend, which he still owns and where he often retreats on weekends. Even though Marla was sweeter appearing and less aggressive than Ivana, that marriage did not last long. Marla was a model just as is his third wife, the current First Lady, Melania.

In the Myers-Briggs Profile, Trump is an ESTP. He's extraverted, confrontational, spontaneous and lives in the moment. He makes choices impulsively and seems to be oblivious to the consequences of those decisions. He seems surprised that there are protest marches, massive opposition to his policies, negative feedback and low approval ratings. He seems to thrive on controversy and is fed by the adoration of his loyal fans.

Go to www.psychologytoday.com/blog/the-situation-lab/201509/the-personality-donald-trump for an excellent article about Donald Trump's traits.

Another valuable and in-depth article: A psychological trap: making sense of Donald Trump's life and Personality by Dan P. McAdams, https://www.theguardian.com/us-news/2016/aug/05/donald-trump-psychology-personality-republicans-election. Here's a part of it:

Despite Republicans urging Trump to be more congenial, his behavior only becomes more erratic – Dan P. McAdams says there are three reasons for this.

"Trump's temperament profile – high extraversion and low agreeableness – derives much of its power from an underlying impulsivity laced with anger. Both George W. Bush and Bill Clinton were highly extraverted presidents who expressed their social dominance in a generally gregarious and friendly way. By contrast, Trump's style is more aggressive and spontaneous, filled with biting humor and a sense that you just don't know what he might do next.

His charisma evokes feelings of danger and excitement. The angry impulsivity, moreover, blocks any expression of care, affection or empathy. He is typically unable or unwilling to squelch the impulse, step back and survey the situation, and focus on another person long enough to appreciate the other's humanity. He seems to live in the angry moment.

Trump's impulsive temperament style dovetails with his central life goal – the narcissistic aim of promoting Donald Trump. Ever since he attended New York Military Academy for high school, Donald Trump has doggedly pursued a motivational agenda of expanding, extolling, displaying and adoring the self. To be fair, it takes no small degree of narcissism to run for United States president. But again, Trump seems extreme compared to other candidates, as witnessed in his near-constant self-references, his over-the-top braggadocio and his desire to plaster his name on skyscrapers, casinos, a so-called "university" and steaks.

In keeping with the narcissism, Trump finds it especially difficult to ignore his impulses and consider the exigencies of situations when he perceives a threat to the self. He couldn't just turn the other cheek, or check his impulsive anger, when Khizr Khan held up his pocket constitution and mocked Trump as somebody who has probably never read America's most sacred document and who has never sacrificed for his country.

Finally, there is Donald Trump's philosophy of life, spelled out first in *The Art of the Deal.* It is a matter of principle for Donald Trump that when you are attacked, you hit back harder. If you want to win the game of life, you must be a counter-puncher. And it does not matter who hits you, even if it is a patriotic American couple who still mourn the loss of their son, or a baby who has the temerity to cry during your speech.

Many people feel safer with a strong authoritative president who promises protection and spouts simple statements without much policy rhetoric or long-range planning. It's hard to admit the boss is defective or that's he not what he pretended to be or do."

Another article that analyzes his Myers-Briggs type in depth. Go to this website for the full article. http://www.personalitypathways.com/article/trump-mbti-type.html

Donald Trump ESTP - Looking Behind the Public Face
Presidential Politics and Personality Type
By Ross Reinhold Jan 2016, PersonalityPathyways.com, Reprinted with the express permission of Ross Reinhold, editor of PersonalityPathways.com

"Bold, Brash, Bombastic! The consummate "entertainer" according to Carly Fiorina. As Danielle Poirier has stated: "Extraverted Sensing personality types [ESTP and ESFP] are pragmatic and realistic with a zest for living life to the fullest."

Trump, The Promoter. As Linda Berens describes ESTPs: "They are highly gifted negotiators, entrepreneurs and salespersons, and they know how to maximize every moment of their waking hours. Indeed, they are people who love life in the fast lane and they are masterful at inching things along in their direction when it comes to interpersonal interactions. They thrive on action and the use of all available resources at hand, sometimes to the point where the goal justifies the means." (Working Together, Isachsen & Berens, 1998)

Born under different circumstances, Trump could have been Richard Sherman, Seattle Seahawks All-Pro cornerback with his flowing dreadlocks, taunting and challenging opponents to throw the ball to the guy he is covering. He is confident he will win; he will beat you.

So, that's the broad brush on Trump and his ESTP profile. It's his dominant Extraverted Sensing mental orientation that is the leading edge of his personality. Being engaged with the outer world with all of the senses feeds his life force. Action and engagement fuel his energy and the more he gets the more he wants.

Because Trump is "out there," speaks boldly, seems quite impulsive and a loose cannon, people wonder "Wow, is this the guy we'd want to have his finger on the Nuclear button? Can we trust this bull in the china shop? He says these nutty things, can we trust him to be piloting this plane?" This is understandable, especially with an ESTP like Trump who loves fun, entertaining with flair, having an impact on others and pulls no punches. His media exposure and extraverted nature so dominates our understanding of who he is."

Trump alters his prior statements, promises and commitments without concern for consistency or reliability. Decisions are made in the moment, seemingly without much concern for negative long-range consequences. He doesn't share much detail of his plans and leaves those details up to others to figure out. His message is, "Trust me." He is authoritarian in nature rather than democratic or inclusive. His aristocratic leaning favors the rich. Trump is bold, outspoken, impulsive and fearless and can highlight others' flaws but seems unaware of his own. Some people seem to like traits of this maverick going against the establishment, and put their trust in him. Others like his prior business success and hope that will create a positive economy. Conflicts of interest between how his business interests effect important presidential decisions, his refusal to divulge his tax information, ties to Russian voting interference, possible collusion to obstruct justice, constitutional questions, issuance of travel bans, desire to dismantle Obama's health care act, and the realities of the new tax plan, will all need to be addressed and sorted in the future.

Trump's insensitivity to hurricane victims of Puerto Rico, his turning a blind eye to white racist groups such as the Ku Klux Klan, his encouragement to police to be rough with alleged criminals, his demand that his cabinet praise him constantly, his disdain at the FBI, the courts, the press, senior officials in his own administration, Congress, even his own Republican Party, his rage at anyone who criticizes him; all speak to an emotionally immature person who demands constant approval. He has set back civil rights, immigration rights, and transgender rights and shows no concern for environmental protection. He's inconsistent in his policy views, knows practically nothing about history or presidential precedent and expects others to solve problems for him. He turns on anyone who doesn't consistently support him. Cabinet members and support staff are often fired or publicly scolded at the whim of the president. His staff tries to control and manage his outbursts and impulsive decisions and keeps him from even knowing the up to date realities of the Mueller investigation into the Russian election tampering for fear of Trump's reactions.

Trump shows the impulsive outspokenness of an immature 8 where anger and the need to be in control mask fear, insecurity and hurt underneath. A mature 8 would have more restraint whereas he seems to have little. Trump skews his facts to support his monochromatic point of view. Loyalty is extremely important, a strong component of most 8s, and he resists feedback that might shed light on his limitations. It's hard for him to accept support from others in any way that sets limits or might trigger self-doubt or self-reflection. Sometimes he seems capable of seeing others' viewpoints, but that can easily shift in the next moment or on another day. He loves to entertain his audience with shocking and self-centered comments and tweets. Tweets fit his short attention span. His fans seem to like it.

Donald Trump's strengths include his directness, persistence, spontaneity, his business success, family loyalty, persuasiveness, entertainment value, and his fearlessness.

Summary of Enneagram types (taken from my book Enneagram Basics)

Each of us has qualities of all the types, though one type for most of us is predominant and more automatic in our thinking, perspective and motivation. This greatly affects our behaviors though the strongest motivation behind the behavior determines the dominant type.

Here's an overview of the nine types of the Enneagram. I'm giving each type three names to show the associated qualities of each type.

Type 1: The Perfectionist/Reformer/Improver. Type 1 has an ideal view of how life should be and wants reality to conform to that view. 1s examine everything, including themselves, with an eye towards correction and perfection.

Type 2: The Helper/Pleaser/Cheerleader. Type 2 wants to help people, as a way to be loved and accepted. 2s need people to need them. A positive personality, the 2 loves to give, but can lay on the guilt if unappreciated.

Type 3: The Success Seeker/Achiever/Winner. Type 3 is the U.S. cultural ideal and focuses on goals, success, accomplishments, winning, and producing. Image is everything, and 3s generally target areas for goal-setting, where they can succeed.

Type 4: The Depth Seeker/Romantic/Searcher. Type 4 is the nonconformist, working to cultivate individuality or specialness, in order to be noticed and admired. The 4 is drawn to beauty, individual self-exploration, and a search for meaning.

Type 5: The Observer/Thinker/Knowledge Seeker Type 5 tends to be private and engaged in thinking, observing, and making sense out of life, particularly in knowledge-gathering, theory making, and integrating different aspects of knowledge and learning.

Type 6: The Questioner/Guardian/Security Seeker. Type 6 tends to question everything, particularly issues of safety and security. 6s worry, analyze in depth, and try to solve concerns in advance. They feel more secure in the truth, no matter how negative, than with positive images.

Type 7: The Optimist/Stimulator/Fun Seeker. Type 7 sees the world in the best possible light. 7s like positive thinking, fun, adventure, and newness. They prefer risk to repetition and like to be around people that are happy, ready for change, and can move on the spur of the moment.

Type 8: The Director/Powerhouse/Challenger. Type 8 likes to be in charge. 8s want control of their own lives and often others' lives, too. 8s act quickly and can't stand ambivalence. They prefer action, directness, and strength.

Type 9: The Peacemaker/Accommodator/Comfort Seeker. Type 9 prefers to avoid conflict. 9s tend not to initiate but "goes with the flow." 9s appear easygoing, and they like comfort, constancy, and little change, unless they initiate it, in stages.

Going a little deeper into understanding the types:

Type 1: The Perfectionist/Reformer/Improver

- Living by the rules
- I'm here to fix me, you, and the rest of the world
- Oh! The pressure to be good is killing me
- Let's see, there's guilt, and resentment, and
- Doing it right - no time to play and relax

Perfectionist/Reformer/Improvers strive to make everything right, have high ideals, and expect the same traits in others. 1s have a hard time with ambivalence and the gray areas of life. It's always an either/or proposition for the 1: black or white, good or evil, right or wrong. That someone could be good and bad at the same time is difficult for the 1 to accept.

Understanding the Type

1s believe there is only one way - the right way! Their ideal vision of how life *must* be lived drives them along on the path toward perfection. We all aim for ideals to some degree, but 1s go overboard in a sink-or-swim effort to do *everything* right. When the results of their best efforts fall short of perfection, guilt and upset haunt them.

Perfectionist **1s** measure everything against how well they're doing to meet often unattainable goals. They focus their attention on what's *not* working more than what *is*. There's an anxious awareness of making a mistake, of being judged, of failing to meet the mark. 1s don't accept that humans are fallible, especially themselves, and they also don't accept that truth and rightness may come in more than one version.

Reformer **1s** make "what is" better. They don't buy into image or surface values. Concerned with ethics, they want to know whether others have hidden selfish motivations cloaked in an image of goodness. They look at what's real and how it can be improved. 1s are often in the forefront of reform, whether religious or political. 1s tend to be one of the dominant types in religion, as they believe in universal values and in good overcoming evil.

***Improver* 1s are** always involved! If it needs to be improved, 1s will improve it, along with everything and anything else that *doesn't* need to be improved. Do you absolutely *have* to straighten a picture that's just a little bit crooked? *Must* you remove dead leaves from a plant in someone else's office or living room? Do folks tell you that you're overly critical? If you notice what's off more than what's on, welcome to your type. You're a 1!

Famous 1s

Famous 1s include Prince Charles, David Thoreau, Tom Brokaw, Peter Jennings, Colin Powell, "Miss Manners," Emily Post, "Felix Unger," Ted Koppel, Margaret Thatcher, William Buckley, Martha Stewart, Al Gore, Bernie Sanders, Ralph Nader, Gandhi, Michelle Obama, Hillary Clinton, Bill Moyers, Noam Chomsky, John Adams, Most common type for US Presidents!

Type 2: The Giver/Pleaser/Cheerleader

- Pleasing yourself while pleasing others
- Where are my needs?
- Sunny on the outside - where are the clouds?
- Relating without helping
- Learning to receive

Helper/Pleaser/Cheerleaders focus on what you want but also on what they want you to be for them. 2s deliver but want credit for it. With your needs highlighted, 2s try to hide their own, and their constant smiles may hide their internal frustration. They aim to please and are disappointed if they can't. Who could refuse such giving?

Understanding the Type

Let me help you! Think of me as the *mother archetype*. I'm really good at helping, and I know what you need. Of course, I am also the punisher who can withhold what you need. Bottom line? I need you to be dependent on me to provide for you, so you will love me. Be dependent on me, yet don't consume me. If this describes your approach to life, welcome to your type. You are a 2!

If you're a 2, you want others to be dependent on you but want your own independence as well. However, you fear others will reject you if you're too independent. If others are taking advantage of your good nature, wanting too much and being ungrateful for your giving or over giving, you may suddenly reach a limit. It comes as a shock to realize you have needs too. Suddenly you can't stand the neediness and demands and may react by doling out the punishments or angrily setting limits.

It's a strange dance, isn't it? You struggle to balance the back and forth between dependence and independence. You can't stand having to need people. It seems like a weakness. Rather, you want people to need *you*. And if they praise you, well, then the sky is the limit. The dance continues.

2s are more likely to be women, though there are plenty of 2 men. Many women think they're 2s, because of the cultural stereotype that women should give. Most mothers need to be a bit 2-seeming, but real 2s have difficulty dropping the caring, nurturing role. They are often devastated when their kids go to college or people no longer need them. To no longer have a giving role is awful. To be rejected is hell. To watch others give to the one you love can bring feelings of jealousy and rejection to the fore. You're upset with yourself if you can't please, and upset with others if you can't win them over.

Famous 2s

Famous 2s include Leo Buscaglia, Kelly Ripa, Ann Landers, Jerry Lewis, Dolly Parton, Desmond Tutu, Eleanor Roosevelt, Monica Lewinsky, Sally Jessy Raphael, Elizabeth Taylor, Nancy Reagan, Kathy Lee Gifford, Richard Simmons, Princess Diana, William McKinley, Elvis Presley, Desmond Tutu, Farrah Fawcett, Amma (the hugging saint)

Type 3: The Success Seeker/Achiever/Winner

- Win at all costs
- Who I am - role and image
- Human being versus human doing
- The inner life of a 3 - where is it?
- Everything is a goal
- The star - no second place

Success Striver/Achiever/Winners want to excel, come in first, and be rewarded. Always focused on success, the word *failure* doesn't exist for 3s. Image and right impression are fundamental and essential. Ever focused on goals and action, 3s produce results.

Understanding the Type

3s are the Success Strivers, doing whatever it takes to accomplish, win, and cross the finish line first. Whether it's reporting to work at 7 A.M., knowing the right connections, or looking the part, the 3 will make sure to complete the task. Nothing blocks the goal. Obstacles? You'll overcome them - and your speed and efficiency accelerate the process. It doesn't have to be perfect; it just has to work, with *you* being recognized for the win.

3s stand out as the models of success. Whatever the family or culture deems worthy of success, 3s are there to accomplish. You'll become a doctor, even if it isn't exactly who you are, because it feels great being admired and reaping the rewards of what is worthy and desired by others. Your worth is what you do, not who you are; though ideally, they mesh. Being who you are is secondary to the symbols of success, the money, and the recognition of being the best.

3s are the family heroes, the rags-to-riches story models, and the stars we admire. 3s are motivated by the dream. In one culture, it's material success; in another it's the equivalent of the Olympic gold medal, the tribal head or shaman or the president of the student council. Image becomes as important as reality. Your goals are measured by outcomes - the roles, the titles, the trophy, the degree. You want people to desire to be like you.

Famous 3s

Famous 3s include Bill Clinton, John Kerry, Mitt Romney, Tony Robbins, Tom Brady, Joe Montana, Dick Clark, Paul McCartney, Tom Cruise, Sharon Stone, Jane Pauley, Demi Moore, Vanna White, Bryant Gumbel, Diane Sawyer, Tiger Woods, George Washington, James Monroe, Condoleezza Rice, Whitney Houston, Lance Armstrong, Demi Moore, Sting

Type 4: The Depth Seeker/Romantic/Searcher

- Living a life of passion
- Everyday living versus living on the edge
- Including pain as part of the mix
- The agony and the ecstasy
- Be authentic or die

Depth Seeker/Romantic/Searchers are characterized by an emotional intensity. Longing for special attention, they want to be perceived as unique, deep, and beautiful, whether female or male. They are looking for love and searching for meaning.

Understanding the Type

Type 4s are true individualists who do not give in easily to group identity or shallow images. 4s hope their unique qualities will captivate others, draw others to them, and cause others to seek them out. Accept the ordinary? Never! The very idea is abhorrent to the 4's romantic nature. If you long to be recognized, appreciated, and adored for your beauty (like Narcissus, in Greek mythology, a beautiful youth condemned by Nemesis to pine away for love of his own reflection), depth, creativity, and emotional intensity, welcome to your type. You are a 4!

As a 4, you're attuned to aesthetic and artistic creation, ideally born from the depths of the soul's suffering. Day-to-day reality is difficult, even boring, so you measure life by those special moments that transcend the mundane, where life soars to special heights or plummets to moments of deep despair. 4s are the emotional junkies and emotional roller coasters of the universe, seeking experiential, spiritual, and relationship thrills and spills to make life worth living.

You teach the other types to feel deeply, to remember we come from spirit, not to give in to normalcy or what others expect of us but rather to live with personality, creativity, romance, drama, and depth. You can give others special attention, too.

You believe that sacrifice for these qualities is worth the cost. As a 4, you don't hide or hold back from your own inner exploration of feelings, thoughts, longings, searching. "Let go of family, cultural, or relationship expectations and be your true self," says the 4.

Famous 4s

Famous 4s include Prince, Johnny Depp, Judy Garland, Tennessee Williams, Edgar Allan Poe, James Dean, Michael Jackson, James Taylor, Angelina Jolie, Eric Clapton, Jimi Hendrix, Francis Ford Coppola, Jackie Kennedy, Marlon Brando, Marilyn Monroe, Abraham Lincoln, Judy Collins, Joni Mitchell, Bob Dylan, Amy Winehouse, Ingmar Bergman, Winona Ryder, Nicholas Cage

Type 5: Knowledge Seeker/Observer/Thinker

- It's all in your head
- I heard you the first time
- Of course I love you - let's talk about astronomy
- Intimacy - let's read or learn something together
- Have you heard the one about the physicist and the aeronautical engineer?

Detached, objective, analytical, and rational, Knowledge Seeker/Observer/Thinkers don't want to be overwhelmed with feelings, personal sharing, or high expectations from others. You are a knowledge seeker par excellence and spend all your time researching the subjects in which you want to become an expert. You may like people but study them first.

Understanding the Type

5s crave the learning experience. Do you tear something apart and put it back together again, just to see how it works? Do you study cause-and-effect relationships and develop theories about them? Do you see yourself as an observer, wondering what is really true and what is conjecture? If objectivity defines you, and you tend not to take things personally, welcome to your type. You're a 5!

5s are reflective. You love the process of analysis and may have a strong scientific or technical bent. Repeat the experiment to check accuracy? Yes, sir! Let's think and not get emotional about it. A healthy skepticism is welcome, and while you approve of tried and true methods, you are also open to new approaches and methods.

Innovations, new perspectives on old ideas, or combining ideas or fields of interest to create new realities are your cup of tea. You use your brain's creative power to unfold new possibilities and then test them with as much proof or logic as possible. 5s are rational and don't fall prey to whimsical thought or personal impulses, though growth includes trusting your intuition as information.

Famous 5s

Some famous 5s include Bill Gates, Ulysses S. Grant, Albert Einstein, George Lucas, Stephen Hawking, Descartes, Friedrich Nietzsche, Karl Marx, Thomas Edison, Georgia O'Keeffe, Jane Goodall, Emily Dickenson, Bobby Fischer, Karl Rove, Daniel Day Lewis, Robert Redford, Thomas Jefferson, James Monroe, Herbert Hoover, Georgia O'Keefe, Julian Assange "Wikileaks", Eckhart Tolle, Emily Dickinson

Type 6: The Questioner/Guardian/Security Seeker

- Fight or flight: fears both real and imagined
- *You* are the authority
- Be prepared!
- Nothing in this life is certain - can you handle it?
- I have a question!

Questioner/Guardian/Security Seekers scan for danger. You can't always trust what is apparently so; you'd better check for deeper motivations and determine what is real. Once tested, 6s tend to be loyal to the max and expect the same from others. Be ready for a lot of questions!

Understanding the Type

All of us are fearful and vigilant, at times, in the face of real or imagined dangers, but 6s live in that state as a preset condition. As a 6, you are wired to prepare for worst-case possibilities. Security comes when you have planned enough and feel ready. But can you tell the difference between real dangers and concerns generated in the mind? If this describes how you think, welcome to your type. You're a 6!

6s have a million questions to ask and there's no end point to the concerns of what might happen. There is no end point in securing the border. You notice the positive, but your mind generates limitless negative possibilities, so your attention is *focused* on problems and problem-solving. Issues of trust, doubting, and fear abound. You are on guard, scanning the environment.

Let's get real - 6s need to prepare! Forget about fantasy and romance and imagination for a moment. There's no time to live in an imagined world. You never know what's around the corner, so it's important to plan for contingencies - constantly. Crisis mode becomes your *modus operandi.* The problem is that you don't see that living in a hyper-aroused state of adrenaline, in case some enemy shows, is just as unrealistic as being totally *un*prepared. Just in case, however, should the enemy appear, you are ready!

You test for danger and may never trust completely. Why should you? You can go back and forth, for and against, for and against. Amidst nature's uncertainties - global warming, earthquakes, snowstorms, outages, avalanches, hurricanes, tornadoes, forest fires, floods, disease - there is no end to danger. And people cause just as much distress: betrayal, death, lies...can anything or anyone be trusted?

You look for certainty in an uncertain world and hope another person or situation can create the solid ground you are looking for. Once you have found that person, group, or cause, your loyalty knows no bounds. This is a Head type, and 6s overmanage in the mind to protect themselves and those they care about. 6s forget to use their bodies to feel secure.

6s are the only type that is divided into two categories:

- *Phobic* 6s run from their fears, which are often irrational. Something is lurking in the shadows! Better get home quick and turn the lights on!

- *Counterphobic* 6s outwardly challenge their real or imagined fears and concerns, either confronting others with probing questions or challenging themselves by meeting their fears head on. Attacking the fear creates a surge of feeling more secure. These are the folks who jump out of airplanes to conquer heights!

Actually, most 6s are a bit of both, but some can be quite one or the other. Think of trial lawyers and stunt men and women as possible counterphobics and lab technicians and insurance analysts as probable phobics.

Famous 6s

Some famous 6s include Robert Kennedy, Spike Lee, Phil Donahue, Joseph McCarthy, "George Costanza" (Seinfeld), Diane Keaton, Julia Roberts, Mary Tyler Moore, Sally Field, Evel Knievel, Johnny Carson, George H.W. Bush, George Bush, Woody Allen, Ellen Degeneres, David Letterman, John Stewart, Richard Nixon, J. Edgar Hoover, Freud

Type 7: The Optimist/Adventurer/Fun Lover

- It's party time!
- Keep the energy high
- Ride the waves - please, no turbulence
- Freedom is my middle name
- Positive ideas cure anything
- The best is yet to come

Always looking on the bright side and seekers of excitement, Optimist/Fun Lovers are fun, entertaining, and always up for something new. 7s don't tolerate painful scenarios. This energized type is chipper, charming and ready for the latest venture, whether it's sports, gala parties and events, or a new and exciting challenge!

Understanding the Type

Optimist/Adventurer/Fun Lovers are the quintessential positive thinkers. Life is what you make it, and 7s choose to make it great! Sure, there are challenges, but you can overcome them. You just have to work at it. The mind can conquer all adversity. Do you refuse to spend much time with the negative side of life - pain, discomfort, bad feelings, or boredom? Do you believe people cause their own misery by having bad attitudes? If this is how you think, welcome to your type. You are a 7!

7 is a Head type, so it's all about *attitude*. You're confident you can think your way out of anything, as long as you keep that affirmative mindset. For 7s, thinking is doing. A good idea, particularly one that's upbeat, can save the day. Unfortunately, ideas aren't executions, and 7s are criticized for merging the two.

Enjoyment, excitement, and adventure are at the heart of 7s. If there's no pleasure in it, why do it? You don't see pain, obstacles, or major difficulties as inevitable parts of the process; rather, they're signs of something major being wrong. Of course, as a 7, you have creative ways of even making pain less painful. Your favorite expressions include:

- Let's look at it this way, from this angle instead.
- It's a learning experience.
- Let's move on.
- It's just a temporary setback.

7s stay stimulated or highly engaged with life, partially to not focus on the bad stuff. As a 7, you can acknowledge pain, but there's no lingering on it, that's for sure. If you focus on what's good, deny what's bad, or reframe your thinking, the pain will lessen or disappear. There's always more fun to be had, thank God, so life is *always* good.

"I have to feel free in order to commit," says the 7. Freedom comes first. It's the foundation of your type. Defined limits cause pain. You need options, the freedom of your individuality, and liberation from limited or dysfunctional situations. More mature 7s realize that limits and some life-ache are just normal parts of life and growth, and not a reflection of something wrong.

You are generally extraverted, social, and engaging, loving to both entertain and be entertained. You know hordes of people but prefer to keep the connecting light. Conversations can be deep, at times, but changing the subject is easy for you, and if things get too serious, well, it's just too serious. Introverted 7s do exist, and the excitement with them may remain in the head as ideas, shared with fewer people.

You have tons of energy and many interests. You not only think but act, though it's hard to complete everything, when your interests are so diverse! You remind us to see the glass as half-full.

Famous 7s

Famous 7s include Timothy Leary, Ram Dass, Mozart, Goldie Hawn, Robin Williams, Elton John, Jim Carrey, Regis Philbin, Jack Nicholson, Howard Stern, Joan Rivers, Benjamin Franklin, Howie Mandell, Steven Spielberg, Carol Burnett, "Indiana Jones," Joe Biden, John Kennedy, FDR, Bette Midler, "Robin Hood," Leonardo da Vinci, Steve Martin, Paris Hilton, Katy Perry, Larry King, Britney Spears

Type 8: The Director/Challenger/Powerhouse

- Live and let live? I don't think so
- The generator: step aside, I'm energized
- Be reasonable - do it my way!
- In charge on the outside, insecure on the inside
- Sorry! I didn't mean to step on you

Director/Challenger/Powerhouses can light up a city with a drive for doing and taking action. Short on patience, what you see is what you get. The most body-instinctive type, 8s tend not to take *no* for an answer. If there's an obstacle in the way slowing down progress, call an 8 for guaranteed action.

Understanding the Type

Preferring action to inaction and driven by impulse, Director/Challenger/Powerhouses have energy to burn and can't stand to wait. No brakes, please. 8s feel easily controlled and are on the alert for that possibility. It's all about the green light and taking charge, so as not to be taken charge of by others. If you test people the way you'd test a new car and push your agenda hard, welcome to your type. You're an 8!

Strength is power. You do whatever it takes to be strong or at least project strength. You hide any weakness, for fear you'll be taken advantage of if you don't. If you're tough with others and yourself, you can manage. Charles Darwin was right - life's a struggle for survival and only the fittest prevail. You have to constantly prove, challenge, and confront.

Who's afraid of a little conflict? Certainly not the 8! You even like conflict if it brings out the truth. You want everything brought to the surface. Unlike the 6, who *mentally* challenges, you *physically* challenge, if needed. You live in your body and are ready to leap, pounce, jump, push, shove - whatever it takes to protect yourself and anyone important to you. You live by your instincts and are the most purely physical of all the types.

You shoot from the hip and lip and only think later, unaware of your power to affect others. You're simply trying to get to the truth and are surprised when others are hurt by your directness. You are being more playful and excited than some people can handle. Bear cubs play rough!

You pull your own weight - so should everyone else! You don't like insecurity, doubt, fear, and weakness of any kind. Open on one hand, guarded on another, you usually are generous, when people are straight with you and particularly need help, but dismissive and confrontational, if people are shirking or taking advantage of you.

Famous 8s

Famous 8s include Martin Luther King, Jr., Donald Trump, Rosie O'Donnell, Geraldo Rivera, Rosanne Barr, Vladimir Putin, Danny DeVito, Mohammad Ali, George Patton, Winston Churchill, Richard Burton, John Wayne, Johnny Cash, Debra Winger, Frank Sinatra, Zorba the Greek, Maya Angelou, Sara Palin, Andrew Jackson, Teddy Roosevelt, Susan Sarandon, Queen Latifah, Ernest Hemingway, Mae West, Serena Williams, Humphrey Bogart, Dr. Phil, Jack Black

Type 9: The Peacemaker/Comfort Seeker

- Standing up for yourself
- Developing a separate identity
- What lies beneath the *nice* guy or gal
- Find your power and your passion

You value peace and harmony above all else, and you want everyone to like you and be nice to you. Your identity changes often, according to the situation at hand and what you perceive others expect from you. Sound familiar? If you've caught tantalizing glimpses of yourself in each of the previous types, but none were an exact fit, welcome to your type. 9s identify who they are by identifying with others. You are a 9!

Understanding the Type

To understand the world of the 9, it's important to know that 9s adapt to the wants of others, accommodate others, and go out of their way to create either real or imagined peace, at least from the type 9 perspective. As a 9, you're generally positive, optimistic, and trusting, although you can get down if you can't create peace. You love life and look for the best in all people and situations.

Sometimes, however, your trust borders on a childlike naiveté and this can cause you problems. Not everyone wants peace, and not everyone's motives are pure or good. As an accommodator, you're sincere and value relationships, so you tend to go along with what others want. However, some may see you as gullible and may take advantage of you, especially since you are easy to talk to, kind, compassionate, welcoming, giving, and agreeable. You defer your own plans and adapt your ideas and wants to those of others. You may seem okay on the surface, but always putting other people first causes your stress level and resentment to build. When you reach your limit, you slam on the brakes or run for your life. People get confused as to why such an agreeable person is suddenly not so agreeable.

Famous 9s

Famous 9s include the Dalai Lama, Laura Bush, Tipper Gore, Walter Cronkite, Norman Rockwell, Tony Bennett, George Burns and Gracie Allen, Jimmy Stewart, Renee Zellweger, Jennifer Aniston, "Gomer Pyle," "Gilligan" on Gilligan's Island, Mr. Rogers, Gerald Ford, Ronald Reagan, Barack Obama, Carl Rogers, Walt Disney, Ron Howard, Princess Grace of Monaco

Enneagram and the Myers-Briggs (taken from my book *Enneagram Beyond the Basics*)

The Myers Briggs is an excellent 16-type system of personality types in its own right. I use the Myers-Briggs as a backup system and sometimes use it more than the Enneagram in counseling sessions, particularly with couples whose differences are addressed more clearly in the Myers-Briggs system than the Enneagram. For instance, the Enneagram doesn't talk about introverted or extraverted versions of each type, though typically each Enneagram type tends to be more introverted or extraverted and the exceptions stand out. Knowing the Myers-Briggs helps explain things the Enneagram doesn't touch.

The Myers-Briggs explains areas of perception in a different way than the Enneagram – the four categories of introversion and extraversion, sensing and intuition, thinking and feeling and perceiving and judging. The Myers-Briggs references a type based on the dominant trait in each pair. For instance: I'm an ENFP – Extraverted Intuitive Feeling Perceiver and my opposite would be ISTJ – Introverted Sensing Thinking Judger. The Myers-Briggs is a great system that explains many things the Enneagram doesn't directly reference. The strength within each category (introverted or extraverted, sensing or intuitive, etc.) explains some of the uniqueness within each Enneagram type.

The Myers-Briggs is an excellent tool to:
1) understand one's individual strengths and limitations
2) coach individuals effectively according to their type differences
3) help teams work together more effectively
4) manage others by supporting their strengths and developing areas that are weak
5) relate effectively to other type differences

The Myers-Briggs theory includes a set of four categories, each of which has a pair of differences and seeming opposites. Every human being, according to Myers-Briggs theory, have a natural and stronger preference for one of those pairs of differences. We may use that natural preference or adapt to the environment by working harder to use the opposite. Below are some of the distinctions of the Myers-Briggs.

The first category is extraversion-introversion.

Extraverts are energized mostly with their major focus of attention on the outer environment, that is, people and objects outside themselves. Stimulation, people contact, communication with others, action, sociability, engagement, dependence on others - are experiences extraverts are looking for and more comfortable with. They talk more than introverts and tend to act before thinking things through. They make choices more by talking things over with others than alone.

Introverts gain energy more from their own inner world of concepts and ideas. Their greatest learning usually takes place when alone. Too much stimulation from people contact and activity is disconcerting and distracting. Usually more reserved, they reflect and think first and act later, while extraverts tend to act first and reflect later if at all. In business, introverts are often slower to talk and act and don't want to act until the concepts and problems are clarified and worked through a bit.

The second category is sensing and intuition.

Sensing types are down to earth; reality based and rely primarily on the five senses. That is, things are what are immediately seen and experienced and if not, you need to "prove it to me." They like facts and details and like things explained step-by-step sequentially. What you see is what you get. They are more "scientific" and need evidence, holding a bit of skepticism. They focus more on the familiar and what is tried and true before attempting something new.

Intuiting types want the big picture first before they deal with details and they get their information through hunches, insights, impressions, images, through a sixth sense. They have a hard time explaining how or why they come to the conclusions they come to. They "know" when something makes sense even if unexplainable. They go from step 1 to step 3 to 6 without a perfect sequence. They "get" it first and fill in the details later.

The third category is thinking/feeling.

Thinkers are more rational, logical, objective, detached, fair and analytical, impersonal, a bit tough-seeming and "cool" and can be perceived as critical. They tend to probe instead of make sensitive comments. In business, they tend to make decisions from their ideas of fairness and principles with less regard to peoples' personal preferences and reactions. They disregard their personal feelings more in preference for objective information and decisions. They are more ok with conflict than feelers.

Feelers are concerned about people's reactions to their decisions. They highly value harmony, good communication and are sensitive to criticism. They thrive on praise, affection, caring language and prefer agreement to disagreement, and don't like conflict and confrontation. Feelers are highly people oriented and want to have peaceful relations. They tend to give up their personal preferences for creating temporary agreement with others.

The fourth category is judging/perceiving.

Judging types are decisive and don't like to wait – let's decide and finish this now. They like order, are efficient, tend to be serious and want to act quickly. They'll make decisions for the future, now. They don't want to be surprised by last minute changes – solve it and be done with it. Make a plan and stick to it. Let's stop changing things and doing things last minute. Not wishy-washy, but solid, reliable and accountable.

Perceivers on the other hand like to keep their options open while collecting more data. They are concerned about potential consequences of premature decisions or missing out on a last-minute better choice. They are adaptable, spontaneous, tend to be cluttered and disordered in their environment and wait to decide when timing seems to be right. They are concerned about "pushing the river." Judgers appear to be "more mature," more adultlike and responsible, while perceivers appear to be more childlike and freer and more playful.

Potential conflicts are rampant between the types:

Extraverts tend to talk too much while the introverts are fuming trying to get a word in edgewise. The extraverts are waiting for the introverts to talk but aren't providing any pauses to make it easy to engage, without cutting in. Extraverts often assume others will cut in! Meanwhile there's a lot of anger and silence. Introverts like to think before they talk and extraverts need to talk as a way to see what they are thinking.

Extraverts need to listen more and pause and ask the introverts what they are thinking. Introverts could jump in more and say what they are thinking.

Sensors want things broken down into steps, categories and details and intuitors want concepts, big picture ideas and brainstorming before the details happen. Intuitors trust their hunches and sensors want information that's verifiable. Both are needed of course. Sensors think intuitors are hair-brained while intuitors think sensors share too many boring details, that they don't try anyone new or share deeper ideas. Intuitors like what's new and different and sensors tend to like what is tried and true.

Sensors need to let intuitors brainstorm more and listen to and see possibilities as exciting and as a kick off to real-life options and intuitors need to listen to and ask questions about sensors' details. Both types need to ask for what they want and realize the limitations and different preferences of their opposite type.

Thinkers tend to be rational and objective in their thinking and decision-making process and have a cool, critical edge. Feelers tend to make decisions from personal feeling and concern for the outcome on people who will be affected by those decisions. Feelers tend to be sensitive and harmonizers and try to find common denominators between people. Thinkers seem cold from the feelers' perspective and feelers seem too personal and not thick-skinned enough from the thinker's perspective. Feelers are perceived as "too sensitive" and thinkers are perceived as "cold and insensitive."

Both perspectives are important. Feelers need to be more objective and approach situations with some rationality and take things less personally, and thinkers need to be more sensitive to the outcome on people of their objective "truthful" statements. Feelers need to accept that some conflict is normal and accept their more self-centered sides, and thinkers can balance by being more personal and harmonizing.

Perceivers seem indecisive and wishy-washy, while judgers seem too controlling. Judgers get upset with perceivers who can't make a definite decision and who are concerned about missing out on options by early decisions, and a perceiver gets upset with judgers who seem to be pushing for decisions too early.

For judgers, earlier decisions relieve tension; and for perceivers, it's just the opposite. Each of their greatest strengths seem like weakness from the other side. If neither perspective were judged as wrong, the best strengths of each perspective would be valued.

Judgers and perceivers can be forever fighting over order also. The judger likes order, cleanliness and more control, and the perceiver can handle the mess and tends to clean up when the time beckons. The perceiver doesn't want to miss out on last-minute opportunities, and the judger wants to know their future in advance and wants order, as that serves their comfort level. Perceivers hate to be pushed and judgers hate loose, indecisive realities where "nothing happens." In reality, we need to use both of these perspectives.

Expect what each type gives and you'll be happier and can predict their tendencies. Ask for what you want in a way that honors the differences. Learn the strengths of the other side, and have friends of each perspective to support your similarities and differences.

The greater one's preference for each category, the tendency may be to judge the "opposite" of that preference. Yet everyone needs some of the qualities of all the categories.

A business that has similar types might sometimes work better, but they might not be addressing the different preferences of many of their clients. If too much of one perspective is dominant, there might be an atmosphere of fear and control regarding those who have a different perspective, thereby causing a lack of creativity in the type that feels left out or criticized. Every "type" tends to control toward what is familiar and what they want, yet each type needs to be flexible for the realities and preferences of others who are different.

Therefore, it is essential to:

1) Understand and value all the preferences as strengths

2) Listen to your "opposite" preference as a missing link for yourself

3) Realize people are often your opposite and it is necessary to relate well to all preferences to create great relationships

4) Your growth is toward enjoying your preferences, yet developing traits of your opposite type to be more well-rounded and to gain the benefits of those different aspects of yourself

The Tendencies of Enneagram types regarding Myers-Briggs preferences:

1s are often TJ (thinking/judging)
2s are often EF (extraverted feelers)
3s generally are EJ (extraverted judgers)
4s are generally more INF (introverted intuitive feelers)
5s are often introverted intuitive thinkers, particularly INTP, yet can also be INTJ, ISTP, ISTJ
6s Can be almost anything yet lean toward Judgers
7s are often EP (extraverted perceivers)
8s are generally more TJ (thinking judgers) yet can be IFP (introverted feeling perceivers)
9s are generally more introverted IFP (introverted feeling perceivers) though can be extraverted and also judgers.

There are plenty of exceptions to these tendencies, and that's why it's important to know a wide range of each Enneagram type to see the many variations that can show up within a type. Enneagram type and their wings explain much more about introversion and extraversion than type alone.

There are exceptions to each rule below but generally speaking:

The 1 with a 9 wing is introverted.
The 1 with a 2 wing is extraverted.

The 2 with a 1 wing is more introverted than the 2/3.
The 2 with a 3 wing is extraverted.

The 3 with a 2 wing is extraverted.
The 3 with a 4 wing is more introverted than 3/2.

The 4 with a 3 wing is extraverted.
The 4 with a 5 wing is more introverted.

The 5, as mentioned, is almost always introverted. They can appear extraverted when talking about their favorite subjects.

The 6 with a 5 wing is introverted.
The 6 with a 7 wing is more extraverted in comparison to 6/5.

The 7 with a 6 wing is more introverted than a 7/8.
The 7 with an 8 wing is extraverted.

The 8 with a 7 wing is extraverted.
The 8 with a 9 wing is more introverted in comparison.

The 9 with an 8 wing is more extraverted than the 9/1.
The 9 with a 1 wing is more introverted.

These tendencies have many exceptions. It's helpful to think about the comparison of introversion and extraversion within the type first; then see if one wing is more introverted or extraverted than the other wing of that type. For instance, a 7/6 can still be an extravert but they will be more introverted than the 7/8. The only type that is almost always introverted is type 5. All other types can be either an introvert or an extravert within the same type and can look exceedingly different! The author is an extraverted 9 with an 8 wing who can easily speak up at times, but an introverted 9 tends to speak up less, particularly with strangers.

Study the Myers-Briggs to understand type distinctions more clearly. You will see exceptions to anything listed below. It's rare to see a type 4 sensing type for instance, but they exist. I've met introverted 7s, though that's rare. There are always exceptions to rules or guidelines as listed below! Thank God people are unique.

More rare types: A Type 1 could be an ENFP, a 2 could be an introvert (yet will extravert when needing to please), a 3 could be an introvert, a 5 could be an INFP 5/4 feeler, 7s can be introverted and more intellectual than highly social. 8 can be introverted and a perceiver which is rarer, and 9s are often NFs and more P but there are plenty of 9 Ss and Js.

Typical correlations of Enneagram type with Myers Briggs though plenty of exceptions:

1 - INTJ, ISTJ, ENTJ, ENFJ INFJ
2 – ESFJ, ESFP, ENFP, ENFJ, INFJ
3 – ENFJ, ENTJ, ESTJ but can be ENTP, ISTJ, INTJ, ISTJ
4 – INFP, INFJ, ENFJ, ENFP
5 – INTP, INTJ, ISTJ, INFP
6 – Just about anything
7 - ENFP, ENTP, ESTP, ESFP, ENFJ
8 – ESTJ, ENTJ, ENTP, ESTP, INTJ
9 – INFP, ISFP, ESFP, ISFJ, ENFP, INTP but can be almost anything, generally F, generally not TJ

I've worked with many couples, for instance a 9/9 couple; with no obvious problems based on the Enneagram type but their Myers-Briggs types are ISTJ (unusual for a 9 but I've seen it on a number of occasions) with an ENFP. Most all their problems would be due to the Myers-Briggs differences. I would work with those differences as much as I'd work with the Enneagram subtype differences which could be part of their problems also. If I have the time, I try to type a couple in both systems, but generally I work with the Enneagram differences first.

Survival Enneagram Subtypes

There are 3 Basic Survival Instincts that we all have:

Self-preservation

Your relationship to staying alive and basic survival instincts for yourself and those important to you – Food/shelter/clothing – security, money, savings, safety, protection, wanting to know things in advance, health, planning for the future, the home, comfort, room temperature, possessions, your physical well-being.

Social

Relates to the herd instinct – your concern about how you fit into the group, whether you are included or excluded, your social ranking, your social image, how you see yourself as related to others, family, groups, organizations, the world, identifying through a group, how you are in socializing with others, your comfort level with groups and your value to a group or as a group member or wanting and investing in changing a social condition.

Intensity, Depth, Relationship, Intimacy

Relates to your mating instinct – your desire for bonding, intimacy with a close other, sexuality, a tendency toward intensity, strong energy, merging, depth, seeking self through another, spirituality, creativity, transformation.

Usually one of the above three survival areas is dominant for you and one that you obsess about and strongly desire; one instinct easier than the other two survival areas and that you are naturally good at; and one instinct you sweep under the rug and neglect and wish you didn't have to deal with.

Dominant Subtype – The instinct that concerns you and that you think about the most, what you worry about when those needs are not met – what feels most important to you, what you want to feel secure in, the one that feels like a survival need, the one most devastating when it doesn't turn out the way you want – for instance, sexual subtype (relationship loss), Social (lack of social recognition or belonging), self-preservation (loss of money and security).

Middle Subtype – This instinct is more natural and easiest of the three subtype areas and requires the least energy, or the one that least concerns you – the one you are often best at but might not pay attention to because it's easier for you than the other two. It's the one that others see you are good at.

Last or Third Subtype – The instinct you pay attention to the least, what you neglect or sweep under the rug, the one that causes difficulty due to avoidance, least interesting to you, hardest to develop, what you don't take care of, what you avoid, what you're not so good at. It's sometimes called the "blind spot."

There are 6 stacking possibilities, one of which subtype stackings or stacking orders most accurately describes you throughout your life, not just related to your current situation. The first or dominant subtype is what absorbs your mind the most and tends to throw you off center strongly when those needs are not met; the second subtype area is the easier one for you and the one in which you are most competent and comfortable; and the last or third subtype is what you neglect and in which you feel least competent.

There are 6 possibilities of subtype stacking:

Self-preservation, Social, Intensity/Relationship/Depth

Self-preservation, Intensity/Relationship/Depth, Social

Social, Self-preservation, Intensity/Relationship/Depth

Social, Intensity/Relationship/Depth, Self-preservation

Intensity/Relationship/Depth, Social, Self-Preservation

Intensity/Relationship/Depth, Self-preservation, Social

There is much more Enneagram information about subtypes available from my other Enneagram books – *Enneagram Basics, Enneagram Beyond the Basics and The Caregiver's Enneagram.*

Wings, Stress, Secure Types

A wing is a numerically adjacent type to your core type, whose mix of the two type traits makes a wingtype (also called dominant wing) different than the wingtype traits on the other side of the core type, such as 7/6 or 7/8 or 4/3 or 4/5. In essence, it appears as 18 wingtypes, two options for each core type. Some people might have equal traits of both wings, though for most people one of the wing's traits is generally dominant and can be quite different than the other wingtype, that is a 4/3 is quite different than a 4/5. The core type description still stands as the foundation of a personality. The dominant wing generally is not your secondary core type, though it could be.

Under continued personal life stress, each type tends to take on the worst traits of another type called the stress type; and when things are secure, going well or one is consciously growing, each type tends to take on the best traits of another type called the secure type. There's much variation in how a dominant type tends to move when stressed or secure, so the below descriptions might not totally fit in every situation. It's good to consciously develop the higher traits of both your stress type and secure type.

Type 1 – 9 wing – The Moralist Philosopher – Usually introverted, philosophical, principled, reserved, passionate about ideas and ideals, teacherly, global in thinking - social cause oriented in theory or practice (often writing or teaching) - Gandhi, Confucius, Thoreau, Prince Charles, Al Gore, Ralph Nader, Bernie Sanders, Jack Kevorkian

Type 1 - 2 wing – The Moralist Helper – Personally engaging with people, one on one, extraverted, persuasive, pushing for right action, helping, sacrificing - religion, banking, health industry, politicians - Jerry Brown, Hillary Clinton, John Bradshaw, Martha Stewart, Pope Paul II, Mary Poppins, Tina Fey

1 to 4 (stress) – Melancholy, self-indulgent, sad, painful, self-pity, fantasy world, emotional outbursts, depressed, withdrawn, moody, feeling out of control, might engage in drinking, affairs, self-destructive behaviors

(Positive move to 4) – Creative, sensual, emotionally tuned in, appreciative of beauty, personal rather than universal, focus on personal needs, self-oriented as well as doing right for others, forgiving, expressive

1 to 7 (secure) – Fun, spontaneous, flexible, excited, humorous, open to more possibilities, tolerant, letting down the guard, more allowing, not in charge so much, trusting, self-oriented, pleasure seeking, balance between work and play

Type 2 – 1 wing – The Serving Giver – More introverted, not as expressive as other wing, more selfless in giving than other wing, principled, teaching, healing or helping professions such as social worker, physical therapist, recreation, advice giver - Eleanor Roosevelt, Desmond Tutu, Ann Landers, Mother Teresa, Ammaji (the hugging saint)

Type 2 – 3 wing – The Success Giver – More personal and self-centered, social, seductive, charming, engaging, ambitious, humorous, more direct about what they want, self-important, my presence and attention should be enough to get appreciation – event planner, interviewer, performer, hostess - Sally Jesse Raphael, Arsenio Hall, Kelly Ripa, Dolly Parton, Cathy Lee Gifford, Jerry Lewis, Celine Dion, Nancy Reagan

2 to 8 (stress) – Controlling, dominating, demanding, rage or betrayal expressed when felt taken advantage of or not appreciated, direct, attacking, blaming, hysteric, felt owed

(**Positive move to 8**) – Clear, direct, needs and expectations expressed, boundaries, self-oriented, limits on giving

2 to 4 (**secure**) – Accepting of all their needs and darker feelings (fear, sadness, insecurities, anger) self-oriented, self-creative projects and interests, more depth, arts focus, time alone, more internally referenced, more aware of self-centered needs

Type 3 – 2 wing – The Achiever/Charmer – In the limelight, social, attract and dazzle, smooth talking, can seem artificial, adaptable, popular – politicians, entertainers, engaged with public - Bill Clinton, Dick Clark, Tony Robbins, Bob Hope, Tom Cruise, Justin Bieber, John Edwards

Type 3 – 4 wing – The Achiever/Feeler – Perfectionistic, professional, ambitious, self-doubting at times, more private than 3/2, serious, darker (sadness, pain) feelings beneath, can be introverted - Barbara Streisand, Werner Erhard, Mitt Romney, John Kerry, Ben Kingsley, Paul McCartney, Oprah Winfrey, Lady Gaga

3 to 9 (stress) – True emptiness shows through – can become disengaged and dissociated like a 9 if they are not doing what they really want – going through the motions of acting but not really behind it – staying with routines, passive, repetitive, less risk-taking

(Positive move to 9) – More relaxed, into "being" as much as doing, accommodating, down time, less into image, tuning into what's really desired, more harmonizing, less rushed and pressured

3 to 6 (secure) – Become more group identified, team player, sacrifice for the whole, look more at their motivations, feelings, insecurities; examine what is richer, deeper & more giving; belonging and being part of a group rather than having to be the star

Type 4 – 3 wing – The Dramatist – Extraverted, success driven, sophisticated, wants recognition, refined, competitive, self-presentation, image oriented, expect attention, can be grandiose & narcissistic, aristocratic, drama queen – Music, poetry, drama, dance, theater, creative types - Judy Garland, Prince, Angelina Jolie, Martha Graham, Kate Winslet, Cher

Type 4 – 5 wing – The Gypsy – Introverted, creative, idiosyncratic, very imaginative, inner world, mysterious, symbolic, dark, personal style, eccentric, rebellious, downbeat, private, minimalistic - Bob Dylan, Vincent Von Gogh, Johnny Depp, Sylvia Plath, James Dean, Edgar Allen Poe, Virginia Woolf, Cat Stevens, Jackie Kennedy (both wings), Rumi

4 to 2 (stress) – Giving to get, needy, need reassurance, clinging, trying to help you, exaggerate their importance to you, jealous, possessive, take credit for you

(Positive move to 2) – Genuine giving without neediness, other focused, positive, upbeat, letting go of amplification of personal story, more focused on needs of others

4 to 1 (secure) – Honest, impersonal, instinctual, non-indulgent, self-disciplined, discriminating, real life rather than imagination, self-sacrificing, secure

Type 5 – 4 wing – The Mental Artist – More emotional than 5/6, introspective, artistic, mixing passion and detachment, unique, independent, surreal, esoteric, can be attracted to dark, forbidden; more drawn to the arts, writing, music, creativity, individuality - David

Lynch, Stephen King, Georgia O'Keefe, Kurt Colbain, Albert Einstein, Daniel Day Lewis, Emily Dickinson, Salvador Dali, Eckhart Tolle, Ulysses S. Grant, Thomas Jefferson

Type 5 – 6 wing – Systems Analyst/Commentator – Systems oriented, detailed, engineering, science, technology, computer technology, philosophy, more practical, disciplined, detached, can be business savvy, very intellectual, analytical, understand the world - Bill Gates, Bobby Fischer, Jane Goodall, Amelia Earhart, Charles Darwin, Descartes, Karl Rove, Herbert Hoover

Type 5 to 7 (Stress) – Become scattered, jumpy, anxious, search for new experiences and variety to avoid stress like 7s, become agitated, look for the bizarre, overly mind oriented, insensitive

(Positive move to 7) – Fun, light, engaging, social positive, upbeat, humorous, less need to be the expert, storytelling

Type 5 to 8 (Secure) – More body oriented, direct, instinctive, intuitive, practical, leadership oriented, responsible, engaging, trusting, act from impressions, in charge

Type 6 – 5 wing - The Intellectual Protector – Serious, smart, independent, systems oriented, danger oriented, scanning, protective, skeptical/rebellious yet loyal to honest authorities, can be reactive, aggressive, protective of established worthy systems and beliefs – political causes, political commentators, community services, security systems - Malcolm X, Gloria Steinem, Woody Allen, Richard Nixon, Helen Palmer, J Edgar Hoover, George H. W. Bush, Robert Kennedy, George Costanza, David Lettermen

Type 6 – 7 wing – People Protector – Likeable, people oriented, less serious, joke around, more dependent, relationship oriented, more humorous than 6/5, buddy, want to be liked - comedians, protective agencies, social work - George W. Bush, Ellen Degeneres, Phil Donahue, Tom Hanks, Mark Twain, Chris Rock, Jay Leno

6 to 3 (Stress) – More image oriented, want to be on winning team or group for safety, frenetic attempt to appear or be successful for protection, active to accomplish a lot but can be scattered, attempt to hide pain, fear and stress, fit in to protect against fear

(Positive move to 3) Be more on their own, more confident, success driven, action oriented, less concern about protection or needing group approval, more individualistic, best case scenario, less concerned about real or imagined danger

6 to 9 (Secure) – More relaxed, trusting, less in the head and more in the body, focus on the positive, enjoyment, the good, what's working, ease, in the moment, let it be

7 with 8 wing – The Fun Driver – Practical, touch minded, materialistic, can be successful, activity oriented, aggressive, less relationship oriented, independent, can appear as an 8; entrepreneurs, leaders, politicians, actors - Joan Rivers, Howard Stern, Regis Philbin, Joe Biden, Timothy Leary, Jack Nicholson, character of Robin Hood, Benjamin Franklin (both wings), Franklin Roosevelt, John Kennedy, Larry King, Suze Orman, Charlie Sheen

7 with 6 wing – The Fun Relater – Relationship oriented, good sense of humor, more positive, cooperative, more aware of insecurity than 7/8, interact easily with people, often in comedy, public relations, advertising, media, travel, entertainment – Robin Williams, Steven Spielberg, Jim Carrey, Goldie Hawn, Carol Burnett, Ram Dass, Britney Spears, Miley Cyrus, Katy Perry

7 to 1 (Stress) - Upset by restriction of freedom/options, critical, righteous, teacherly, preacherly like a 1, rigid in thinking and action, demanding that others be positive

(Positive move to 1) More serious minded, focused, sacrificing for rightness, sees the whole, less self-absorbed about constant fun and excitement, creating positive limits that add depth, can face pain as part of growth, attempt to be more structured

7 to 5 (Secure) - Quieting and focusing the mind to go deeper, less scattered, less need for constant stimulation, patience, reflection; more clear and insightful, value inner process, limit to options, learning in depth

8 with 7 wing – The Powerhouse – Realistic, dominating, hyperactive, wants to have impact on world, very action oriented, impulsive, engaging, adventurous, risk taking, overconfident, sociable, talkative, impatient, winners, leaders, loud, strong – Donald Trump, Andrew Jackson, Don Imus, Lyndon Johnson, Zorba the Greek, Frank Sinatra, Queen Latifah, Serena Williams

8 with 9 wing – The Mother Bear – Grounded, often more introverted, quieter, steady, protective, less wheeler-dealer than 8/7, calming, friendly, strong, steady, mediating, can be explosive suddenly, patient but strong - Martin Luther King, Golda Meir, John Wayne, Sean Connery, Winston Churchill, Jesse Jackson, John McCain, Susan Sarandon

8 to 5 (Stress) - Can become cynical like 5s, private, secretive, withdraw from others in their pain, not seeking help, too analytical, stay hurt, strategize to get back at someone, not seek help, evaluate others contemptuously

(Positive move to 5) – Be more objective, detach, think first before action, spend time going inside instead of fixing others outside, meditating, waiting, patient, getting help

8 to 2 (Secure) – Giving, sensitive to personal and unique needs of others, more forgiving, generous without demanding loyalty, heart oriented more than power oriented, accept weakness of others and themselves, not take over, connect to their own needs and vulnerability, aware of dependence on others, interdependent

9 with 1 wing – The Unifier – Wanting an ideal world, want external order, precise, less adventurous and more reserved than 9/8, quieter, introverted, more restraint with anger, more respectable, perfectionist, moral code, conflict adverse - Norman Rockwell, Walt Disney, Laura Bush, Dalai Lama, Mr. Rogers, Jimmy Stewart, Queen Elizabeth

9 with 8 wing – The Coach – Agreeable but with endurance and strength, powerful and gentle, easygoing, more impulsive than 1 wing, more sociable, sensual, comfort seeking, stubborn, can have tempers if stressed, can be blunt on occasion, can zone out - Ronald Reagan, Gerald Ford, Walter Cronkite, Kevin Costner, Geena Davis, Herb Pearce!

9 to 6 (Stress) – Obsessive, negative thinking, fearful, passive, worst case scenarios, frozen, paranoid, passive aggressive, blaming

(Positive move to 6) Be more cautious, less trusting of users, plan in advance, let go of naivete, be select, more self-oriented, more noticing and alert, don't assume something will go away on its own, be more assertive and express needs clearly, set boundaries

9 to 3 (Secure) - Focused, goal and action oriented, self-oriented, can-do attitude, values good aspects of image and presentation, values their own importance, vital, assertive

Summary of Presidents and Type

George Washington	Type 3, ISTJ
John Adams	Type 1, INTJ
Thomas Jefferson	Type 5, INTP
James Madison	Type 5, INTP
James Monroe	Type 3, ISTJ
John Quincy Adams	Type 1, INTJ
Andrew Jackson	Type 8, ESTP
Martin Van Buren	Type 2, ESFP
William Henry Harrison	Type 3, ESTJ
John Tyler	Type 1, ISTJ
James Polk	Type 1, ISTJ
Zachary Taylor	Type 8, ISTP
Millard Fillmore	Type 9, ISFJ
Franklin Pierce	Type 7, ESFP
James Buchanan	Type 6, ISFJ
Abraham Lincoln	Type 4, INTP
Andrew Johnson	Type 1, ESTJ
Ulysses S. Grant	Type 5, INTJ
Rutherford B. Hayes	Type 1, ESTJ
James Garfield	Type 7, ESFP
Chester Arthur	Type 8, ESFP
Grover Cleveland	Type 8, ESTJ
Benjamin Harrison	Type 1, ISTJ
William McKinley	Type 2, ESFJ
Teddy Roosevelt	Type 8, ESTP
William Howard Taft	Type 9, ISFJ
Woodrow Wilson	Type 1, INTJ
Warren Harding	Type 6, ESFP
Calvin Coolidge	Type 1, ISTJ
Herbert Hoover	Type 5, INTJ
Franklin Roosevelt	Type 7, ESTP
Harry S. Truman	Type 1, ISTJ
Dwight Eisenhower	Type 1, INTJ
John F. Kennedy	Type 7, ESTP
Lyndon Baines Johnson	Type 8, ESTP
Richard M. Nixon	Type 6, INTJ

Gerald Ford	**Type 9, ESFJ**
Jimmy Carter	**Type 3, ISTJ**
Ronald Reagan	**Type 9, ENFJ**
George H.W. Bush	**Type 6, ISFJ**
Bill Clinton	**Type 3, ESFP**
George W. Bush	**Type 6, ESTJ**
Barack Obama	**Type 9, ENFJ**
Donald Trump	**Type 8, ESTP**

The most dominant Enneagram type president is Type 1, followed by Type 8. Over one-half the presidents are body types (8-9-1) who focus on attunement to body instinct, and a preference for directness. Next are the head types (5-6-7) who focus primarily on knowledge and learning, followed by the image types (2-3-4) who focus on impression and concern for how others see them. Any Enneagram type can be a leader. The least common type represented is Type 4.

Number of US Presidents per Enneagram type:
Type 1 - eleven
Type 2 - two
Type 3 - five
Type 4 - one
Type 5 - four
Type 6 - five
Type 7 - four
Type 8 - seven
Type 9 - five

Number of US Presidents most to least Enneagram type:
Type 1 – eleven
Type 8 – seven
Type 3 - five
Type 9 – five
Type 6 - five
Type 5 - four
Type 7 - four
Type 2 - two
Type 4 – one

I question the type of a few presidents such as Martin van Buren who could have been either a 2 or 3, or James Garfield who might have been a 1, counterphobic 6, 7 or 8. I type him as a 7 with wings on either side. I slightly question Zachary Taylor as an 8. Andrew Johnson presented like an 8 (which was probably his secondary type) but I believe he was a 1. The other presidents I feel fairly confident about. I think it's valuable to take a fresh look at the typing of the presidents, as it's easy to assume prior assessments by others are accurate. It's always good to reexamine prior determinations in depth, including my own assessments here.

As far as the Myers-Briggs, the most dominant types are ISTJ, INTJ and ESTP, followed by ESTJs. TJs are fairly dominant as would be expected for leader types. ESTPs also often take on a leadership role. There are about the same number of introverts and extraverts. There are many more sensing types than intuitive types, more thinkers than feelers and more judgers than perceivers. This makes sense, as presidents are more down-to-earth as sensors, tough minded as thinkers and make quick decisions like judgers. Certainly, there are many exceptions to these tendencies.

It's certainly a challenge to type people you don't know. I can't guarantee that each Myers-Briggs type is perfectly accurate though I did my best to conjecture based on research and personal stories. The Presidents' type accuracy I question more than others include Martin van Buren, James Garfield and Chester Arthur who could be ESTPs instead of ESFPs as I labelled them. They seemed close on the T/F scale. I question Zachary Taylor's type though ISTP seems the best fit. I do think Abraham Lincoln is an INTP though it's unusual for an Enneagram 4 to be a T. There's a chance he could be an INFP which is more typical of 4s. I still debate whether Barack Obama is an introvert or extravert.

Number of US Presidents per Myers-Briggs type:

```
ISTJ - 8
INTJ - 7
ESTP - 6
ESFP - 6
ESTJ - 5
ISFJ - 4
INTP - 3
ESFJ - 2
ENFJ - 2
ISTP - 1
```

Bibliography

Some references are listed separately within the book chapters.

Websites: For most of the websites below, I did a separate reading for each president.

biography.com

whitehouse.gov/1600/Presidents

millercenter.org

brittanica.com

classroomhelp.com/lessons/Presidents/nicknames.htm

history.com/topics/us-presidents

en.wkipedia.org

presidentialprofiles.com

presidents.usa.net

presidentialham.com

historynet.com

spangledwithstars.com

60-Second Presidents/PBS

pbs.org/newshour/spc/character/essays/

c-span.org/series/?bookTv (numerous book lectures about presidents)

Full name of each president, followed by .org

Books:

Our Country's Presidents by Ann Bausum

Our Country's First Ladies by Ann Bausum

The Look It-Up Book of Presidents by Wyatt Blassingame

The Complete Book of U.S. Presidents by William A. Gregorio

Presidential Temperament (related to Myers-Briggs temperaments) by Ray Choiniere and David Keirsey, one of best books on the personalities of Presidents

Don't Know Much About the American Presidents by Kenneth C. Davis

The Secret Lives of U.S. Presidents by Cormac O'Brien

Recarving Rushmore by Ivan Eland

Presidential Campaign Posters from the Library of Congress

The First Ladies of the United States of America by Allida Black with foreword by Michelle Obama

Confounding Father – Thomas Jefferson's Image in His Own Time by Robert M.S. McDonald

A People's History of the United States by Howard Zinn

A People's History of the American Revolution by Ray Raphael edited by Howard Zinn

Home Life in Colonial Days by Alice Morse Earle

The Virgin Vote: How Young Americans Made Democracy Social, Politics Personal, and Voting Popular in the Nineteenth Century by Jon Grinspan

The Fireside Chats, edited by Russell D. Buhite and David W. Levy (about Franklin Roosevelt)

TV and DVD series:

The Presidents: 3 DVD series by The History Channel

The Ultimate Guide to the Presidents: 3 DVD series by The History Channel

National Geographic Classics: American Presidents DVD series

PBS television series – The American Experience, separate series of each of below – Clinton, George H. W. Bush, Reagan, Carter, Nixon, JFK, Eisenhower, FDR, TR, U.S. Grant: The Warrior; Abraham and Mary Lincoln: A House Divided; John and Abigail Adams; The Roosevelts: An Intimate History; Murder of a President: James Garfield;

John Adams Miniseries on TV (extensive readings regarding the accuracy of details)

www.pbs.org/newshour/spc/character/essays/ (essays about many 20th century presidents

imdb.com/title/tt1567215/mediaviewer/rm1863498496 miniseries on the Kennedys

Historical visits:

Personal attendance of numerous lectures about different presidents as a member of The Boston Historical Society, www.masshist.org, Boylston St., Boston, MA

Play, "45 Presidents" at the Merrimack Repertory Theater, Lowell Theater (attended twice), 2016

8-day trip visiting Presidential Mansions in Virginia – Mt Vernon, Monticello, Montpelier, Berkeley Plantation; Old City Alexandria, Ash Lawn-Highland, Sherwood Forest Plantation in June of 2016

A guide to Virginia's presidential estates and plantations

washingtonpost.com/goingoutguide/virginias-presidential-estates-a-planning-guide

Visits to the Adams Peacefield Estate and John Adams and John Quincy Adams birthplaces in Quincy, Massachusetts, Calvin Coolidge Homestead in Plymouth, Vermont and Franklin Pierce Birthplace and Estate in Hillsborough, NH and home in Concord, New Hampshire in 2017

Membership and attendance at Sturbridge Village for 40 years in Massachusetts, many visits to historical villages in Deerfield MA, Strawberry Banke in Portsmouth, NH, Mystic Seaport in Mystic, Connecticut

Attendance of historical reenactors of George Washington, James Madison, Abraham Lincoln, Ulysses S. Grant

Myers-Briggs and Enneagram websites:

typologycentral.com/forums/popular-culture-and-type/32260-typing-presidents.html

9types.com/writeup/enneagram_leadership.html

9types.com/writeup/enneagram_lists.html (lists of some of the Presidents' Enneagram types)

PersonalityPathways.com

theenneagraminbusiness.com

celebritytypes.com/ about Myers-Briggs types

whichmbtitype.wordpress.com/2012/12/14/which-mbti-type-are-all-the-american-presidents/

brain-and-mind.com/2012/06/is-obama-introvert-or-extrovert.html

thesixteentypes.tumblr.com/tagged

truity.com/personality-type

thoughtcatalog.com/lorenzo-jensen-iii/2015/06/44-presidents-1-myers-briggs-test/

myersbriggs.org/my-mbti-personality-type/mbti-basics/the-16-mbti-types.htm

typologycentral.com/forums/popular-culture-and-type/17587-types-presidents-12.html

Websites (add www.) - YouTube historical lectures and articles in order of presidents:

youtube.com/watch?v=vkwZDRB3tZo, The Truth about George Washington by Stefan Molyeux

thepresidentsatbigmo.blogspot.com/search/label/George%20Washington (assessment of George Washington and short summary of first 13 presidents)

bostonglobe.com/lifestyle/travel/2014/11/08/tracing-washington-steps/zVj0BRpOKRHtEC3KlUHojM/story.html

channel.nationalgeographic.com/explorer/videos/george-washington-revealed/
click on next video clip after first one, 10 different clips

Many lectures by historian John Ferling on YouTube about George Washington

youtube.com/watch?v=LZmF79LOcqM (interview of author of book about John Adams, The Character and Legacy about John Adams, 1993)

featherfoster.wordpress.com/2013/08/05/mrs-adams-goes-to-paris/

youtube.com/watch?v=7LRZ3AaBlt0 interview about John Adams by David McCullough

youtube.com/watch?v=8Rf-kW1fKic American Experience about Jefferson

Many YouTube history lectures and lectures of Presidents by Stefan Molyeux about Founding Fathers

youtube.com/watch?v=thin1LeCrxY about Founding Fathers

c-span.org/video/?301621-1/james-madison

James Madison by Richard Brookhiser – book review lecture on C-Span

youtube.com/watch?v=YbKNq529yWQ (lecture about James Monroe)

deadpresidents.tumblr.com/post/79923126144/washington-vs-monroe-the-feuding-presidents-of

thepresidentsatbigmo.blogspot.com/2007/06/number-12-zachary-taylor.html

jameskpolk.com/james-polk-biography.php

millardfillmore.org

celebrities-galore.com/celebrities/millard-fillmore/personality-number/

history.com/topics/first-ladies/jane-pierce

nps.gov/nr/travel/presidents/franklin_pierce_homestead.html

Franklin Pierce and Bowdoin College Associates Hawthorne and Hale, essay by Peter A. Wallner

The President's Wife, Jane Mean Appleton Pierce: A Woman of Her Time, essay by Jane Walter Venzke and Craig Paul Venzke

Myths and Truths of the Pierce Administration: Notes from a lecture at the Pierce Manse by Peter Wallner, Author of Franklin Pierce, New Hampshire's Favorite Son and Franklin Pierce, Martyr for the Union,

The Pierce Manse: Home of Franklin Pierce, 14th President of the United States, pamphlet

presidentprofiles.com/Washington-Johnson/James-Buchanan-Foreign-policy-the-imperialist.html

thoughtco.com/president-james-buchanan-the-secession-crisis-1773714

pbs.org/wgbh/aia/part4/4p2952.html (about Bleeding Kansas)

theatlantic.com/magazine/archive/2005/10/lincolns-great-depression/304247/ (about depression of Lincoln)

youtube.com/watch?v=0-4mwF1S18k (about Lincoln)

abrahamlincolnsclassroom.org/abraham-lincoln-in-depth/abraham-lincolns-stories-and-humor/

answers.com/Q/What_is_Ulysses_S._

presidentprofiles.com/Grant-Eisenhower/Benjamin-Harrison-Presidential-style-and-appointments.html

granthomepage.com/grantlincoln.htm

historynet.com/ulysses-s-grant

granthomepage.com/frederick_dent_grant.htm

libguides.css.edu/usgrant/home/upclose

granthomepage.com/nellie_grant.htm

libguides.css.edu/usgrant/home/quotes

pbs.org/wgbh/americanexperience/features/timeline/garfield/

youtube.com/watch?v=-Nf4EQrxyf8 (about Chester Arthur)

tvtropes.org/pmwiki/pmwiki.php/UsefulNotes/ChesterAArthur

let.rug.nl/usa/biographies/william-howard-taft/

en.wikipedia.org/wiki/Helen Herron Taft

youtube.com/watch?v=yLOhByiwdfE (Woodrow Wilson)

nps.gov/nr/travel/presidents/calvin_coolidge_homestead.html

biography.com/people/calvin-coolidge-9256384#policies

youtube.com/watch?v=iynPkBEE0wE (about John Kennedy)

pbs.org/newshour/spc/character/essays/kennedy.html (Richard Reeves essay on Kennedy)

abcnews.go.com/US/14-things-jfk/story?id=20633994 (about John F. Kennedy)

dailymail.co.uk/news/article-3403196/The-tragic-tale-JFK-s-charming-rebellious-sister-Kick-Kennedy.html

pbs.org/wgbh/americanexperience/features/kennedy-wealth/

buzzfeed.com/kevinjamesshay/jfk-faced-plots-in-tampa-chicago-other-cities-du-1wwul?utm_term=.ekJQjDAAV#.mk5QAaqqx (Kennedy assassination plots) abc7chicago.com/archive/9315215/ (Kennedy assassination plots)

kennedysandking.com/john-f-kennedy-articles/the-three-failed-plots-to-kill-jfk-the-historians-guide-on-how-to-research-his-assassination

theatlantic.com/magazine/archive/2013/08/jfk-vs-the-military/309496/

jfklibrary.org/Asset-Viewer/Wyn_KJvaFUOgyG_1-dY3eQ.aspx (Kennedy's Navy Medals)

pbs.org/newshour/spc/character/essays/johnson.html about Lyndon Johnson

nixonfoundation.org

history.com/this-day-in-history/gerald-ford-marries-elizabeth-bloomer

youtube.com/watch?v=yVYtIdUcYqY (about Ronald Reagan)

youtube.com/watch?v=KrXr1zksNEs (about Nixon)

alternet.org/election-2016/15-ways-bill-clintons-white-house-failed-america-and-world

content.time.com/time/politics/article/0,8599,1847723,00.html article "Putting Bill Clinton on the Couch"

learningenglish.voanews.com/a/father-bush-critiques-sons-presidency-in-new-book/3050341.html

thoughtco.com/george-hw-bushisms-2734321

nbcnews.com/id/28482517/ns/politics-white_house/t/analysis-bushs-personality-shapes-his-legacy/#.WgdBDWhSyM8 (about George W. Bush)

partners.nytimes.com/library/politics/camp/061000wh-bush.html

politicaltypes.com/bush_type.html (George W. Bush's Myers-Briggs type) prezi.com/f8x23rmwhcfd/the-leadership-characteristics-of-president-barack-obama/

washingtonmonthly.com/magazine/marchapril-2012/obamas-top-50-accomplishments/

brain-and-mind.com/2012/06/is-obama-introvert-or-extrovert.html

youtube.com/watch?v=w4BhRx5EQyg (excellent interviews of Barack Obama) and justification for type 9

jcsd-cl-obama.weebly.com/obamas-leadership--character-traits.html

aol.com/article/news/2017/02/17/barack-obama-ranks-near-the-top-of-new-c-span-list-of-best-u-s/21716499/

psychologytoday.com/blog/the-career-within-you/201407/president-obama-enneagram-type-9-part-1

today.law.harvard.edu/obama-first-made-history-at-hls/ article about Obama in law school

blackdoctor.org/483712/job-well-done-first-lady-16-accomplishments-of-michelle-obama/

wwnorton.com/college/history/america7/content/multimedia/ch15/research_01.htm

oxfordbibliographies.com/view/document/obo-9780190280024/obo-9780190280024-0022.xml (about black integration of federal offices)

senate.gov/artandhistory/history/common/generic/Feature_Homepage_TreatyVersailles.htm

huffingtonpost.com/entry/a-running-list-of-the-women-whove-accused-donald-trump-of-sexual-misconduct_us_57ffae1fe4b0162c043a7212

motherjones.com/politics/2016/10/donald-trump-obsessed-with-revenge psychologytoday.com/blog/the-situation-lab/201509/the-personality-donald-trump

theguardian.com/us-news/2016/aug/05/donald-trump-psychology-personality-republicans-election (written by Dan P. McAdams)

youtube.com/watch?v=SnSMBwjZaGY (about Trump's grandfather)

youtube.com/watch?v=SnSMBwjZaGY (about Trump)

bostonglobe.com/lifestyle/2016/08/21/donald-trump-wore-hat-would-crown/EpgYKtD98hE9PK8aiDdSOM/story.html (Boston Globe article about my Enneagram work)

www.youtube.com/watch?v=y4hOkLk8fyE (PBS show about Trump)

youtube.com/watch?v=_xFovzUrCcg 10 Top Presidents

youtube.com/watch?v=_xFovzUrCcg 10 Worse Presidents

youtube.com/watch?v=BXXqCOKMQcY about all the Presidents

firstladies.org/biographies/firstladies.aspx?biography=27

history.stackexchange.com/questions/23236/what-portion-of-northerners-were-against-slavery-for-humanitarian-reasons-in-186

en.wikipedia.org/wiki/Interracialmarriage

Youtube about every president on bio.com

blackpast.org/primary/declaration-independence-and-debate-over-slavery

presidential-power.org/quotes-by-presidentsfactcheck.org/2008/03/presidents-winning-without-popular-vote/

Other books by Herb Pearce:

Enneagram Basics

Enneagram Beyond the Basics

The Caregiver's Enneagram

Herb's Tips for Living: Wise Tips for Daily Living

Lessons from the River: What I've Learned from Whitewater Canoeing and Camping on Maine's Rivers

Herb's likely next book will be First Ladies from Martha Washington to Melania Trump: Enneagram Types

Books available from Amazon or Kindle or email: herb@herbpearce.com to request a book

Contact Herb Pearce for consultations, psychotherapy, life coaching, phone and Skype/Zoom counseling, personality typing, workshops and trainings. Trainings available in the Boston and New England area, though Herb is happy to travel to any location.

Sign up for his weekly free email newsletter with an article, tips to improve daily life and Herb's schedule of Enneagram workshops and events. Email or call to order books. Send your email address to herb@herbpearce.com and request to be on the newsletter list.

www.herbpearce.com

herb@herbpearce.com

781 648 3737

Made in the USA
Columbia, SC
30 March 2019